MW01015751

PC LEARNING LABS TEACHES MICROSOFT POWERPOINT FOR WINDOWS 95

PLEASE NOTE—USE OF THE CD-ROM AND THE PROGRAMS INCLUDED ON THE CD-ROM PACKAGED WITH THIS BOOK AND THE PROGRAM LISTINGS INCLUDED IN THIS BOOK IS SUBJECT TO AN END-USER LICENSE AGREEMENT (THE "AGREEMENT") FOUND AT THE BACK OF THE BOOK. PLEASE READ THE AGREEMENT CAREFULLY BEFORE MAKING YOUR PURCHASE DECISION. PURCHASE OF THE BOOK AND USE OF THE CD-ROM, PROGRAMS, AND PROGRAM LISTINGS WILL CONSTITUTE ACCEPTANCE OF THE AGREEMENT.

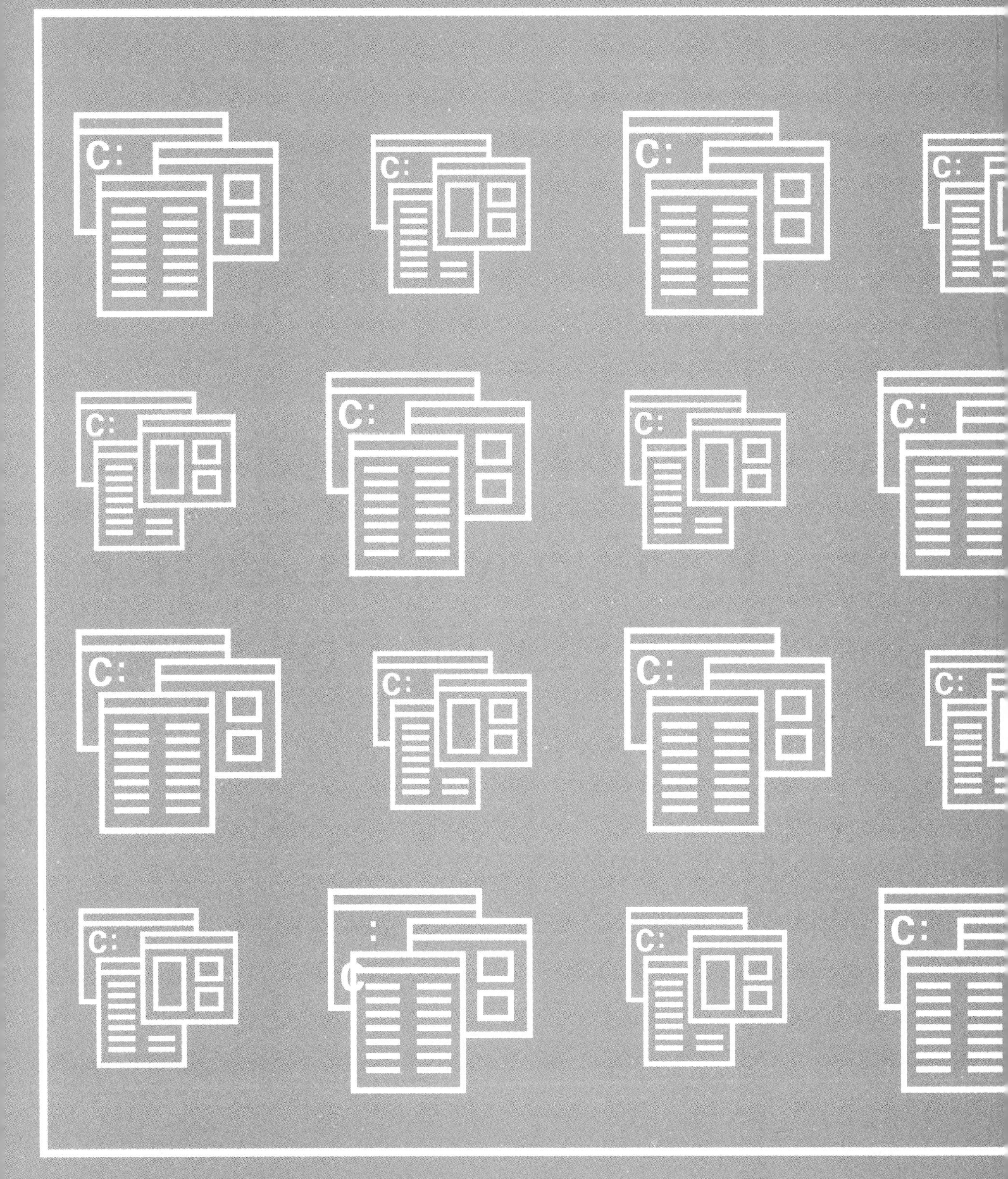

PC LEARNING LABS TEACHES MICROSOFT POWERPOINT FOR WINDOWS 95

By Sue Reber and Charles Blum for

Writers	Sue Reber and Charles Blum
Curriculum Development	Logical Operations
Editor	Jeannie Smith
Technical Reviewer	Leslie Caico
Project Coordinators	Ami Knox and Barbara Dahl
Production Coordinator, Logical Operations	Marie Boyers
Cover Illustration and Design	Regan Honda
Book Design	Laura Lamar/MAX, San Francisco
Technical Illustration	Steph Bradshaw
Word Processing	Howard Blechman
Page Layout	Janet Piercy
Indexer	Carol Burbo

Ziff-Davis Press, ZD Press, PC Learning Labs, and PC Learning Labs Teaches are licensed to Macmillan Computer Publishing USA by Ziff-Davis Publishing Company, New York, New York.

Ziff-Davis Press imprint books are produced on a Macintosh computer system with the following applications: FrameMaker®, Microsoft® Word, QuarkXPress®, Adobe Illustrator®, Adobe Photoshop®, Adobe Streamline™, MacLink®*Plus*, Aldus® FreeHand™, Collage Plus™.

If you have comments or questions or would like to receive a free catalog, call or write:
Macmillan Computer Publishing USA
Ziff-Davis Press Line of Books
5903 Christie Avenue
Emeryville, CA 94608
1-800-688-0448

Copyright © 1996 by Macmillan Computer Publishing USA. All rights reserved.
PART OF A CONTINUING SERIES

All other product names and services identified throughout this book are trademarks or registered trademarks of their respective companies. They are used throughout this book in editorial fashion only and for the benefit of such companies. No such uses, or the use of any trade name, is intended to convey endorsement or other affiliation with the book.

No part of this publication may be reproduced in any form, or stored in a database or retrieval system, or transmitted or distributed in any form by any means, electronic, mechanical photocopying, recording, or otherwise, without the prior written permission of Macmillan Computer Publishing USA, except as permitted by the Copyright Act of 1976 and the End-User License Agreement at the back of this book, and except that program listings may be entered, stored, and executed in a computer system.

EXCEPT FOR THE LIMITED WARRANTY COVERING THE PHYSICAL DISK(S) PACKAGED WITH THIS BOOK AS PROVIDED IN THE END-USER LICENSE AGREEMENT AT THE BACK OF THIS BOOK, THE INFORMATION AND MATERIAL CONTAINED IN THIS BOOK ARE PROVIDED "AS IS," WITHOUT WARRANTY OF ANY KIND, EXPRESS OR IMPLIED, INCLUDING WITHOUT LIMITATION ANY WARRANTY CONCERNING THE ACCURACY, ADEQUACY, OR COMPLETENESS OF SUCH INFORMATION OR MATERIAL OR THE RESULTS TO BE OBTAINED FROM USING SUCH INFORMATION OR MATERIAL. NEITHER MACMILLAN COMPUTER PUBLISHING USA NOR THE AUTHOR SHALL BE RESPONSIBLE FOR ANY CLAIMS ATTRIBUTABLE TO ERRORS, OMISSIONS, OR OTHER INACCURACIES IN THE INFORMATION OR MATERIAL CONTAINED IN THIS BOOK, AND IN NO EVENT SHALL MACMILLAN COMPUTER PUBLISHING USA OR THE AUTHOR BE LIABLE FOR DIRECT, INDIRECT, SPECIAL, INCIDENTAL, OR CONSEQUENTIAL DAMAGES ARISING OUT OF THE USE OF SUCH INFORMATION OR MATERIAL.

ISBN 1-56276-379-2

Manufactured in the United States of America
10 9 8 7 6 5 4 3 2 1

CONTENTS AT A GLANCE

TABLE OF CONTENTS

INTRODUCTION

Welcome to *PC Learning Labs Teaches PowerPoint 7.0 for Windows 95*, a hands-on instruction book designed to help you attain a high level of PowerPoint fluency in the shortest time possible. And congratulations on choosing PowerPoint 7.0, an easy-to-use, feature-packed desktop presentation program that will enable you to create professional-quality presentations with a minimum amount of training.

We at PC Learning Labs believe this book to be a unique and welcome addition to the ranks of "how to" computer publications. Our instructional approach stems directly from over a decade of successful teaching in a hands-on, classroom environment. Throughout the book, we mix theory with practice by presenting new techniques and then applying them in hands-on activities. These activities use specially prepared sample PowerPoint files, which are stored on the enclosed Data Disk.

When you're done working your way through this book, you will have a solid foundation of skills in

- Creating, editing, and enhancing presentations
- Working with text, images (drawings and clip art), color schemes, and charts (graphs)
- Importing and exporting data from/to other programs
- Printing presentation slides, notes, handouts, and outlines

This foundation will enable you to quickly and easily create sophisticated, professional-quality desktop presentations.

READ THIS BEFORE YOU PROCEED

We strongly recommend that you read through the rest of this Introduction before beginning Chapter 1.

WHO THIS BOOK IS FOR

This book was written with the beginner in mind. Although experience with desktop presentation and personal computers is certainly helpful, little or none is required. You should know how to turn on your computer and use your keyboard. We explain everything beyond that.

HOW TO USE THIS BOOK

This book is designed to be used as a learning guide, a review tool, and a quick reference.

AS A LEARNING GUIDE

Each chapter in this book covers one broad topic or set of related topics. Chapters are arranged in order of increasing proficiency; skills you acquire in one chapter are used and elaborated on in later chapters. For this reason, you should work through the chapters in sequence.

Each chapter is organized into explanatory topics and step-by-step activities. Topics provide the theory you need to master PowerPoint; activities allow you to apply this theory to practical, hands-on examples.

AS A REVIEW TOOL

Any method of instruction is only as effective as the time and effort you are willing to invest in it. For this reason, we strongly encourage you to spend some time reviewing the book's more challenging topics and activities.

AS A QUICK REFERENCE

General procedures such as opening a new presentation or changing a presentation's color scheme are presented as a series of bulleted steps; you can find these bullets (•) easily by skimming through the book.

These procedures can serve as a handy reference. At the end of every chapter, you'll find a quick reference that lists the mouse and keyboard actions needed to perform the techniques introduced in that chapter.

WHAT THIS BOOK CONTAINS

This book is divided into the following 13 chapters and 3 appendices:

Chapter 1	Getting Started
Chapter 2	Beginning a Presentation
Chapter 3	Working with Slide Text
Chapter 4	Drawing on Your Slides
Chapter 5	Clip Art and Color Schemes
Chapter 6	Slide Masters and Templates
Chapter 7	Working with Organization Charts
Chapter 8	Working with Column Charts
Chapter 9	Working with Pie Charts
Chapter 10	Advanced Templates and Slide Masters
Chapter 11	Importing and Exporting
Chapter 12	Presentation Options
Chapter 13	Printing
Appendix A	Installation
Appendix B	Toolbar Reference
Appendix C	Keystroke Reference

To attain full PowerPoint fluency, you should work through all 13 chapters. The appendices are optional.

SPECIAL LEARNING FEATURES

The following features of this book will facilitate your learning:

- Carefully sequenced topics that build on the knowledge you've acquired from previous topics
- Frequent hands-on activities that sharpen your PowerPoint skills
- Numerous illustrations that show how your screen should look at key points during these activities
- The Data Disk, which contains all the files you will need to complete the activities (as explained in the next section)
- Easy-to-spot, bulleted procedures that provide the general, step-by-step instructions you'll need to perform PowerPoint tasks
- A quick reference at the end of each chapter, listing the mouse/keyboard actions needed to perform the techniques introduced in the chapter

WHAT YOU NEED TO USE THIS BOOK

To run PowerPoint 7.0 and complete this book, you need a computer with a hard disk and at least one floppy-disk drive, a monitor, a keyboard, and a mouse (or compatible tracking device). Although you don't absolutely need a printer, we strongly recommend that you have one. Windows 95 must be installed on your computer; if it is not, see your Windows reference manual for installation instructions. (PowerPoint 7.0 must also be installed; for help, see Appendix A.)

COMPUTER AND MONITOR

You need an IBM or IBM-compatible personal computer and monitor that are capable of running Microsoft Windows 95.

You need a hard disk with at least 17 megabytes of free storage space (if PowerPoint 7.0 is not yet installed) or 5 megabytes of free space (if PowerPoint 7.0 is installed) and a CD-ROM drive.

Finally, you need an EGA or higher (VGA, SVGA, and so on) graphics card and monitor to display Windows and PowerPoint at their intended screen resolution. (**Note:** The PowerPoint screens shown in this book are taken from a VGA monitor. Depending on your monitor type, your screens may look slightly different.)

KEYBOARD

IBM-compatible computers come with various styles of keyboards; these keyboards function identically but have different layouts. Figures I.1, I.2, and I.3 show the three main keyboard styles and their key arrangements.

Figure I.1 **IBM PC–style keyboard**

Figure I.2 **XT/AT–style keyboard**

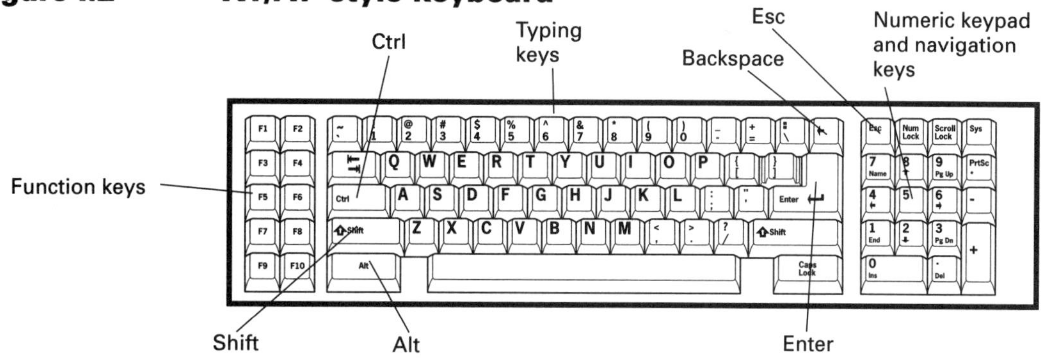

Ctrl
Typing keys
Esc
Backspace
Numeric keypad and navigation keys
Function keys
Shift
Alt
Enter

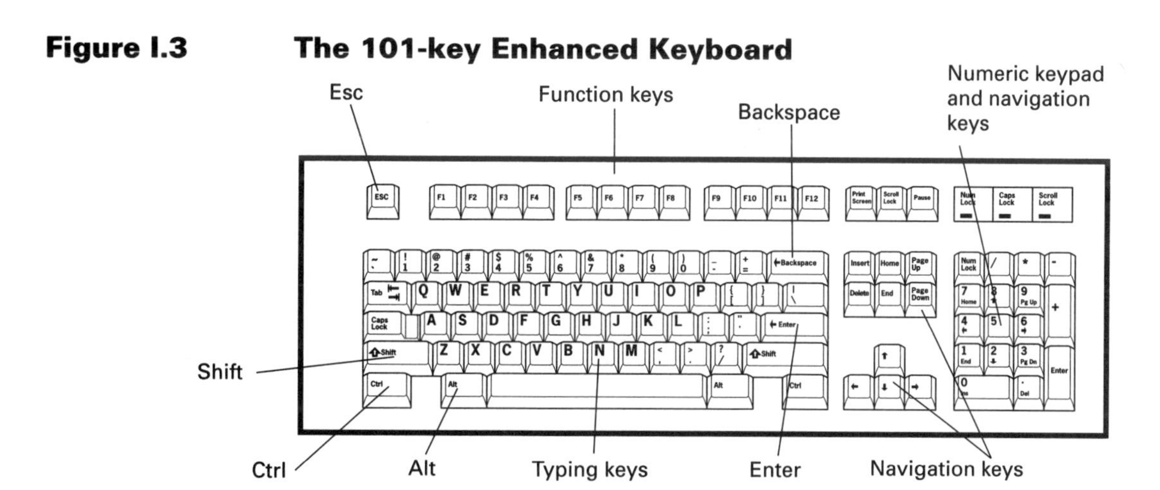

Figure I.3 **The 101-key Enhanced Keyboard**

Esc
Function keys
Backspace
Numeric keypad and navigation keys
Shift
Ctrl
Alt
Typing keys
Enter
Navigation keys

- The *function keys,* which enable you to access PowerPoint's special features. On the PC-, XT-, and AT-style keyboards, there are 10 function keys at the left end of the keyboard; on the 101-key Enhanced Keyboard, there are 12 keys at the top of the keyboard.
- The *typing keys,* which enable you to enter letters, numbers, and punctuation marks. These keys include the Shift, Ctrl, and Alt keys, which you will need to access several of PowerPoint's special features. The typing keys are located in the main body of all the keyboards.

- The *numeric keypad*, which enables you either to enter numeric data or to navigate through a document. When Num Lock is turned on, you use the numeric keypad to enter numeric data, just as you would on a standard calculator keypad. When Num Lock is turned off, you use the numeric keypad to navigate through a document by using the cursor-movement keys: Up, Down, Left, and Right Arrows; Home, End, PgUp (Page Up), and PgDn (Page Down). To turn Num Lock on/off, simply press the Num Lock key. To enter numeric data when Num Lock is off, use the number keys in the top row of the typing area.
- The *cursor-movement keypad*, which is available only on the Enhanced Keyboard, enables you to navigate through a document by using the Home, End, Page Up, and Page Down keys. The cursor-movement keypad works the same when the Num Lock is turned on or off. This enables you to use the numeric keypad for numeric data entry (that is, to keep Num Lock on) and still have access to cursor-movement keys.

MOUSE OR COMPATIBLE TRACKING DEVICE

You need a mouse or other type of tracking device to work through the activities in this book. Any standard PC mouse or tracking device (a trackball, for example) will do.

Note: Throughout this book, we direct you to use a mouse. If you have a different tracking device, simply use your device to perform all the mousing tasks: pointing, clicking, dragging, and so on.

PRINTER

Although you don't absolutely need a printer to work through the activities in this book, we strongly recommend that you have one. A laser printer is ideal, but an ink-jet or dot-matrix will do just fine.

CONVENTIONS USED IN THIS BOOK

The following conventions used in this book will help you learn PowerPoint 7.0 easily and efficiently.

- Each chapter begins with a short introduction and ends with a summary that includes a quick-reference guide to the techniques used in the chapter.
- Main chapter topics (large, capitalized headings) and subtopics (headings preceded by a cube) explain PowerPoint features. Hands-on activities allow you to practice using these features.

In these activities, keystrokes, menu choices, and anything you are asked to type are printed in boldface. Here's an example from Chapter 2:

1. Click on the Slide Show button.

- Activities adhere to a cause-and-effect approach. Each step tells you what to do (cause) and then what will happen (effect). From the example above:

Cause:	Click on the Slide Show button.
Effect:	The slide show begins.

- A plus sign (+) is used with the Shift, Ctrl, and Alt keys to indicate a multi-key keystroke. For example, press **Ctrl+R** means "Press and hold down the Ctrl key, press the R key, and then release them both."
- To help you distinguish between steps presented for reference purposes (general procedures) and steps you should carry out at your computer as you read (specific procedures), we use the following system:
  - A bulleted step, like this, is provided for your information and reference only.

1. A numbered step, like this, indicates one in a series of steps that you should carry out in sequence at your computer.

BEFORE YOU START

Each chapter's activities proceed sequentially. In many cases, you cannot perform an activity until you have performed one or more of the activities preceding it. For this reason, we recommend that you allot enough time to work through an entire chapter in one session.

Feel free to take as many breaks as you need. Stand up, stretch, take a walk, drink some decaf. Don't try to absorb too much information at one time. Studies show that people assimilate and retain information most effectively when it is presented in digestible chunks and followed by a liberal amount of hands-on practice.

You are now ready to begin. Good learning and...*bon voyage!*

CHAPTER 1: GETTING STARTED

A Quick Review of Mousing Skills

Creating Your Work Folder

Starting PowerPoint

Please Read This, It's Important

Exploring the Application and Presentation Windows

Opening a Presentation File

Moving between Slides in Slide View

Changing the View

Closing a Presentation File

Exiting from PowerPoint

Welcome to the world of computerized desktop presentation! PowerPoint 7.0 for Windows 95 is a feature-rich, easy-to-use program that enables you to create presentation slides that combine text, charts (graphs), drawings, and clip-art graphics. You can display your PowerPoint slides on a computer screen, print them on paper or overhead transparencies, or process them as 35-millimeter slides.

This first chapter gets you up and running in PowerPoint and introduces you to the PowerPoint working environment. When you're done working through this chapter, you will know

- How to start PowerPoint
- How to open a presentation file
- How to move between slides in Slide view
- How to change the view
- How to close a presentation file
- How to exit from PowerPoint

A QUICK REVIEW OF MOUSING SKILLS

The *mouse* is a hand-operated device that enables you to communicate with PowerPoint by manipulating (selecting, deselecting, moving, deleting, and so on) graphical and text objects that are displayed on your computer screen. When you move the mouse across the surface of your mousepad (or roll a trackball in its base), a symbol called the *mouse pointer* moves across the screen. You use this mouse pointer to point to the on-screen object that you want to manipulate. The mouse has two or more buttons. You use these buttons to communicate with PowerPoint in various ways, as detailed in Table 1.1.

Note: Read through the following table to familiarize yourself with standard PowerPoint mousing techniques. Do not, however, try to memorize these techniques. Instead, use this table as a quick reference, referring to it whenever you need to refresh your memory.

Table 1.1 Mousing Techniques

Technique	How to Do It
Point	Move the mouse until the tip of the mouse pointer is over the desired object. "Point to the word *File*" means "Move the mouse until the tip of the mouse pointer is over the word *File*."

Table 1.1 **Mousing Techniques (Continued)**

Technique	How to Do It
Click	Press and release the left or right mouse button. When we want you to click the left mouse button, we'll simply say "Click." For example, "Click on the word *File*" means "Point to the word *File* and then press and release the left mouse button." When we want you to click the right mouse button, we'll say so. For example, "Point to the Standard toolbar and click the right mouse button."
Double-click	Press and release the left mouse button twice in rapid succession. "Double-click on the Preview1 file" means "Point to the file name Preview1 and then press and release the left mouse button twice in rapid succession."
Choose	Click on a menu command or a dialog-box button. "Choose File, Open" means "Click on the word *File* (in the menu bar) and then click on the word *Open* (in the File menu)."
Drag	Press and hold the left mouse button while moving the mouse. "Drag the scroll box upward" means "Point to the scroll box, press and hold the left mouse button, move the mouse upward, and then release the mouse button."
Scroll	Click on a scroll arrow or within a scroll bar, or drag a scroll box.
Select	Click on an object (to select the entire object) or drag over part of a text object (to select part of the text). "Select the Chapter 2 file" means "Click on the file name Chapter 2." "Select the first three letters of the label *Last Name*" means "Drag over the letters *Las*."
Check	Click on a check box to check (turn on) that option. "Check the Match Case option" means "Click on the Match Case check box to check it."
Uncheck	Click on a check box to uncheck (turn off) that option. "Uncheck the Match Case option" means "Click on the Match Case check box to uncheck it."

CREATING YOUR WORK FOLDER

Throughout this book, you will be creating, editing, and saving several files. In order to keep these files together, you need to create a work folder for them on your hard disk. Your work folder will also hold the sample files contained on the enclosed Data Disk.

Follow these steps to create your work folder. (**Note:** If PowerPoint 7.0 is not currently installed on your computer, please install it now, before you create your work folder. See Appendix A for instructions.)

1. Turn on your computer. After a brief, internal self-check, Windows 95 will load and prompt you for a password. Type your password and press **Enter**. (See Figure 1.1)

Figure 1.1 **The Windows 95 desktop**

2. From the Windows 95 desktop, click on the **Start** button. Point to Programs and select **Windows Explorer**. The Windows Explorer can be used to manage the folders and files on your computer.

3. In the Tree pane, click on the plus sign (**+**) to the left of the My Computer branch to expand it so that you can view the floppy disk drive and the hard drive. (The branch might already be expanded.) This branch may also contain folders, such as the Control Panel and Printers folders.

4. Click on the hard-disk icon (**C**:). From the menu bar, choose **File, New, Folder** to create a new folder. You will copy the contents of the Data Disk into this folder. The new folder is displayed in the Contents pane and is highlighted so that you can rename it now. Type **Power Work** and press **Enter** to assign a new name to the folder.

5. Select the hard-disk icon (**C**:) and choose **File, Properties** to view the amount of available hard-disk space. On the General tab, the number of free bytes is displayed.

   If you have fewer than 5,000,000 (5MB) free bytes, you will not be able to create your work folder and perform the hands-on activities in this book (while maintaining an adequate amount of free hard-disk space for your other computer activities). Click on **Cancel** to close the Properties dialog box. Before going any further, you must delete enough files from your hard disk to increase the free-byte total to at least 5,000,000. For doing this, refer to your Windows 95 reference manual, or better yet, enlist the aid of an experienced Windows 95 user. (**Note:** Make sure you back up all your important files before deleting them!)

6. Remove the Data Disk from its envelope at the back of this book. Insert the Data Disk (label up) into the CD ROM drive. Determine whether this is drive D or drive E.

7. The easiest way to copy the files from the CD ROM to your Power Work folder is by dragging them. Display the contents of the **CD-ROM (D: or E:) branch.** (Use the same technique that you used in step 3.) Then select all of the files (Ctrl+D or Ctrl+E is a keystroke shortcut) in the Contents pane.

8. Drag the selected files to the Power Work folder in the Tree pane. Release the mouse button to copy the files into the Power Work folder. The folder name should be highlighted

before you release the mouse button. As the files are copied, you will see a graphical display of the files flying from one folder to another.

9. Choose **File, Close**—that is, click on **File** and then click on **Close**—to close the Windows Explorer window.

Now all the files that you need for this book are stored in the PowerPoint work folder.

Important Note: The hands-on activities in this book assume that your work folder is on the hard drive and is named Power Work. If you specified a different location for the folder or a different name, remember to substitute this location and/or name whenever we mention the PowerPoint work folder.

STARTING POWERPOINT

Before you start PowerPoint 7.0, it must be installed on your hard disk. If it is not installed, please install it now. For help installing PowerPoint 7.0, see Appendix A of this book.

You also need to have created a work folder on your hard disk and copied the files from the enclosed Data Disk to this directory. If you have not done this, please do so now; for instructions, see the previous section, "Creating Your Work Folder."

Note: In this book, we present two types of procedures: bulleted and numbered. A *bulleted procedure*—one whose steps are preceded by bullets (•)—serves as a general reference; you should read its steps without actually performing them. A *numbered procedure*—one whose steps are preceded by numbers (1., 2., and so on)—is a specific hands-on activity; you should perform its steps as instructed.

To start PowerPoint,

- Turn on your computer.
- Enter your Windows 95 password.
- From the Start menu, highlight *Programs* and select *Microsoft PowerPoint*. If you have installed Microsoft Office, you might need to move through additional layers of the Start menu to locate PowerPoint.

Let's follow this procedure to start PowerPoint:

1. Now that Windows 95 is running, you can start PowerPoint. In order to do this, you must locate the program Microsoft PowerPoint in the Start menu. Because Windows 95 is a customizable program, we cannot know the details of your Windows 95 setup. So please bear with us as we search for your Microsoft PowerPoint program. Let's begin by clicking on the **Start** button in the taskbar.
2. Point to **Programs** to display the available programs. Depending on your Windows 95 setup, you might need to search through a few layers of menus to find Microsoft PowerPoint. (If PowerPoint was installed as part of Microsoft Office, then you will probably find PowerPoint in the Microsoft Office menu as shown in Figure 1.2.)

Figure 1.2 **The Start menu with cascading menus**

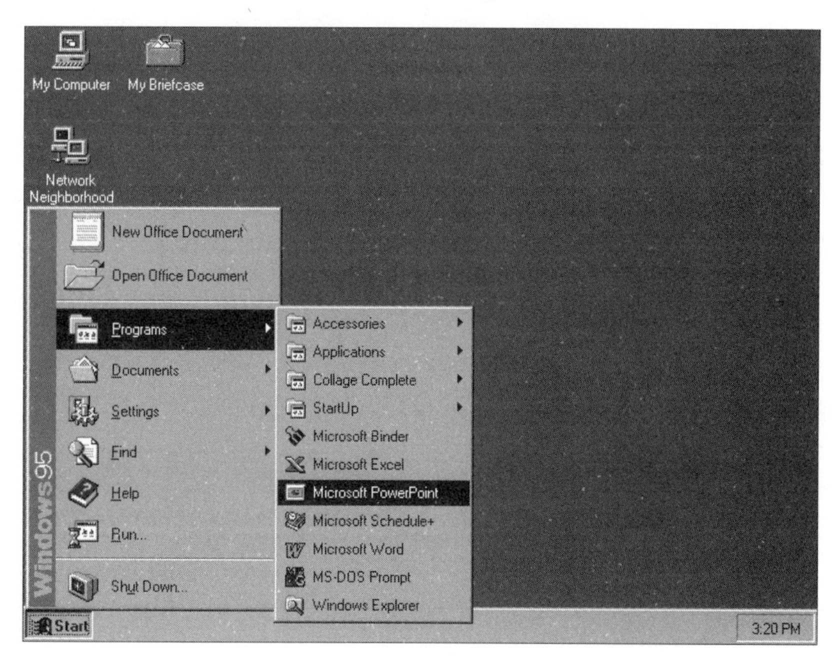

3. When Microsoft PowerPoint is visible, click on it to begin the PowerPoint program. A Tip Of The Day window that you must respond to may appear. If you find this feature distracting, you can turn it off by clicking in the Show Tips At Startup box. Another window will appear asking you to choose a starting point for your presentation. For now, click on **Cancel** (we'll open existing presentations and work with templates later) (see Figure 1.3).

Figure 1.3 **PowerPoint 7.0, after startup**

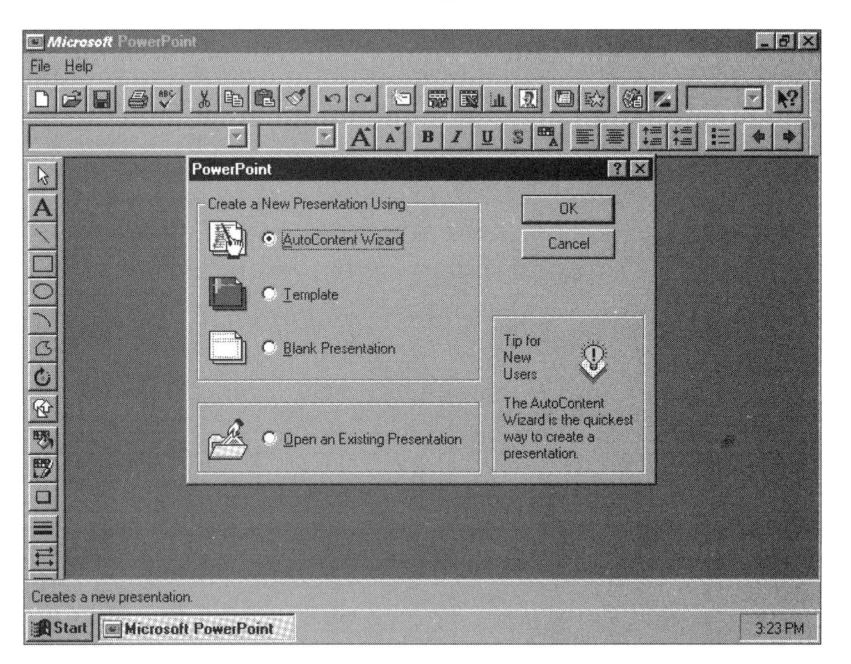

PLEASE READ THIS, IT'S IMPORTANT

Like Windows 95, PowerPoint can be customized. And depending on how you (or perhaps a colleague) have set up your PowerPoint program, it may look very different from another user's PowerPoint setup, or from the PowerPoint setup used in this book. When faced with the daunting task of writing for an "invisible" audience—with hundreds, if not thousands, of different PowerPoint setups—we decided to make the following assumption:

- We assume that you are running PowerPoint with the same *default* (standard) settings that were automatically chosen when you first installed PowerPoint 7.0.

Of course, this assumption may not be true. You or a colleague may have customized your PowerPoint program to show additional toolbars, display on-screen text as 20-point Antique English, hide the status bars, and so on.

Here's our recommendation. First of all, relax. Chances are that your program settings are fine. But if you should run into a snag while working through this book—for example, if your screen displays differ markedly from ours, or if tools that we ask you to use are missing from your screen—simply use your increasing PowerPoint expertise to make the changes necessary to match your PowerPoint setup with ours.

EXPLORING THE APPLICATION AND PRESENTATION WINDOWS

A *window* is a rectangular area on the screen, in which you view a program (PowerPoint, for example) or a document (a PowerPoint slide, for example). PowerPoint uses two windows, one nestled snugly within the other. The outer window is called the *application window* because it contains the PowerPoint program's main options and commands. (**Note**: The terms *application* and *program* are synonymous.) The inner window is called the *presentation window*, because it contains the current presentation file and the tools, options, commands, and messages associated with this file. The next two sections discuss the PowerPoint application and presentation windows in detail.

THE APPLICATION WINDOW

Let's explore the PowerPoint application window. Think of the application window as a project supervisor that provides you with a set of options and commands to create and edit your presentations. Observe the elements shown in Figure 1.4 and Table 1.2.

Figure 1.4 **The PowerPoint application window**

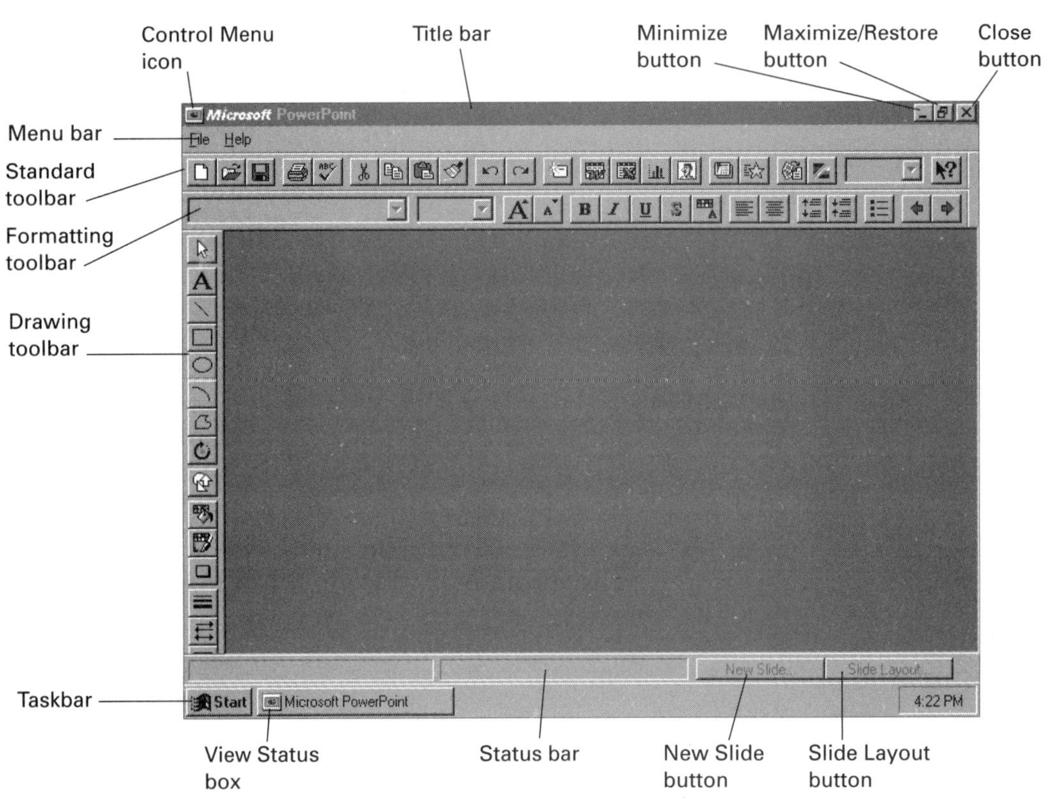

Table 1.2 **PowerPoint Application-Window Elements**

Element	Description
Control Menu icon	Use it to change the size and position of the application window or to close it.
Title bar	Contains the application title, Microsoft PowerPoint.
Menu bar	Displays PowerPoint's menu options.
Minimize button	Shrinks the application window to a program icon (the same type of program icon observed earlier in this chapter).

Table 1.2 **PowerPoint Application-Window Elements (Continued)**

Element	Description
Maximize/ Restore button	Maximizes or restores (shrinks) the application window.
Close button	Use this button to close the application window. The Close button has the same function as the Close command in the Control menu.
Standard toolbar	Click on its buttons to issue frequently used commands and utilities.
Formatting toolbar	Click on its buttons to issue frequently used formatting commands.
Drawing toolbar	Use its buttons to draw on slides.
Status bar	Reports information about the currently selected command.
View Status box	Reports information about the current slide and view.
New Slide button	Use it to create a new slide. Note that this button is *dimmed* (displayed in light letters) because it is unavailable in the current working context. You cannot create a new slide when no presentation is open.
Slide Layout button	Use it to change a slide's layout. Note that this button is dimmed for the same reason as given above.

Let's take a moment to explore some application-window elements:

1. Observe your Maximize/Restore button (the button in the upper-right corner of the window). If your application window is maximized (enlarged to full screen size), this button contains two windows, one in front of the other; clicking on this button restores (shrinks) the application window to its nonmaximized size and location. If your application window is not maximized, this button contains a single window; clicking on it maximizes the window.

2. Click on the **Maximize/Restore** button a few times to toggle your application window between its maximized and non-maximized states.
3. Place the application window in its nonmaximized state. The Maximize/Restore button should now contain a single window. Click once on the **Control Menu** icon (the icon to the left of the PowerPoint title bar) to open the drop-down Control menu. (Do not double-click on the Control Menu icon, as this will cause you to exit from PowerPoint.) Observe the various commands for moving and resizing the window. Click once again on the **Control Menu** icon to close the drop-down Control menu.
4. Click on thc **Maximize/Restore button** to maximize the application window. Click on the **Control Menu** icon to reopen the drop-down Control menu. Note that several commands are now dimmed (Move, Size, and Maximize). In this case, you cannot move, size, or maximize your application window, because it is already maximized. Click once again on the **Control Menu** icon to close the drop-down Control menu.

THE PRESENTATION WINDOW

Now let's open the PowerPoint presentation window, so that we can examine it:

1. Click on the **New** icon (the first icon from the left) in the Standard toolbar dialog box.
2. Click on **OK** to open a new presentation window.
3. Observe your presentation window's Maximize/Restore button. If your presentation window is maximized, this button contains two windows, one in front of the other.
4. If your presentation window is maximized, click on the **Maximize/Restore** button to restore the window to its nonmaximized size and location. Your presentation window should now match (or closely resemble) that shown in Figure 1.5.

Think of the PowerPoint presentation window as a workspace in which you create and edit your presentation slides. Observe the window elements, as described in Table 1.3 and shown in Figure 1.5.

Figure 1.5 **PowerPoint Presentation-Window Elements**

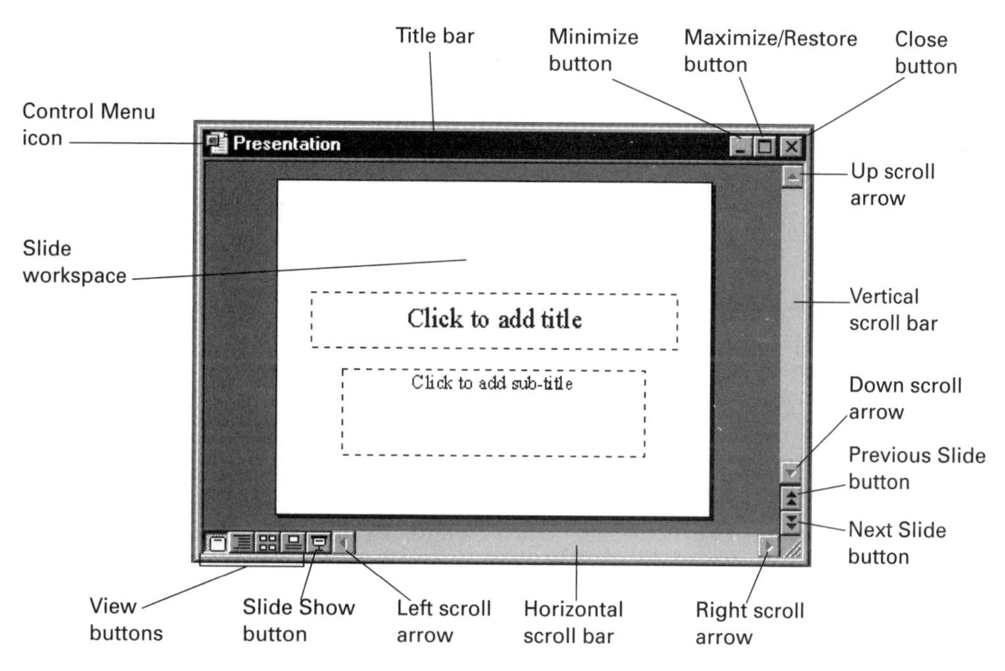

Table 1.3 **PowerPoint Presentation-Window Elements**

Element	Description
Control Menu icon	In a maximized presentation window, this is an icon to the left of the menu bar. In a nonmaximized presentation window (as shown in Figure 1.5), this is an icon to the left of the title bar. These boxes are equivalent; only their locations differ. You use the Control Menu icon to change the size and position of the presentation window or to close it.

Table 1.3 PowerPoint Presentation-Window Elements (Continued)

Element	Description
Title bar	Contains the presentation's title. Since you have not yet given a title to the new presentation you created in step 1, PowerPoint gives it the default title, Presentation.
Minimize button	Use this button to shrink the presentation window to an icon.
Maximize/Restore button	In a maximized presentation window, this button contains two windows, one in front of the other; use this button to restore the presentation window to its nonmaximized size and location. In a nonmaximized presentation window (as shown in Figure 1.5), this button contains a single window; use it to maximize the presentation window.
Close button	Use this button to close the presentation window. The Close button has the same function as the Close command in the Control menu.
Slide workspace	The large white area in the middle of the window where you view, create, and edit presentation slides.
View buttons	Use these buttons to change the *view* in which the current presentation is displayed. (More about views in the upcoming section, "Changing the View.")
Slide Show button	Use this button to run a slide show of the current presentation.
Horizontal scroll bar, left/right scroll arrows	Use these to scroll (move) the current slide contents right or left.
Vertical scroll bar, up/down scroll arrows	Use these to scroll (move) the current slide contents up or down and to move between slides in the current presentation.

Table 1.3 **PowerPoint Presentation-Window Elements (Continued)**

Element	Description
Previous Slide button	Use this to display the previous slide in the current presentation.
Next Slide button	Use this to display the next slide in the current presentation.

Let's take a closer look at some of these presentation-window elements:

1. Observe the presentation-window title bar. As mentioned earlier, since you have not yet named your new presentation, PowerPoint has given it the default title, Presentation.
2. Click once on the presentation-window **Control Menu** icon to the left of the presentation-window title bar. (Make sure you click on the presentation-window Control Menu box, not the application-window Control Menu box.) Note that the presentation-window Control Menu commands are virtually identical to the application-window Control menu commands you viewed in an earlier activity. Click again on the **Control Menu** box to close the Control menu.
3. Click on the Maximize/Restore button (as shown in Figure 1.5) to maximize your presentation window.
4. Observe the changes to your screen display, as shown in Figure 1.6. The presentation window enlarged to fill all the available space within the application window, the presentation-window title bar disappeared, and the current file name moved up to the application-window title bar—Microsoft PowerPoint - Presentation. The presentation-window Control Menu icon moved to the left end of the menu bar (directly below the application-window Control Menu icon), and the presentation-window Maximize/Restore button moved to the right end of the menu bar (directly below the application-window Maximize/Restore button).
5. Choose **File, Close**—click on **File**, then click on **Close**—to close the presentation window. The application window is left alone on screen.

Figure 1.6 **Maximized PowerPoint presentation window**

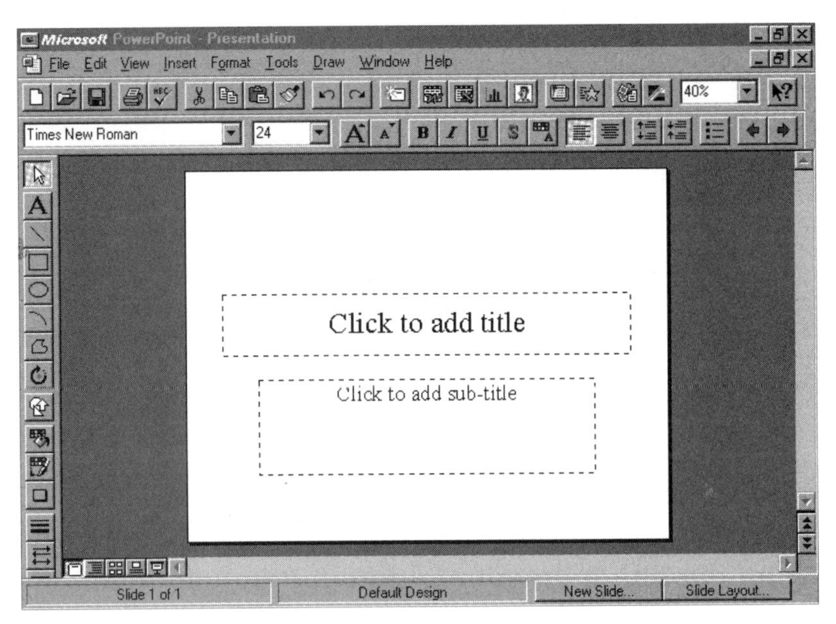

OPENING A PRESENTATION FILE

A *file* is a collection of data (information) stored on a hard or floppy disk. A PowerPoint *presentation file* consists of one or more slides. Each slide can contain text, charts (graphs), drawings, and clip-art graphics. In order to view, edit, add, or delete slides in an existing presentation, you must first open the presentation file in which these slides are stored.

Here's the general procedure for opening a presentation file:

- Choose *File, Open* to open the Open dialog box.
- If necessary, change the current drive to the drive that contains the presentation file you want to open.
- If necessary, change the current folder to the folder that contains the presentation file you want to open.
- In the File Name list box, select the name of the presentation file that you want to open.
- Click on *OK*.

Let's open a presentation file stored in the Power Work work folder that you created in the Introduction. First, we'll take a closer look at PowerPoint's menu commands:

1. Click on **File** to open the drop-down File menu. Observe the commands in this menu. Note that some are followed by an *ellipsis* (...), and others are not. When you choose a command that is followed by an ellipsis (for example, Open...), PowerPoint displays a dialog box prompting you for further information that it needs to carry out your command. When you choose a command not followed by an ellipsis (for example, Exit), PowerPoint performs the command without displaying a dialog box. (**Note**: For the sake of clarity, we've chosen not to print command ellipses in this book. For example, when we ask you in step 3 to choose the File, Open... command, we'll simply say, "Choose File, Open.")
2. Click on **File** again to close the drop-down File menu.
3. Choose **File, Open** to open the File Open dialog box, as shown in Figure 1.7.

Figure 1.7 **The File Open dialog box**

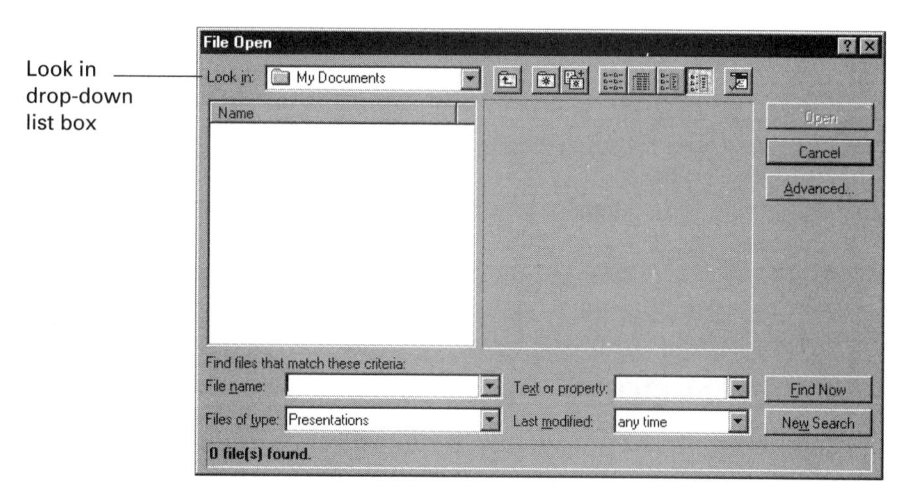

1. Observe the current folder, as reported in the Look in drop-down list box at the top of the dialog box. In Figure 1.7, this drop-down list box displays *My Documents;* your drop-down

list box may be different. You must now change the current folder to that of your Power Work work folder.

2. Change the current drive to the drive on which you created your Power Work directory. To do this, click on the **down arrow** to the right of the Look In drop-down list box to open the drop-down list of available drives, and then click on the desired drive. The Look in drop-down list box reports the new drive.
3. To change the current folder to your Power Work folder, locate the Power Work entry in the Name list box. You may need to scroll down through the list to find Power Work; if so, click on the **down scroll arrow** (the downward-pointing arrow in the lower-right corner of the list box) as many times as needed.
4. Double-click on **Power Work** to change your current folder to Power Work. The Look in drop-down list box should now read *Power Work;* if it doesn't, repeat steps 3 through 6. This is the work folder that you created earlier in this chapter.

Now that you've changed to your Power Work folder, you can select and open a presentation file that is stored in it:

1. In the Name list box, select (click once on) **Preview1**. The file name is *highlighted* (displayed in reverse video). In addition, a miniature representation of the first slide of Preview1 appears on the right side of the dialog box.
2. Click on **Open** to open Preview1. The mouse pointer changes to an hourglass to indicate that PowerPoint is busy and you cannot interrupt it. After a moment, the normal mouse pointer returns and the first slide of the presentation file Preview1 appears, as shown in Figure 1.8. This is the same slide you saw in miniature when you selected Preview1 in the Open dialog box.

MOVING BETWEEN SLIDES IN SLIDE VIEW

PowerPoint provides four different *views* (working environments) in which you can work on your presentation slides. You are currently in Slide view; you use this view to work in detail on one slide at a time. (You'll learn about the remaining views in the upcoming section, "Changing the View.") When you are in Slide view, you can use the mouse or the keyboard to move between slides in the current presentation.

Figure 1.8 **Preview1, newly opened**

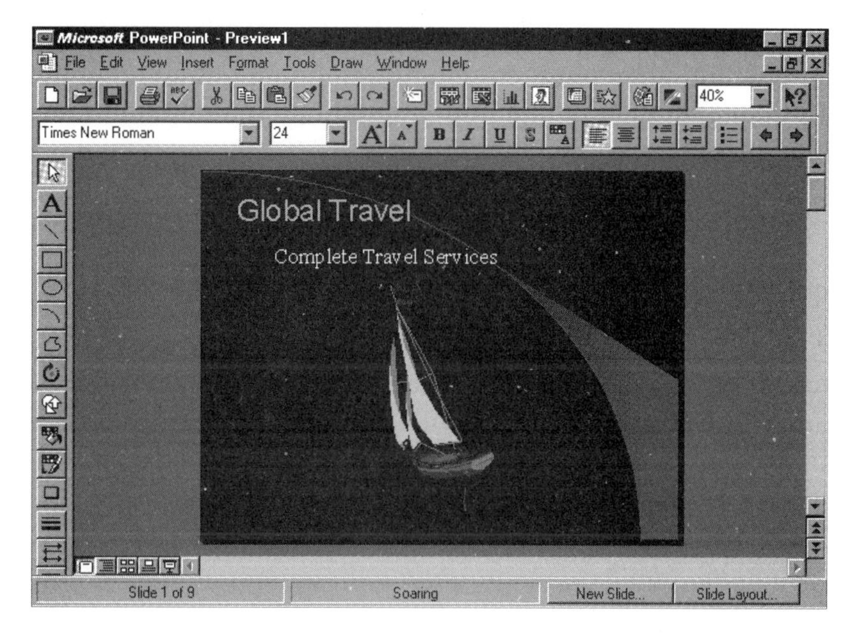

Here's the general procedure for using the mouse to move between slides:

- To move to the next slide, click on the *Next Slide* button (as shown in Figure 1.9).
- To move to the previous slide, click on the *Previous Slide* button.
- To move forward or back more than one slide, drag the *vertical scroll box* until desired slide number appears.

Here's the general procedure for using the keyboard to move between slides:

- To move to the next slide, press *Page Down* (or *PgDn* on the numeric keypad).
- To move to the previous slide, press *Page Up* (or *PgUp* on the numeric keypad).
- To move to the first or last slide in the presentation, press Ctrl+Home or Ctrl+End, respectively.

Figure 1.9 **Using the mouse to move between slides**

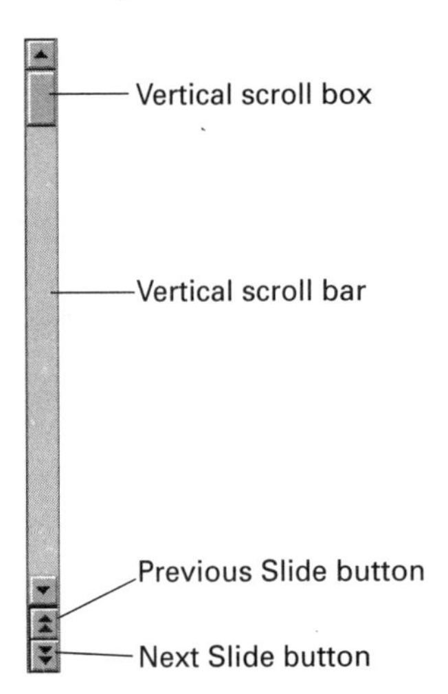

Let's practice using the keyboard to move between the slides of Preview1:

1. Observe the View Status box. It reports the current slide number, 1.
2. Press **Page Down** (or **PgDn**) to move to the next slide. (If you use the PgDn key on the numeric keypad, make sure that Num Lock is off.) Note that the View Status box reports your new slide number.
3. Repeat step 2 until you reach the last slide of the presentation, slide 9.
4. Press **Page Up** (or **PgUp**) to move to the previous slide, slide 8.
5. Repeat step 4 until you reach the first slide of the presentation.

Now let's use the mouse to display this same sequence of slides:

1. Click once on the **Next Slide** button (as shown in Figure 1.9) to move to the next slide.
2. Repeat step 1 until you reach the last slide of the presentation, slide 9.
3. Click once on the **Previous Slide** button to move to the previous slide, slide 8.
4. Repeat step 3 until you reach the first slide of the presentation.

Let's end this activity by using the vertical scroll box to move between nonconsecutive slides. Suppose you wanted to move directly to slide 5, without displaying any of the slides in between:

1. Point to the vertical scroll box (as shown in Figure 1.9).
2. Press and hold down the **left mouse button** to "grab" the vertical scroll box. Note that the current slide number is displayed (slide 1). Do not release the mouse button until we tell you to do so in step 4.
3. Move the mouse downward until *slide 5* is displayed.
4. Release the mouse button to display slide 5.

Note: The four-step procedure you just performed—pointing to an object, pressing and holding the left mouse button to "grab" the object, moving the mouse in the desired direction, and then releasing the mouse button—is called *dragging* an object (as explained in Table 1.1).

PRACTICE YOUR SKILLS

1. Use the keyboard to move to the following succession of consecutive slides:

   6, 7, 8, 9, 8, 7, 6, 5, 4, 3, 2, 1, 2

2. Use the mouse to move to the following succession of consecutive and nonconsecutive slides:

   6, 1, 4, 2, 7, 8, 9, 6, 5, 4, 2, 5, 3, 2, 1

CHANGING THE VIEW

As mentioned, PowerPoint provides four different views in which you can display, create, and edit your presentation slides. These are Slide view, Outline view, Slide Sorter view, and Note Pages view. Each view lends itself to certain types of tasks:

- *Slide view* allows you to work in detail on one slide at a time. You can view a slide, create a new slide, and create/edit/delete slide text, graphs, clip art, and drawings.

- *Outline view* allows you to work with an overview of the presentation's text. You can create new slides and enter/edit slide text.
- *Slide Sorter view* allows you to work with an overview of the entire set of slides in the presentation. Slides are displayed in miniature, making it easy for you to rearrange, copy, and delete them.
- *Notes Pages view* allows you to create notes for your individual slides. You can then use these notes as "cue cards" when narrating the presentation.

Here's the general procedure for changing the view:

- Click on *View* to open the drop-down View menu, and then click on the desired view: *Slides, Outline, Slide Sorter,* or *Notes Pages.*
- Or, click on the *Slide View* button, the *Outline View* button, the *Slide Sorter View* button, or the *Notes Pages View* button (as shown in Figure 1.10).

Figure 1.10 **The View buttons**

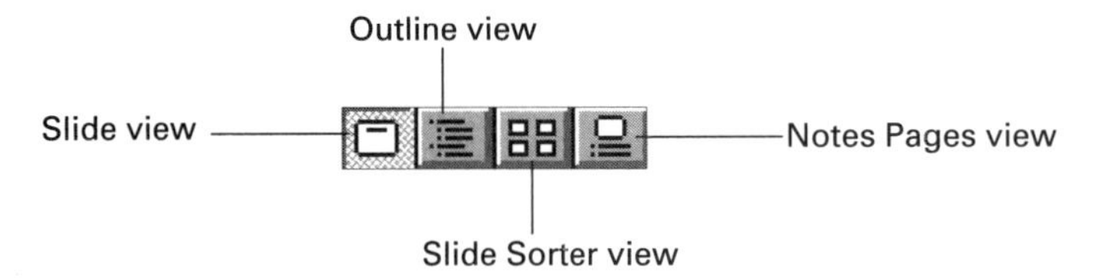

Let's practice changing views by using the View menu:

1. Click on **View** to display the drop-down View menu. Note that Slides is selected (preceded by a bullet).
2. Click on **Outline** to change to Outline view (as shown in Figure 1.11).
3. Observe the textual information on your screen. Scroll down to the end of the outline. (To do this, click repeatedly on the **down scroll arrow** in the bottom-right corner of the presentation window.) Now scroll back up to the beginning. (Click repeatedly on the **up scroll arrow.**) This is all the text in the Preview1

Figure 1.11 Preview1 in Outline view

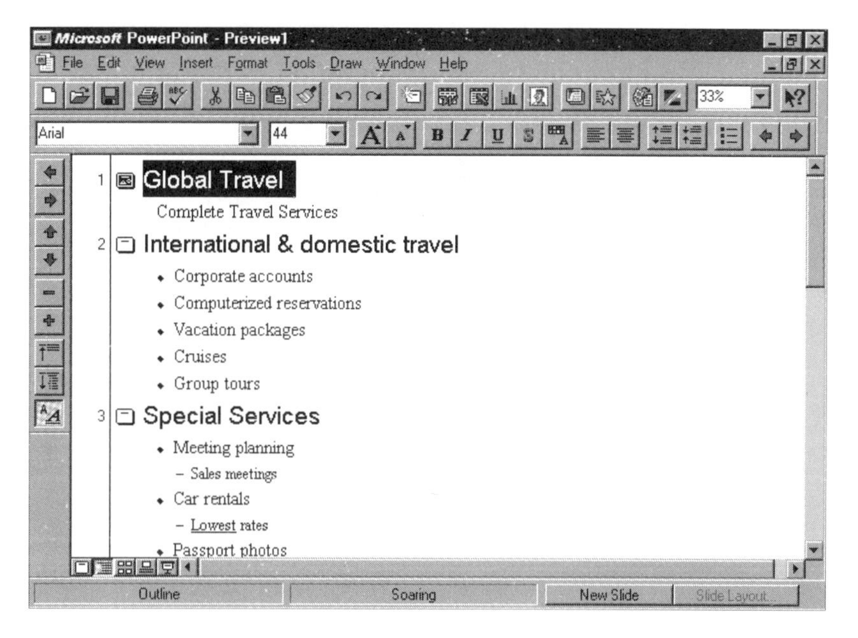

presentation. Note the numbers (1 through 9) on the left side of the screen; these represent the nine slides of Preview1.

4. Observe the View buttons along the bottom of the presentation window. Note that the Outline View button (the one showing a miniature outline) is selected.
5. Choose **View, Slide Sorter** to change to Slide Sorter view. Note that all nine slides of Preview1 are displayed in miniature, as shown in Figure 1.12. Later on, you'll learn how to copy and rearrange slides in the Slide Sorter.
6. Observe the View buttons. Note that the Slide Sorter View button (the one showing four miniature slides) is now selected.

Now let's use the View buttons to change views:

1. Click on the **Slide View** button (as shown in Figure 1.10) to change to Slide view.
2. Click on the **Slide Sorter View** button to change back to Slide Sorter view.

Figure 1.12 Preview1 in Slide Sorter view

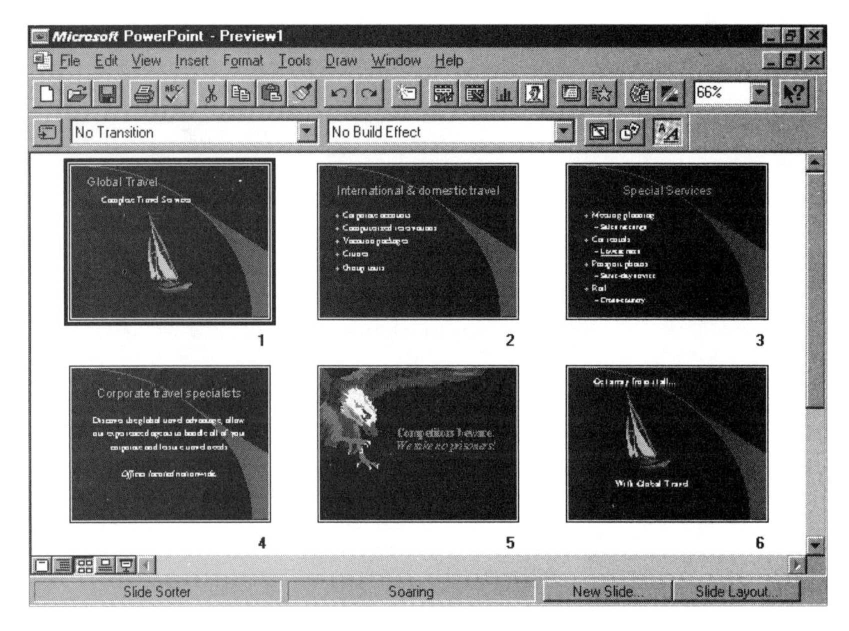

PRACTICE YOUR SKILLS

1. Use the View buttons to change to Notes Pages view.
2. Use the View buttons to return to Slide view.

CLOSING A PRESENTATION FILE

When you are finished working on a presentation file, you should close it. Opening a file places a copy of it in your computer's active memory (RAM); closing the file removes it from memory, freeing this memory for use by another presentation.

Here's the general procedure for closing a presentation file:

- Choose *File, Close*.

Let's close the current presentation file, Preview1:

1. Choose **File, Close**. (If you are asked whether to "Save changes to Preview1," click on No.) The Preview1 presentation window disappears, and the application window remains alone on the screen.

EXITING FROM POWERPOINT

When you finish a PowerPoint work session and want to turn off your computer or to run another program, you must first exit from PowerPoint. Here's the general procedure to do this:

- Choose *File, Exit*.

Let's end this chapter by exiting from PowerPoint:

1. Choose **File, Exit**. You are returned to the Windows 95 environment. You may now start another program from Windows, or exit and turn off your computer. For more information, see your Windows 95 reference manuals.

SUMMARY

Congratulations on successfully working through this first chapter; you're well on your way to PowerPoint mastery! You now know how to start PowerPoint, how to open a presentation file, how to move between slides in Slide view, how to change the view, how to close a presentation file, and how to exit from PowerPoint.

Here's a quick reference for the techniques you learned in this chapter:

Desired Result	How to Do It
Start PowerPoint	Turn on your computer; after Windows 95 loads, click on **Start, Programs, Microsoft PowerPoint**
Open a presentation file	Choose **File, Open** to open the File Open dialog box; if necessary, change the current folder to the folder that contains the presentation file you want to open; select the name of the presentation file you want to open; click on **Open**
Move between slides using the mouse	To move to the next slide, click on the **Next Slide** button; to move to the previous slide, click on the **Previous Slide** button; to move ahead or back more than one slide, drag the vertical scroll box

Desired Result	How to Do It
Move between slides using the keyboard	To move to the next slide, press **Page Down** (or **PgDn**); to move to the previous slide, press **Page Up** (or **PgUp**); to move to the first slide, press **Ctrl+Home**; to move to the last slide, press **Ctrl+End**
Change the view	Click on **View** to open the drop-down View menu, then click on the desired view (**Slides, Outline, Slide Sorter**, or **Notes Pages**); or, click on the desired View button (**Slide, Outline, Slide Sorter**, or **Notes Pages**)
Close a presentation file	Choose **File, Close**
Exit from PowerPoint	Choose **File, Exit**

A NOTE ON HOW TO PROCEED

If you wish to stop here, please feel free to do so now. If you feel energetic and wish to press onward, please proceed directly to the next chapter. Remember to allot enough time to work through an entire chapter in one sitting.

CHAPTER 2: BEGINNING A PRESENTATION

Running a Slide Show

Creating a Presentation: An Overview

Opening a New, Blank Presentation

Creating Slides and Entering Text in Slide View

Saving a New Presentation

Creating Slides and Entering Text in Outline View

Saving an Existing Presentation

In Chapter 1, you learned basic PowerPoint survival skills. In this chapter, you'll put these skills into action by beginning work on the nine-slide presentation that you'll create over the course of this and the four following chapters. After learning the general procedure for creating a presentation, you'll open a new presentation, create blank slides, enter text in these slides, and save the presentation to a file on your hard disk.

When you're done working through this chapter, you will know

- How to run a slide show
- How to open a new presentation
- How to create slides and enter text in Slide view
- How to save a new presentation
- How to create slides and enter text in Outline view
- How to create nonbulleted body text
- How to save an existing presentation

RUNNING A SLIDE SHOW

You can display a presentation on your computer screen by running a slide show. One slide is displayed at a time; the application and presentation windows disappear to allow each slide to fill the entire screen. You can advance the slides manually, or have PowerPoint advance them automatically.

Here's the general procedure for running a slide show manually:

- If it is not already open, open the presentation file containing the slides you want to show.
- Click on the *Slide Show* button to begin the slide show.
- To move forward one slide, click the *left mouse button,* press *Enter,* or press *Page Down.*
- To move backward one slide, press *Page Up.*
- When the last slide in the presentation is displayed, click the *left mouse button* or press *Enter* to end the show.
- During a slide show, you can click the right mouse button and have a menu containing a new set of tools at your fingertips. At the bottom of the menu is the End Show command. Clicking on this command with either mouse button ends the slide show, regardless of whether you're at the end of the slide show or not.

Note: You'll learn how to get PowerPoint to run a slide show automatically in Chapter 12.

SNEAK PREVIEW

Over the course of Chapters 2 through 6, you will create a nine-slide presentation that makes use of many of PowerPoint's basic slide creation and editing features. We'll begin this chapter by showing you a sneak preview of this presentation. As you observe these nine slides, remember that you'll soon possess the technical mastery to create them yourself!

Let's start PowerPoint, then run a slide show of Preview1, a presentation that contains copies of the nine slides you'll create in this and the next four chapters:

1. If you are not running PowerPoint, please start it now. For help, see "Starting PowerPoint" in Chapter 1 or the quick reference section at the end of Chapter 1.
2. If the Tip Of The Day dialog box appears, read your tip, then click on **OK** to close the dialog box.
3. In the PowerPoint dialog box, select the **Open An Existing Presentation** option. Click on **OK** to display the File Open dialog box. This is the same dialog box that appeared in Chapter 1 when you chose the File, Open command.
4. Open **Preview1** from your Power Work folder. As you'll recall from Chapter 1, you need to perform the following steps to do this:
    - If necessary, change from the current drive to the drive containing Power Work.
    - If necessary, change the current folder to **Power Work.**
    - Select (click on) the file **Preview1** in the File Name list box.
    - Click on **Open**.
5. If your application and presentation windows are not maximized, please do so now.

In order to run the slide show, you'll need to click on the Slide Show button. (Please don't do this yet.) You've probably noticed that the PowerPoint screen is overflowing with arcane-looking buttons. Locating the button for a given task is not always easy, especially during your initial learning period—that's where the *ToolTips* feature comes in. You can use ToolTips to display the name of a button by simply pointing to that button, as follows:

1. Point to—but don't click on—the leftmost button in the Standard toolbar (directly below the menu bar). After a moment, the word *New* pops up. This is the name of the button.
2. Observe the status bar. It reads

   ```
   Creates a new presentation based on the
   Blank Presentation template.
   ```

   This is a brief description of the New button's function.
3. Spend a few minutes using the ToolTips feature to tour your on-screen buttons. (Again, point to the buttons, but don't click!) Don't forget to observe the status bar.
4. PowerPoint displays status-bar descriptions for menu commands as well as buttons. Click on **File** to open the drop-down File menu. Point to—but don't click on—the New command. Note that the status bar displays a brief description of the File, New command (a similar description as the one displayed for the New button in step 1).
5. Press the **down arrow key** to select the *Open* command, and observe the description in the status bar. (If you had clicked the mouse on Open to select it, you would have *executed* the command, not just selected it.)
6. Use the technique outlined in steps 4 and 5 to take a quick tour of PowerPoint's menu system. (Use the mouse to open the drop-down menus Edit, View, Insert, Format, and so on. Use the arrow keys to select the individual commands in these menus.) Note that the status-bar descriptions appear for both available and dimmed commands.

Let's get back to the topic at hand, running a slide show of Preview1:

1. Use the ToolTips feature to locate the Slide Show button. (Hint: It's near the View buttons.)
2. Click on the **Slide Show** button to begin. The first slide of the presentation is displayed in full-screen view (as shown in Figure 2.1). This slide contains large title text (Global Travel), smaller nonitalicized subtitle text (Complete Travel Services), clip art (the sailboat), background graphics (the silhouetted boat and plane), and background shading (dark blue to light blue).

Figure 2.1 **Slide 1 of the Preview1 slide show**

3. Click the **left mouse button** to display the next slide. It contains large title text (International & domestic travel), a bulleted list with yellow, diamond-shaped bullets and text (Corporate accounts, Computerized reservations, and so on), and the same background graphics and shading as the previous slide.
4. Press **Enter** to display the next slide. You can advance to the next slide by pressing Enter, by clicking the left mouse button, or—as you'll see in the next step—by pressing Page Down. This slide contains large title text, a two-level bulleted list with yellow, diamond-shaped bullets, and the same background as the previous two slides.

Notice a pattern here? Although the text and layout differ from slide to slide, several elements remain the same: title-text size and style, bullet color and shape, bulleted-text size and style, and background graphics and shading. These recurring elements give the presentation unity. You'll learn more about unifying your presentation slides in Chapter 6. Now let's get back to our slide show:

1. Press **Page Down** to display the next slide. Note the title text, the body text (in this case, not formatted as a bulleted list), and the familiar background.
2. Display the next slide. (Use whichever technique you feel most comfortable with—the mouse, **Enter**, or **Page Down**.) Now here's something totally different! A black background, a fierce eagle, and text that is in neither the standard title-text nor body-text location. PowerPoint allows you to "override" the unified style of a presentation in order to make a dramatic point—which this slide admirably succeeds in doing.
3. Display the next slide. It contains text and background, along with the sailboat.
4. Display the next slide. It contains just the background and a picture of the sailboat.
5. Display the next slide. It contains an assortment of predefined shapes. You'll create a similar slide in Chapter 4.
6. Display the next slide. This—the ninth and last slide in the presentation—contains an assortment of *free-form shapes*. You'll create a similar slide in Chapter 4.
7. Click the **left mouse button** (or press **Enter** or **Page Down**) to end the slide show. (You can also click the right mouse button and then click on **End Show** at the bottom of the menu.)
8. Choose **File, Close** to close Preview1.

CREATING A PRESENTATION: AN OVERVIEW

All the skills you'll learn in this book are geared toward helping you produce sophisticated, professional-quality slide presentations. The following five bulleted steps represent the general procedure you'll use in Chapters 3 through 6 to create the nine-slide presentation that you just previewed.

- Open a new, blank presentation in which to create your slides.
- In the newly opened presentation, create new, blank slides and enter their text.

- Save the presentation to a file on your disk; continue to save this file every 10 or 15 minutes while you're working on it.
- Add design elements by drawing on slides, adding charts (graphs) to slides, adding clip art to slides, and laying out slides.
- Generate output by running a slide show of the presentation; printing slides, notes, or handouts; and/or processing the presentation as 35-millimeter slides.

In this chapter, you'll learn how to begin a presentation by performing the first three steps of this procedure: opening a new presentation, creating slides and entering text, and saving the presentation. The remaining steps will be covered in Chapters 3 through 6.

OPENING A NEW, BLANK PRESENTATION

Your first step in creating a slide presentation is to open a new, blank presentation. Here's the general procedure for doing this:

- Choose *File, New* to open the New Presentation dialog box.
- Select *Blank Presentation* from the General tab in the New Presentation dialog box. There are two other tabs in the New Presentation dialog box: *Presentation Designs* and *Presentations,* both of which provide various templates to help you create presentations (templates will be covered in Chapter 6.)
- Click on *OK.* The New Slide dialog box appears.
- Select your desired autolayout for the new presentation's first slide.
- Click on *OK.*

The following procedure outlines a quicker and simpler way to create a new, blank presentation:

- Click on the *New* button in the Standard toolbar. A New Slide dialog box opens.
- Select your desired autolayout for the new presentation's first slide.
- Click on *OK.*

Use this procedure when you want to create a new presentation, but you don't care to use a design template. There is a way to apply design templates later as we'll see in Chapter 6.

Let's open a new presentation:

1. Your screen should be empty, except for a maximized PowerPoint application window. If any presentations are open, please close them.
2. Click on the **New** button in the Standard toolbar to open the New Slide dialog box.
3. Verify that the top-left autolayout option is selected. This is the layout of the title slide, as indicated in the lower-right corner of the dialog box. A title slide—usually the first slide in a presentation—contains the presentation's title and (optionally) subtitle.
4. Click on **OK** to open a new, blank presentation beginning with a title slide (as shown in Figure 2.2).

Figure 2.2 **Opening a new, blank presentation**

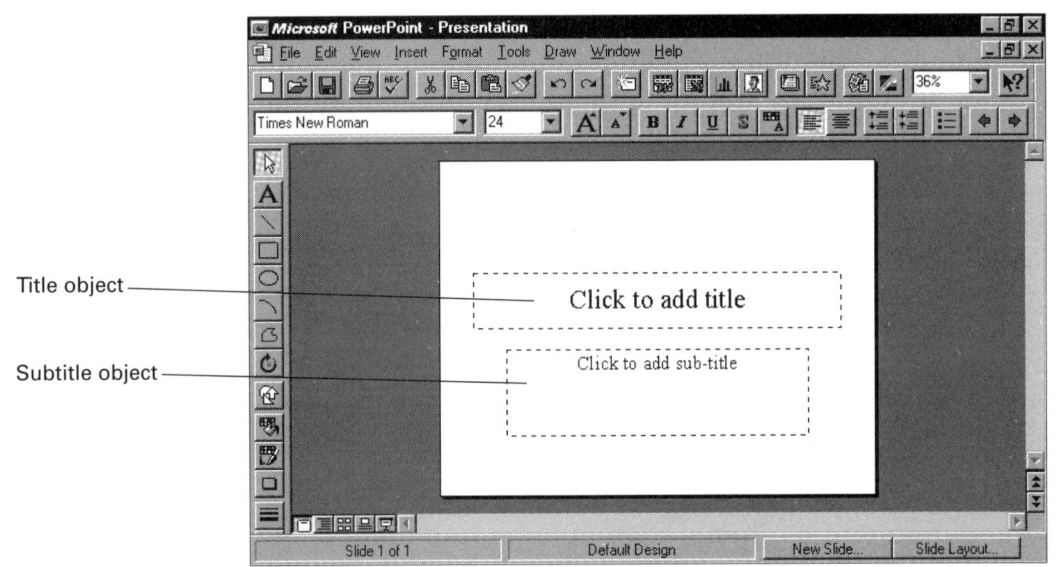

5. Observe that the new presentation's name, *Presentation* (as shown in the title bar), is the default name for the first new presentation. Subsequent new presentations are named *Presentation2, Presentation3,* etc., by default. Soon you'll learn how to rename a presentation and save it to a file on your hard disk.

CREATING SLIDES AND ENTERING TEXT IN SLIDE VIEW

After opening a new presentation, your next step in creating a presentation is to create blank slides and enter text in them. You can do this either in Slide view or in Outline view.

The advantage of entering your slide text in Slide view is that you can see what the actual slides look like (the text size, style, layout, and so on); the disadvantages are that you can see only one slide at a time, and that it is somewhat harder to enter and edit your text than in Outline view.

The advantages of entering your slide text in Outline view are that you can see an overview of all the text in your presentation, and that it is somewhat easier to enter and edit your text than in Slide view; the disadvantage is that you cannot see what the actual slides look like.

Beginning PowerPoint users often prefer to enter their slide text in Slide view, while more advanced users often prefer to enter their slide text in Outline view.

Over the next few sections, we'll show you how to create slides and enter text in Slide view. In the second half of the chapter, we'll show you how to perform these same tasks in Outline view. By the end of the chapter, you should have a good idea in which view you feel more comfortable entering text.

CREATING NEW SLIDES IN SLIDE VIEW

Here's the general procedure for creating a new slide in Slide view:

- Display the slide directly *after* which you want to add your new slide to appear.
- Click on the *New Slide* button or choose *Insert, New Slide* to open the New Slide dialog box.

- Select the desired autolayout for your new slide.
- Click on *OK.*

Let's use this simple procedure to add a new slide to our presentation:

1. Observe the View Status box (in the lower-left corner of the screen). The current slide is slide 1.
2. Click on the **New Slide** button (in the lower-right corner of the screen) to open the New Slide dialog box.
3. Verify that the Bulleted List autolayout is selected (the top choice in the center column of autolayouts).
4. Click on **OK** to create a new, bulleted-list slide. This slide is designed to hold a title and a list of bulleted items.

ENTERING SLIDE TEXT IN SLIDE VIEW

When you are in Slide view, PowerPoint provides three different types of *objects* in which you can enter slide text. You enter a title in a *title object*, a subtitle in a *subtitle object*, and body text (bulleted items, descriptive paragraphs, and so on) in a *bulleted-list object.* We'll explore these three types of objects in a moment.

Here's the general procedure for entering text in Slide view:

- Select (click on) the desired title, subtitle, or bulleted-list object.
- Type your desired title, subtitle, or body text.
- Press *Esc* to enter the text into the selected object.
- To deselect the object, press *Esc* again.

TEXT FORMATTING AND THE SLIDE MASTER

The format of the text you enter in a title, subtitle, or bulleted-list object is determined by the format settings in a special slide called the *Slide Master.* For example, the text you enter in a bulleted-list object is automatically formatted as a bulleted list, because this is the format of the bulleted-list text in the Slide Master. The bullet shape, size, and color, as well as the alignment of the bullet text items (left, right, center, or justified) are all determined by the Slide Master settings.

The Slide Master guarantees that all the title, subtitle, and bulleted-list text in your presentation will be identically formatted, thus lending an overall consistency to the presentation. You'll learn more about the Slide Master in Chapter 6.

Let's enter a title for the first slide of our new presentation:

1. Display slide 1. (Use the **vertical scroll box** or the **Page Up** key.)
2. Point to (but don't click on) the **title object**, the dotted box containing the placeholder *Click to add title*. Note that the mouse pointer changes to an I-beam; this pointer appears whenever you enter or edit text.
3. Click inside the **title object** to select it. The placeholder disappears, and PowerPoint outlines the object to indicate that it is selected.
4. Type the title, **Global Travel**. Note that your text is automatically centered within the title object, because the title-object text in the Slide Master is set to be centered.
5. Press **Esc** to enter your title in the title object. (Pressing Enter would have added a new line to the title object; please do *not* do this.)

Now let's enter a subtitle:

6. Click inside the **subtitle object**, the dotted box containing the placeholder *Click to add sub-title*.
7. Type the subtitle, **Complete Travel Services**. Note that the text is smaller than the title text and centered between the left and right borders of the subtitle object.
8. Press **Esc** to enter your subtitle.
9. Press **Esc** again to deselect the subtitle object. Your screen should match that shown in Figure 2.3.

Now let's enter a title and some bulleted-list text for slide 2:

1. Display slide 2 and select the **title object** (by clicking within it).
2. Type **International and domestic travel** and then press **Esc** to enter your slide title. Note that the text is automatically centered within the title object, just as it was in slide 1. The Slide Master causes all the title, subtitle, and bulleted-list text in your presentation to be identically formatted.

Figure 2.3 **Entering a title and subtitle in Slide view**

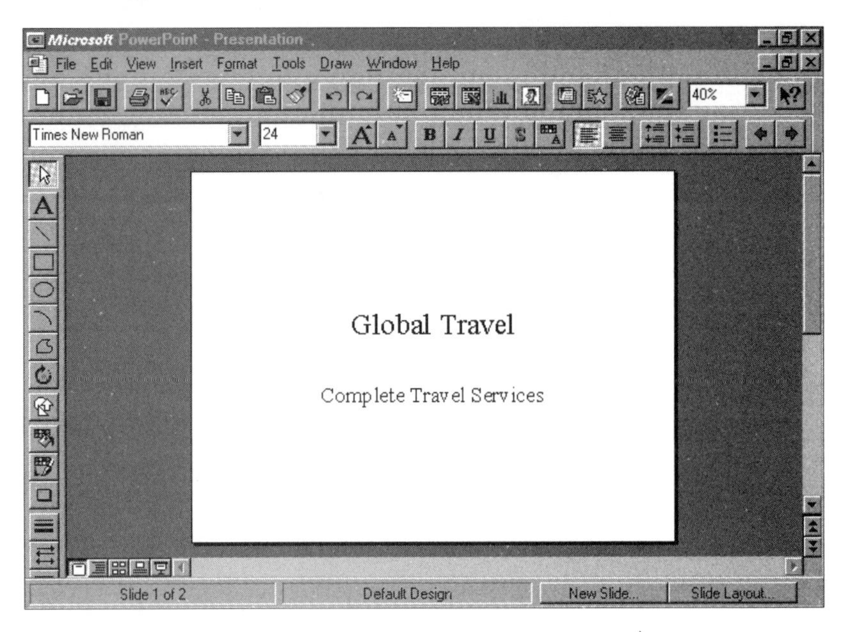

3. Select the **bulleted-list object**.
4. Type **Corporate accounts** to enter your first line of bulleted-list text. Note that the text is automatically formatted as a bulleted item. As mentioned, this is the format of the bulleted-list text in the Slide Master. (Later on, you'll learn how to change the format of your title and bulleted-list text.)
5. Press **Enter** to create a new bulleted item.
6. Type **Computerized reservations**.

PRACTICE YOUR SKILLS

1. Add the following two bulleted items to your list.

   Vacation packages

   Group tours

2. Press **Esc** to enter your bulleted-text items. Press **Esc** again to deselect the bulleted-list object. Your screen should match that shown in Figure 2.4.

Figure 2.4 **Entering a title and bulleted items for slide 2**

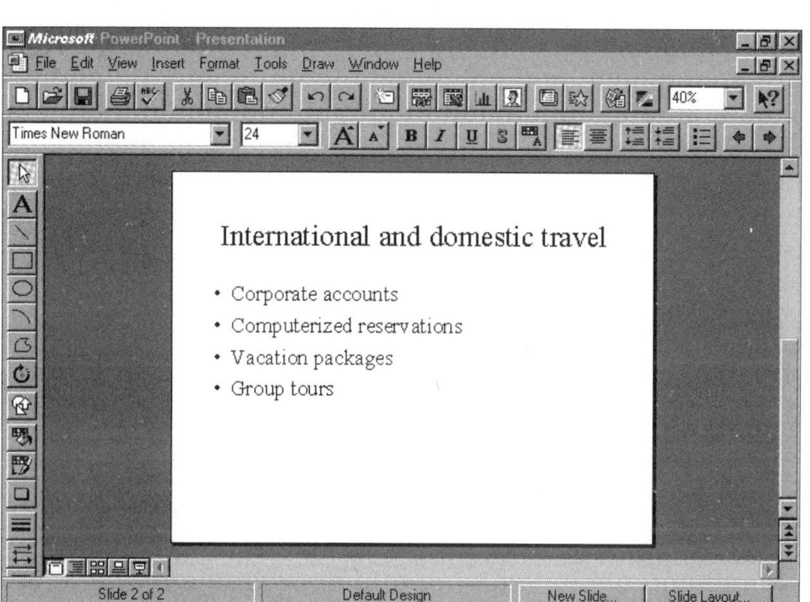

SAVING A NEW PRESENTATION

Until you save a new presentation, it exists only in computer memory (RAM), a temporary storage place. For permanent storage, you must save the presentation to a file on a disk. To save a new presentation for the first time, you use the *File, Save As* command. Here's the general procedure for doing this:

- Choose *File, Save As* to open the File Save dialog box.
- If necessary, change the current drive and folder to the drive and folder in which you want to save your presentation.
- In the File Name text box, type your desired file name. A file name can contain from up to 255 characters (letters and numbers, including spaces). Choose a descriptive file name to help you remember your presentation's contents. Do *not* include a *file-name extension*, a period followed by three letters (.PPT, for example). PowerPoint automatically adds the extension .PPT to your presentation's file name.

  Note: While all PowerPoint files contain a .PPT extension, you can hide file extensions in Windows 95. You may have noticed that none of our PowerPoint files display the .PPT extension. This is because we have hidden the file extensions. To hide file extensions, click on **Start, Programs, Windows Explorer** to run the Windows Explorer program. Then click on View, Options. If you want the file extensions hidden, make sure the second of the three check boxes at the bottom of the window is checked.

- Click on *OK.*
- If the Summary Info dialog box appears, fill in your desired summary information and click on OK.

Let's use File, Save As to save our new presentation:

1. Choose **File, Save As** to open the Save As dialog box. Note the similarity between this and the File Open dialog box (the dialog box that appears when you choose File, Open).
2. Observe the drop-down list box to the right of heading *Save in:*. Note that the current folder is already set to Power Work. Why? Earlier in this chapter, you changed your current location to the Power Work folder so that you could open the presentation file Preview1. PowerPoint "remembers" these changes and uses them as the new default settings.
3. Type **mypres1** in the File Name text box.
4. Click on **Save**. PowerPoint saves the presentation to a disk file named mypres1 in your C:\Power Work folder. As mentioned, PowerPoint automatically adds the extension .PPT to the end of a presentation file name. Note that the title bar reports your file name, Microsoft PowerPoint - [mypres1].

A NOTE ON WORKING WITH POWERPOINT 4.0 FILES

You can save files created in PowerPoint 7.0 for Windows 95 in the PowerPoint 4.0 for Windows 3.1 file format. If you do this, however, you run the risk of losing some of the PowerPoint 7.0 features. For this reason, we recommend that you save any PowerPoint 4.0 file that you revise as a PowerPoint 7.0 file. To do this,

- Open the PowerPoint 4.0 file.
- Choose *File, Save As.*
- In the Save As Type list box, select the *Presentations* option. This option saves the file as a PowerPoint 7.0 file.

- Give the file a new name. PowerPoint 4.0 files can be opened in PowerPoint 7.0, but only as read-only files. If you wish to save them, you must rename them.
- Click on *Save.*

CREATING SLIDES AND ENTERING TEXT IN OUTLINE VIEW

In the first half of this chapter, you learned how to create slides and enter text in Slide view. Now you'll learn how to perform these same tasks in Outline view.

CREATING NEW SLIDES IN OUTLINE VIEW

Here's the general procedure for creating a new slide in Outline view:

- Place the insertion point anywhere within the text of the slide after which you want to add your new slide.
- Click on the *New Slide* button or choose *Insert, New Slide.*

Let's create a new slide in Outline view:

1. Click on the **Outline View** button (use the ToolTips feature to find it) to change to Outline view.
2. Observe the differences between Outline view and Slide view. (You may want to switch back and forth between these two views while reading this step.) The Drawing toolbar has been removed because you cannot draw on a slide in Outline view. In its place appears the Outline toolbar, containing buttons for creating and editing outline text. The mouse pointer—when it is within the slide workspace—appears as an I-beam. Finally, and most dramatically, the slides are no longer displayed in their actual "slide" form (as they are in Slide view or in a slide show); instead, only an outline of the slides' text is displayed.
3. Return to Outline view, if necessary.
4. Move the I-beam until it is positioned anywhere within the text of slide 2. Click the **left mouse** button to place the insertion point in the text.
5. Click on the **New Slide** button to create a new slide (slide 3).
6. Type **My Slide** to assign a temporary title to this slide.

Now let's use the Insert, New Slide command to create a new slide:

1. Place the insertion point anywhere within the text of slide 2.
2. Choose **Insert, New Slide** to add a new slide after slide 2. Your screen should match that shown in Figure 2.5. Note that My Slide was moved down to slide 4 to make room for your new (untitled) slide. When you add a new slide to a presentation, PowerPoint inserts it *directly* after the currently displayed slide.

Figure 2.5 **Creating slides in Outline view**

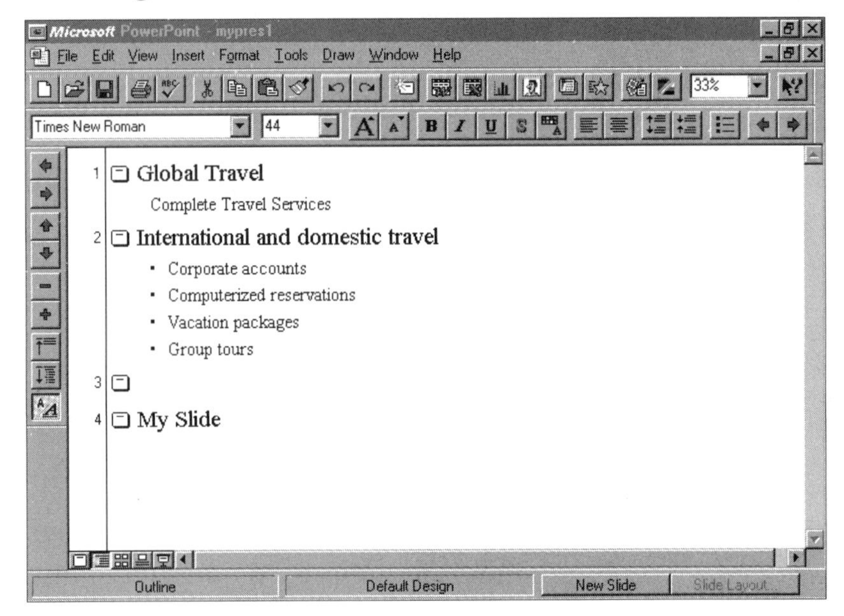

ENTERING SLIDE TEXT IN OUTLINE VIEW

As you know, in Slide view, you enter title text in the title object and body text in the bulleted-list object. In Outline view, you still work with title and body text; however, this text is defined not by its location within a box, but by its degree of indentation within the outline.

Title text is not indented; that is, it appears leftmost in the outline. You can see this in the Figure 2.5 titles, *Global Travel, International & domestic travel,* and *My Slide*.

Bulleted-list text is indented from one to five levels to the right of title text. The first level of indentation corresponds to a standard bulleted item on the slide. In Figure 2.5, the body-text items *Corporate accounts, Computerized reservations, Vacation packages,* and *Group tours*—all of which are indented one level—correspond to the four standard bulleted items shown in Figure 2.4. The second through fifth levels of body-text indentation correspond to level-2 through level-5 bulleted items. Figure 2.6 shows a sample slide in Outline view with all five levels of indentation; Figure 2.7 shows this same slide in Slide view.

Figure 2.6 **Level-1 through level-5 bulleted items in Outline view**

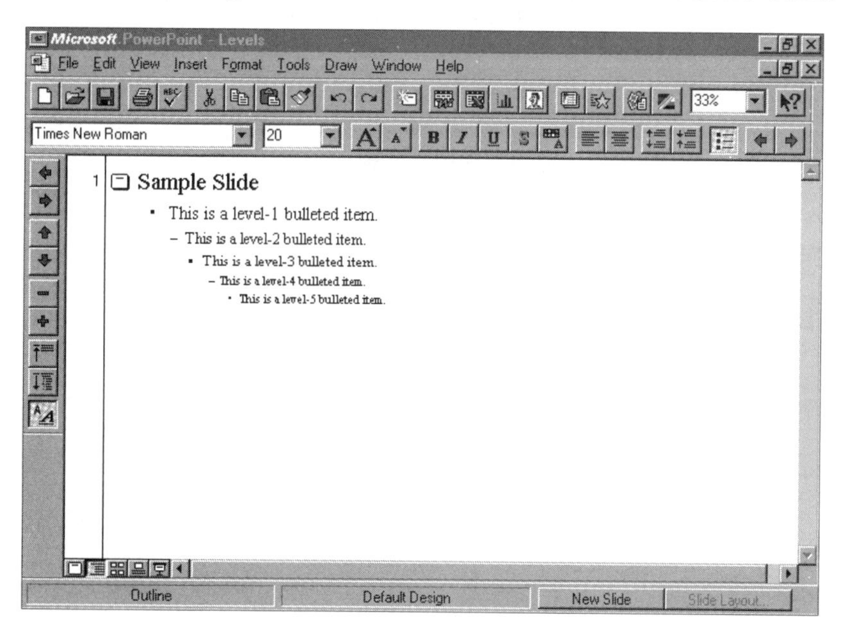

Here's the general procedure for entering text in Outline view:

- To enter title text, place the insertion point to the right of the slide icon and type your desired text.
- To enter bulleted-list text, place the insertion point at the end of the line after which you want to enter your text, press *Enter* to create a new line, press *Tab* or *Shift+Tab* (if necessary) to change your new line to the desired indentation level, and type your desired text.

Figure 2.7 **Level-1 through level-5 bulleted items in Slide view**

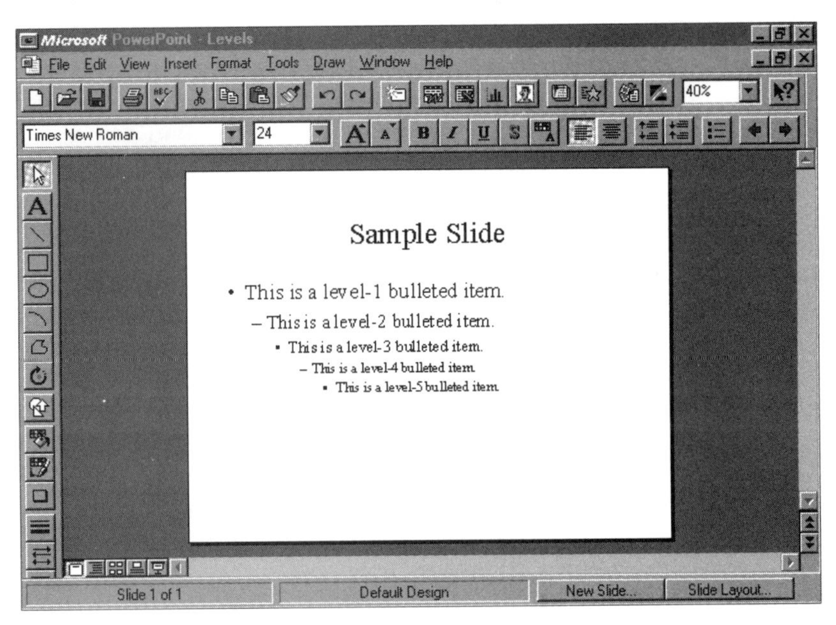

- To *promote* a line (that is, to *decrease* its indentation by one level), place the insertion point in the line and click on the *Promote* button (in the Formatting toolbar) or press *Shift+Tab.*
- To *demote* a line (that is, to *increase* its indentation by one level), place the insertion point in the line, and click on the *Demote* button (also in the Formatting toolbar) or press *Tab.*

Let's use this procedure to create a two-level bulleted list for slide 3. First, we'll enter the slide title:

1. If necessary, place the insertion point directly to the right of the slide 3 icon.
2. Type **Special Services** to enter the title for slide 3.

Now we'll enter the body text, a two-level bulleted list:

1. Press **Enter** to create a new line (and a new slide). We need to demote this line by one level to make it body text.
2. Click on the **Demote** button (the second button from the top in the Outline toolbar) to increase the line's indentation by one level, from title text to level-1 body text. Note that the

new slide icon disappears, and your new line becomes the first bulleted item of slide 3.

3. Type **Meeting planning** to enter the text for this first bulleted item.
4. Press **Enter** to create a new line. Observe that this is a level-1 bulleted item. We want to change it to a level-2 bulleted item, a *sub-bullet* under the level-1 bullet (*Meeting planning*) you just created. To do this, you need to demote the line by one level.
5. Press **Tab** to demote the line from a level-1 to a level-2 bulleted item. To demote a line, you can either click on the Demote button (as you did in step 2) or press Tab.
6. Type **Sales meetings** to enter the text for the level-2 bulleted item.
7. Press **Enter** to create a new, level-2 bulleted item. We need to promote this to a level-1 bulleted item.
8. Click on the **Promote** button (above the Demote button) to do this. You could also have pressed Shift+Tab to perform the promotion.
9. Type **Passport photos** to enter the text for the bulleted item.
10. Press **Enter** to create a new level-1 bulleted item, and then press **Tab** to demote it to a level-2 bulleted item.
11. Type **Same-day service** to enter the text for this bulleted item.

PRACTICE YOUR SKILLS

1. Add the following pair of level-1 and level-2 bulleted items to slide 3:

   Rail

      Cross-country

   Your screen should now match that shown in Figure 2.8.

Figure 2.8 **Creating a two-level bulleted list**

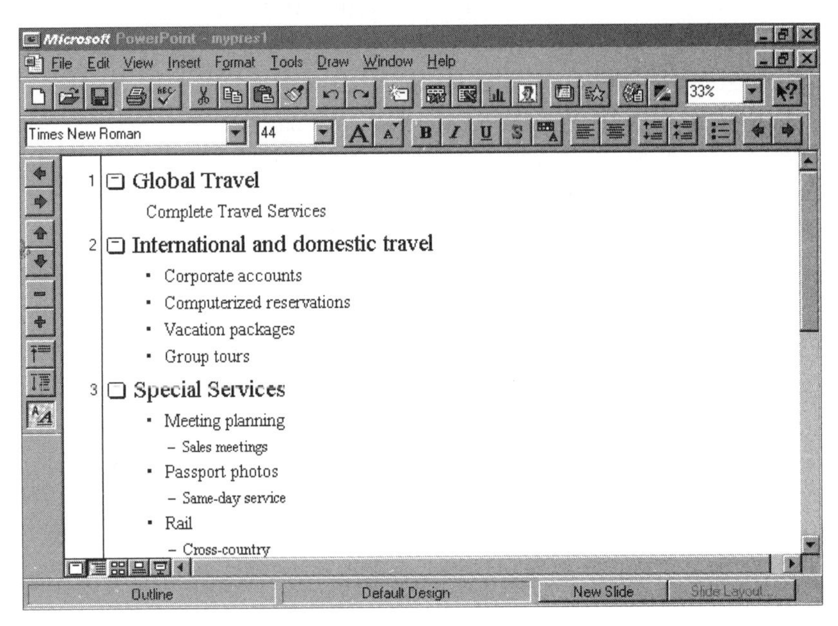

CREATING NONBULLETED BODY TEXT

As you know, PowerPoint formats the text you enter in a bulleted-list object as a bulleted list by default. There may be times, however, when you want to create nonbulleted body text. For example, you might find that a nonbulleted descriptive paragraph communicates a slide's message better than a bulleted list does.

Here's the general procedure for removing bullets from your body text:

- Select the body text whose bullets you want to remove. To select a single bulleted item, place the insertion point anywhere within the item. To select two or more adjacent bulleted items, drag from anywhere within the top item to anywhere within the bottom item.
- Click on the *Bullet On/Off* button (in the Formatting toolbar).
- To restore bullets to your body text, select the bulleted-list object and click on the *Bullet* button. Clicking on the Bullet button once removes the bullets; clicking on it a second time restores the bullets.

Let's enter a new title and two nonbulleted paragraphs for slide 4:

1. Select (drag over) **My Slide**, the current title of slide 4. The title is highlighted to indicate that it is selected.
2. Type **Corporate travel specialists** to enter a new title. Note that your new text replaced your old text (*My Slide*). Whenever you select text and then type, the new text replaces the selected text.
3. Press **Enter** and then press **Tab** to create a level-1 bulleted item under your new title.
4. Observe the Bullet On/Off button (the third button from the right in the Formatting toolbar). Note that it is selected. Click on the **Bullet** button to remove the bullet from your new bulleted-list line. Note that the button is now deselected.
5. To enter your nonbulleted body text, type **Discover the Global Travel advantage; allow our experienced agents to handle all of your corporate and leisure travel needs.** (Include the period!) Note that the text automatically wraps around to a second line after the word *of*, and that this second line is indented. (Depending on how PowerPoint is set up, your text may wrap at a different word.)
6. Press **Enter** twice to create two new level-1 body-text lines. Note that both of these lines inherit the nonbulleted attribute of their parent line, *Discover the Global Travel advantage....*
7. Type **Offices located nationwide.** (including the period) to enter a second nonbulleted body-text line. Your screen should match that shown in Figure 2.9.

Now let's change to Slide view to see what the two slides we just created in Outline view actually look like:

1. Change to Slide view. Slide 4 should be displayed; if not, display it now. Your screen should match that shown in Figure 2.10.
2. Observe the slide workspace. This is an accurate representation of how slide 4 will look when you display it in a slide show, print it out, or process it as a 35-millimeter slide.
3. Observe the first paragraph of body text. Note that it wraps around twice, once after *allow* and once after *your*. (Again, your text may wrap at different words.) In Outline view, as

Figure 2.9 **Creating nonbulleted body text**

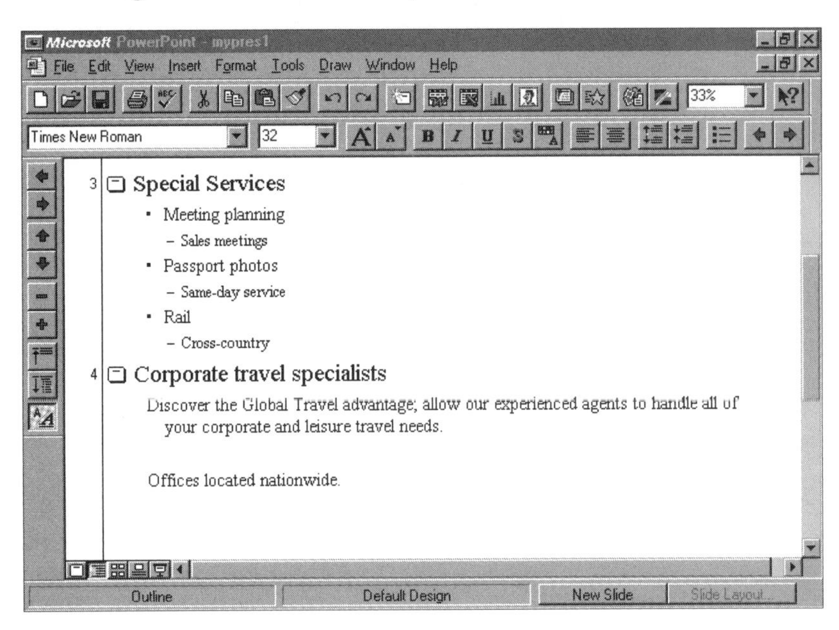

Figure 2.10 **Slide 4 in Slide view**

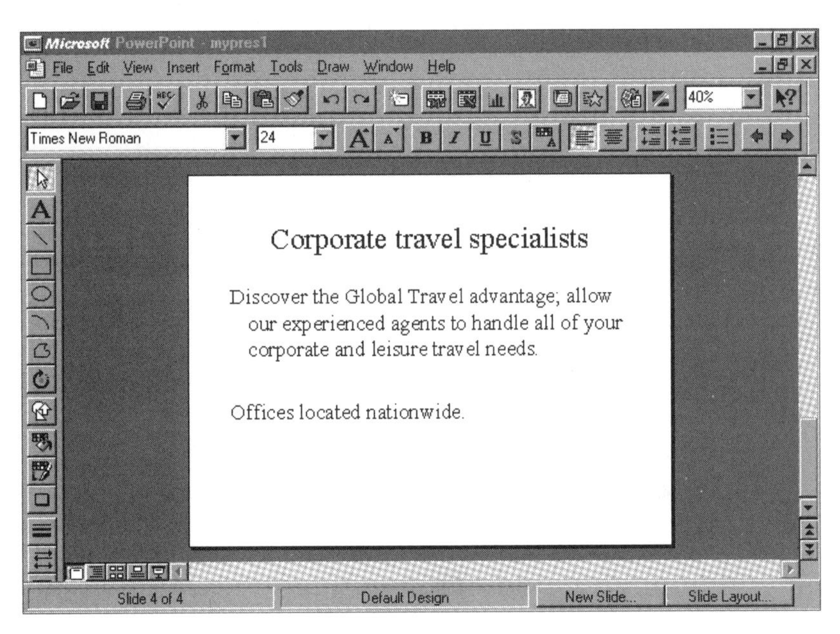

you'll recall, this paragraph wrapped around just once, after *of.* Change to Outline view to verify this. Outline view does not provide an accurate representation of how your text will look on the actual slide. Slide view does.

4. Return to Slide view. Display slide 3. It should match that shown in Figure 2.11.

Figure 2.11 Slide 3 in Slide view

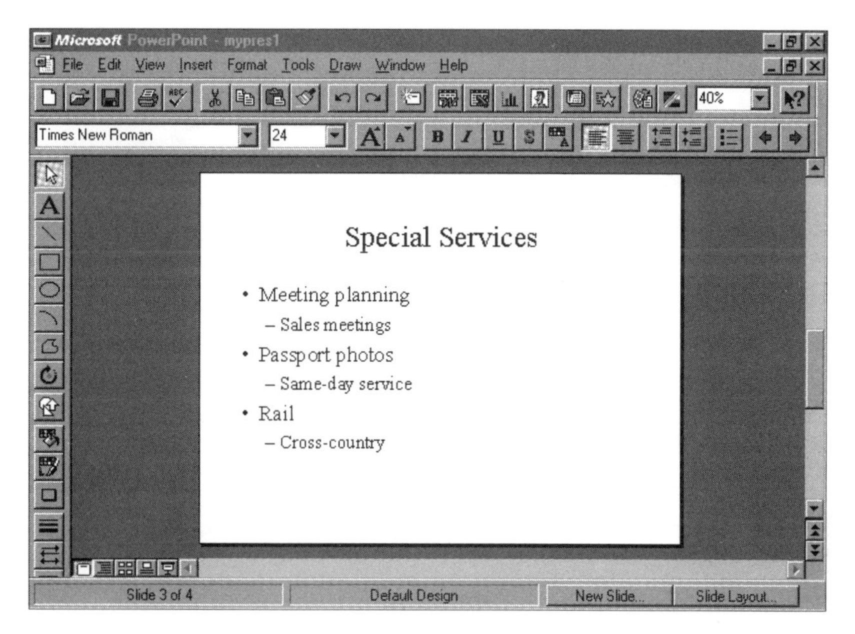

5. Switch back and forth between Outline view and Slide view to observe the differences in how slide 3's text is displayed in these two views.

SAVING AN EXISTING PRESENTATION

As you learned earlier in this chapter, to save a new presentation for the first time, you use the File, Save As command. To save changes to an existing presentation—a presentation that you've already saved at least once—you use the File, Save command. When you choose File, Save, PowerPoint saves the current version of your presentation under the same name and to the same disk location (folder and drive) that you specified when you used File, Save As to save the new presentation.

Here's the general procedure for saving an existing presentation:

- Choose *File, Save*, or click on the *Save* button, or press *Ctrl+S*.

Let's use the first of these techniques to save the current presentation, mypres1:

1. Choose **File, Save** to save the current version of your presentation under the same file name (mypres1) and to the same disk location (C:\Power Work) used for the previously saved version. Note that no dialog box appears. PowerPoint already knows all the salient information (file name, disk drive and folder), so it can perform your command without any further input from you.

Now we'll use the Save button to save the current presentation:

2. Click on the **Save** button (the third tool from the left in the Standard toolbar) to save your presentation again.

Most PowerPoint tasks are designed to be performed with a mouse. Some users, however, prefer to use the keyboard. PowerPoint provides avid keyboardists with a large selection of *keyboard shortcuts:* keystroke combinations that issue commands and execute actions normally performed with the mouse. Keyboard shortcuts are generally listed in the drop-down menus. Let's take a look:

3. Click on **File** to open the drop-down File menu. Observe the Save command; note that its keyboard shortcut, Ctrl+S, appears next to it. (Hint: To learn PowerPoint's keyboard shortcuts, refer to your drop-down menus; or better yet, refer to Appendix C for a complete listing.)
4. Click on **File** again to close the File menu.

Let's use the Ctrl+S keyboard shortcut to save the current presentation:

5. Press **Ctrl+s** (press and hold the **Ctrl** key, press **s**, then release both) to save your presentation again. Note that you don't need to capitalize the letter in a keyboard shortcut; pressing Ctrl+s is equivalent to pressing Ctrl+S.

Now you've used all three techniques for saving an existing presentation (as listed above in the general procedure): choosing File, Save; clicking on the Save tool; and pressing Ctrl+S. You'll find that PowerPoint usually provides two or more methods for performing the same task. To avoid cluttering this book (and your mind!) with these alternatives, we'll take the following tack: We'll mention the various methods for performing a given task in the general procedure for that task. But when it comes to actually performing the task in a numbered, hands-on activity, we'll have you use the most convenient method.

One more thing to do before we end this chapter's activities:

6. Close **mypres1**. Always remember to close files when you're done working on them. Your computer will appreciate it.

FILE-SAVING GUIDELINES

You should get into the habit of saving your presentation files frequently. As a rule of thumb, save your current presentation every 10 to 15 minutes. That way, if your computer accidentally shuts off (due to a power outage, for example), you'll lose only 10 to 15 minutes of work. Never wait longer than a half hour before you save a file; to do so is to invite trouble!

KEEPING DIFFERENT VERSIONS OF THE SAME PRESENTATION

When you use File, Save to save an existing presentation, the current presentation file *overwrites* the previous version of the file, permanently erasing the previous file from your disk. If all you want to keep is your current version, this is fine. However, if you also want to keep the previous version, you must use File, Save As to save the current presentation file under a new name.

SUMMARY

In this chapter, you began work on your mypres1 presentation by creating four simple text slides. You learned how to run a slide show, how to open a new presentation, how to create slides and enter text in Slide view and in Outline view, how to create nonbulleted body text, and how to save both a new presentation and an existing presentation.

Here's a quick reference for the techniques you learned in this chapter:

Desired Result	How to Do It
Run a slide show manually	If necessary, open the presentation file; click on the **Slide Show** button; to move forward one slide, click the **left mouse button**, press **Enter**, or press **Page Down**; to move backward one slide, press **Page Up**; to end the show, display the last slide and click the **left mouse** button, press **Enter**, or press **Page Down;** You can also end the show by clicking anywhere with the right mouse button and then using either mouse button to click on **End Show**
Create a slide presentation	Open a new, blank presentation; create blank slides and enter their text; save the presentation (continue to save it every 10 or 15 minutes); add design elements by drawing on slides and adding charts (graphs) and clip art to slides, and then lay out slides; generate output by running a slide show, printing slides, notes, or handouts, or processing a presentation as 35-millimeter slides
Open a new presentation	Choose **File, New** to open the New Presentation dialog box; select **Blank Presentation** from the General tab in the New Presentation dialog box; click on **OK** to open the New Slide dialog box; select your desired autolayout for the first slide; click on **OK.** For a quicker and simple method, click on the **New** button in the Standard toolbar
Create a new slide in Slide view	Display the slide after which you want to add your new slide; click on the **New Slide** button or choose **Insert, New Slide**; select desired autolayout; click on **OK**
Enter text in Slide view	Select the **title**, **subtitle**, or **bulleted-text object**; type desired text

Desired Result	How to Do It
Save a new presentation	Choose **File, Save As**; if necessary, change the current drive and directory; enter your desired file name; click on **OK**
Create a new slide in Outline view	Place the insertion point anywhere within the text of the slide after which you want to add your new slide and click on the **New Slide** button or choose **Insert, New Slide**
Enter text in Outline view	For title text, place the insertion point to the right of the slide icon and type your desired text; for bulleted-list text, place the insertion point at the end of the line after which you want to enter your text, press **Enter** to create a new line, use **Tab** or **Shift+Tab** (if necessary) to change your new line to the desired indentation level, and type your desired text
Promote/demote an outline line	To promote a line, place the insertion point in the line and click on the **Promote** button or press **Shift+Tab**; to demote a line, place the insertion point in the line and click on the **Demote** button or press **Tab**
Remove/restore bullets from your bulleted-list text	Select the desired text and click on the **Bullet On/Off** button
Save an existing presentation	To keep only the current version of the presentation, choose **File, Save**, or click on the **Save** button, or press **Ctrl+S**; to keep both the current version and the previous version of the presentation, choose **File, Save As**, enter your new file name and/or drive and/or folder, and click on **OK**

In the next chapter, we'll show you how to work with slide text. You'll learn how to get general and dialog-box help, how to edit slide text, how to rearrange bulleted items, how to apply text attributes, how to change indents, how to align text, how to change line spacing, and how to spell-check a presentation.

CHAPTER 3: WORKING WITH SLIDE TEXT

Getting Help

Editing Slide Text

Spell-Checking a Presentation

In Chapter 2, you learned how to begin a presentation by creating slides and entering text in Slide view and in Outline view. In this chapter, you'll expand your slide-creation skills by learning how to further manipulate your slide text. We'll show you how to edit (modify) your text, rearrange it, change its appearance, and check its spelling. Mastery of these topics is crucial, as a presentation is only as good as its words and images.

When you're done working through this chapter, you will know

- How to get help
- How to edit slide text
- How to add bulleted items to your slides
- How to rearrange bulleted items
- How to apply text attributes
- How to change indents
- How to align text
- How to change line spacing
- How to change text case (capitalization)
- How to spell-check a presentation

GETTING HELP

Before diving into the main topic of this chapter, working with slide text, we'd like to introduce you to PowerPoint's on-line reference tools, *Tip Of The Day* and *Help*.

TIP OF THE DAY

The Tip Of The Day dialog box—which appears automatically when you start PowerPoint—provides you with tips and shortcuts for using PowerPoint. Let's take a few minutes to explore this feature:

1. If you are already running PowerPoint, please exit it now.
2. Start PowerPoint. The Tip Of The Day dialog box appears.
3. Observe the buttons on the right side of the Tip Of The Day dialog box. You have three choices: clicking on OK closes the dialog box; clicking on Next Tip displays another PowerPoint tip and clicking on More Tips displays a comprehensive list of tips.
4. Read your tip, then click on **Next Tip** to display another tip. Repeat this to display several more tips. You can use this flashcard-like technique to obtain random information about PowerPoint.
5. Click on **More Tips** to open a Help window that consists of the Index tab and the Find tab. By default, the Index tab is

selected. The insertion point is positioned in the text box, enabling you to get help on any words that you type in the text box. (You'll learn more about Help windows in the next section.) There is a second list box containing the word *tips*, which you can double-click on to open the PowerPoint tips window. Browse through the choices in the PowerPoint tips window, and then exit by clicking on the **Close** button (the button in the upper-right corner of the PowerPoint tips window). The Tip Of The Day dialog box reappears.

6. Observe the *Show Tips At Startup* option at the bottom of the dialog box. When this option is checked, the Tip Of The Day dialog box appears automatically every time you start PowerPoint. While these tips are certainly edifying, you may not want to see them every time you start PowerPoint.
7. Uncheck the **Show Tips At Startup** option and click on **OK**. Now the Tip Of The Day dialog box will no longer open automatically when you start PowerPoint.
8. Click on **Cancel** to close the PowerPoint dialog box.

If you find the Tip Of The Day feature useful, feel free to activate it at anytime during a PowerPoint session (by choosing Help, Tip Of The Day) or to turn the Show Tips At Startup option back on when you're done working through this book (by choosing Help, Tip Of The Day and checking the Show Tips At Startup option).

HELP

You can use Help to get information about PowerPoint (commands, concepts, procedures, and so on) at any point during your work session. Think of Help as a very knowledgeable tech-support person sitting in the background and waiting patiently to answer your questions.

You can use Help to get both *general help* and *dialog-box help*. General help provides information on a vast array of PowerPoint topics. For example, let's say you forgot how to run a slide show of a presentation; you could refresh your memory by running Help and viewing the *Hints for Creating and Running Slide Shows* topic. Dialog-box help provides information on the active dialog box. For example, let's say you opened the Slide Show dialog box and didn't fully understand the Advance option; you could run Help to get information on Advance.

General Help

Here's the procedure for getting general help:

- Choose *Help, Microsoft Power Point Help Topics* or press F1 to open the Help Topics window. By define it, you will be placed in the Contents tab of the Help Topics window.
- To view the Help window for a particular topic, click on that topic.
- To search for a topic you want help with, click on the *Index tab*; locate the desired index word by typing the initial part of the word or by scrolling through the index-word list; double-click on the desired index word to show its associated topics; double-click on the desired topic to view its Help window.
- To view previous Help windows, click on the *Back* button.
- To view the Help Topics window, click on the *Help Topics* button.
- To exit from Help, click on the Close button in the Help Topic window.

Let's get general help for some of the topics already covered in this book:

1. Choose **Help, Microsoft PowerPoint Help Topics** to open the Help Topics window. By default, the Contents tab of the Help Topics window is opened, as shown in Figure 3.1. Click on the **Contents** tab if it isn't currently opened.

   The next five steps (2 through 6) are a miniprimer on scrolling. You can use these techniques to scroll through any Power-Point window with scroll bars.

2. In the Help Topics window, click on the **down scroll arrow** (as shown in Figure 3.2) to scroll the window down one line. Click two more times to scroll down two more lines.
3. Point to the **up scroll arrow**, and press and hold the **left mouse button** to scroll up to the top of the window. Do the same thing with the **down scroll arrow** to scroll back to the bottom.
4. Inside the scroll bar, click once above the scroll box to scroll up one full screen of topics. (If less than one full screen is visible, it will scroll that amount.)
5. Use this technique to scroll down to the bottom, then back to the top of the window.

Figure 3.1 **Help Topics window**

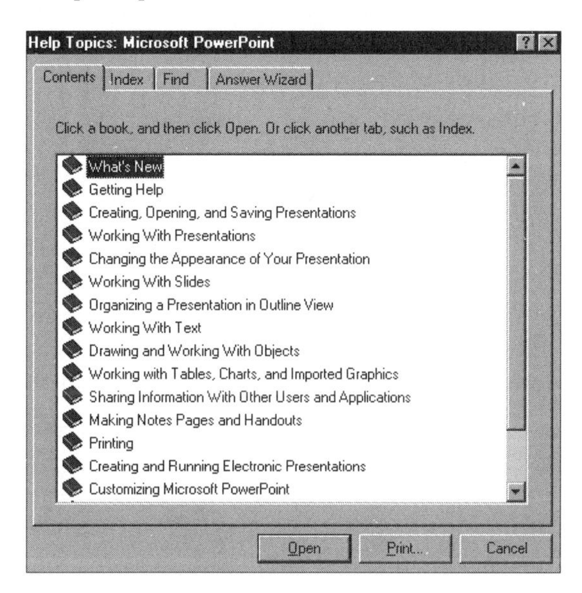

Figure 3.2 **Scrolling terminology**

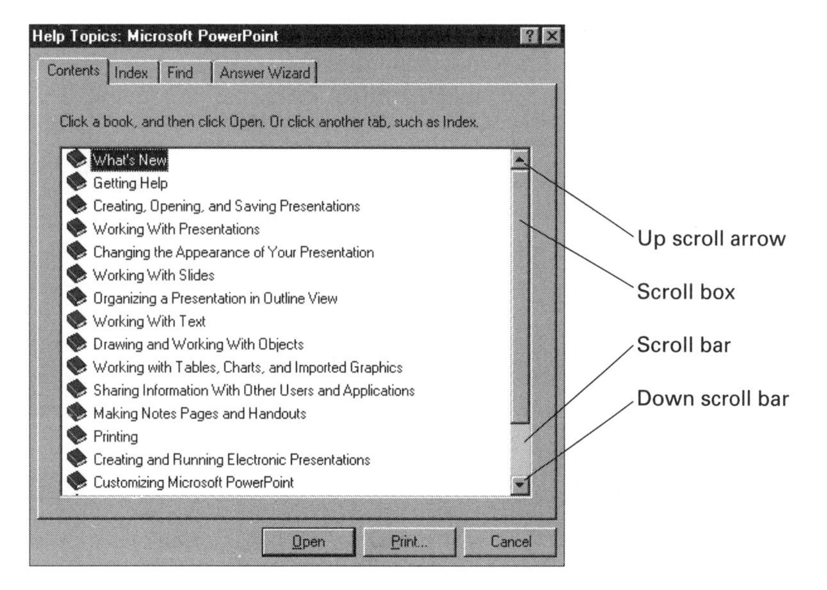

6. Drag the **scroll box** down to the middle of the scroll bar to move halfway to the end of the window. Use this technique to move to the bottom, and then back to the top.

Now that you're comfortable with scrolling, let's select a topic and get help for it:

1. Select the topic **Creating, Opening and Saving Presentations** and then click on **Open**. The book icon next to the Creating, Opening, And Saving Presentations topic is now opened, and several other books are displayed within it.
2. Select **Saving and Closing Presentations** and then click on **Open**. As in step 2, the selected line's book icon opens to reveal several lines beginning with question mark icons.
3. Select **Naming presentations** and then click on **Display**. A Help window appears, as shown in Figure 3.3.

Figure 3.3 **Help window for naming presentations**

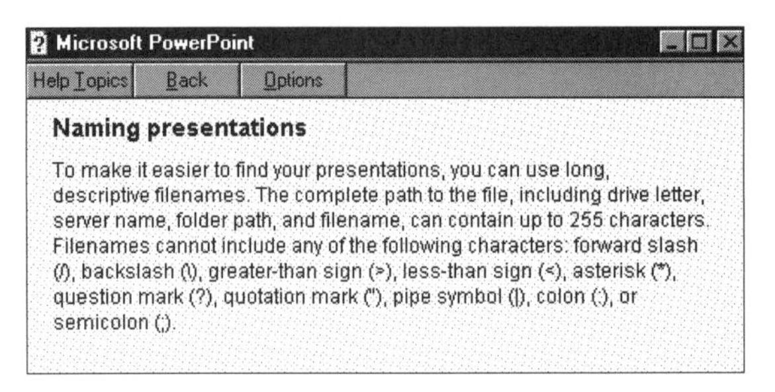

While we successfully obtained help for naming a presentation, we had to know where to click. Most of the time, you will use the Search feature in the Index tab to get help. Let's use the Search feature to find out how to name a presentation:

1. Click on **Help Topics** in the small Help window shown in Figure 3.3. This returns you to the Help Topics window.
2. Click on the **Index** tab. Your screen should match Figure 3.4.
3. Type **naming** in the text box to scroll the display list to *naming presentations*. Note that in this case you had to type just the first six letters of your desired search word (*naming presentations*) to find it. In other cases, you may only need to type the first couple of letters.

Figure 3.4 **The Index tab of the Help Topics window**

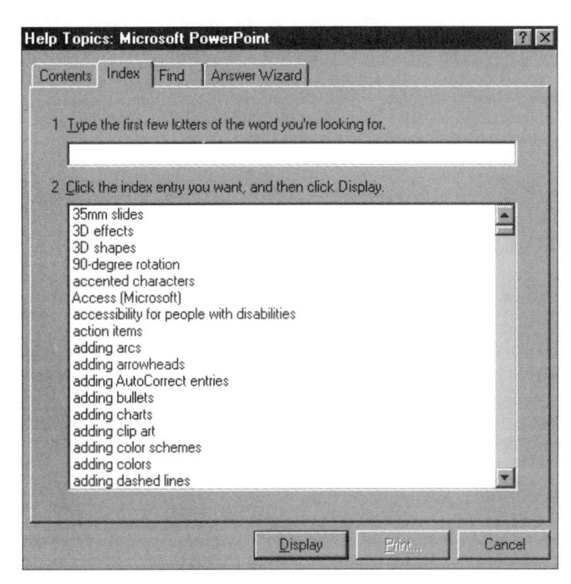

4. Click on **Display** to show the topics associated with naming presentations. In this case, there are no associated topics, so just the Help window describing how to name presentations is displayed.
5. Click on the **Close** button in the Help window to exit from Help.

DIALOG-BOX HELP

Now that you know how to get general help, let's find out how to get its counterpart, dialog-box help. Here's the general procedure for getting help for the active dialog box:

- Click on the *question mark* icon to the left of the Close button, as shown in Figure 3.5. Note how the cursor changes. A question mark now appears to the right of the arrow cursor.
- Point to and then click on the feature in the dialog box for which you would like help.

Let's use this technique to get information on the Open dialog box:

1. Click on the **Open** button (if necessary, use ToolTips to find it) to display the File Open dialog box. Note that the dialog box's Title bar is highlighted, indicating that it is active.

Figure 3.5 **The dialog-box Help button**

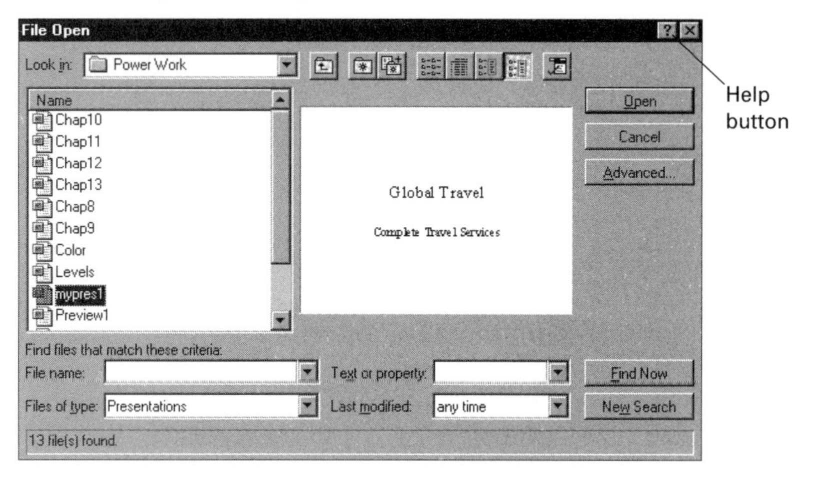

2. Point at the text box to the right of the text, *Look in:*.
3. Click the **right mouse button** to display the help text shown in Figure 3.6.

Figure 3.6 **Dialog-box Help text**

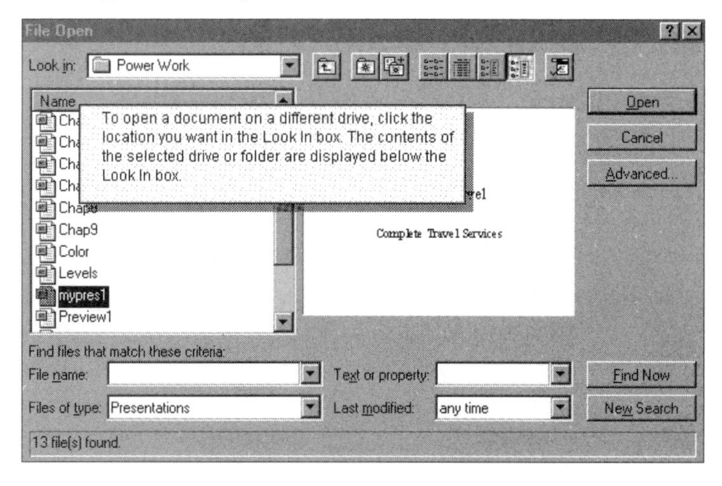

4. Click on the **Close** button to close the File Open dialog box.

PRACTICE YOUR SKILLS

1. Get general help for the following PowerPoint features. When you are finished getting help for the last feature, exit from Help.

   Formatting text

   Line spacing

   Selecting objects

   Deleting slides

EDITING SLIDE TEXT

In Chapter 2, you learned how to enter text in Slide view and in Outline view. Here, you'll learn how to *edit* (modify) your slide text in both of these views. Over the next several sections, we'll show you how to

- Add bulleted items to your slides
- Rearrange bulleted items
- Apply text attributes
- Change indents
- Align text
- Change line spacing
- Change text case (capitalization)

ADDING BULLETED ITEMS

Here's the general procedure for adding a bulleted item to a slide in Slide view or in Outline view:

- Place the insertion point at the end of the bulleted item after which you want to add your new bulleted item.
- Press *Enter* to create the new bulleted item.
- If necessary, press *Tab* or *Shift+Tab* to change the indent level of your new bulleted item.
- Type your desired bullet text.

Let's open mypres1 and add a bulleted item to slide 2 in Outline view:

1. Open **mypres1** from your Power Work folder. Maximize the presentation window, if necessary.
2. Change to Outline view.
3. Place the insertion point at the end of the level-1 bulleted item *Computerized reservations*.
4. Press **Enter** to create a new level-1 bulleted item.
5. Type **Cruises** to enter the text for this bulleted item. Your screen should match that shown in Figure 3.7.

Figure 3.7 **Adding a bulleted item in Outline view**

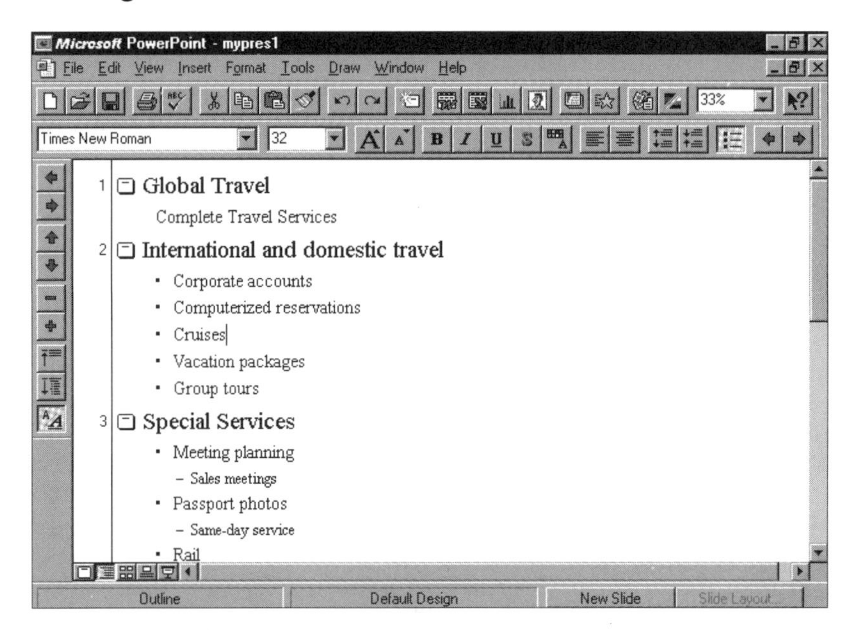

Now let's add a pair of bulleted items to slide 3 in Slide view:

1. Select slide 3 by clicking on the number **3** in the left margin of the outline.
2. Change to Slide view. Verify that slide 3 is displayed.
3. Place the insertion point at the end of the level-2 bulleted item *Same-day service*.

4. Press **Enter** to create a new level-2 bulleted item, and then press **Shift+Tab** to promote this to a level-1 bulleted item.
5. Type **Car rentals** to specify the text for this bulleted item.
6. Press **Enter** and press **Tab** to create a new level-2 bulleted item.
7. Type **Lowest rates** to specify the text for this bulleted item.
8. Press **Esc** twice; once to enter the text and once more to deselect the bulleted-list object. Your screen should match that shown in Figure 3.8.
9. Choose **File, Save** to save the modified file.

Figure 3.8 Adding bulleted items in Slide view

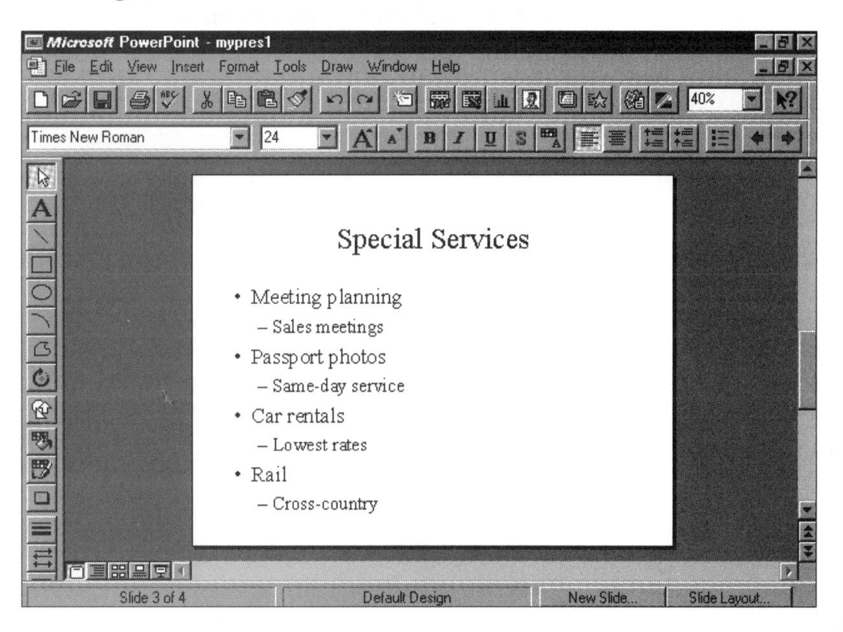

REARRANGING BULLETED ITEMS

PowerPoint allows you to quickly and easily rearrange the order of a slide's bulleted items in Slide view or in Outline view. You can do this either by dragging the bulleted items (in both views) or by selecting the items and clicking on the *Move Up* and *Move Down buttons* (in Outline view only).

Here's the general procedure for rearranging the order of bulleted items by dragging:

- If you are in Slide view, place the insertion point anywhere within the bulleted list.
- Point to the bullet of the bulleted item you want to move. The mouse pointer changes to a four-headed arrow.
- Press and hold down the *left mouse button* to grab this bulleted item (and all the sub-bulleted items beneath it).
- Drag the bulleted item(s) up or down to your desired new position, then release the mouse button.

Note: As you'll see in the next activity, when you move a bulleted item by dragging, you move the selected bulleted item along with all the sub-bulleted items beneath it.

Here's the general procedure for rearranging the order of bulleted items in Outline view by using the Move Up and Move Down buttons:

- Select the bulleted item(s) you want to move. To select a single bulleted item, place the insertion point anywhere within the item. To select two or more adjacent bulleted items, drag from anywhere within the top item to anywhere within the bottom item.
- Click as many times as necessary on the *Move Up* or *Move Down* button to move the selected bulleted item(s) to your desired new position in the bulleted list.

Let's move a slide 3 bulleted item and its accompanying sub-bulleted item by dragging in Slide view:

1. Place the insertion point anywhere within the bulleted text of slide 3.
2. Point to the bullet of the *Car rentals* bulleted item. Note that the mouse pointer changes to a four-headed arrow.
3. Press and hold the **left mouse button** to "grab" this bullet. (Don't release the mouse button until we tell you to do so in step 5.) Note that both *Car rentals* and its sub-bulleted item *Lowest rates* are selected. As mentioned, when you move a bulleted item by dragging, you also move all the sub-bulleted items beneath it.

4. Drag upward until the *position marker* (the horizontal line extending across the Body object) is above the Passport photos bulleted item.
5. Release the mouse button to move the *Car rentals* and *Lowest rates* bulleted items to above *Passport photos*.

Now let's move a bulleted item in Outline view:

1. Change to Outline view.
2. Place the insertion point anywhere within the bulleted item *Vacation packages* in slide 2.
3. Click on the **Move Up** button (the third button from the top in the Outline toolbar) to move *Vacation packages* above *Cruises*.
4. Save the file.

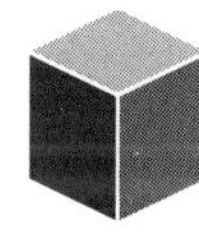

APPLYING TEXT ATTRIBUTES

Text attributes determine the appearance of your slide text. PowerPoint's text attributes include *font* (typeface, such as Times Roman or Courier), *font size* (in points, where 72 points equals 1 inch in height), *style* (bold, italic, underlined, shadow, and so on), and *color* (black and white, grays, and a full spectrum of colors). To change the attributes of your text, simply select the text and *apply* the desired new attributes. You can do this in Slide view or in Outline view, with two exceptions: You cannot change text shadowing or color in Outline view. All text attributes are visible in both views (again, except for shadowing and color, which are visible only in Slide view).

Here's the general procedure for applying text attributes:

- Select the desired text. In Slide view, to select some of an object's text, drag over the desired text; to select all the object's text, select the entire object (by placing the insertion point in the object and pressing Esc). In Outline view, to select some of a slide's text, drag over the desired text; to select all the slide's text, click on the slide number.
- Click on the desired text-editing button (as shown in Figure 3.9). Or, press the desired keyboard shortcut: *Ctrl+B* to bold; *Ctrl+I* to italicize; *Ctrl+U* to underline.

Figure 3.9 **Text-editing buttons**

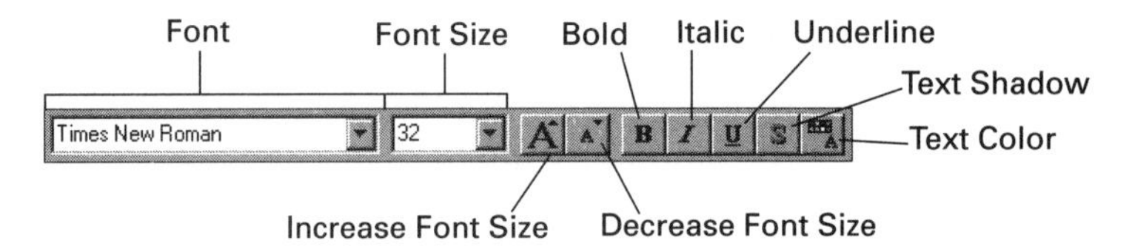

Let's practice applying text attributes in Outline view. We'll begin by using the Underline button to underline a word:

1. In Outline view, double-click on the word **Lowest** in slide 3 to select it. (Double-clicking a word selects that word; Cltr+clicking on a word selects the entire sentence; triple-clicking on a word selects the entire paragraph.)
2. Click on the **Underline** button (as shown in Figure 3.9) to underline *Lowest*.
3. Deselect the text (by placing the insertion point elsewhere). Note that the underline attribute is visible in Outline view.

Now we'll use the Font Size buttons to change the size of slide 2's text:

1. Click on the number **2** in the left margin to select all of slide 2's text.
2. Click on the **Increase Font Size** button (as shown in Figure 3.9) to increase the size of slide 2's text. Observe this change in the outline and in the Font Size list box (to the left of the Increase Font Size button).
3. Click on the **Increase Font Size** button again to increase the text size by another step.
4. Click on the **Decrease Font Size** button twice to return slide 2's text to its original size.

Now let's change the font of slide 2's text:

1. If necessary, select all of slide 2's text (by clicking on **2** in the left margin).
2. Observe the current font, as displayed in the Font list box. Jot down its name; you'll need it in a moment.
3. To open the list of available fonts, click on the **down arrow** to the right of the Font list box.

4. Click on any other font in this list to change the font of slide 2's text. Observe this change in the outline.
5. Use the procedure laid out in steps 3 and 4 to try out a few other fonts. When you've had enough, return slide 2's text to its original font (the one you jotted down).

Now let's practice applying text attributes in Slide view:

1. Change to Slide view and display slide 4.
2. Triple-click on the nonbulleted item **Offices located nationwide** to select it.
3. Click on the **Italic** button (as shown in Figure 3.9).
4. Press **Esc** twice to deselect the bulleted-list object. Your screen should match that shown in Figure 3.10.
5. Save the file.

Figure 3.10 Italicizing text in Slide view

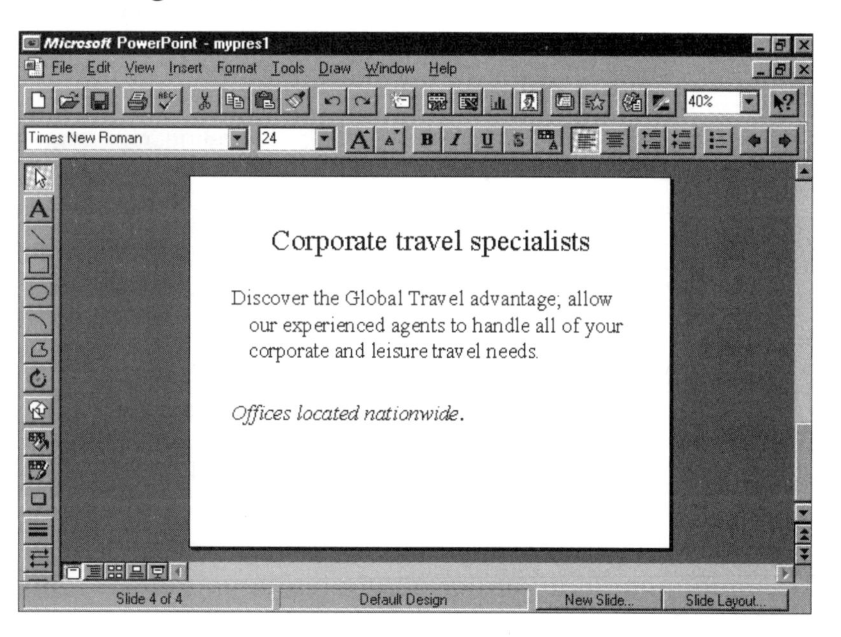

CHANGING INDENTS

Before you learn about indents, you need to understand what PowerPoint means by the term *paragraph*. A paragraph is a unit of text that begins with a character and ends with a *carriage return*. A carriage return is the invisible character that you insert by pressing Enter; it creates a new line of text (or a new bulleted item).

Paragraphs can consist of a single text line or of several lines. Let's verify this by taking a quick tour through the slides of mypres1:

1. In Slide view, press **Ctrl+Home** to display slide 1. The Title object contains one paragraph (*Global Travel*), as does the subtitle object (*Complete Travel Services*).
2. Display slide 2. The Title object contains one paragraph; the bulleted-list object contains five paragraphs (five separate bulleted items).
3. Display slide 3. The Title object contains one paragraph; the bulleted-list object contains eight paragraphs (four bulleted items and four sub-bulleted items).
4. Display slide 4. The Title object contains one paragraph. The bulleted-list object contains three (not two!) paragraphs:
    - The nonbulleted, three-line item beginning with *Discover* and ending with *needs*. You pressed Enter only after typing this entire item; PowerPoint wrapped the text automatically.
    - The *Offices located nationwide.* item.
    - The blank line between these two text items.

Now that you understand paragraphs, we can move on to indents. *Indents* determine how far the lines of a paragraph are shifted to the right. A slide's bulleted-list text, as you'll remember, has up to five levels of text. Each of these levels has, in turn, two types of indents: The *first-line indent* (marked by the upper indent triangle, as shown on the ruler in Figure 3.11) is the place where the first line of a paragraph at that level will start; the *trailing-line indent* (sometimes called the left indent and marked by the lower indent triangle) is the place where any subsequent lines of a paragraph at that level will start.

Note: Every text object on a slide has a ruler associated with it. Normally, these rulers are kept hidden, because they clutter the

Figure 3.11 Indents, as shown on the ruler

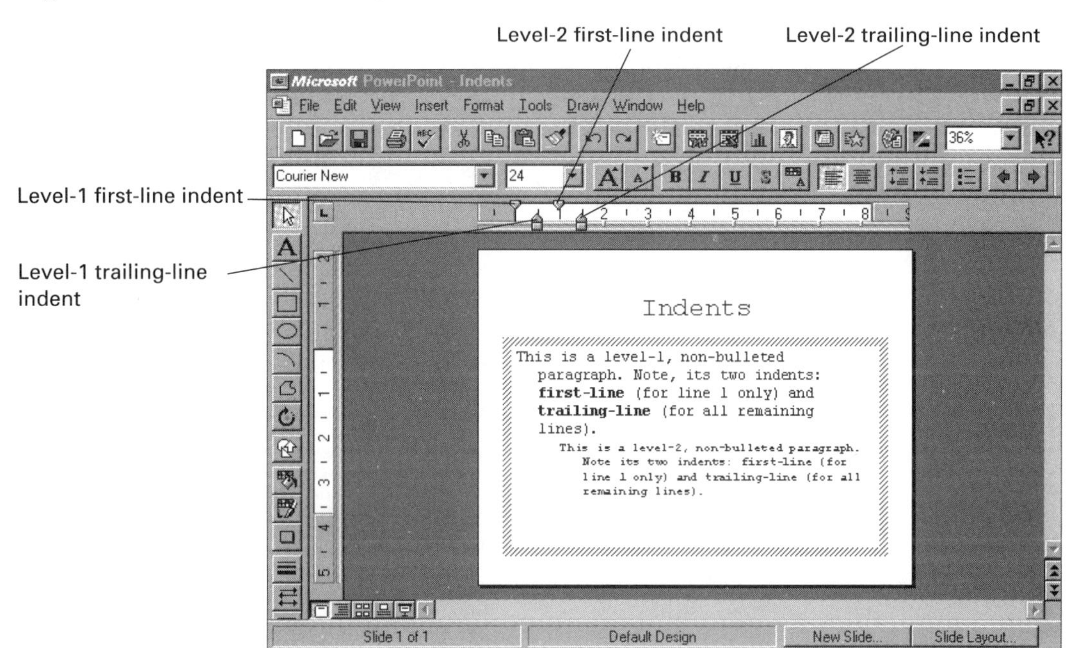

screen. To change the indents of the text in a given text object, however, you need to display the ruler of this text object.

Here's the general procedure for changing indents:

- Place the insertion point in the text object whose indents you want to change.
- Choose *View, Ruler* to display the ruler for this text object.
- To change the first-line indent for an indent level, drag that level's upper indent triangle to the desired position on the ruler.
- To change the trailing-line indent for an indent level, drag that level's lower indent triangle to the desired position on the ruler.
- To change both the first-line indent and the trailing-line indent for an indent level, drag the rectangle below the lower indent triangle to move both triangles to the desired position.
- Choose *View, Ruler* to remove the ruler.

Let's use this procedure to change the indents of slide 4's bulleted-list paragraphs:

1. Place the insertion point in slide 4's bulleted-list object.
2. Choose **View, Ruler** to display the ruler for the text object. Note the two level-1 indent triangles. (The level-2 through level-5 indent triangles are not displayed, because this bulleted-list object contains only level-1 text.) The upper triangle marks where the first line of the selected paragraphs starts. Point to the upper triangle, and press and hold the **left mouse button** (without dragging!) to verify this. The lower triangle marks where the remaining lines start. Press and hold the **left mouse button** on the lower triangle to verify this.
3. Drag the **upper indent triangle** rightward until it points to the ½-inch mark on the ruler. The first-line indent is now set to half an inch. Observe the change in your paragraphs' layouts, as shown in Figure 3.12. The first line is now indented more than the remaining lines.

Figure 3.12 **Changing the first-line indent**

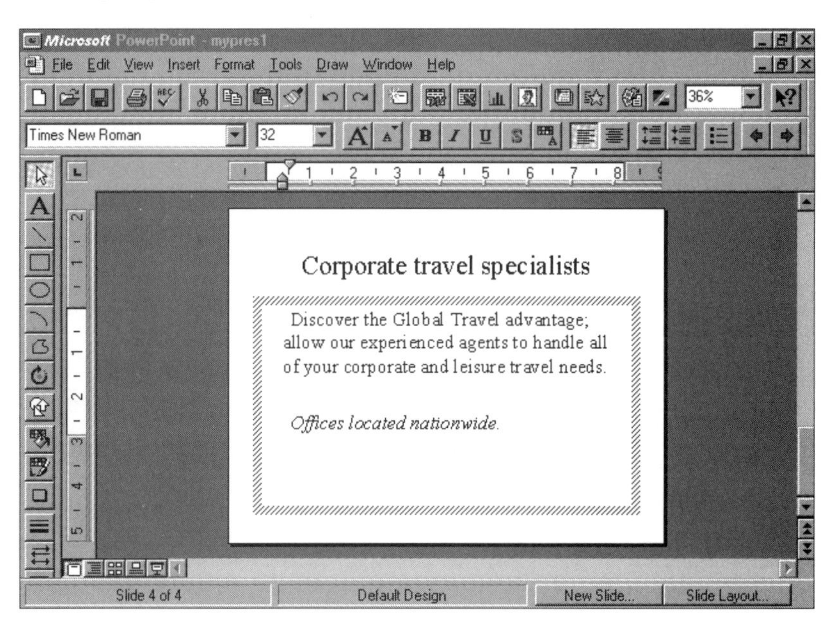

4. Drag the **lower indent triangle** (*not* the rectangle below it!) rightward until it points to the 1-inch mark on the ruler. The trailing-line indent is now set to 1 inch. Observe the change in your paragraphs' layouts.
5. Drag the **rectangle** beneath the lower indent triangles as far left as possible. Note that dragging this rectangle moves both triangles as a unit, without changing the distance between them. The first-line indent is now set to 0 inches, and the trailing-line indent is set to half an inch.
6. Drag the **lower indent triangle** to the leftmost edge of the ruler. Both the first-line indent and the trailing-line indent are now set to 0 inches. Your screen should match that shown in Figure 3.13.

Figure 3.13 **Changing both indents to 0 inches**

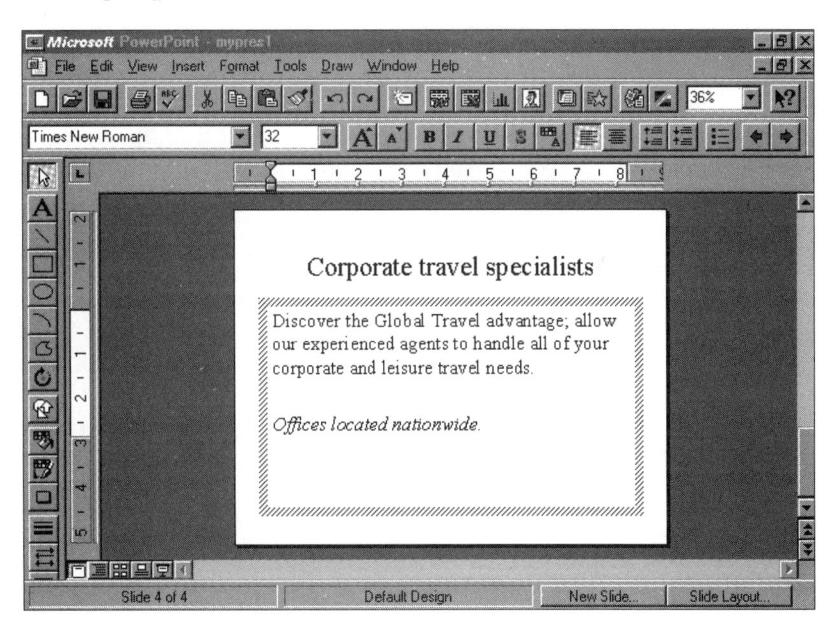

7. Choose **View, Ruler** to hide the ruler.
8. Deselect the bulleted-list object (by pressing **Esc** twice).
9. Save the file.

ALIGNING TEXT

Alignment determines the position of your slide text within its text-object box. Text can be left-aligned, right-aligned, centered, or justified, as follows (see Figure 3.14):

Figure 3.14 **Alignment types**

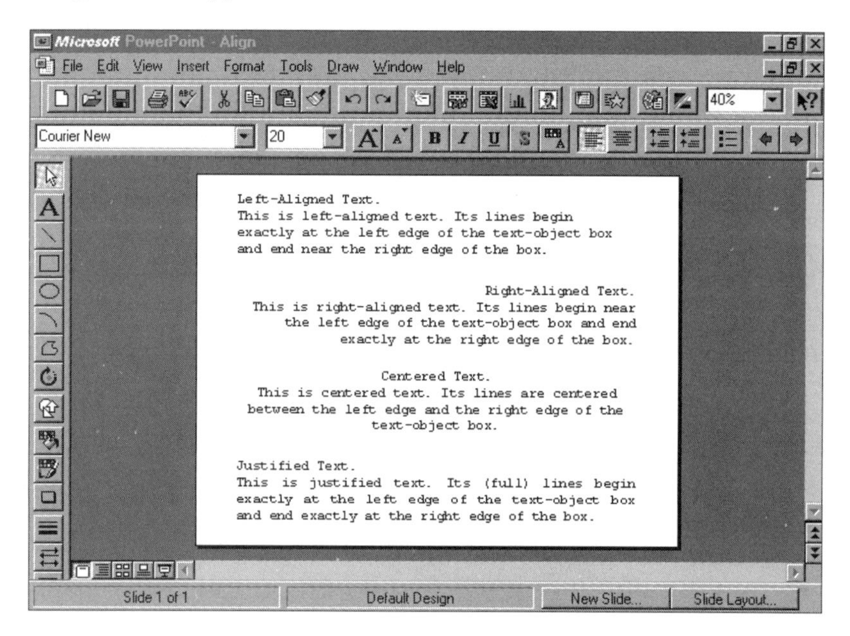

- *Left-aligned* text lines begin at the left edge of the text-object box.
- *Right-aligned* text lines end at the right edge of the text-object box.
- *Centered* text lines are centered between the left and right edges of the text-object box.
- *Justified* text lines begin at the left edge and end at the right edge of the text-object box.

Here's the general procedure for aligning text:

- Select the text to be aligned.
- Choose *Format, Alignment* to open the Alignment submenu, and click on the desired alignment (*Left, Center, Right,* or *Justify*).

- Or, press *Ctrl+L* (to left-align), *Ctrl+R* (to right-align), *Ctrl+E* (to center), or *Ctrl+J* (to justify).
- Or, click on the *Left-Alignment* button or the *Center-Alignment* button (in the Formatting toolbar).

Let's use the first of these methods to change the alignment of slide 4's bulleted-list text:

1. Select the entire bulleted-list object of slide 4 (by placing the insertion point in the object, then pressing **Esc**). Note the black *selection squares* that enclose the bulleted-list object. These indicate that the entire object is selected.
2. Choose **Format, Alignment** to open the Alignment submenu.
3. Observe that the current alignment setting is Left. By default, PowerPoint left-aligns bulleted-list text.
4. Click on **Right** to right-align the selected text within its bulleted-list object box.

PRACTICE YOUR SKILLS

Slide 4's text layout looks imbalanced, like it's tipping over to the right. Let's try a different alignment:

1. Use the menu to justify the bulleted-list text. This layout looks better, but is still somewhat off.
2. Use a Formatting toolbar button to center the bulleted-list text. Now we've got it!
3. Save the file.

CHANGING LINE SPACING

Line spacing determines two things: the amount of space between the individual lines of a multiline paragraph and the amount of space between paragraphs. Here's the general procedure for changing the line spacing of your slide text:

- Select the paragraph(s) whose line spacing you want to change.
- Choose *Format, Line Spacing* to open the Line Spacing dialog box.

- To change the spacing between lines of a multiline paragraph, click on the Line Spacing *up arrow* (to increase the spacing) or the *down arrow* (to decrease the spacing).
- To change the spacing between separate paragraphs, click on the Before Paragraph or After Paragraph *up arrow* (to increase the spacing) or the *down arrow* (to decrease the spacing). Before Paragraph determines the amount of space before each paragraph; After Paragraph determines the space after each paragraph.
- To preview your new line spacing (without closing the Line Spacing dialog box), click on *Preview.*
- Click on *OK.*

Let's change the spacing between the lines of a paragraph:

1. Select the first paragraph of slide 4's bulleted-list text by placing the insertion point anywhere within the paragraph.
2. Choose *Format, Line Spacing* to open the Line Spacing dialog box. Observe the current line-spacing value, *1* line.
3. Click on the Line Spacing **up arrow** ten times to increase the line spacing to 1.50 lines. (You could also have typed **1.5** in the Line Spacing text box.)
4. Move the Line Spacing dialog box (by dragging on the title bar) away from the center of the slide, so that the selected paragraph is mostly visible.
5. Click on **Preview** (in the dialog box) to see how your new line spacing affects the selected paragraph.

PRACTICE YOUR SKILLS

We've overdone it; the paragraph looks too loose. Let's tighten things up a bit:

1. Change the first paragraph's line spacing to 1.25 lines.
2. Preview the results. There, that looks better.
3. Click on **OK** to apply your new line spacing and close the dialog box. Your screen should match that shown in Figure 3.15.
4. Save the file.

Figure 3.15 **Changing a paragraph's line spacing**

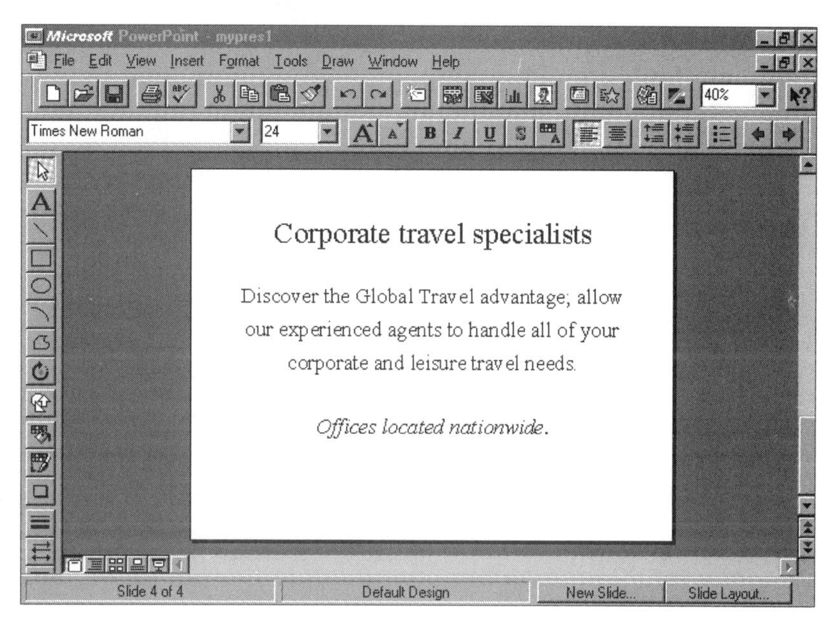

CHANGING TEXT CASE

PowerPoint's Change Case command allows you to easily change the *case* (capitalization) of your slide text. This nifty little feature can be a real life-saver in some situations. For example, let's say your boss reviewed your meticulously prepared, wonderfully creative 100-slide presentation and asked you to make one small change—to capitalize all of the slide text. In pre-PowerPoint 4.0 days, this would have meant manually retyping the text (with the Caps Lock key on) for all 100 slides. Ughh! Now you can simply select all the presentation text (in Outline view) and use Change Case to capitalize it—a 10-second task, tops!

Here's the general procedure for changing text case,

- Select the desired text.
- Choose *Format, Change Case* to open the Change Case dialog box.
- Select your desired option: *Sentence case.* capitalizes the first letter of each selected sentence and changes the remaining letters to lowercase; *lowercase* changes all the selected letters to

lowercase; *UPPERCASE* changes all selected letters to uppercase; *Title Case* capitalizes the first letter of each selected word; and *tOGGLE cASE* reverses the case of all selected letters.

- Click on *OK.*

Let's try out these case options:

1. Drag to select the entire contents of slide 4's bulleted-list object. Note that when the insertion point reaches a new word, PowerPoint selects the whole word, rather than its individual characters. This makes it easy to select large blocks of text. If, however, you'd prefer to select individual characters by dragging, simply choose Tools, Options and uncheck *Automatic Word Selection.*
2. Choose **Format, Change Case** to open the Change Case dialog box.
3. Select the **UPPERCASE** option, and click on **OK** to change the selected text to uppercase letters (as shown in Figure 3.16). See how easy that was!

Figure 3.16 **Changing selected text to UPPERCASE**

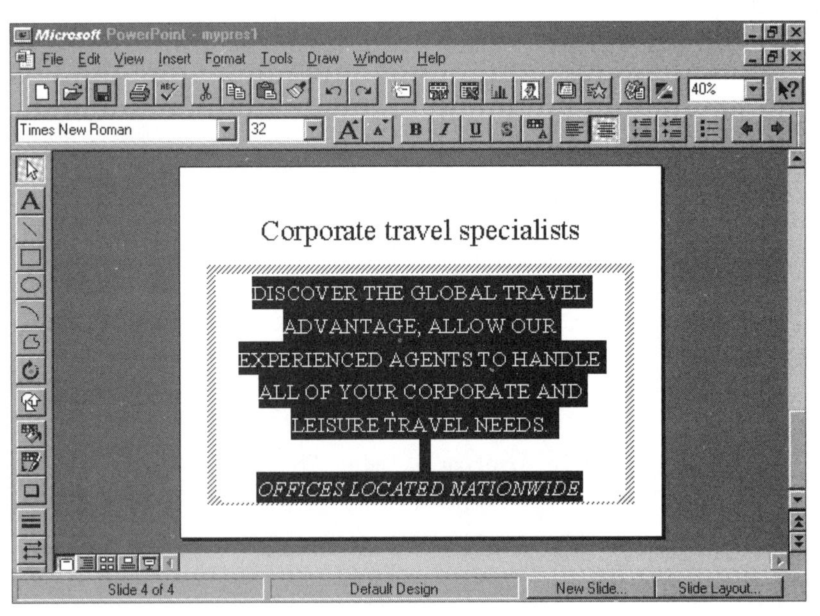

4. Choose **Format, Change Case** to reopen the Change Case dialog box.
5. Select the **lowercase** option, and click on **OK** to change the selected text to lowercase. Your slide now resembles an e. e. cummings poem.

PRACTICE YOUR SKILLS

1. Change the selected text to **Title Case**. This option capitalizes the first letter of each word, as in titles.
2. Change the selected text to **tOGGLE cASE**. This option reverses the case of all selected letters; looks a little goofy, hmmmm?
3. Change the selected text back to **Sentence case.** (its original case).
4. Change the words *THE*, *TO*, *OF*, and *AND* to **lowercase**, if necessary.
5. Save the file.
6. Close the file.

SPELL-CHECKING A PRESENTATION

Correct spelling is a vital part of a successful presentation. No matter how impressive a slide looks, if its title is misspelled, you'll lose credibility with your audience. PowerPoint provides a spell checker that searches your entire presentation—all the text objects in all of your slides, outlines, notes, and handouts—for spelling errors.

Here's the general procedure for spell-checking a presentation:

- Change to Outline view. (You can spell-check in Slide view, but doing so in Outline view is easier.)
- Press *Ctrl+Home* to move the insertion point to the top of the outline.
- Choose *Tools, Spelling* or click on the *Spelling* button (in the Standard toolbar), or press *F7* to open the Spelling dialog box.
- When PowerPoint finds a misspelled or unrecognized word (a word that is not in its internal dictionary), it highlights the word in the outline and displays the word in the Not In Dictionary

text box (as shown in Figure 3.17). At this point, you have several choices:

- If the word is misspelled and you know the correct spelling, type the correctly spelled word in the Change To text box and then click on the *Change* button to correct the word in the outline.
- If the word is misspelled and the correct spelling is in the Suggestions list box, click on the correct spelling (you may need to scroll through the list), and then click on the *Change* button.
- If the word is misspelled and the correct spelling is not in the Suggestions list box, click on the *Suggest* button to display more suggestions, click on the correct spelling (if it's there), and then click on the *Change* button.

Figure 3.17 Spelling dialog box

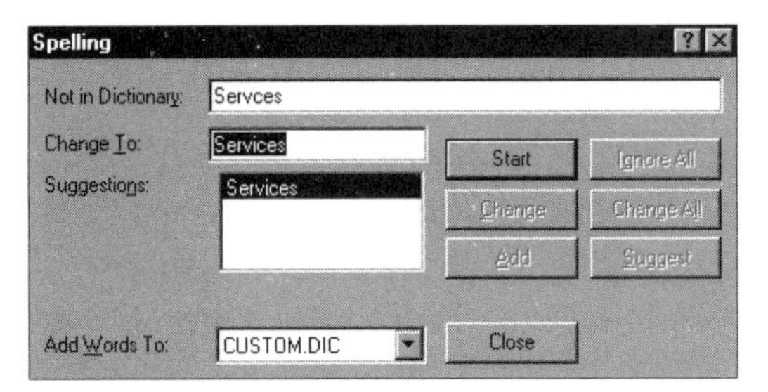

- If the word is not misspelled (for example, if it is a correctly spelled proper name that is not in PowerPoint's dictionary), click on the *Ignore* button to leave the word as is.
- If you want to add the word in the Not In Dictionary text box to your custom dictionary, click on the *Add* button; the next time the spell checker encounters the word (in this or any other presentation), it will consider the word correctly spelled. (**Note:** You can *add* words to a custom dictionary, but you cannot remove words from it.)

- To exit from the spell checker, click on the *Close* button. You can do this at any time during the spell-checking procedure.

Let's open a presentation file from the Power Work directory and spell-check it:

1. Open **spell** from your Power Work directory.
2. Change to Outline view and press **Ctrl+Home** to move the insertion point to the top of the outline.
3. Click on the **Spelling** button (fifth button from the left in the Standard toolbar) to open the Spelling dialog box.
4. PowerPoint highlights the word *Servces* in the outline and displays it in the Not In Dictionary text box. This is obviously a misspelling of *Services*. PowerPoint then suggests services as the correct spelling.
5. Click on **Change** to change the misspelled word in the outline (*Servces*) to the correctly spelled word you typed in the Change To text box (*Services*).
6. PowerPoint highlights the word *MacArthur* and displays it in the Not In Dictionary text box. The proper name *MacArthur* is not in PowerPoint's dictionary.
7. Click on **Ignore** to leave *MacArthur* as is. (You could have clicked on Add if you'd wanted to leave *MacArthur* as is *and* add it to your custom dictionary.) PowerPoint now displays the word *Incantive* in the Not In Dictionary text box.
8. Let's say you weren't sure how to spell this word correctly. Observe the Suggestions list box; note the correct spelling, *Incentive*.
9. Click on *Incentive* to select it (it may already be selected). Note that *Incentive* is now displayed in the Change To text box.
10. Click on **Change** to change *Incantive* in the outline to *Incentive*.
11. PowerPoint displays the message *Finished spell checking entire presentation*. All done!
12. Click on **OK** to close the Spelling dialog box.

Now let's add add *MacArthur* to the custom dictionary:

1. Click on the **Spelling** button to reopen the Spelling dialog box. PowerPoint displays *MacArthur* in the Not In Dictionary text box.
2. Click on **Add** to add *MacArthur* to the custom dictionary.

3. When the *Finished spell checking* message appears, click on **OK**.
4. Browse through the presentation in Slide view to verify that the spelling changes were made.
5. Save the file as **myspell** (Hint: Use the File, Save As command.)
6. Close the file.

SUMMARY

In this chapter, you learned how to work with your slide text. You now know how to get general and dialog-box help, how to edit slide text, how to rearrange bulleted items, how to apply text attributes, how to change indents, how to align text, how to change line spacing, how to change text case, and how to spell-check a presentation.

Here's a quick reference for the techniques you learned in this chapter:

Desired Result	How to Do It
Get general help	Choose **Help, Microsoft PowerPoint Help Topics** or press **F1**; to view a topic, click on the **Contents** tab and then click on the particular topic; to search for a topic, click on the **Index** tab and either type in the search word or double-click on the desired search word, double-click on the desired topic; to view previous Help windows, click on the **Back** button; to view the Index, click on the **Index** button; to exit from Help, click on the **Close** button
Get help for the active dialog box	Click on the dialog box's **Help** button and then click on the item for which you need help
Add a bulleted item to a slide	Place the insertion point at the end of the bulleted item after which you want to add your new bulleted item; press **Enter** to create the new bulleted item; if necessary, press **Tab** or **Shift+Tab** to change the indent level of your new bulleted item; type your desired bullet text

Desired Result	How to Do It
Rearrange the order of bulleted items by dragging	If you are in Slide view, place the insertion point anywhere within the bulleted list; point to the bullet of the bulleted item you want to move; drag the bullet (and all its sub-bulleted items) to your desired new position
Rearrange the order of bulleted items by using the Move Up and Move Down buttons (in Outline view)	Select the bulleted item(s) you want to move and click as many times as necessary on the **Move Up** or **Move Down** button to move the selected bulleted item(s) to your desired new position
Apply text attributes	Select the desired text; click on the desired text-editing button or press the desired keyboard shortcut (Ctrl+B to bold, Ctrl+I to italicize, Ctrl+U to underline)
Change indents	In Slide view, place the insertion point in the desired text object; choose **View, Ruler** to display its ruler; drag the desired first-line indent triangles and/or trailing-line indent triangles to the desired position on the ruler; choose **View, Ruler** to remove the ruler
Align text	Select the desired text; choose **Format, Alignment** and select the desired alignment (**Left**, **Center**, **Right**, or **Justify**); or press the desired keyboard shortcut (Ctrl+L to left align, Ctrl+R to right align, Ctrl+E to center, or Ctrl+J to justify)
Change line spacing	Select the desired paragraph(s); choose **Format, Line Spacing**; to change the spacing between lines of a multiline paragraph, click on the Line Spacing **up arrow** or **down arrow**; to change the spacing between separate paragraphs, click on the Before Paragraph or After Paragraph **up arrow** or **down arrow**; click on **OK**

Desired Result	How to Do It
Change text case	Select the desired text; choose **Format, Change Case**; select desired option (Sentence case, lowercase, UPPERCASE, Title Case, or tOGGLE cASE); click on **OK**
Spell-check a presentation	Change to Outline view; press **Ctrl+Home** to move to the top of the outline; choose **Tools, Spelling**, click on the **Spelling** button, or press **F7**; follow the prompts; to exit from the spell checker, click on its **Close** button

In the next chapter, you'll find out how to draw and create text objects on your slides. You will learn how to draw basic shapes (lines, rectangles, squares, ellipses, circles, and arcs), how to draw other predefined shapes (arrows, triangles, stars, diamonds, and so on), how to draw free-form objects, and how to create text objects. You will also learn how to edit objects (select and deselect, resize, move, align, and delete them), how to undo your last action, and how to enhance objects (change their shapes, fill colors, shadows, and line styles).

CHAPTER 4: DRAWING ON YOUR SLIDES

Drawing Primer

Creating Text Objects

Editing Objects

Enhancing Objects

A strong presentation consists of both effective words and effective images. In Chapters 2 and 3, you learned the fundamentals of working with words. In these next two chapters, you'll learn how to work with images. We'll begin by showing you how to draw on your slides and how to edit and enhance your drawn objects.

Note: Normally, we ask you to work through an entire chapter in one sitting. However, since this chapter is so long, we've given you an opportunity to work through it in two separate sittings. You'll find a section entitled "If You Want to Pause Here" about halfway through the chapter. You can decide then whether to pause or continue.

When you're done working through this chapter, you will know

- How to draw basic shapes—lines, rectangles, squares, ellipses, circles, and arcs
- How to draw other predefined shapes—arrows, triangles, stars, diamonds, and so on
- How to draw free-form objects
- How to create text objects
- How to edit objects—select and deselect, resize, move, align, and delete them
- How to undo your last action
- How to enhance objects—change their shapes, fill colors, shadows, line styles, and angles of rotation

DRAWING PRIMER

PowerPoint's Drawing toolbar contains fifteen drawing tools, as shown in Table 4.1 and Figure 4.1.

Table 4.1 Drawing Tools

Tool	Used To
Selection tool	Select and edit objects
Text tool	Create text objects
Line tool	Draw straight lines
Rectangle tool	Draw rectangles and squares
Ellipse tool	Draw ellipses (ovals) and circles
Arc tool	Draw arcs (curved lines)

Figure 4.1 **Drawing tools**

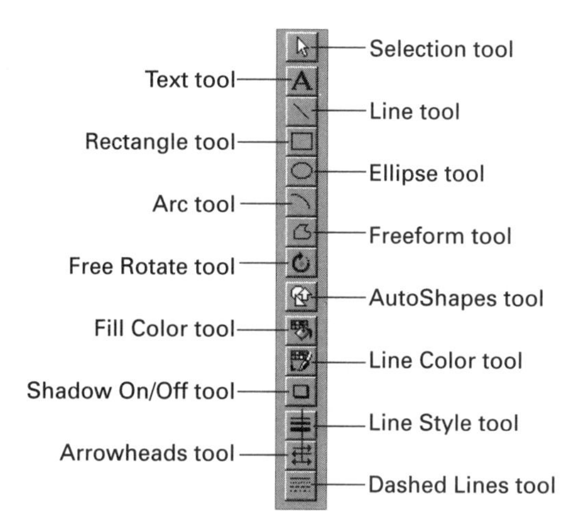

Table 4.1 **Drawing Tools (Continued)**

Tool	Used To
Freeform tool	Draw free-form shapes
Free Rotate tool	Rotate objects
AutoShapes tool	Draw predefined shapes (autoshapes)
Fill Color tool	Change or remove fill color from objects
Line Color tool	Change or remove line color from objects
Shadow On/Off tool	Add or remove default shadow color from objects
Line Style tool	Change the thickness of a line
Arrowheads tool	Add arrowheads to selected line, arc, or open freeform line
Dashed Lines tool	Change the style of selected line to dashed

In addition to the Drawing toolbar, PowerPoint provides a Drawing+ toolbar that allows you to do such things as group and ungroup objects; flip objects; and so on. Discussion of the Drawing+ toolbar is beyond the scope of this book; drawing enthusiasts should refer to their PowerPoint documentation.

DRAWING STRAIGHT LINES

Here's the general procedure for drawing straight lines on a slide:

- Click (or double-click) on the *Line* tool to select it. Clicking once on the tool allows you to draw a single line only; double-clicking on it allows you to draw multiple lines.
- To draw a horizontal, vertical, or diagonal line, press and hold the *Shift* key.
- Press and hold the *left mouse button.*
- Drag in the slide to draw the line.
- Release the mouse button.
- If necessary, release the *Shift* key.

If you are not running PowerPoint, please start it now. If the Tip Of The Day dialog box or the PowerPoint dialog box is displayed, close it. If any presentations are open, close them. A maximized application window should be displayed alone on your screen.

Let's begin by using a handy shortcut for opening mypres1:

1. Click on **File** to open the drop-down File menu.
2. Note that several files are listed at the bottom of the menu above the Exit menu selection. These are your most recently used PowerPoint files. One of them should be mypres1. (**Note:** If you created/edited several files since working through the last chapter of this book, mypres1 may not appear in the list.)
3. Click on **mypres1** to open it. (Or, if mypres1 is not listed, click on **Open** and use the standard method to open mypres1.)

Now let's create a new slide and draw some lines on it:

1. Display slide 4, the last slide of the presentation.
2. Click on the **New Slide** button (at the bottom of the screen) to add a new slide after slide 4. The New Slide dialog box appears. PowerPoint is asking you to select an autolayout for

your new slide. Note that the currently selected autolayout is *Bulleted List* (as shown in the lower-right corner of the dialog box), the same autolayout as slide 4.

3. Click on **OK** to create a new bulleted-list slide (slide 5). Hmmmm.... Something's not quite right. We want to *draw* on this slide, not enter a title or a bulleted list. What we really need is a blank slide.
4. Click on the **Slide Layout** button (next to the New Slide button) to open the Slide Layout dialog box. Select (click on) the **Blank** layout, the bottom layout of the rightmost column (you might have to scroll).
5. Click on **Apply** to change slide 5's layout from bulleted list to blank. There, that's much better: a clean slate to work on! You can use the Layout button to change the layout of a slide without losing any of its contents.

Let's draw a straight line that slants up slightly to the right:

1. Select the **Line** tool (use Figure 4.1 or ToolTips to find it) by clicking once on it.
2. Move the mouse pointer onto the slide workspace. Note that the pointer changes to a cross hair. Position the center of the cross hair about half an inch below and to the right of the upper-left corner of the slide. (**Note**: In the slide workspace of a maximized presentation window, the actual slide is represented by the white area, not by the gray area surrounding it.)
3. Press and hold the **left mouse button**. Drag rightward and slightly upward to draw a slanting straight line resembling the one shown in Figure 4.2. Release the mouse button to complete the line.

Now let's draw a horizontal line:

1. If necessary, move the mouse pointer back onto the slide workspace. Note that the pointer is now an arrow, not a cross hair. Note also that the Line tool is no longer selected. As mentioned in the general procedure, you must double-click on a drawing tool if you want to use it more than once. Because you clicked just once on the Line tool (in step 1 of the previous activity), PowerPoint automatically deselected the tool after you drew your line.
2. Double-click on the **Line** tool to select it.

3. Position the mouse cross hair about half an inch below the left end of the line you just drew.
4. Press and hold the **Shift** key. Press and hold the **left mouse button**.
5. Drag to the right to draw a horizontal line resembling the one shown in Figure 4.2. (As long as you are holding down Shift, you do not need to drag absolutely horizontally to do this.)

Figure 4.2 **Drawing a slanting line and a horizontal line**

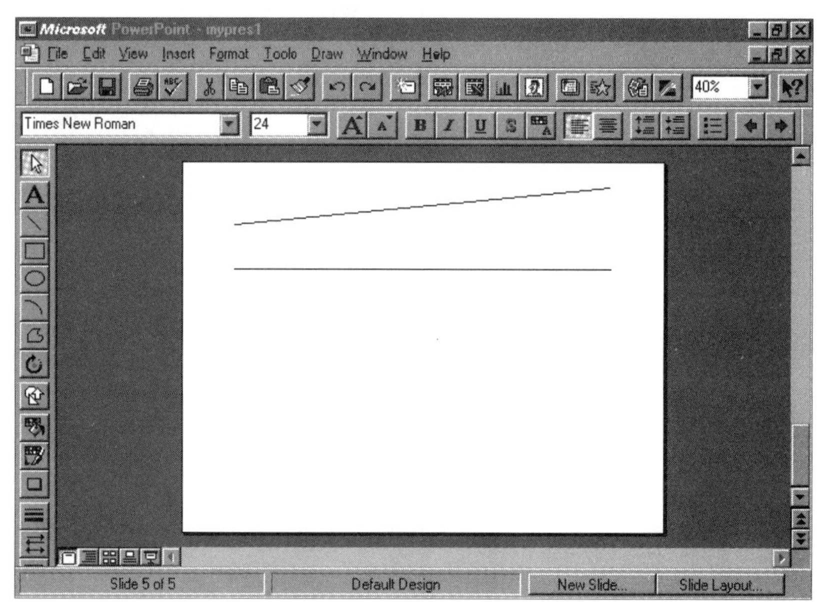

6. Release the mouse button, and then release the Shift key to complete the line. (Make sure to release the mouse button *before* you release the Shift key, or your line may not turn out exactly horizontal.)
7. Note that the mouse pointer is still a cross hair and the Line tool is still selected. You *could* draw more lines without reselecting the Line tool. We won't, however, do this right now.
8. Click on any blank area of the slide to deselect your newly drawn line. Note that this also deselects the Line tool. Your screen should match (or closely resemble) that shown in Figure 4.2.

DRAWING RECTANGLES AND SQUARES

Here's the general procedure for drawing a rectangle or a square on a slide:

- Click (or double-click) on the *Rectangle* tool to select it.
- To draw a square, press and hold the *Shift* key.
- Press and hold the *left mouse button.*
- Drag in the slide to draw the rectangle or square.
- Release the mouse button.
- If necessary, release the Shift key.

Let's draw a rectangle on our new slide:

1. Double-click on the **Rectangle** tool (as shown in Figure 4.1) to select it. This will allow you to draw the rectangle in this activity and the square in the next without reselecting the Rectangle tool.
2. Position the mouse cross hair about half an inch below the left end of the horizontal line you drew in the last activity.
3. Press and hold the **left mouse button**.
4. Drag down and to the right to draw a long, thin rectangle resembling the one shown in Figure 4.3.
5. Release the mouse button to complete the rectangle. Note that PowerPoint automatically fills the rectangle with the current default fill color.

Now let's draw a square:

1. Position the mouse cross hair about half an inch to the right of the upper-right corner of the rectangle you just drew.
2. Press and hold the **Shift** key. Press and hold the **left mouse button**.
3. Drag down and to the right to draw a square resembling the one shown in Figure 4.3.
4. Release the mouse button, and then release the Shift key. (Make sure to release the mouse button *before* you release the Shift key, or your square may not turn out perfectly square.)

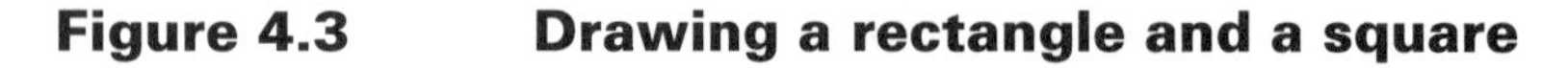

Figure 4.3 Drawing a rectangle and a square

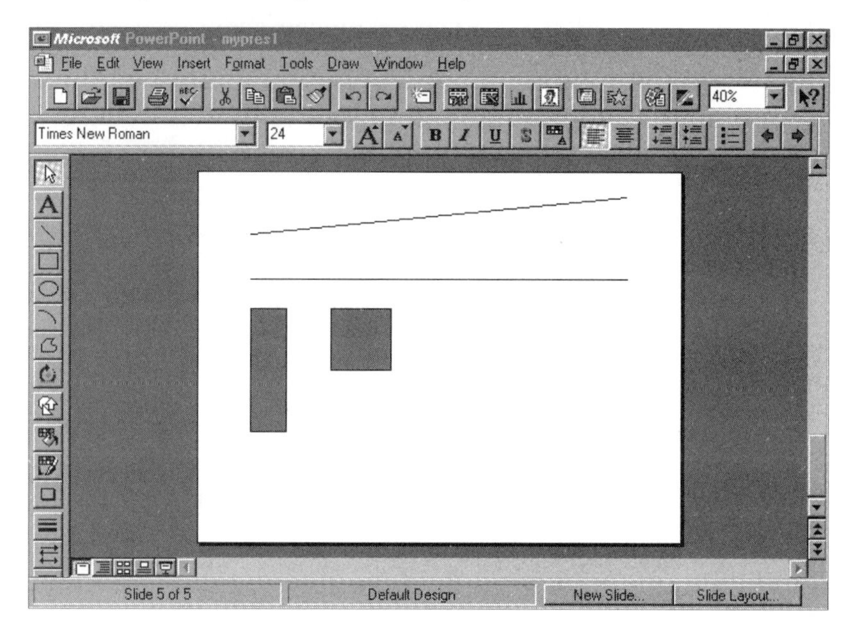

5. Deselect your square (by clicking on a blank area of the slide). Your screen should match (or closely resemble) that shown in Figure 4.3.

DRAWING ELLIPSES AND CIRCLES

Here's the general procedure for drawing an ellipse (oval) or a circle on a slide:

- Click (or double-click) on the *Ellipse* tool to select it.
- Drag in the slide to draw an ellipse. *Shift+drag* to draw a circle.

Let's add an ellipse to our slide:

1. Double-click on the **Ellipse** tool to select it.
2. Position the mouse cross hair about half an inch to the right of the upper-right corner of the square you drew in the last activity.
3. Drag to the right and down to draw a long, thin ellipse resembling the one shown in Figure 4.4.

Figure 4.4 **Drawing an ellipse and a circle**

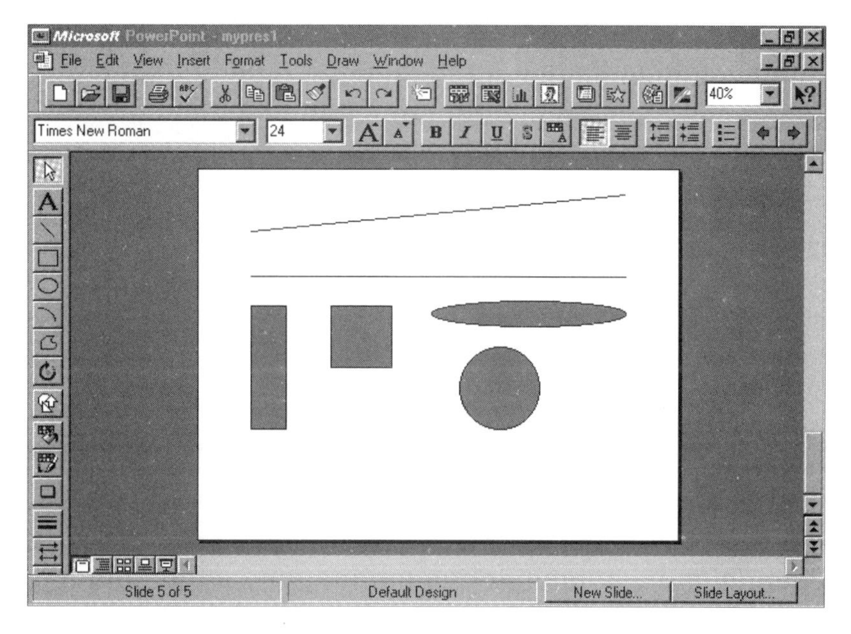

Now let's draw a circle:

1. Position the mouse cross hair about half an inch below the left end of the ellipse you just drew.
2. *Shift+drag* (hold the **Shift** key while dragging) down and to the right to draw a circle resembling the one shown in Figure 4.4. (Remember to release the mouse button *before* the Shift key.)
3. Deselect the circle. Your screen should match (or closely resemble) that shown in Figure 4.4.

DRAWING ARCS (CURVED LINES)

Technically, an *arc* is a 90-degree (quarter) segment of an ellipse or a circle. In effect, though, an arc is simply a curved line. Here's the general procedure for drawing an arc on a slide:

- Click (or double-click) on the *Arc* tool to select it.
- Drag in the slide to draw an elliptical arc. *Shift*+drag to draw a circular arc.

Let's add an elliptical arc to our slide; that is, an arc with the curve of an ellipse rather than a circle:

1. Double-click on the **Arc** tool to select it.
2. Position the mouse cross hair about half an inch below the lower-left corner of the rectangle.
3. Drag up and to the right to draw an elliptical arc resembling the one shown on the left in Figure 4.5. Observe that the arc's curve is that of an ellipse (oval), rather than that of a circle.

Figure 4.5 **Drawing an elliptical arc and a circular arc**

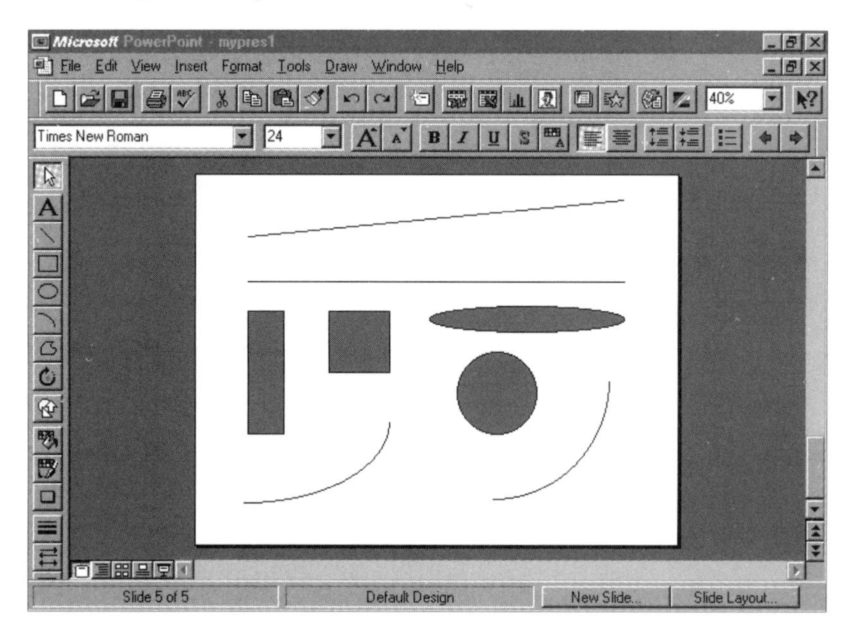

Now let's draw a circular arc:

1. Position the mouse cross hair about half an inch below the lowest point of the circle.
2. **Shift**+drag up and to the right to draw a circular arc resembling the one shown in Figure 4.5. Observe that the arc's curve is that of a circle, rather than that of an ellipse.

3. Deselect the circular arc. Your screen should match (or closely resemble) that shown in Figure 4.5.
4. Choose **File, Save** to save the presentation file.

DRAWING AUTOSHAPES

Thus far, you've learned how to draw four types of objects on your slides: lines, rectangles/squares, ellipses/circles, and arcs. Although the size and proportions of these objects vary, their basic shapes are predefined. For example, you can use the Rectangle tool to draw a long narrow rectangle, a short wide rectangle, or a perfect square, but you can't use it to draw a butterfly. In this section, you'll learn how to use the AutoShapes tool to draw other predefined shapes (called *autoshapes*), including arrows, triangles, stars, diamonds, and three-dimensional boxes.

Here's the general procedure for drawing an autoshape on a slide:

- Click (once!) on the *AutoShapes* tool to open the *AutoShapes tool palette.*
- Click (or double-click) on the desired *AutoShapes* tool.
- Drag in the slide to draw the selected autoshape. *Shift*+drag to maintain the proportions of the autoshape.
- To close the AutoShapes tool palette, click on the *AutoShapes* tool.

Let's create a new slide and fill it with autoshapes:

1. Click on the **New Slide** button to open the New Slide dialog box. Note that the Blank autolayout is selected. (If not, please select it.) This is what we want, so click on **OK** to create the new slide (slide 6).
2. Click once on the **AutoShapes** tool to open the AutoShapes tool palette, which contains PowerPoint's 24 predefined autoshape tools.
3. Double-click on the **Isosceles Triangle** tool (use the ToolTips to locate the tool) to select it.
4. If necessary, move the AutoShapes tool palette out of the way, so you can draw freely. Position the mouse cross hair about half an inch below and to the right of the upper-left corner of the slide.

5. Press and hold the **left mouse** button. Do not release this button until we tell you to do so in the next step. Drag all around the slide to get a feeling for how you can change the size and proportions of the triangle.
6. Continue dragging until your triangle resembles the thin, left triangle in Figure 4.6, and then release the mouse button.

Figure 4.6 **Drawing isosceles triangle autoshapes**

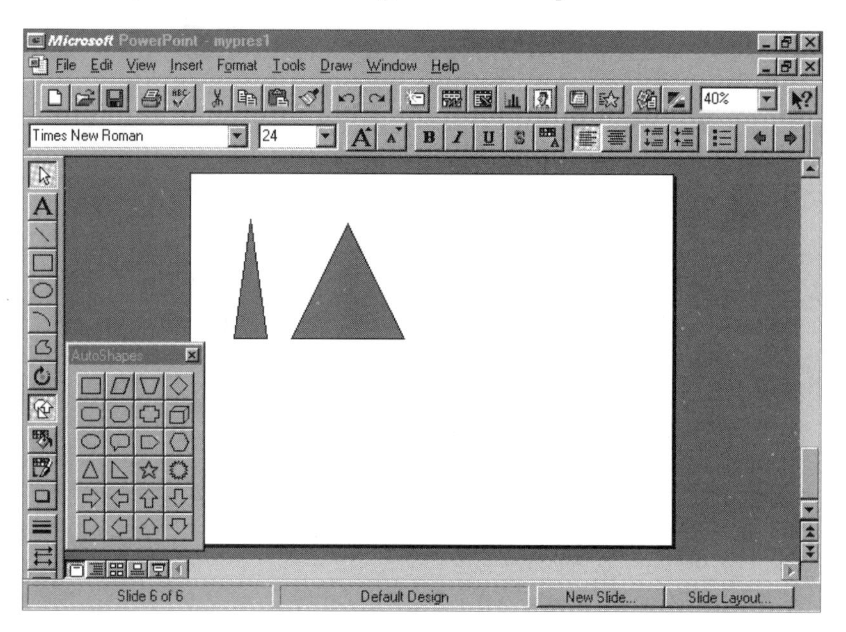

Observe that the proportions of your triangle do not match the proportions of the triangle displayed in the Isosceles Triangle tool; your triangle is much thinner. As mentioned, you need to Shift+drag in order to maintain the proportions of your selected autoshape. Let's do this now:

1. Position the mouse cross hair about an inch to the right of the top of the triangle you just drew.
2. **Shift**+drag down and to the right to draw a triangle resembling the one to the right in Figure 4.6. Note that this triangle has the same proportions as the one displayed in the Isosceles Triangle tool.

3. Deselect the triangle. Your screen should match (or closely resemble) that shown in Figure 4.6.

PRACTICE YOUR SKILLS

1. Time to have fun! Using the procedure just described, fill slide 6 with as many autoshapes as you have the stamina to draw. Don't worry about overlapping objects; it's perfectly okay to do this.
2. When you're done drawing, close the AutoShapes tool palette.
3. Click on the **Slide Show** button to display the slide in full-screen view. Compare your slide with the one we created in Figure 4.7. Who wins?

Figure 4.7 **A cornucopia of autoshape delights**

4. Press **Esc** to return to Slide view.
5. Save the file.

DRAWING FREE-FORM OBJECTS

All the objects you've drawn thus far have been predefined PowerPoint shapes (lines, rectangles/squares, ellipses/circles, arcs, and autoshapes). In this section, you'll learn how to use the Freeform tool to draw *free-form* shapes. Here's the general procedure for doing this:

- Click (or double-click) on the *Freeform* tool to select it.
- Position the mouse cross hair where you want to start drawing.
- Drag to draw your free-form object.
- Complete your free-form object in either of the following ways:
    - To create an *open object*—one whose end point does not connect to its starting point, such as a spiral—double-click on your desired end point for the object.
    - To create a *closed object*—one whose end point connects to its starting point, such as a circle—click on the starting point of the object.

Let's draw some open free-form objects:

1. Use the **New Slide** button to create a new, blank slide (slide 7).
2. Double-click on the **Freeform** tool to select it.
3. Position the mouse cross hair in the center of the slide.
4. Press and hold the **left mouse button**. Without releasing the button, drag in ever-widening circles to draw a spiral object resembling the one shown in Figure 4.8.
5. When you've reached the end point of your spiral, release the mouse button and—without moving the pointer—double-click to complete the object. This is an open object; its end point does not connect to its starting point.
6. Follow the technique outlined in steps 4 and 5 to draw an open object resembling the boot-like object on the right side of the slide in Figure 4.8.

Now let's draw a closed free-form object:

1. Do your best to draw a perfect circle in the lower-left quadrant of the slide. When you've reached the end point of your circle (which should be right on top of the starting point), release the mouse button and click on the starting point to connect these two points, thus closing the object.

Figure 4.8 **Drawing open and closed freeform objects**

2. Observe your results. Note how difficult (impossible!) it is to use the Freeform tool to draw a perfect circle (as evidenced by our woeful attempt in Figure 4.8). The moral is this: To draw a precise geometric shape (rectangle/square, ellipse/circle, and so on), use the appropriate drawing tool (Rectangle tool, Ellipse tool, and so on), not the Freeform tool.

DRAWING STRAIGHT FREE-FORM LINES

The free-form objects you just drew are composed almost exclusively of curved lines. You may at times, however, want to draw one or more straight lines in a free-form object. You can do this in either of the following ways:

- While drawing your free-form object, drag in a straight line. You'll need a very steady hand to achieve good results using this technique, particularly if you are attempting to draw lines that are neither exactly horizontal nor vertical.
- Or, while drawing your free-form object, release the mouse button, move the pointer to draw the straight line, and then

press and hold the left mouse button to continue drawing in free-form (or click to begin drawing another straight line). (**Note**: To draw a horizontal, vertical, or diagonal line, hold down the Shift key while you move the mouse pointer.)

Let's use each of these techniques to draw a closed free-form object composed of both free-form and straight lines. In order to do this, you must press, hold, and release the left mouse button and the Shift key at precisely the right times, so please be sure to follow our directions exactly:

1. The Freeform tool should still be selected. If not, please select it now.
2. Position the cross hair about half an inch above the uppermost point in your imperfect circle.
3. Press and hold down the **left mouse button**. Do not release the button until we tell you to do so in step 8.
4. Begin drawing the object depicted in the upper-left quadrant of Figure 4.8 by dragging a curved line up and to the right about 1 inch. (Don't release the mouse button!)
5. Now attempt to draw a straight horizontal line by dragging left about half an inch (refer to Figure 4.8).
6. Attempt to draw a straight diagonal line by dragging diagonally up and to the right about half an inch. Note how difficult it is to draw a nonhorizontal, nonvertical straight line by dragging.
7. Attempt to draw a straight vertical line by dragging up about half an inch.
8. Release the mouse button (finally!) but do not move the mouse.

Now we'll use the second technique to draw a copy of these three straight lines:

1. Press and hold the **Shift** key. Do not release this key until we tell you to do so in step 2 of the next activity.
2. Draw a straight horizontal line by moving the mouse pointer (*without* pressing the mouse button) about half an inch to the left (refer to Figure 4.8).
3. Without moving the mouse pointer, click to begin another straight line.

4. Draw a straight diagonal line by moving the mouse pointer diagonally about half an inch up and to the right. Note how much easier it is to draw a diagonal line by using this technique than by dragging.
5. Click to begin another straight line.
6. Draw a straight vertical line by moving the mouse pointer up about half an inch. Observe how much better these straight lines look than the ones you drew by dragging.

Now we'll return to free-form drawing and complete the object depicted in Figure 4.8:

1. Press and hold the **left mouse button**.
2. Release the Shift key.
3. Drag to draw the rest of the object in Figure 4.8.
4. Close the object by clicking on its starting point.

CREATING TEXT OBJECTS

In Chapters 2 and 3, you learned how to add text to your slides' title, subtitle, and bulleted-list objects. PowerPoint does not limit your slide text to these predefined text objects. Just as you can create any number of drawn objects on a slide, you can create any number of text objects.

You create text objects to add text that does not belong to the title, subtitle, or bulleted-list categories—for example, a caption for a piece of clip art, or a footnote for a bulleted-list item.

Here's the general procedure for creating a text object on a slide:

- Click (once) on the *Text* tool to select it.
- Position the mouse pointer where you want your text to begin on the slide.
- Click to create a text object that does *not* automatically wrap the words you type. Or, drag to create a text object that *does* wrap your words.
- Type your desired text.
- When you are finished typing, click on any blank area of the slide to complete your text object.

Let's use this procedure to create a simple word-wrapped text object:

1. Use the **New Slide** button to create a new, blank slide (slide 8).
2. Click on the **Text** tool to select it. (PowerPoint only allows you to create one text object at a time, whether you click or double-click on the Text tool.) Move the mouse pointer onto the slide workspace and note its shape, a variation of the standard insertion point.
3. Position the mouse pointer about half an inch below and to the right of the upper-left corner of the slide.
4. Drag to create a box about half as wide as the slide and an inch high. As you'll see in the next step, it doesn't matter how high you make your box, because PowerPoint reduces it to a one-line-high text box, when you release the mouse button.
5. Release the mouse button. A dotted text object appears. Its width is the width you dragged in the previous step; its height, as mentioned, is one line. Observe the blinking insertion point in the text object. This marks where your text will appear.
6. Type the following paragraph (without pressing Enter). As you type, observe how PowerPoint automatically wraps the text to fit your text-object width. Observe also how PowerPoint automatically expands the text object vertically to accommodate all of your text lines.

   Discover the Global Travel advantage; allow our experienced agents to handle all of your corporate and leisure travel needs.

7. Click on any blank area of the slide to complete your text object. The object is deselected, as shown in Figure 4.9. (Your lines may wrap at different places than ours.)

PRACTICE YOUR SKILLS

1. Create the other text object shown in Figure 4.9. Do this by creating a text object that does *not* automatically wrap words (by selecting the Text tool and clicking in the workspace, not dragging). Use your Enter key to wrap the text as shown. See how tedious it is to wrap text manually! (For this

Figure 4.9 **Creating text objects**

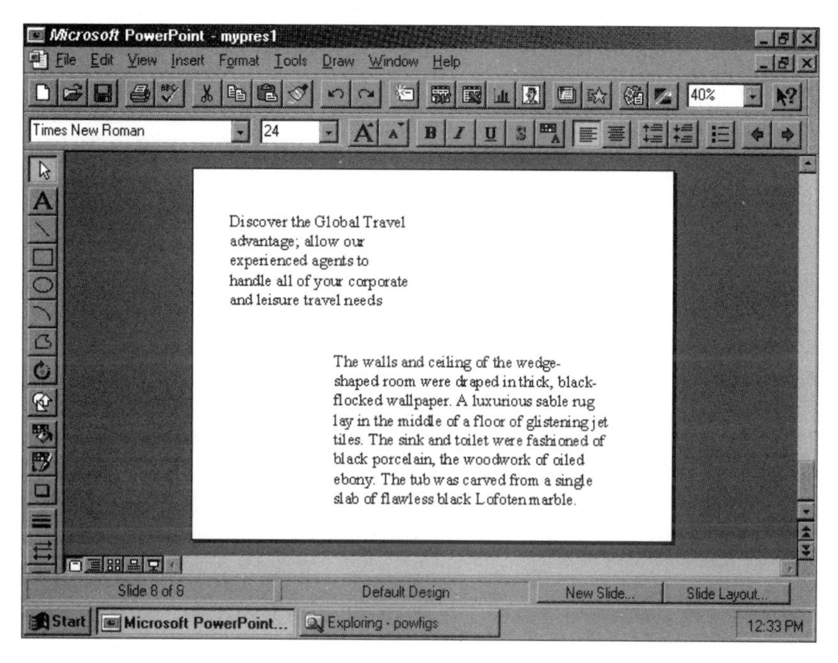

reason, you normally only use a non-wrapping text object to create a simple, one- or two-line text label.)

2. Save the file.

EDITING OBJECTS

Now that you know how to draw objects and create text objects on your slides, it's time to learn how to edit them. Over the next several sections, you'll learn how to:

- Select and deselect objects
- Undo your last action
- Resize objects
- Move objects
- Align objects
- Delete objects

SELECTING AND DESELECTING OBJECTS

In order to edit an object, you must first select it. Here's the general procedure for doing this:

- Click on the *Selection* tool to select it (if it is not already selected).
- To select a graphic (drawn) object, click on it. To select a text object with an insertion point in it, press *Esc*; to select a text object with no insertion point, *Shift*+click on the object. Square selection handles appear around the object to indicate that it is selected.
- To deselect the currently selected object, press *Esc* or click on any blank area of the slide.

You may, at times, want to select multiple objects. For example, later in this chapter you'll add a shadow effect to several objects by selecting them all and then applying a shadow to the entire group at once (rather than selecting one object, applying a shadow, selecting the next object, applying a shadow, and so on). Here's the general procedure for selecting multiple objects:

- *Shift*+click (hold the Shift key and click the left mouse button) on all desired objects, one by one.
- Or, to select all objects in a slide, choose *Edit, Select All* (or press *Ctrl+A*).
- To remove (deselect) an object from a multiple selection, *Shift*+click on it.
- To deselect all objects in a multiple selection, press *Esc* or click on any blank area of the slide.

Let's begin by selecting and deselecting single objects:

1. Display slide 5, the slide that contains the simple objects you drew at the beginning of this chapter.
2. Select the slanted line at the top of the slide by clicking on it. Note the selection handles that appear at the ends of the line to indicate that it is selected.
3. Deselect the line by pressing **Esc**.
4. Use this technique to select and deselect first the square, then the circle, and finally the elliptical arc.

Now let's create and modify a multiple selection:

1. All of slide 5's objects should be deselected. If they are not, press **Esc** to do this.
2. **Shift**+click on the two lines, the rectangle, the square, the ellipse, and the circle to select them. (You don't have to release the Shift key between each Shift+click.)

Let's say you decided to add the two arcs to your multiple selection:

1. **Shift**+click on the two arcs to add them to the selection. All eight objects on your slide should now be selected, as shown in Figure 4.10.

Figure 4.10 **Selecting all of slide 5's objects**

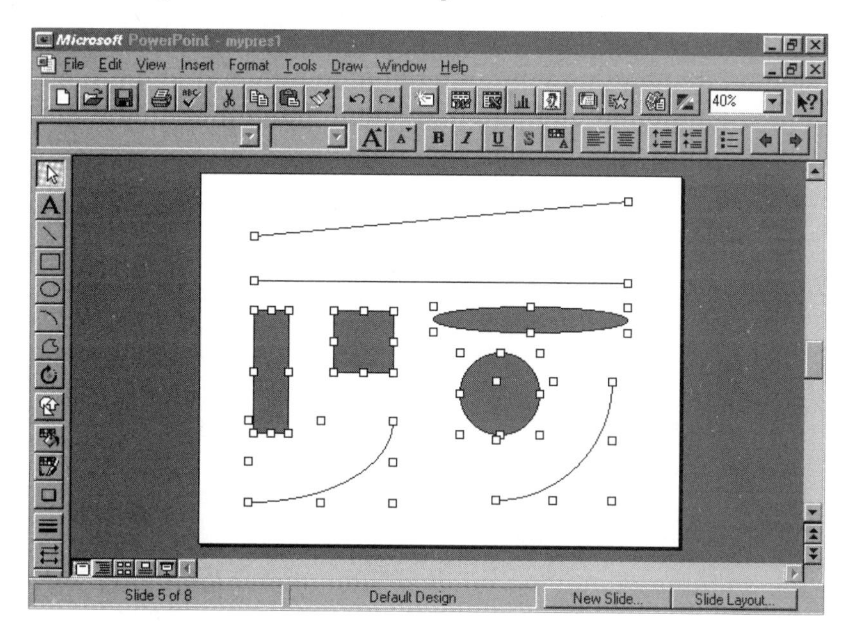

Now let's say you wanted to remove the circle from your multiple selection:

1. **Shift**+click on the circle to remove it from the multiple selection.

Let's finish up by deselecting all the objects in your multiple selection:

1. Press Del. Oh no! You've made a terrible mistake. Instead of deselecting the objects, you've deleted them! Relax... PowerPoint provides a very handy command that can rescue you from potential calamities like this. (Please don't touch your keyboard or mouse until we tell you to do so in the next activity.)

UNDOING YOUR LAST ACTION

You can use the *Edit, Undo* command to undo (reverse) your last PowerPoint action. There are twenty levels of Undo by default. You can increase or decrease the number of levels by choosing Tools, Options and then clicking on the Advanced tab. Here's the general procedure for doing this:

- Immediately after performing the action you want to reverse, choose Edit, Undo. Or click on the *Undo* button (in the Standard toolbar) or press *Ctrl+Z*.
- To reverse your last Undo command, choose **Edit, Redo.** Click on the Redo button (to the right of the Undo button) or press **Ctrl+Y.**

Let's use Edit, Undo to recover our lost objects:

1. Choose **Edit, Undo Clear** to reverse the last action you performed, deleting all the objects in your multiple selection. The deleted objects reappear!
2. Choose **Edit, Redo Clear.** again to reverse the Undo command you just issued. The objects are again deleted.
3. This time, click on the **Undo** button (the curved arrow near the middle of the Standard toolbar) to reverse the second Undo command. The objects reappear. You can use the Undo and Redo commands in this manner to toggle between the "before" and "after" conditions of an action. (Clicking on the Undo button or pressing Ctrl+Z is exactly equivalent to choosing Edit, Undo.)
4. Save the file.

IF YOU WANT TO PAUSE HERE

As mentioned, because this chapter is so long, we're giving you an opportunity to work through it in two sittings. If you want to pause here and finish the chapter later, close the file and exit PowerPoint. When you're ready to finish the chapter, start PowerPoint and open mypres1 from your Power Work directory.

RESIZING OBJECTS

Once you've drawn an object or created a text object on a slide, you may find that you need to reduce or enlarge the object to fit the overall slide layout. PowerPoint enables you to resize objects quickly and easily. Here's the general procedure for doing this:

- Select the object.
- To reduce the object, drag a selection handle toward the center of the object. To enlarge the object, drag a selection handle away from the center of the object. To maintain the original proportions of the object as you resize it, *Shift*+drag a corner selection handle.

Let's practice resizing objects:

1. Display slide 5, if necessary.
2. Select the circle. Observe the selection handles—you can drag any of these handles to resize the circle.
3. Enlarge the circle by dragging its lower-right corner selection handle about an inch diagonally away from the center of the circle. Feel free to overlap the arc, if it gets in your way.
4. Observe your enlarged circle carefully. Is it, in fact, still a perfect circle? Or have you subtly distorted its proportions, turning it into a nearly circular ellipse?

If you have a good eye and a steady hand, it's possible to maintain the proportions of a object you resize by dragging along the true diagonal. However, it's much easier—and more reliable—to hold down the Shift key while resizing.

Let's try this technique. First, we'll return the enlarged circle to its original size and proportions. Rather than dragging to do this, we'll use the Undo command:

1. Click on the **Undo** button to undo your circle-resizing action.

2. Select the circle, if necessary.
3. **Shift**+drag the corner handle about 1 inch diagonally away from the center of the square. Voilà! An enlarged perfect circle, as shown in Figure 4.11.

Figure 4.11 **Enlarging a circle proportionally**

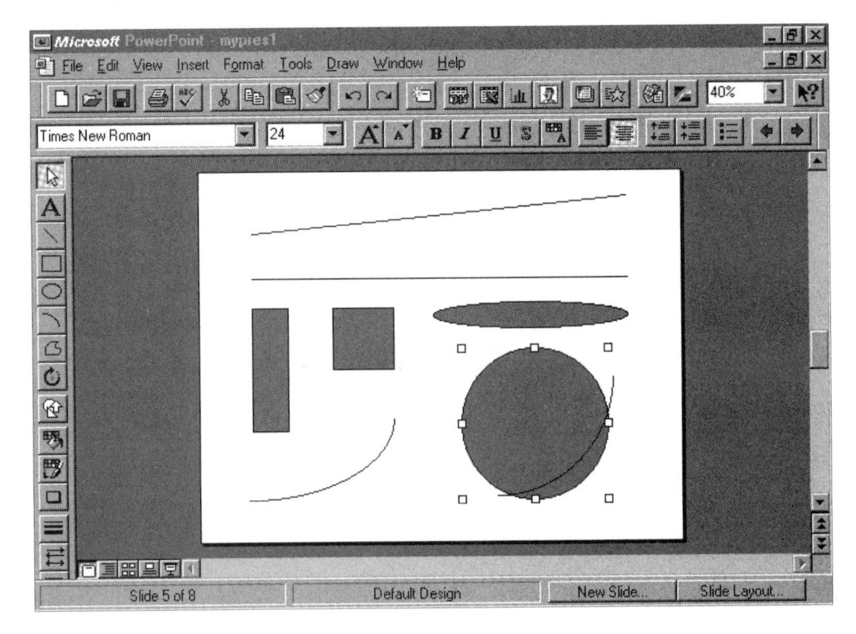

PRACTICE YOUR SKILLS

Using Figure 4.12 as a guide, perform the following steps:

1. Proportionally enlarge the rectangle by Shift+dragging its lower-right corner selection handle.
2. Proportionally enlarge the ellipse by Shift+dragging its lower-left corner handle.
3. Proportionally reduce both arcs by Shift+dragging their upper-right corner handles. (Hint: Drag toward—not away from—the center of the arc objects.)

4. Press **Esc** to deselect. Your screen should resemble that shown in Figure 4.12.
5. Save the file.

Figure 4.12 **Proportionally resizing objects**

MOVING OBJECTS

Along with resizing your objects, you may want to move them to improve the slide layout. Here's the general procedure for doing this:

- Select the object.
- To move a graphic object, point to its middle (not to a selection handle). To move a text object, point to its selection box outline (again, not to a handle).
- Drag the object to your desired new location. *Shift*+drag to move the object exactly horizontally or vertically.
- Or, press your arrow keys (left, right, up, or down) to move the object in small, discrete steps.

PRACTICE YOUR SKILLS

1. Use the above procedure to move the objects on slide 5 to resemble the arrangement shown in Figure 4.13. Try using the mouse *and* the arrow keys; which method do you prefer?

Figure 4.13 **Moving objects**

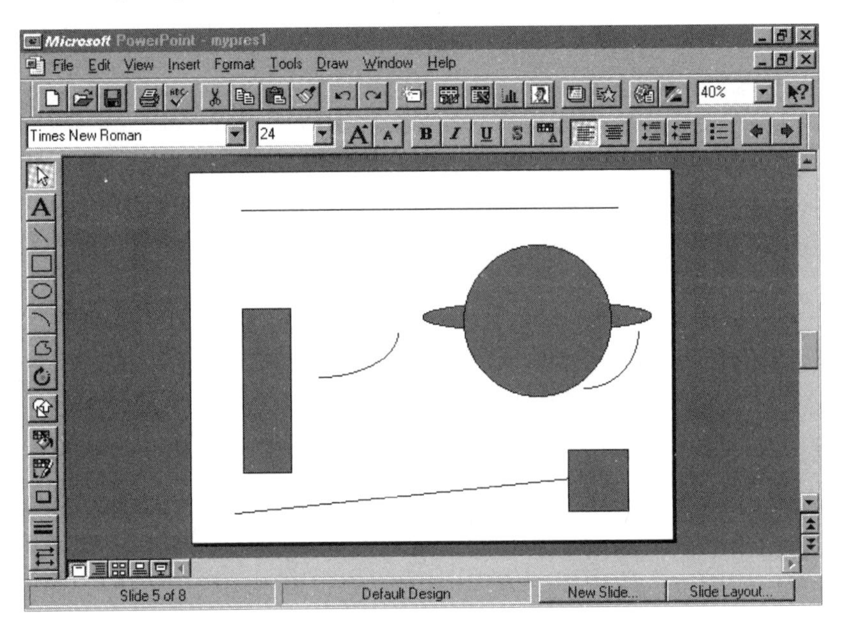

2. Save the file.

ALIGNING OBJECTS

Sloppily laid-out objects can seriously undermine the effectiveness of a slide. To help you optimize the clarity and harmony of a slide's layout, PowerPoint enables you to align its objects; that is, it allows you to position these objects so that they line up precisely across or down the slide. For example, in an organization chart depicting the hierarchical structure of a company, you'd want to horizontally align the text boxes of employees who are at the same level. PowerPoint provides two utilities that allow you to easily align objects in your slides: the *grid* and *guides*.

The grid is an invisible crosshatch of vertical and horizontal lines (12 to an inch) that covers the entire slide workspace. When the *Draw, Snap To Grid* option is turned on, the edge of any object that you move will *snap* (move automatically) to the nearest grid line. (**Note**: To temporarily turn off Snap To Grid—in order to move an object in increments less than 1/12 of an inch—hold Alt as you move the object.)

The guides are a single vertical and a single horizontal line, both extending across the entire slide workspace. When the *View, Guides* option is turned on, the center or edge of any object that you move near either guide will snap to that guide.

Let's create a new slide, draw a number of rectangles on it, and then use the grid to align their top edges:

1. If necessary, display slide 5. Use the **New Slide** button to create a new, blank slide (slide 6). Once again, note that you can insert a new slide between two existing slides (in this case, between slides 5 and 7).
2. Using Figure 4.14 as a guide, draw five rectangles of different sizes from left to right across the slide. (Your rectangles needn't match ours exactly.) Make sure to leave a gap at the right, as shown in Figure 4.14.
3. Click on **Draw** to open the drop-down Draw menu. Observe the Snap To Grid option. If it is already turned on (preceded by a check), click on **Draw** again to close the Draw menu, and then skip the rest of this step. Otherwise, click on the **Snap To Grid** option to turn it on.
4. Move the first (leftmost) rectangle to the upper-left corner of the slide, as shown in Figure 4.15.
5. Now move the second rectangle (proceeding from left to right) so that its top edge aligns with the first rectangle's top edge. Note that it is quite easy to align the two objects, because the Snap To Grid option causes the rectangles to snap to the invisible grid lines (12 to an inch) as you drag.
6. Align the top edges of the remaining three rectangles with those of the first two. (If you have trouble doing this with the mouse, try using the arrow keys.) Space the rectangles equidistantly *across* the slide also, as shown in Figure 4.15.

Figure 4.14 Drawing five rectangles

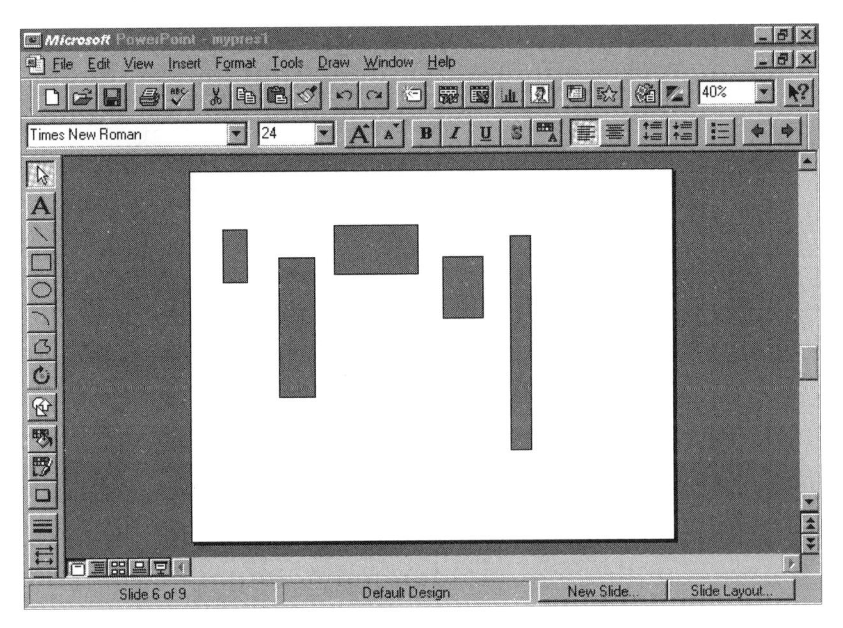

Figure 4.15 Using the grid to align the rectangles' top edges

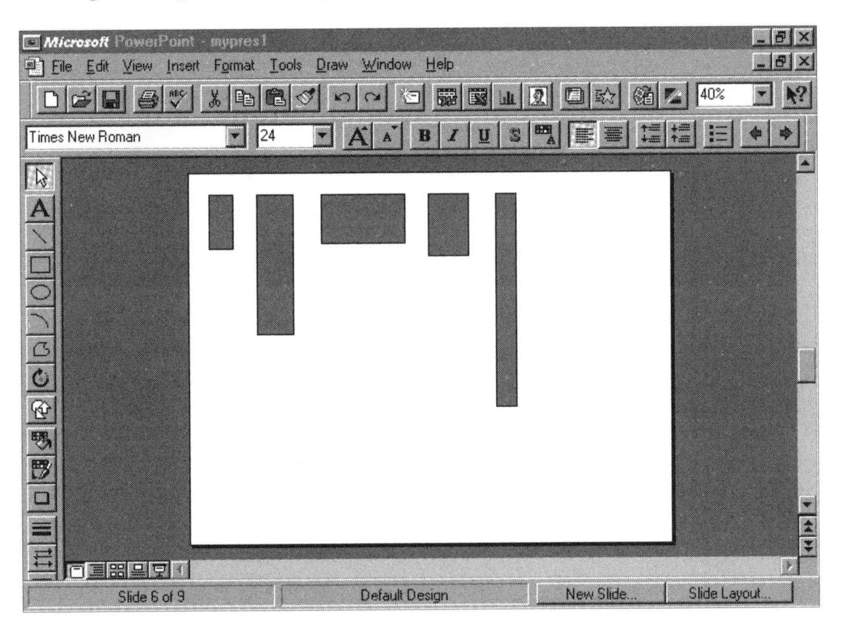

Now let's create some circles and attempt to align their centers by using the grid:

1. In the gap at the right side of the slide, draw five perfect circles (not ellipses), resembling those shown in Figure 4.16.

Figure 4.16 Attempting to align circles' centers by using the grid

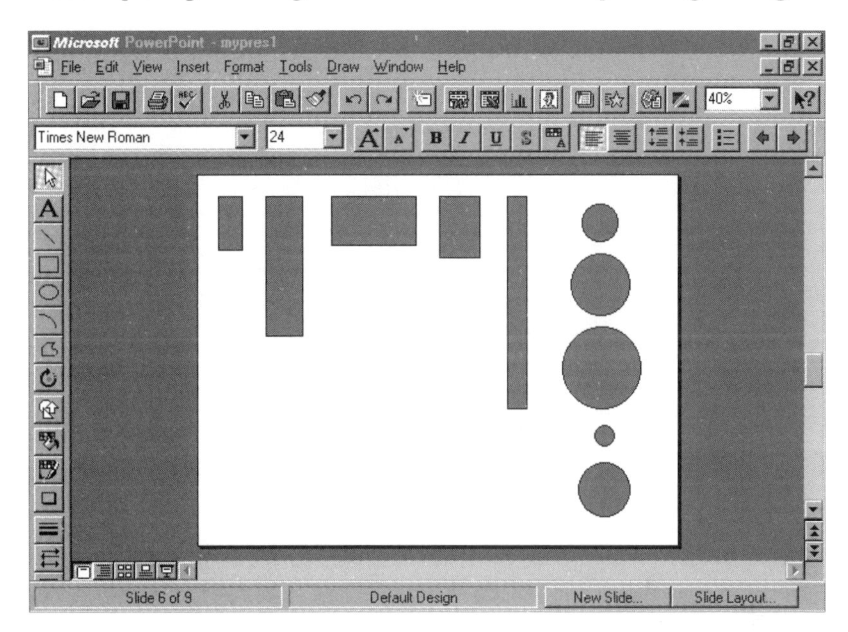

2. Attempt to align the centers of the circles along an imaginary vertical line down the right side of the slide, as shown in Figure 4.16. Space the circles equidistantly down the slide. Note that—try as you might—you cannot align the circles' centers exactly. Why not? Because the grid aligns objects' edges, not their centers.

In order to align the circles by their centers, you must use the guides. Let's do this now:

1. Click on **View** to open the drop-down View menu. Observe the Guides option; it should be turned off. If, instead, it is turned on (preceded by a check), click on **View** to close the View menu, and then skip the rest of this step. Otherwise, click on the **Guides** option to turn it on.

2. Dotted vertical and horizontal lines appear in your slide workspace. These are the PowerPoint guides. They are used as drawing aids, and will not show up when you print the slide or display it in a slide show.
3. Drag the **vertical guide** to the right until it lines up as closely as possible with the centers of your five circles.
4. Drag the **horizontal guide** upward as far as you can; the position indicator will read *3.75* (meaning that the guide is 3.75 inches above the center of the slide). We want to put this guide aside before we begin aligning the circles with the vertical guide. If, instead, you let the horizontal guide overlap (or come near) a circle, the circle might accidentally snap to the horizontal guide as well as the vertical guide. This, in turn, might cause uneven spacing between your circles.
5. Point to the uppermost circle. Press and hold the **left mouse button**; do not move the mouse. If your vertical guide is close enough to the circle's center, the center will automatically snap to the guide, without your having to drag. If this does not happen, drag the circle until its center snaps to the vertical guide. Release the mouse button.
6. Repeat this for the remaining four circles. Your circles should match those shown in Figure 4.17.

PRACTICE YOUR SKILLS

Now let's use the horizontal guide to realign the top edges of our five rectangles:

1. Drag the **horizontal guide** downward until the position indicator reads *2.75*. This is where we'll realign the top edges of our rectangles.
2. **Shift**+drag the leftmost rectangle downward—holding Shift ensures it won't slide left or right—until its top edge snaps to the horizontal guide.
3. Repeat this for the four remaining rectangles. (Hint: make sure to release the Shift key after moving each rectangle.) Your screen should match that shown in Figure 4.17. As you can see, aligning to a guide is easier (and more reliable) than aligning to a grid line.

Figure 4.17 **Using the guides to align objects**

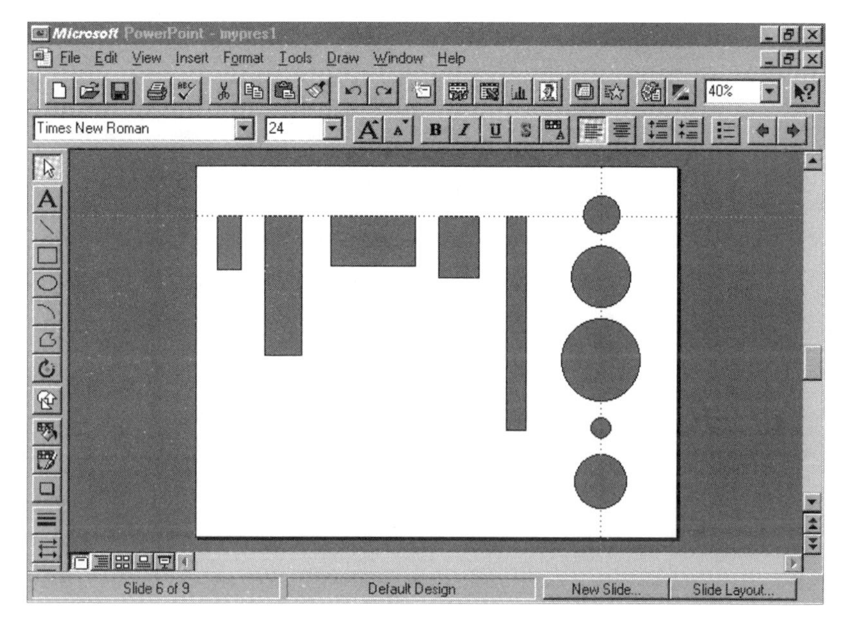

4. Choose **View, Guides** to remove the guides from the screen.
5. Save the file.

DELETING OBJECTS

Earlier in this chapter, you had a near-traumatic, object-deletion experience. We're sure that you'll never forget how to delete objects; however, for the record, here's the general procedure:

- Select the object(s) you want to delete.
- Press *Del.*

PRACTICE YOUR SKILLS

Hone your already formidable object-deletion skills by deleting all the objects from slides 5 and 6. Yes, this time we really mean it! (Hint: To select all of a slide's objects, choose **Edit, Select All** or press **Ctrl+A**.)

ENHANCING OBJECTS

We'll finish up this chapter by showing you how to enhance the appearance of your slide objects. Over the next several sections, you'll learn how to:

- Change the shape of an object
- Change or remove an object's fill color
- Add a shadow to an object
- Change the style of the line with which an object is drawn
- Rotate an object

CHANGING OBJECT SHAPES

You may, at times, want to change the shape of a drawn object. For example, you might want to change a simple rectangle to a more dramatic, three-dimensional rectangle, or to change a simple five-pointed star to a glorious, multipointed starburst.

You could do this by deleting the old object and drawing the new object in its place. This technique, however, is tedious and time-consuming. It's far more convenient to use the *Draw, Change AutoShape* command. Choosing this command allows you to quickly and easily change the shape of any object that you've drawn with the Rectangle, Ellipse, or AutoShapes tools (but *not* with the Freeform tool). Here's the general procedure for doing this:

- Select the object.
- Choose *Draw, Change AutoShape* to open the AutoShapes palette.
- Select your desired new shape.

Let's use this technique to change the shape of an object you drew on slide 7:

1. Display slide 7, your cornucopia of autoshape objects.
2. Select a prominent object that is not overlapped by another object.
3. Choose **Draw, Change AutoShape** to open the AutoShapes palette. These are the same 24 autoshapes that are contained in the palette associated with the AutoShapes tool.

4. Select a new shape of your choice in the AutoShapes palette. Observe that the selected object changes to this new shape, while maintaining its original size and proportions.

PRACTICE YOUR SKILLS

1. Use this technique to change the shape of several of the objects in slide 7.
2. When you've had enough of shape-shifting, save the file.

CHANGING OR REMOVING AN OBJECT'S FILL COLOR

You can use the *Format, Colors And Lines* command or the *Fill Color* and *Line Color* buttons on the Drawing toolbar to change the fill color of a closed object. Here's the general procedure for doing this:

- Select the desired object.
- Choose *Format, Colors And Lines*—or, click on the *Fill Color* or *Line Color* button—to open the Colors And Lines dialog box.
- Open the Fill drop-down list box.
- Select a color from the palette in this list box. Or, click on Other Color, select a color from the extended palette, and click on *OK*. **Note:** The default (automatic) Fill Colr is green.
- In the Colors And Lines dialog box, click on *OK* to apply the color to your object.

Shortcut menus are drop-down menus that appear when you click the *right* mouse button on a screen element (a toolbar, a graphic or text object, the slide workspace, and so on). A shortcut menu lists the most commonly used commands for the element you click on. For example, you can open a shortcut menu by clicking the right mouse button on one of your drawn objects; this menu will list the most commonly used commands for working with drawn objects: Cut, Copy, Paste, Colors And Lines, and so on. To choose one of these commands, you simply click the left mouse button on it, just like choosing a command from the menu bar. Once you get the hang of shortcut menus, you'll find them convenient and time-saving.

You can use the *Fill Color* tool to change an object's fill color. Here's the general procedure for doing this:

- Select the desired object.
- Click on the *Fill Color* button to display the color palette.
- Click on the desired color or click on *No Fill* to remove the fill color.

Let's use the Colors And Lines command to fill some of the objects in slide 8:

1. Display slide 8, your free-form jamboree.
2. Select a prominent closed object, preferably one that overlaps other objects but is not itself overlapped.
3. Choose **Format, Colors And Lines** to open the Colors And Lines dialog box, and then press **Esc** to close it. Instead of using the menu bar, let's use a shortcut menu to open this same dialog box.
4. Click the **right mouse button** on your selected object to open a shortcut menu. Click on **Colors And Lines** to open the Colors And Lines dialog box. Convenient, yes?
5. Open the Fill drop-down list box (by clicking on its **down arrow**).
6. Select (click on) the **lavender color** in the upper-right corner of the list box.
7. Click on **OK** to fill your object with this lavender color.

Now let's choose a color from the extended palette:

1. If necessary, select the same object you just colored.
2. Use the shortcut menu to choose the **Colors And Lines** command for the object. (Click the **right mouse button** on it, then click on **Colors And Lines**.) **Note**: You can also click on the Fill Color button, if you prefer.
3. Open the Fill drop-down list box.
4. Click on **Other Color** to open the Colors dialog box.
5. Select a color of your choice from the extended palette, and click on **OK** to return to the Colors And Lines dialog box. **Note**: If you used the Fill Color button, you won't have a Colors And Lines dialog box to close.

6. Click on **OK** again to apply your color to the selected object.
7. Choose the **Colors And Lines** comand for the same object, and open the Fill list box. Note that the color you selected from the extended palette is displayed at the bottom of the list box, making it easy for you to choose this same color again.
8. Click on **OK** to close the dialog box.

Now let's use the Fill On/Off tool to remove your object's fill color:

1. If necessary, select the object.
2. Click on the **Fill Color** tool, and then click on the words **No Fill** to remove the object's fill color. Note that the object becomes transparent (devoid of fill color), revealing those objects that it overlaps.
3. Click on the **Fill Color** tool again and select a color to fill the object with the default fill color. Note that the object once again hides the objects it overlaps.

PRACTICE YOUR SKILLS

1. Fill several of the closed objects in slide 8 with colors of your choice. Make sure to use some colors from the extended palette.
2. Select the spiral in the middle of slide 8 and fill it with a color. (If your spiral is not visible, select and fill any other open object.) Observe the results. To fill an open object, PowerPoint first closes the object by connecting its end point and starting point, thus distorting the original shape.
3. Click on the **Undo** button to remove the spiral's fill color and return it to its original (open) shape.
4. Save the file.

ADDING A SHADOW TO AN OBJECT

PowerPoint enables you to add a shadow effect to an object. Here's the general procedure for doing this:

- Select the desired object.
- Click on the *Shadow On/Off* tool (in the Drawing toolbar) to apply the default shadow color to your selected object.

- To change the shadow color, choose *Format, Shadow,* select your desired color from the Color list box, and click on *OK.*
- To remove an object's shadow, select the object, then click on the *Shadow On/Off* tool.

Let's add a shadow to several of the objects in slide 8:

1. In slide 8, select a prominent object.
2. Click on the **Shadow On/Off** tool (the fourth tool from the bottom in the Drawing toolbar) to add a default gray shadow to the selected object.
3. Click again on the **Shadow On/Off** tool to remove the object's shadow. The Shadow On/Off tool acts as a toggle; clicking on it either adds or removes the selected object's shadow.
4. Using the technique outlined in steps 1 and 2, add a default gray shadow to several objects.

Now let's change the shadow color for these objects:

1. **Shift**+click to select all your shadowed objects.
2. Choose **Format, Shadow** to open the Shadow dialog box.
3. Open the Color list box, and select the **black color** in the second row of colors.
4. Click on **OK** to change the shadow for all your selected objects from gray to black. Press **Esc** to deselect. Note that the multiple selection you performed in step 1 allowed you to accomplish this task in one step, instead of several.

CHANGING AN OBJECT'S LINE STYLE

You can use the Colors And Lines command to change the style of the line with which an object is drawn. Here's the general procedure for doing this:

- Select the desired object.
- Choose *Format, Colors And Lines* (or choose *Colors And Lines* from the shortcut menu) to open the Colors And Lines dialog box.
- Select your desired line style from the Line Styles palette and click on *OK.*

- To hide the line with which an object is drawn, select the object, then click on the *Line Color* tool (in the Drawing toolbar). In the Line Color pop-up menu, click on *No Line.*

Let's change the line style of a few of slide 8's objects:

1. In slide 8, select a nonshadowed object.
2. Choose **Colors And Lines** from the shortcut menu to open the Colors And Lines dialog box.
3. Click on the **down arrow** of the Line Style drop-down menu.
4. Select the third style from the top, and click on **OK** to increase the thickness of the line with which the selected object is drawn.
5. Click on the **Line Color** tool and then click on **No Line** to hide the selected object's line.
6. Click on the **Line Color** tool again and then click on **Automatic** to redraw this line. Note that the line doesn't return to its original thickness, but retains the thickness you applied in step 3. To change the line width back to its original thickness, click on **Format, Colors And Lines,** and then select the first line width in the Line Style drop-down menu.

PRACTICE YOUR SKILLS

1. Change the line style of several other nonshadowed and shadowed objects in slide 8.
2. Save the file.

ROTATING AN OBJECT

One more drawing treat: You can use the Free Rotate tool to rotate a selected object to any desired angle. Here's the general procedure:

- Select the desired object.
- Click (once) on the *Free Rotate* tool (in the Drawing toolbar) to select it.
- Point to any of the object's selection handles, and drag to rotate the object around its center point. *Shift*+drag to constrain the rotation angle to 45-degree (1/8-turn) increments.
- When you're done rotating, click on the *Free Rotate* tool to deselect it.

PRACTICE YOUR SKILLS

1. Rotate the objects in slide 8 to your heart's content! If an object extends beyond the slide workspace, move it back into the workspace.
2. When you're done, save the file and then close it.

SUMMARY

In this chapter, you began working with slide images. You learned how to draw basic shapes (lines, rectangles, squares, ellipses, circles, and arcs), how to draw autoshapes (arrows, triangles, stars, diamonds, and so on), how to draw free-form objects, and how to create text objects. You also learned how to edit objects (select and deselect, resize, move, align, and delete them), how to undo your last action, and how to enhance objects (change their shapes, fill colors, shadows, line styles, and angles of rotation).

Here's a quick reference for the techniques you learned in this chapter:

Desired Result	How to Do It
Draw a straight line	Select the **Line** tool; drag (or **Shift**+drag) in the slide
Draw a rectangle or a square	Select the **Rectangle** tool; drag (or **Shift**+drag) in the slide
Draw an ellipse or a circle	Select the **Ellipse** tool; drag (or **Shift**+drag) in the slide
Draw an arc	Select the **Arc** tool; drag (or **Shift**+drag) in the slide
Draw an autoshape	Select the desired tool from the AutoShapes palette; drag (or **Shift**+drag) in the slide
Draw a free-form object	Select the **Freeform** tool; drag to draw your free-form object; to create an open object, double-click on the desired end point; to create a closed object, click on the starting point

Desired Result	How to Do It
Draw a straight line in a free-form object	Drag in a straight line; or, release the mouse button, move the pointer to draw the straight line, and then press and hold the **left mouse** button to continue drawing in free-form or click to begin drawing another straight line
Create a text object	Select the **Text** tool; drag to create a word-wrap object or click to create a non-word-wrap object; type your desired text; press **Esc** or click on any blank area of the slide to complete the text object
Select a drawn object	Select the **Selection** tool and click on the desired object
Select a text object	If the insertion point is in the object, press **Esc**; if not, **Shift**+click on the object
Select multiple objects	**Shift**+click on all your desired objects
Remove object(s) from a multiple selection	**Shift**+click on the selected object(s) that you want to remove
Deselect all currently selected objects	Click on any blank area of the slide, or press **Esc**
Undo your last PowerPoint action	Choose **Edit, Undo**, or click on the **Undo button**, or press **Ctrl+Z**
Resize an object	Select the object; drag (or **Shift**+drag) the desired selection handle
Move an object	Select the object and drag it (by its middle for a graphic object or by its selection outline for a text object) to your desired new location; or use **arrow keys**
Align objects using the grid	Turn on the **Draw, Snap To Grid** option and move the objects to align their edges to the grid lines; to temporarily turn off Snap To Grid, hold **Alt**

Desired Result	How to Do It
Align objects using the guides	Choose **View, Guides** (or choose **Guides** from the shortcut menu); move the guides to your desired positions; move the objects to align their edges or centers to the guides
Delete an object	Select the object and press **Del**
Change an autoshape's shape	Select the autoshape object; choose **Draw, Change AutoShape**; select your desired new shape from the AutoShapes palette
Change an object's fill color	Select the desired object; click on the **Line Color** button, choose **Format, Colors And Lines** or choose **Colors And Lines** from the shortcut menu; select the desired fill color
Remove or add an object's default fill color	Select the desired object; click on the **Fill Color** tool, and click on **No Fill**
Add a shadow to an object	Select the desired object; click on the **Shadow On/Off** tool; to change the shadow color, choose **Format, Shadow** and select your desired shadow color; to remove or add the default shadow, click on the **Shadow On/Off** tool
Change the line style of an object	Select the desired object; choose Format, Colors And Lines (or choose **Colors And Lines** from the shortcut menu); select your desired line style; to hide the default line, click on the **Line Color** tool and then click on **No Line;** to show the default line, click on the **Line Color** tool, and then click on **Automatic**
Rotate an object	Select the desired object; select the **Free Rotate** tool; drag (or **Shift**+drag) one of the object's selection handles
Copy an object	Select the desired object; choose **Edit, Duplicate**

Desired Result	How to Do It
Flip an object	Select the desired object; choose **Draw, Rotate/Flip**; click on **Flip Horizontal** or **Flip Vertical**
Add text to a drawn object	Select the object and type the desired text

In the next chapter, you'll complete our two-part series on working with images by exploring clip art and color. You'll learn how to add clip art to a slide, and how to resize, crop, ungroup, and scale your clip art. You'll also learn how to change an entire color scheme, how to change individual color-scheme colors, how to recolor clip art, and how to uncrop clip art.

CHAPTER 5: CLIP ART AND COLOR SCHEMES

Clip Art

Working with Color

Exiting PowerPoint with an Open, Unsaved File

In Chapter 4, you learned how to draw objects on your slides and how to edit and enhance these objects. In this chapter, the second in our two-part series on working with images, you'll learn how to add *clip art* (predrawn, precolored graphic images) to your slides; how to resize, crop, and recolor clip art; and how to change your presentation's *color scheme* (the palette of colors used to draw the various elements of a slide—title text, bulleted-list text, lines, fills, and so on).

When you're done working through this chapter, you will know

- How to add clip art to a slide
- How to resize clip art
- How to crop clip art
- How to ungroup clip art into its component parts
- How to scale clip art
- How to change an entire color scheme
- How to change individual colors of a color scheme
- How to recolor clip art
- How to uncrop clip art

CLIP ART

In Chapter 4, you added images to your slides by drawing them yourself. In some cases, this was easy (as when you were working with autoshapes); in others, a bit more challenging (as when you created free-form shapes). Here you'll learn how to add sophisticated predrawn, precolored images to your slides without doing any drawing at all. These images are called *clip-art objects* or simply *clip art*. PowerPoint provides you with a generous library of clip art, including images of animals, people, household objects, humorous cartoons, evocative hand gestures, and much more.

ADDING CLIP ART TO A SLIDE

Here's the general procedure for adding clip art to a slide:

- In Slide view, display the slide to which you want to add the clip art.
- Choose *Insert, Clip Art* or click on the *Insert Clip Art* button (in the Standard toolbar) to open the Clip Art gallery.
- Select the desired category of clip art (in the Categories list box).
- Select the desired clip-art image from the gallery.
- Click on *OK*.

If you are not running PowerPoint, please start it now. If any dialog boxes or presentations are open, please close them. A maximized application window should be displayed alone on your screen. Let's begin this chapter's activities by adding a clip-art object to slide 1 of mypres1:

1. Open **mypres1** from your Power Work directory. (Hint: Use the Most Recently Used File list shortcut you learned in Chapter 4.)
2. Display slide 1, if necessary.
3. Choose **Insert, Clip Art** to open the Clip Art gallery.

   (**Note:** If you are opening the Clip Art gallery for the very first time, PowerPoint must "build" the gallery from scratch. Follow the dialog box prompts to do this.)
4. In the Categories list box, select **Transportation** (you'll have to scroll to the bottom). Observe that the Pictures list box displays transportation clip-art images.
5. In the Pictures list box, select the **sailboat** image.
6. Click on **Insert** to add the sailboat image to your slide. Oops...the sailboat looks great, but it's obscured our title and subtitle text (as shown in Figure 5.1).

Figure 5.1 **Oops...**

7. Click on the **Undo** button to remove the sailboat image.

Let's make room for the sailboat by moving the title and subtitle to the top of the slide:

1. If the Draw, Snap To Grid option is not selected (preceded by a check), please turn it on now. We'll be using the grid to move the title and subtitle objects in discrete steps.
2. **Shift**+click on the **subtitle object** (*Complete Travel Services*) to select it. Remember, if a text object has an insertion point in it, press **Esc** to select it; if it has no insertion point, **Shift**+click on it to select it.
3. Press the **up arrow key** eight times to move the subtitle closer to the title. Moving the subtitle object with the up arrow key ensures that it won't veer left or right.
4. Without deselecting the subtitle, **Shift**+click on the **title object** to select it. Both the title and subtitle should now be selected.
5. Move the title and subtitle to the top of the slide.

Now let's reinsert the sailboat clip art:

1. Click on the **Insert Clip Art** button (the bulbous-nosed man in the Standard toolbar) to open the Clip Art gallery.
2. Select the **sailboat** image (you remember how!), and click on **Insert** to add it to the slide. You may want to move the sailboat down a little.
3. Press **Esc** to deselect. Your screen should match that shown in Figure 5.2. Effective, yes?

RESIZING CLIP ART

You resize a clip-art object just as you would resize any other PowerPoint object. Here's the general procedure for doing this:

- Select the clip-art object.
- To reduce the object, drag a selection handle toward the center of the object. To enlarge the object, drag a handle away from the center of the object. Drag a corner handle to maintain the proportions of the object. *Ctrl*+drag a corner handle to keep the object centered as you resize it (as explained below).

Figure 5.2 **Now that's more like it**

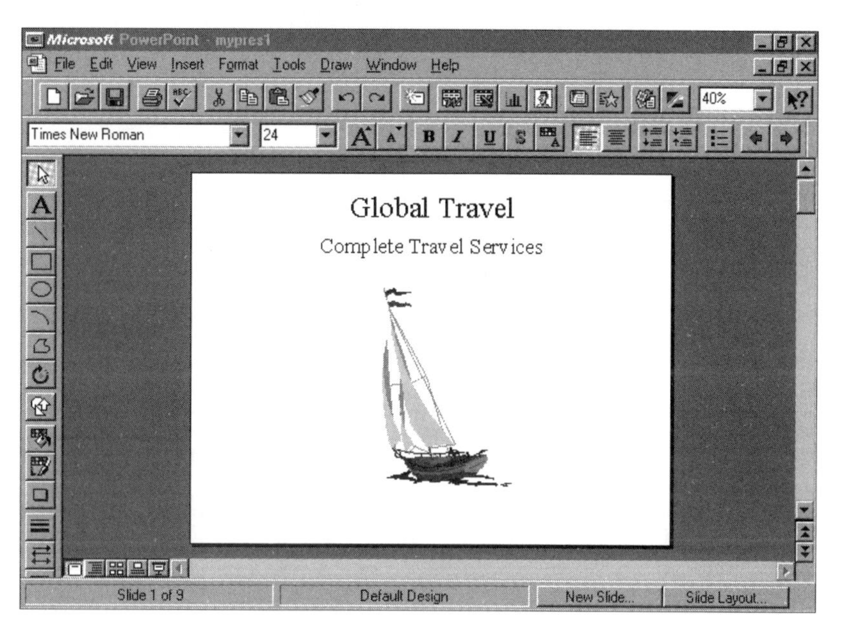

This is the same procedure you used in Chapter 4 to resize your drawn and text objects, with the addition of one very useful technique. By holding down the Ctrl key while you drag a corner selection handle, you resize the object from the center outward (or inward); that is, the center of the object remains fixed as you enlarge (or reduce) the object. This technique is not limited to clip art; you can use it on any resizable PowerPoint object (drawn object, text object, and so on).

Let's enlarge our clip-art sailboat nonproportionally:

1. Select the **sailboat** object.
2. Drag the middle-right selection handle about half an inch to the right to enlarge the sailboat object horizontally. Observe that this significantly distorts the object's original proportions.
3. Click on the **Undo** button to return the object to its original proportions.
4. Drag the middle-bottom selection handle about half an inch downward to enlarge the object vertically. This also distorts the object's proportions.

5. Click on the **Undo** button to return the object to its original proportions. As mentioned in Chapter 4, you can use the Undo command to toggle between the "before" and "after" conditions of an action, a feature we'll take full advantage of in this activity.

Now let's enlarge the sailboat proportionally:

1. Drag the lower-right corner selection handle to enlarge the object proportionally by about half an inch.
2. Observe the results, shown in Figure 5.3. You've enlarged your sailboat proportionally, but in doing so, you've changed its position on the slide.

Figure 5.3 **Enlarging proportionally without using the Ctrl key**

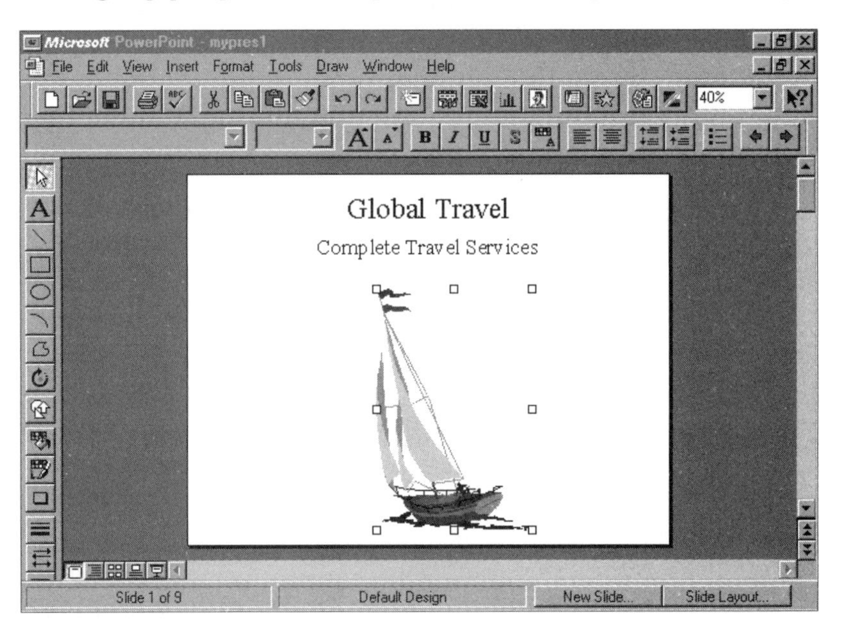

3. Click on the **Undo** button to return the object to its original size and position.

Now let's use the Ctrl key to enlarge the sailboat from the center outward, without changing its position:

1. **Ctrl**+drag the lower-right selection handle to enlarge the object proportionally by about half an inch.

2. Observe the results, shown in Figure 5.4. You've enlarged your sailboat proportionally without changing its centered position on the slide.

Figure 5.4 Enlarging proportionally using the Ctrl key

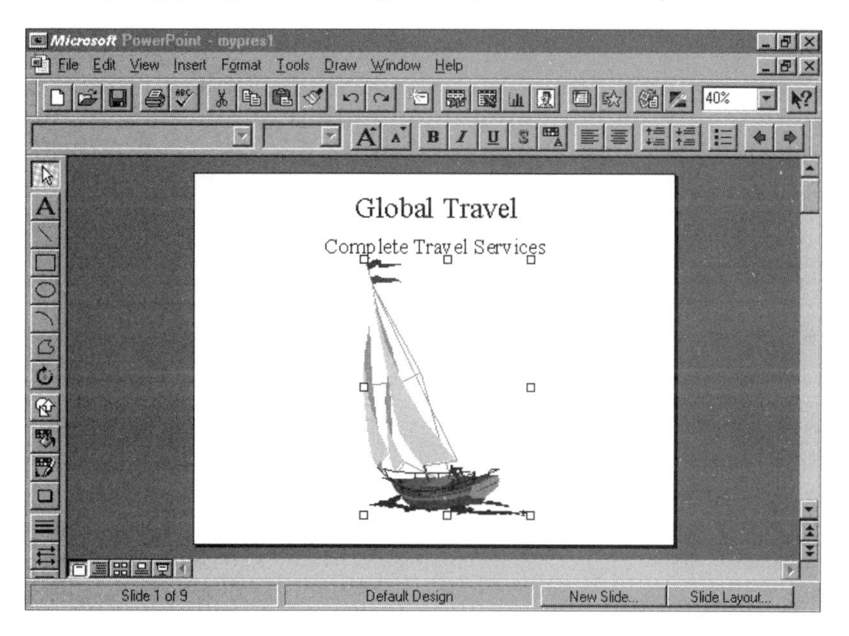

3. Click on the **Undo** button to return the object to its original size.

PRACTICE YOUR SKILLS

1. Without changing its position, reduce the sailboat proportionally to about the size of a postage stamp.
2. Click on the **Undo** button to return the sailboat to its original size. This is the size we'll use for the actual slide.

CROPPING CLIP ART

PowerPoint allows you to quickly and easily *crop* (trim) a clip-art object. You use this feature just as photographers and layout artists do: to remove the undesirable part of an image in order to emphasize the part that remains. For example, in the next activity, you'll crop a clip-art image of an eagle so that only the head and feet remain. Then you'll enlarge the cropped image and use it as a dramatic illustration in a slide.

Here's the general procedure for cropping a clip-art object:

- Select the clip-art object.
- Choose *Tools, Crop Picture* or choose *Crop Picture* from the shortcut menu. The mouse pointer becomes a *Cropping tool.*
- Drag one of the clip-art object's selection handles to crop the image as desired.
- If necessary, repeat the previous step until the image is cropped to your satisfaction.
- Click on any blank area of the slide (or press Esc) to deselect both the clip-art object and the Cropping tool.

(**Note**: At the end of this chapter, you'll learn how to uncrop a cropped clip-art object.)

Let's use this procedure to create the cropped eagle object, as described earlier in this section. We'll begin by pasting the eagle clip art onto a blank slide:

1. Display slide 5. This blank slide originally contained several simple objects (lines, rectangles, ellipses, and so on) that you drew at the beginning of Chapter 4.
2. Click on the bulbous-nosed **Insert Clip Art** button to open the Clip Art gallery.
3. Select the **Animals** category.
4. Observe the gallery; it contains several different clip-art animals. Observe the eagle. This is the animal that we want to select for slide 5.
5. Select the **eagle**, and click on **Insert** to insert it on slide 5 (as shown in Figure 5.5).

Now let's crop the eagle until only its head and feet remain:

1. Choose **Tools, Crop Picture**. Move the mouse pointer onto the slide. Note that the pointer changes to the squarish Cropping tool.
2. Using this tool, grab the eagle's upper-left corner selection handle and drag downward until the top, dashed line of the

Figure 5.5 **The original eagle clip-art object**

object box is about one-quarter of an inch above the top of the eagle's head (the white part).

3. Release the mouse button and observe the results. Your cropped eagle should resemble the one shown in Figure 5.6. If it doesn't, click on the **Undo** button and repeat step 2.
4. Using the **Cropping tool**, drag the eagle's lower-left selection handle to the right until the dashed vertical line is about one-eighth of an inch to the left of the leftmost edge of the eagle's feet (the orange part), as shown in Figure 5.7.
5. Drag the eagle's lower-right selection handle to the left until the dashed vertical line is about one-eighth of an inch to the right of the rightmost edge of the eagle's beak, as shown in Figure 5.7.

Now let's proportionally enlarge our cropped eagle:

1. Click on any blank area of the slide to deselect both the eagle clip-art object and the Cropping tool.
2. Reselect the **eagle**, and proportionally enlarge it (by dragging the upper-right corner selection handle) until the object box is about three-quarters as high as the slide, as shown in Figure 5.8.

Figure 5.6 **The eagle, after one round of cropping**

Figure 5.7 **The eagle, fully cropped**

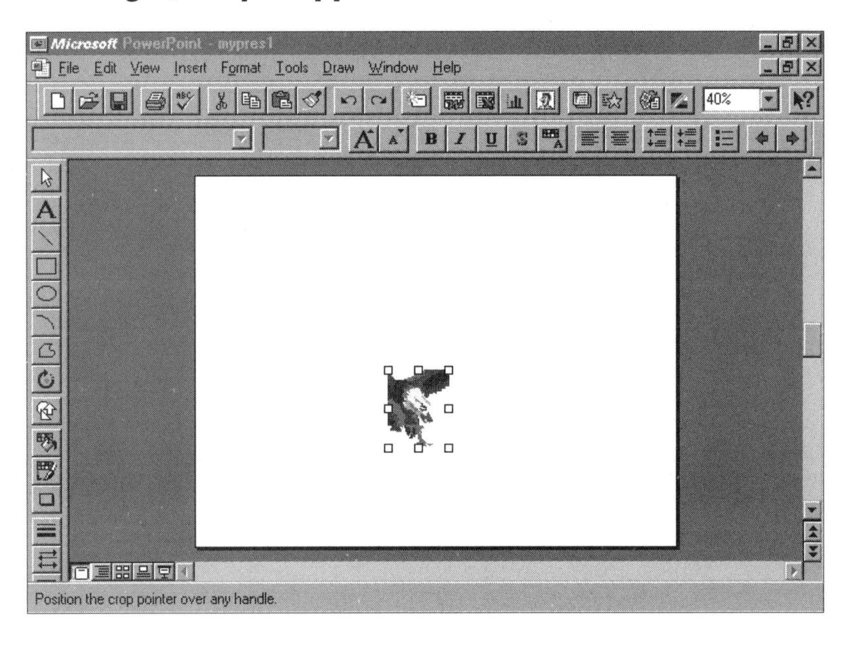

Figure 5.8 **Proportionally enlarging the cropped eagle**

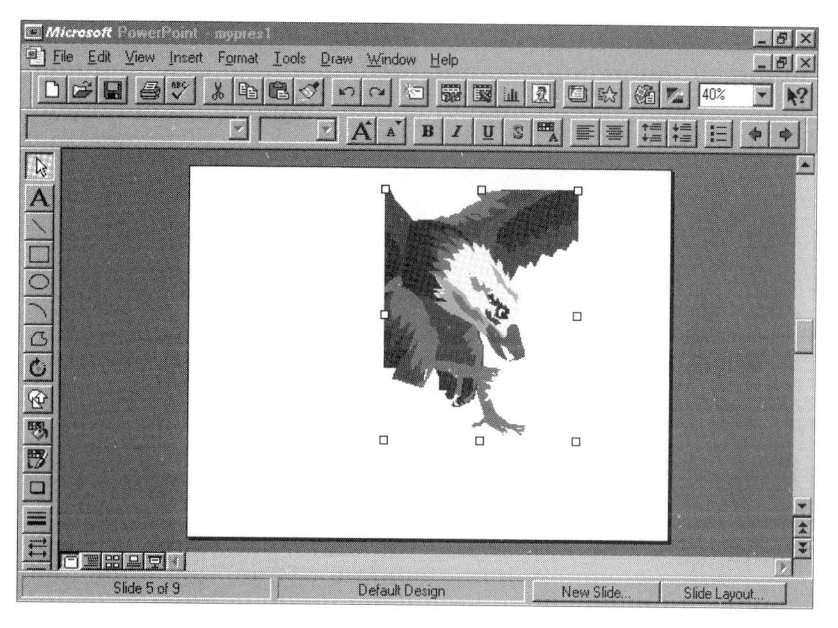

Now let's relocate our cropped, enlarged eagle and add some appropriate text to the slide:

1. Move the **eagle** object to the upper-left corner of the slide, as shown in Figure 5.9. (Hint: To move the eagle right to the edge of the slide workspace, hold the Alt key as you drag or press the arrow keys. This temporarily turns Snap To Grid off, allowing you to move the eagle object in fine increments.)
2. Create a word-wrapped text object consisting of the following two paragraphs:

   Competitors beware:

   We take no prisoners!

3. Center and bold both paragraphs. Italicize the second paragraph.

Figure 5.9 **Moving the eagle and adding text**

4. Increase the font size to 40 points. Resize the text box, if necessary, to make the lines break as they do in Figure 5.9. Move the text box to the location shown in Figure 5.9.
5. Use the **Text Color** button (eighth button from the right in the Formatting toolbar) to change the text color to **pink**. Your screen should match that shown in Figure 5.9.
6. Save the file.

GROUPING AND UNGROUPING OBJECTS

There are times when you have several objects that you want to treat as a single entity. For example, you may wish to combine a graphic and the text that refers to it, particularly if you need to move the graphic and text a lot. Similarly, you can ungroup a collection of objects and treat each individual object as a single entity.

Here's the general procedure for grouping objects:

- Select the objects.
- Choose *Draw, Group.*

Let's group a clip-art image with some text:

1. Display slide 6, another blank slide whose contents you deleted in Chapter 4.
2. Click on the **Insert Clip Art** button to open the Clip Art gallery.
3. Select **Transportation** from the Categories list.
4. Select the **sailboat** and click on **Insert** to insert it into slide 6.
5. Double-click on the **Text** tool and then click somewhere above the sailboat. Type **Get away from it all...**
6. Click somewhere below the sailboat and then type **With Global Travel**.
7. Click on **Edit, Select All**. The objects aren't grouped. Your screen should look like Figure 5.10.

Figure 5.10 **Clip art with ungrouped text**

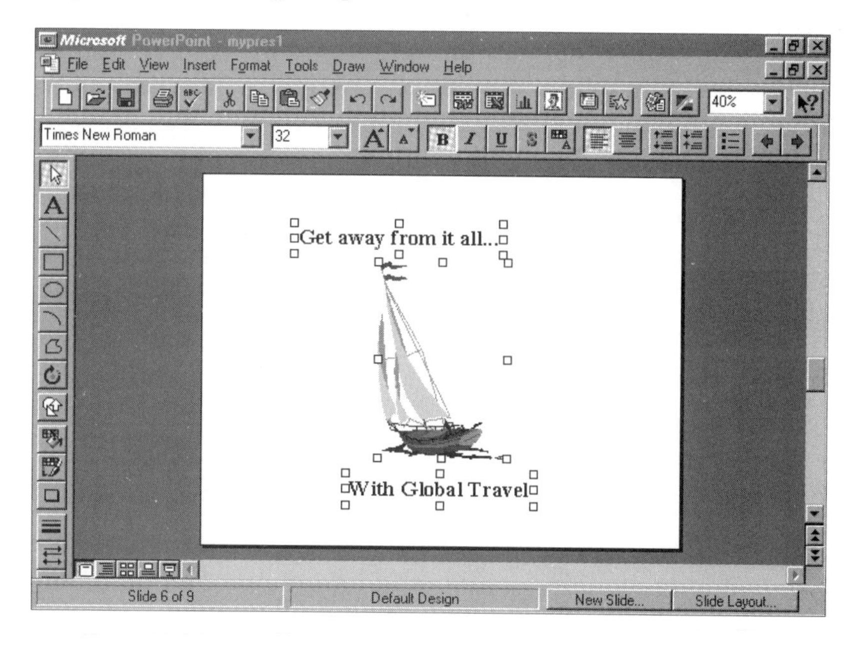

8. Click on **Draw, Group**. The clip art and text are now one entity. Prove this by moving the object around on the slide.
9. Choose **Draw, Ungroup**. The objects are no longer grouped.
10. Save the file.

SCALING CLIP ART

Earlier in this chapter, you learned how to proportionally resize a clip-art object around a fixed center point by holding down the Ctrl key as you dragged one of the object's corner selection handles. Here you'll learn how to *scale* a clip-art object; that is, how to proportionally resize the object around a fixed center point by specifying a *scale percentage*. Specifying a scale of 200 percent doubles the size of the selected object; specifying 50 percent halves the size of the object; and so on.

Here's the general procedure for scaling a clip-art object:

- Select the clip-art object.
- Choose *Draw, Scale* to open the Scale dialog box.
- In the Scale To box, specify your desired scale percentage.
- Click on *Preview* to observe the results. Repeat the previous step, if necessary.
- Click on *OK* to apply your scaling.

Note: You can use this procedure to scale any resizable PowerPoint object.

Let's create a new slide, copy the sailboat object to it, and then practice scaling this object:

1. Verify that slide 6 is displayed. Use the **New Slide** button to create a new, blank slide (slide 7).
2. Display slide 6 again.
3. Select the sailboat object and click on the **Copy** button (seventh from the left in the Standard toolbar). This copies the sailboat object to the *Clipboard*, a behind-the-scenes Windows storage area.
4. Display slide 7.
5. Click on the **Paste** button (to the right of the Copy button) to *paste* the sailboat object from the Clipboard to slide 7. Use the Copy and Paste commands to copy an object from one slide to another. Use the *Duplicate* command to copy an object to the same slide (as outlined in the Practice Your Skills activity at the end of Chapter 4).

6. Choose **View, Guides** to display the guides. Use them to center the sailboat within the slide. Choose **View, Guides** again to remove the guides.
7. Select the sailboat object, if necessary. Choose **Draw, Scale** to open the Scale dialog box. Check **Relative to Original Picture Size.**
8. Type **50** (without pressing Enter) to scale the sailboat down to 50 percent of its original size; that is, to proportionally reduce the sailboat object by half without changing its slide position.
9. Click on **Preview** to view the results. Chances are that the Scale dialog box is blocking your view of the scaled-down sailboat. Let's fix that.
10. Move the dialog box (by dragging its title bar) to the upper-left corner of your screen to free up as much of the slide workspace as possible, as shown in Figure 5.11. It's perfectly okay to move the dialog box on top of other PowerPoint elements (toolbars, menu bar, title bar, and so on).

Figure 5.11 **Moving the Scale dialog box out of the way**

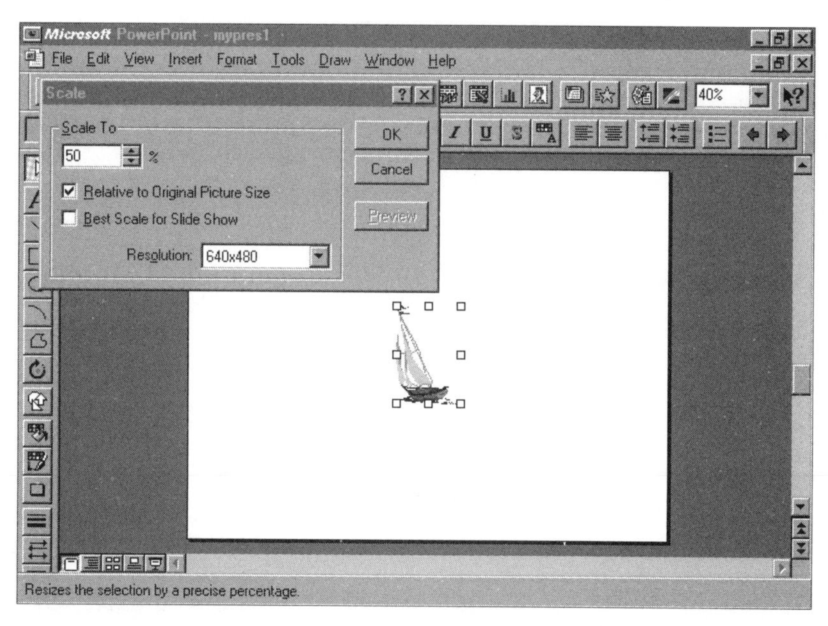

11. Change the scale size to **25** (without pressing Enter) to scale the sailboat down to 25 percent of its original size.
12. Click on **Preview** to observe this change on your slide.

Now let's scale the sailboat to fill the entire slide:

1. Change the scale size to **150** to increase the sailboat's size one and a half times. Click on **Preview**.
2. Click on **OK** to apply your scaling changes and close the Scale dialog box.
3. Save the file.

WORKING WITH COLOR

Color is a critical (and, sadly, often neglected) factor in the overall effectiveness of a presentation. For example, a vivid palette of colors—one consisting, perhaps, of neon blues, reds, and yellow—could be just what you need to wake up a sleepy audience. Conversely, an understated palette—one consisting of black, white, and gray shades—might be perfect for a sedate business crowd.

Over the next several sections, we'll introduce you to the exciting world of slide colors by showing you how to change your presentations' color schemes and how to recolor your clip art.

CHANGING AN ENTIRE COLOR SCHEME

Every PowerPoint presentation has a *color scheme*, a set of eight compatible colors that are used for specific slide elements. Table 5.1 lists these eight colors by element and provides a brief description of each.

Table 5.1 **Color-Scheme Colors**

Color Name	**Description**
Background	The color of a slide's background (the area behind the slide's objects)
Text & Lines	The color of drawn lines (ellipses, squares, straight lines, free-form objects, and so on), bulleted-list text, and text created with the Text tool

Table 5.1 **Color-Scheme Colors (Continued)**

Color Name	Description
Shadows	The color of objects' shadows
Title Text	The color of the title-object text
Fills	The color inside filled objects
Accents	The set of three colors used for graphs (bar-chart bars, pie-chart slices, and so on) and for secondary slide items

Here's the general procedure for changing an entire color scheme:

- Change to *Slide* view or *Slide Sorter* view. (You can also change the color scheme in Outline view, but doing so in Slide view or Slide Sorter view lets you see your new color scheme immediately.)
- If you are changing the color scheme of a single slide, select this slide.
- Choose *Format, Slide Color Scheme* (or choose *Slide Color Scheme* from the shortcut menu) to open the Slide Color Scheme dialog box.
- Click on the *Standard* tab to view the Standard color schemes.
- Select a color scheme.
- To change the color scheme of the current slide only, click on *Apply*. To change the color scheme of all the presentation's slides, click on *Apply To All*.

Let's begin this activity by opening a new presentation file and exploring a very useful PowerPoint feature:

1. Observe that mypres1 is open. We're not done working on this presentation, so we won't close it yet.
2. Open the **Color** file from your Power Work folder. You now have two presentation files open at the same time, mypres1 and Color. Mypres1 is currently hidden behind the active file, Color.

3. Verify this by clicking on **Window** to open the drop-down Window menu. Your two open files, mypres1 and Color, are listed at the bottom of the drop-down menu. The numbers preceding the file names (*1* and *2*) indicate the order in which you opened the files. The check preceding Color indicates that it is the active file. The unchecked file, mypres1, is hidden.
4. Click on **1 mypres1** to make it the active file. Color disappears; the file is not closed, however, just hidden.
5. Choose **Window, 2 Color** to make Color the active file again.

You can use the procedure just outlined in steps 2 through 5 to work on two or more presentations at the same time. You'll find this feature particularly useful when you're working on interdependent presentations or when you're copying objects between different presentations.

Now let's examine Color's color scheme:

1. Display slide 4 of Color.
2. Choose **Format, Slide Color Scheme** to open the Color Scheme dialog box. The Custom tab is selected by default. Observe the set of eight colors (Background, Text & Lines, Shadows, and so on) that make up the current color scheme.
3. Move the **Color Scheme** dialog box to the lower-right corner of the screen, as shown in Figure 5.12, so that you can see the slide and the color-scheme colors at the same time.
4. Observe the current background color in the dialog box (light yellow). Now observe this color in the background of the slide.
5. Repeat step 4 for the remaining seven color-scheme colors. (**Note:** There are no shadowed objects on the slide, so the shadow color is not used.) Observe that the fill color and the three accent colors are used to color the four slices of the pie chart.

Now let's practice changing the color scheme. First we'll create a sedate, black/white/gray scheme:

1. Click on the **Standard** tab in the Color Scheme dialog box. There are seven standard color schemes in the Color Schemes list box.

Figure 5.12 Moving the Color Scheme dialog box out of the way

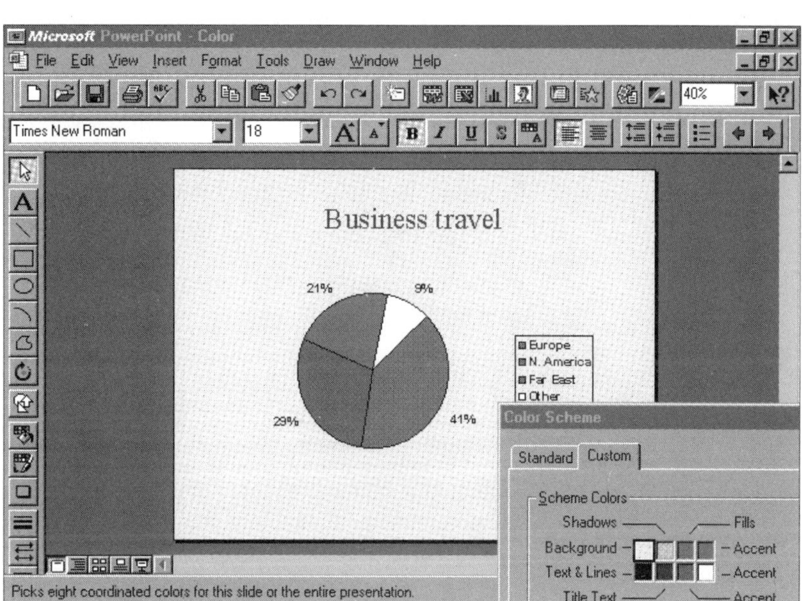

2. Click on the gray and black color scheme (the first scheme in the second row).
3. Click on **Preview**. Chances are that the Color Scheme dialog box is in front of your slide. Move the dialog box out of the way so you can see how your sedate colors look.
4. Click on **Apply To All**. All of the slides in the presentation now have the sedate color scheme. If you wanted to change only slide 4's color, you would click on Apply rather than Apply To All.

PRACTICE YOUR SKILLS

Experiment with the other Standard color schemes. Practice applying color schemes to individual slides in addition to the entire presentation. When you're done, close the file without saving changes.

CHANGING INDIVIDUAL COLORS OF A COLOR SCHEME

In the previous section, you learned how to change an entire color scheme (all eight colors). PowerPoint also allows you to change individual color-scheme colors. This handy feature lets you fine-tune a color scheme quickly and easily, without having to recreate the entire scheme. Here's the general procedure for changing individual color-scheme colors:

- Change to *Slide* view or *Slide Sorter* view.
- If you are changing the color scheme of a single slide, select this slide.
- Choose *Format, Slide Color Scheme* (or use the shortcut menu) to open the Color Scheme dialog box.
- Select the *Custom* tab.
- Select the color that you want to change (Background, Text & Lines, Shadows, and so on), and click on *Change Color* to open that color's Color dialog box.
- Select the desired color in the color grid.
- In the Color dialog box, click on *OK* to return to the Color Scheme dialog box.
- If necessary, repeat the above steps to change additional color-scheme colors.
- In the Color Scheme dialog box, click on *Apply* or *Apply To All.*

Let's use this procedure to change the background color of our eagle slide from white to black:

1. In Slide view, display slide 5, the eagle slide.
2. Click the **right mouse button** on a blank area of the slide to open the shortcut menu, then choose **Slide Color Scheme** to open the Color Scheme dialog box. Make sure that the Custom tab is selected
3. Select the current **Background** color (white), and click on **Change Color** to open the Background Color dialog box.
4. Select the color **black** (the oversized color box at the bottom of the palette).
5. Click on **OK** to return to the Color Scheme dialog box.

6. Click on **Apply** to apply your modified color scheme to slide 5—not to the rest of the slides. Observe the results, as shown in Figure 5.13. Your eagle looks even fiercer against a black background.

Figure 5.13 **Changing the background of the eagle slide to black**

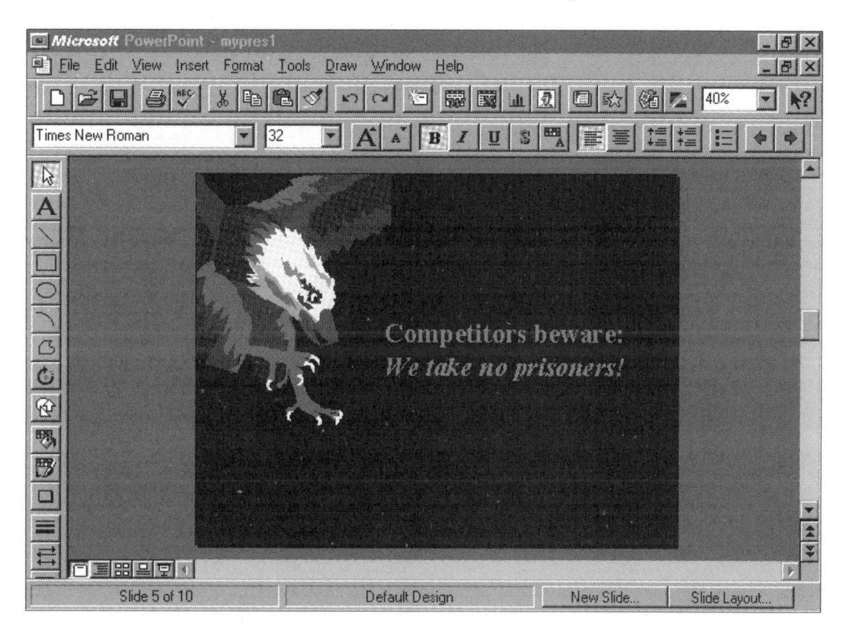

RECOLORING CLIP ART

As you know, clip-art images are precolored. You do not, however, have to accept these colors. PowerPoint allows you to change a clip-art object's colors, just as it allows you to change a presentation's color scheme. Here's the general procedure for recoloring a clip-art object:

- In *Slide* view, select the desired clip-art object.
- Choose *Tools, Recolor* (or choose *Recolor* from the shortcut menu) to open the Recolor Picture dialog box.
- To change any color in the object (line, background, or fill), select the *Colors* option in the Change box. To change only the background or fill colors, select the *Fills* option.

- To change a color, locate it in the Original column (you may need to scroll), and then select your new color from the drop-down list box in the corresponding New column.
- Click on the *Preview* button to view your recolored object (in the dialog box).
- Repeat the previous three steps for each color that you want to change.
- To restore an element to its original color, uncheck the box in front of the color.
- When you're finished, click on *OK* to apply your new colors.

Let's fine-tune our cropped eagle's colors:

1. Display slide 5 and select the eagle object.
2. Click on **Tools** to open the drop-down Tools menu.
3. Click on Recolor to open the Recolor Picture dialog box. Observe that the entire eagle is displayed in the Preview box. Although you cropped the eagle clip-art object quite severely, PowerPoint still "remembers" the original (uncropped) object. You'll learn how to use this fact to your advantage in the next section, "Uncropping Clip Art."
4. In the Change box, select the **Fills** option. Selecting this option allows you to change the eagle's background and fill colors—which is what we want to do in this activity—rather than to change the eagle's line colors.
5. Observe the third fill color from the top of the Original column, an egg-shellish off-white. This is the color of the eagle's head and talons.
6. In the corresponding New column (the third from the top), click on the **down arrow** to display the palette of available colors.
7. Click on the **pink** color to change the eagle's off-white color to a pink. Note that the box preceding the Original column is checked, indicating that you have changed this color. The change is reflected in the Preview box as well.
8. Click on the **Preview** button to see the actual slide.
9. Click on **OK** to close the Recolor Picture dialog box. Observe the slide. Our suspicions were correct. Pink is definitely the wrong color for the head and talons.

10. Select the eagle object, if necessary. Choose **Recolor** from the shortcut menu to reopen the Recolor Picture dialog box.
11. Select the **Fills** option.
12. Uncheck the box of the color you changed in step 7 (third color from the top).
13. Click on the **Preview** button. By unchecking the box, you've returned the head and talons to their original off-white color.

Let's finish up by changing the color of the eagle's eye:

1. Observe the first color in the list, pure white. This is the color of the eagle's eye.
2. Click on the **down arrow** of the corresponding New box to display the palette of available colors. This time we'll select a color from the Other Color list.
3. Click on **Other Color** to open the Colors dialog box.
4. Select the **bright green** color.
5. Click on **OK** to close the Other Color dialog box.
6. Click on the **Preview** button to see how your eagle will look with its new eye color. Unfortunately, the Preview feature isn't very helpful this time, because the eagle's eye is too small. We'll just have to look at the actual slide.
7. Click on **OK** to apply your color change. Observe the slide. Deselect the eagle to get the full effect. Nice eye!
8. Save the file.

UNCROPPING CLIP ART

When you crop a clip-art object, PowerPoint hides—but does not delete—the cropped part of the object. That's why the entire eagle appeared in the Recolor Picture dialog box in the last activity, even though you'd severely cropped the eagle earlier in this chapter. Because the entire object remains intact after you crop it, PowerPoint allows you to *uncrop* it; that is, to restore part or all of what you previously cropped. To do so, you follow the same procedure as when cropping a clip-art object. Let's try this out:

1. Select your cropped **eagle** object.
2. Choose **Crop Picture** from the shortcut menu. (Are you getting the hang of the shortcut menus? Aren't they useful?)

3. Use the **Cropping** tool to drag the upper-right selection handle as far right as possible. Take care not to change the height of the object.
4. Deselect the eagle object and observe the results. You've uncropped part of the eagle wing, making your slide even more effective.
5. Click on the **Slide Show** button to view your eagle slide in its full glory, exactly as it would appear in a slide show. Your screen should match that shown in Figure 5.14.

Figure 5.14 The uncropped eagle object in slide-show view

6. Press **Esc** to return to Slide view.

EXITING POWERPOINT WITH AN OPEN, UNSAVED FILE

We've taught you to always save and close a presentation file when you're finished working on it. You may, however, occasionally forget to do this. To prevent accidental data loss if this should happen, PowerPoint will not allow you to exit without first giving you the opportunity to save your open, unsaved files.

Mypres1 is open and unsaved (you did not save it after uncropping the eagle). Let's issue a File, Exit command and see what happens:

1. Choose **File, Exit** to exit PowerPoint. A dialog box asks whether you want to save the changes you made to mypres1, as shown in Figure 5.15. As mentioned, PowerPoint will not let you exit without first giving you the opportunity to save your open, unsaved files.

Figure 5.15 **Exiting PowerPoint with an open, unsaved file**

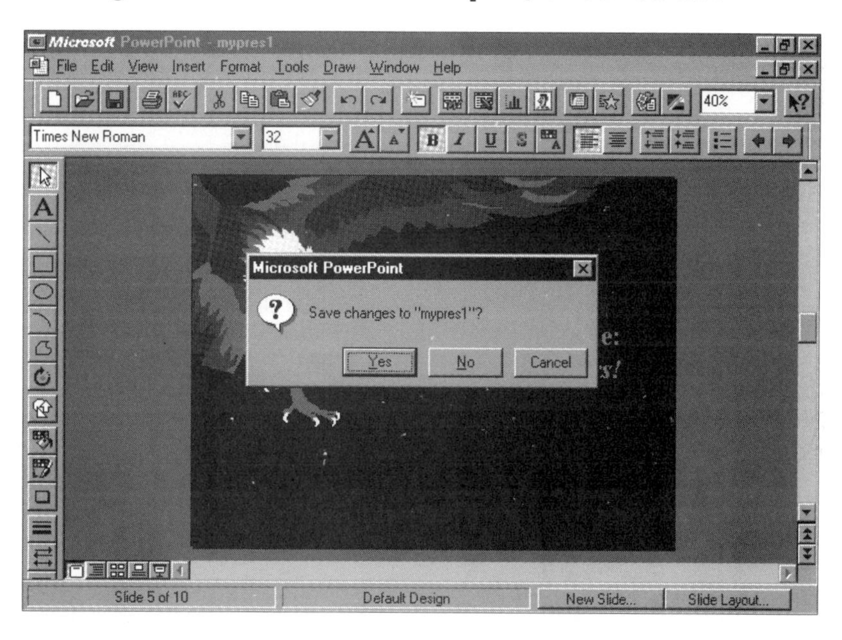

2. Click on **Yes** to save your latest version of mypres1 and to exit from PowerPoint.

Note: Please don't take this as encouragement to leave your presentation files unsaved and/or unclosed. We strongly recommend that you *always* save and close a file when you're done working on it. However, if you should forget, we want you to know that PowerPoint will catch your oversight when you attempt to exit.

SUMMARY

In this chapter, you completed our two-part series on working with images by exploring clip art and color. You now have a solid repertoire of image creation and enhancement techniques. You learned how to add clip art to a slide, how to resize clip art, how to crop clip art, how to group and ungroup objects (including clip art), and how to scale clip art. You also learned how to change an entire color scheme, how to change individual color-scheme colors, how to recolor clip art, and how to uncrop clip art.

Here's a quick reference for the techniques you learned in this chapter:

Desired Result	How to Do It
Add clip art to a slide	Display the slide in Slide view; click on the **Insert Clip Art** button or choose **Insert Clip Art**; select the desired category and image; click on **OK**
Resize a clip-art object	Select the object; to reduce the object, drag a selection handle toward the object's center; to enlarge the object, drag a handle away from the center; drag a corner handle to resize proportionally
Crop a clip-art object	Select the object; choose **Tools, Crop Picture** (or choose **Crop Picture** from the shortcut menu); use the **Cropping** tool to drag a selection handle to crop the image as desired; if necessary, repeat the previous step; click on any blank area of the slide (or press **Esc**) to deselect the object and the Cropping tool
Group objects	Select the objects and choose **Draw, Group** (or use the shortcut menu)
Ungroup an object	Select the object; choose **Draw, Ungroup** (or use the shortcut menu); if a dialog box asks whether you want to convert the imported object to PowerPoint objects, click on **OK**
Scale a clip-art object	Select the object; choose **Draw, Scale**; type your desired scale percentage; click on **Preview** to see the results; click on **OK**

Desired Result	How to Do It
Change an entire color scheme	Change to Slide view or Slide Sorter view; if you are changing the color scheme of a single slide, select this slide; choose **Format, Slide Color Scheme** (or use the shortcut menu); click on the **Standard** tab; click on one of the standard color schemes; click on **Apply** (for a single slide) or **Apply To All** (for all slides)
Change individual color-scheme colors	Change to Slide view or Slide Sorter view; if you are changing the color scheme of a single slide, select this slide; choose **Format, Slide Color Scheme** (or use the shortcut menu); click on the **Custom** tab; select the color that you want to change; click on **Change Color**; select the desired new color in the color grid; then click on **OK** to return to the Color Scheme dialog box; if necessary, repeat the above steps to change additional colors; in the Color Scheme dialog box, click on **Apply** (for a single slide) or **Apply To All** (for all slides)
Recolor a clip-art object	In Slide view, select the object; choose **Tools, Recolor** (or use the shortcut menu); select the **Colors** option (to change any color) or the **Fills** option (to change the background or fill colors); to change a color, locate it in the Original column and select your new color in the corresponding New column; click on the **Preview** button to view your recolored object; repeat the previous three steps for each color that you want to change; to restore a color back to its original, uncheck the box preceding the Original column; click on **OK**

In the next chapter, you'll explore two closely related topics, slide masters and templates. You'll learn how to change the Slide Master's font size, bullet character, and bullet indent; how to enhance the Slide Master; how to apply a template to a presentation; and how to create the default template.

CHAPTER 6: SLIDE MASTERS AND TEMPLATES

Working with Slide Masters

Working with Templates

In the first five chapters of this book, you learned how to create, edit, and enhance *individual* slides within a presentation. In this chapter, you'll learn how to edit and enhance *all* the presentation's slides at once. We'll explore two closely related features, slide masters and templates, and show you how to use these features to unify the overall appearance of your presentation. At the end of the chapter, you'll complete the nine-slide presentation that you previewed in Chapter 2.

When you're done working through this chapter, you will know

- How to change the Slide Master's font size, bullet character, and bullet indent
- How to enhance the Slide Master
- How to apply a template to a presentation
- How to create the default template

WORKING WITH SLIDE MASTERS

As you learned in Chapter 2, the format of a presentation's title and bulleted-list text is determined by the format settings in the presentation's *Slide Master*. For example, when you enter title text on a slide, it is automatically formatted as 44-point centered because the title text in the Slide Master is formatted this way.

The Slide Master also sets the presentation's color scheme; the background graphics (such as borders, lines, and logos); and automatic page numbering and date and time stamping. In doing this, the Slide Master ensures that all your presentation's slides will have a similar appearance; for example, the same color scheme, background logo, and text fonts. This helps to unify the overall presentation and increase its clarity and effectiveness.

CHANGING THE SLIDE MASTER

The Slide Master's title object and bulleted-list object are called the *Title Area for AutoLayouts* and the *Object Area for AutoLayouts*. The Title Area determines the font, size, color, style, and alignment of the text in all your presentation's title objects. The Object Area determines the font, size, color, style, and alignment of the text; the bullet size and bullet character; and the first-line and trailing-line indents for each of the five levels of text in all your presentation's bulleted-list objects.

Over the next few sections, you'll learn how to change the font size of your Title Area and Object Area text and how to change the bullet character and indents of your Object Area text. In Chapter 10, you'll learn how to change other Slide Master elements, including border, lines, logos, and date/time/page-number stamps.

Changing the Font Size

Here's the general procedure for changing the font size of your Title Area and Object Area text:

- Choose *View, Master, Slide Master* or *Shift*+click on the *Slide View* button to display the Slide Master.
- To resize all the title or body text, select the entire *Title Area* object or *Object Area*. To resize part of the bulleted-list text (for example, levels 4 and 5 only), select this text.
- To change the size of your selected text, use the Increase and Decrease Font Size buttons or the Font Size list box. (**Note:** As explained below, do not use the Font Size list box to resize the *entire* Object Area, unless you want all five levels of your bulleted-list text to be the same size.)

The Object Area contains five levels of text. In your current PowerPoint setup, these five levels are divided into four progressively smaller font sizes: Level-1 text is 32 points; level-2 text is 28 points; level-3 text is 24 points; and level-4 and level-5 text are both 20 points.

When you select the entire Object Area and use the Increase/Decrease Font Size buttons to resize its text, PowerPoint maintains this size differential. For example, if you resize the entire Object Area text by clicking once on the Increase Font Size button, the level-1 text is increased to 36 points, the level-2 text to 32 points, the level-3 text to 28 points, and the level-4 and level-5 text to 24 points.

If, however, you select the entire Object Area and use the Font Size list box command to resize its text, PowerPoint sets all five levels of text to the same size. For example, if you resize the entire Object Area text by selecting 28 points from the Font Size list box, all five text levels are set to 28 points.

The moral is this: Don't use the Font Size list box to resize an entire Object Area, unless you want all five levels of your presentation's body text to be the same size. (This is normally *not* desirable.)

If you are not running PowerPoint, please start it now. If any dialog boxes or presentations are open, please close them. A maximized application window should be displayed alone on your screen.

Let's open mypres1 and use both methods for changing the size of its Title Area and Object Area text:

1. Open **mypres1** from your Power Work folder.
2. Display slide 3, the Special Services slide. Observe its title text and bulleted-list text to get a sense of their font sizes.
3. Choose **View, Master, Slide Master** to display the Slide Master, shown in Figure 6.1. Observe the Title Area, which contains the title text, and the Object Area, which contains the five levels of bulleted-list text.

Figure 6.1 **The WordPerfect typing area**

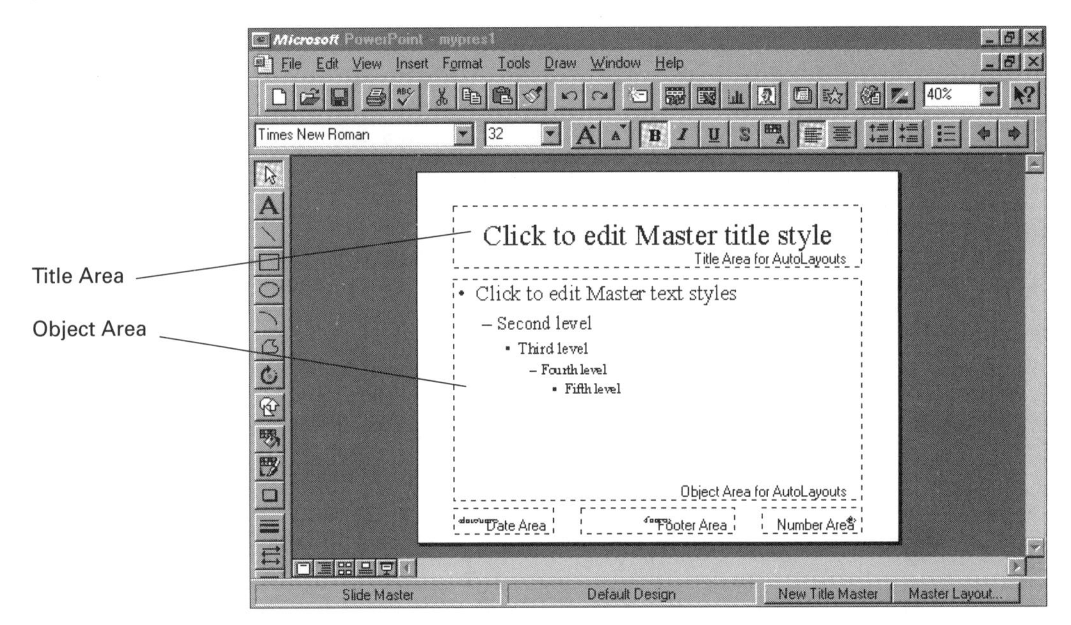

4. Select the entire **Title Area** object (by Shift+clicking on it). Observe the Font Size list box. The Title Area text size is set to 44 points.
5. Click repeatedly on the **Decrease Font Size** button to decrease the font size to 20 points.
6. Change to Slide view. Observe slide 3's title. It reflects the change you made to the Slide Master.

7. Display slide 2 and observe its 20-point title. When you change the Slide Master, you change all the slides in your presentation.

Let's undo our font-size change:

1. Choose **View, Master, Slide Master** to redisplay the Slide Master.
2. Click on the **Undo button**. The font size changes to 24. Click on **Undo** again. This time the font size changes to 28. Hmmm. PowerPoint seems to remember how you incrementally reduced the font size. Clicking on the Undo button a few more times returns the text to its original size of 44. This multiple-undo feature is new with PowerPoint 7.0. It's useful whenever you're performing incremental actions. Your Title Area's font size should now be 44.

Now let's practice resizing the Object Area text:

1. Deselect the Title Area, then select the **Object Area**.
2. As mentioned, the five levels of your Object Area text are divided into four progressively smaller font sizes. Verify this by placing the insertion point in each of the five levels and observing the Font Size list box.
3. Press **Esc** to reselect the entire Object Area. Observe the Font Size list box. It displays 20+, which means that the Object Area contains two or more font sizes, all greater than or equal to 20 points.
4. Click on the **Increase Font Size** button to increase the Object Area's font sizes to 24+ points (24 points or larger.) Verify this by using the procedure outlined in step 2.
5. Press **Esc** to reselect the entire Object Area.
6. Click on the **Decrease Font Size** button to return the font sizes to their original 20+ points.

Now let's use the Font Size list box to resize the Object Area text:

1. In the Font Size drop-down list, select **24** to change all five levels of the Object Area text to 24 points. Verify this visually, without using the insertion-point technique.
2. Click on the **Undo** button to return the font sizes to their original 20+ points.
3. Save the file.

Changing the Bullet Character

By default, your Object Area uses two different characters for its bullets: the level-1, level-3, and level-5 bullets use the • character; the level-2 and level-4 bullets use the – character. PowerPoint allows you to change the bullet character for each of these five text levels. Here's the general procedure for doing this:

- Display the Slide Master.
- Place the insertion point in the bulleted-text level whose bullet character you want to change.
- Choose *Format, Bullet*, or choose *Bullet* from the shortcut menu to open the Bullet dialog box.
- Proceed as follows:
    - To change the font from which you select the bullet character, select a new font in the Bullets From list box.
    - To select the bullet character, click on any of the characters in the character grid.
    - To increase or decrease the size of the bullet character, increase or decrease the percentage value in the Size box.
    - To change the color of the bullet character, check the *Special Color* option, and then choose your desired new color from the list box.
    - Click on *OK*.

Let's change the level-1 bullet character in our Object Area:

1. Place the insertion point anywhere within the Object Area level-1 text, which reads *Click to edit Master text styles*.
2. Choose **Format, Bullet** to open the Bullet dialog box.
3. Observe the character that is selected in the character grid (•). This is your current level-1 bullet character.
4. Click on the Bullets From **down arrow** to display the drop-down list of available fonts.
5. Click on **Monotype Sorts** to select this font. The character grid fills with a new set of characters.
6. Observe the shadowed square character shown in Figure 6.2.

Figure 6.2 **Selecting a new level-1 bullet character**

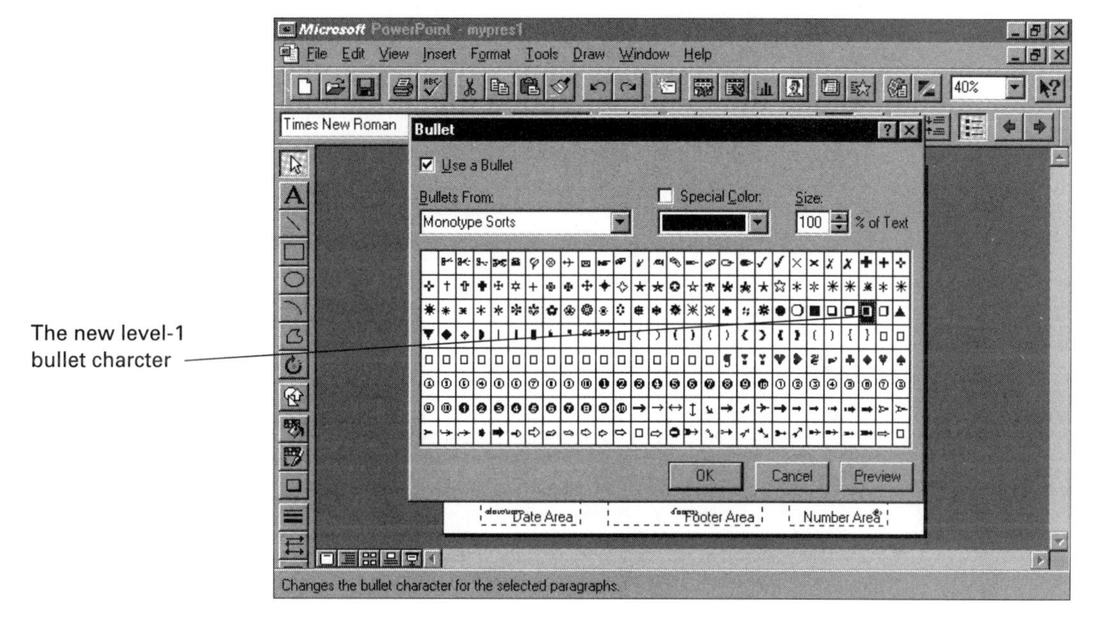

7. Click on this character to select it. Note that PowerPoint displays it in magnified view. You can use this technique to get a better look at any of the characters in the grid.
8. Click on **OK** to apply your new level-1 bullet character to the Object Area. Observe the results. Very nice, except for one thing: The bullet's a bit too large. Let's reduce it.
9. If necessary, place the insertion point within the level-1 text.
10. Use the shortcut menu to reopen the Bullet dialog box.
11. Click repeatedly on the Size box **down arrow** to decrease the bullet character's font size to 80 percent of the level-1 text's font size.
12. Click on **OK** to apply your change to the Object Area. Well done! The bullet looks much better now.

PRACTICE YOUR SKILLS

1. Change the Object Area level-2 bullet character to the Monotype Sorts diamond-shaped character shown in Figure 6.3. Specify a size of **80** percent.

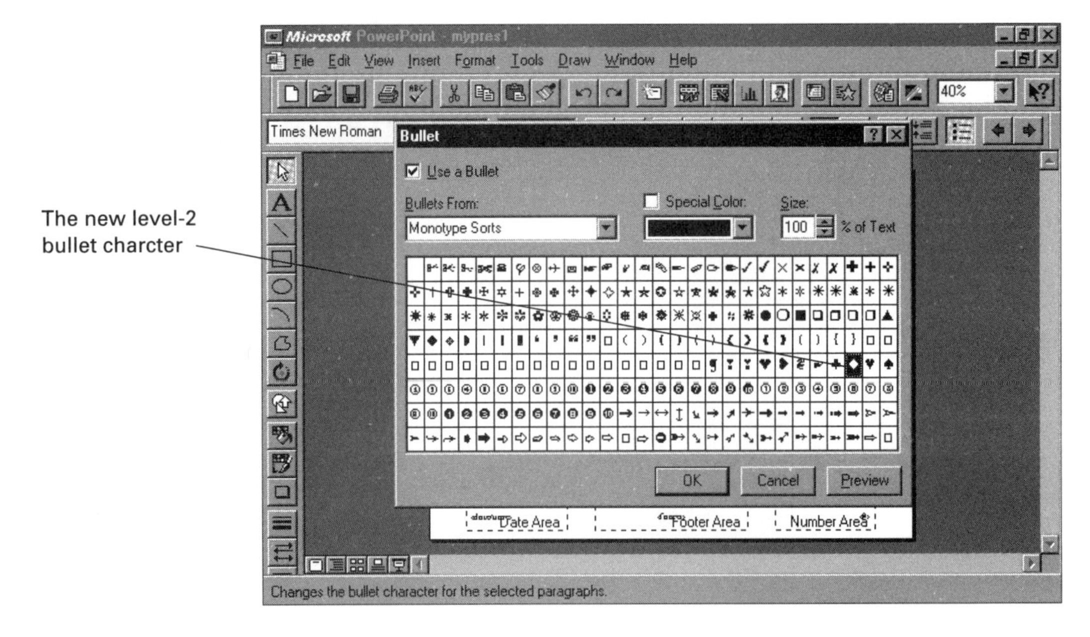

Figure 6.3 **Selecting a new level-2 bullet character**

2. Change to Slide view. Display slide 3 and observe your two new bullets, as shown in Figure 6.4. Looks good, yes?
3. Save the file.

Changing the Bullet Indent

In Chapter 3, you learned how to change your bulleted-list indents by dragging the indent triangles on the text ruler. You can use this same technique to adjust the amount of space between a bullet and its accompanying text. Here's the general procedure:

- In the Slide Master, place the insertion point in the Object Area.
- Display the ruler.
- Locate the pair of indent triangles for the level whose bullet indent you want to change. Drag the trailing-line indent triangle (the lower triangle) to your desired new position on the ruler.
- Remove the ruler.

Figure 6.4 **Changing the level-1 and level-2 bullet characters**

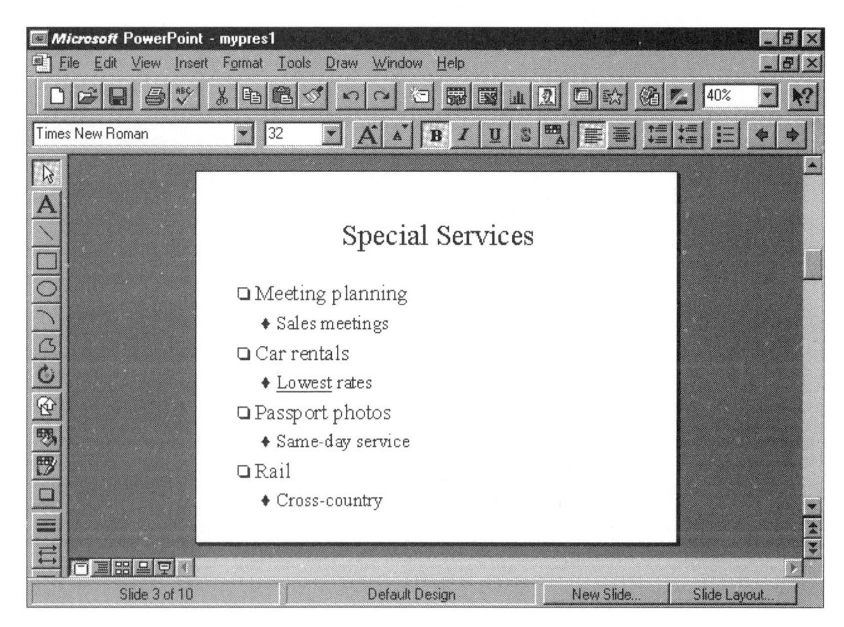

Let's use this simple procedure to fine-tune our level-1 and level-2 bullet indents:

1. Display the Slide Master, and place the insertion point in the Object Area.
2. Choose **View, Ruler** to display the ruler.
3. Observe the ruler. It displays the first-line and trailing-line indent triangles for all five levels of Object Area text.
4. Drag the level-1 **trailing-line indent triangle** (the leftmost lower indent triangle) to the half-inch mark.
5. Drag the level-2 **trailing-line indent triangle** to the 1-inch mark.
6. Choose **View, Ruler** to remove the ruler.
7. Change to Slide view and observe your fine-tuned bullet indents on slide 3, shown in Figure 6.5. A subtle, but effective change, as you can see by comparing Figures 6.4 and 6.5.
8. Save the file. If the Summary Info dialog box appears, deal with it as you will.

Figure 6.5 **Changing the level-1 and level-2 bullet indents**

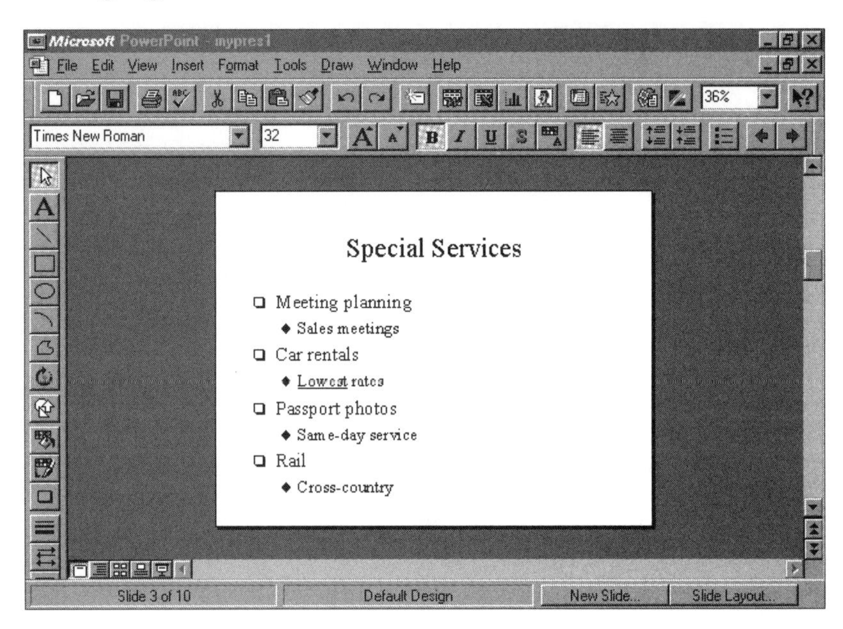

ENHANCING THE SLIDE MASTER

By enhancing the appearance of your presentation's Slide Master, you enhance the appearance of the entire presentation. You can enhance many different aspects of a Slide Master, including its color scheme; its Title Area and Object Area fonts, sizes, styles, and colors; the locations, sizes, and borders of its Title Area and Object Area boxes; and its background graphics (clip art).

Let's create a new presentation and enhance its Slide Master. We'll begin by changing the background color. (**Note:** This group of activities is unusually long and involved. Figure on spending an uninterrupted hour working through it.)

1. Choose **File, New**.
2. In the New Presentation dialog box, select the **General** tab and then select the **Blank Presentation** option and click on **OK**. In the New Slide dialog box, select the **Bulleted List** autolayout and click on **OK**. Slide 1 of a new presentation appears.
3. Display the Slide Master of your new presentation.

4. Choose **Format, Slide Color Scheme** to open the Color Scheme dialog box.
5. Click on the **Custom** tab.
6. Double-click on the current **Background** color (white) to open the Background Color dialog box. (Double-clicking on a color is a shortcut for selecting the color and then clicking on Change Color.)
7. Select the **black** color (at the bottom of the dialog box) to change the background color to black, and then click on **OK** to return to the Color Scheme dialog box.
8. Click on **Apply** to apply your black background to the Slide Master.
9. Use **File, Save As** to name your new presentation file **mymaster**.

Now we'll change the fill colors of the Title Area and Object Area:

1. **Shift+click** to select both the Title Area and the Object Area.
2. Choose **Format, Colors And Lines** to open the Colors And Lines dialog box.
3. In the Fill drop-down list, select the **light gray** color (in the second row).
4. Click on **OK**.

Let's add our eagle clip-art object to the Slide Master. This object is in mypres1, which is hidden behind mymaster:

1. Choose **Window, 1 mypres1** to make mypres1 the active presentation.
2. Display slide 5, the eagle slide.
3. Select the **eagle** object, and then click on the **Copy** button to copy it to the Clipboard.
4. Press **Ctrl+F6** to make mymaster the active presentation. (Ctrl+F6 is the keyboard shortcut for activating a different open presentation.)
5. Click on the **Paste** button to paste the eagle object from the Clipboard onto the Slide Master.
6. Drag the lower-right selection handle to proportionally reduce the eagle to the size shown in Figure 6.6.

Figure 6.6 **Mymaster, after resizing the eagle**

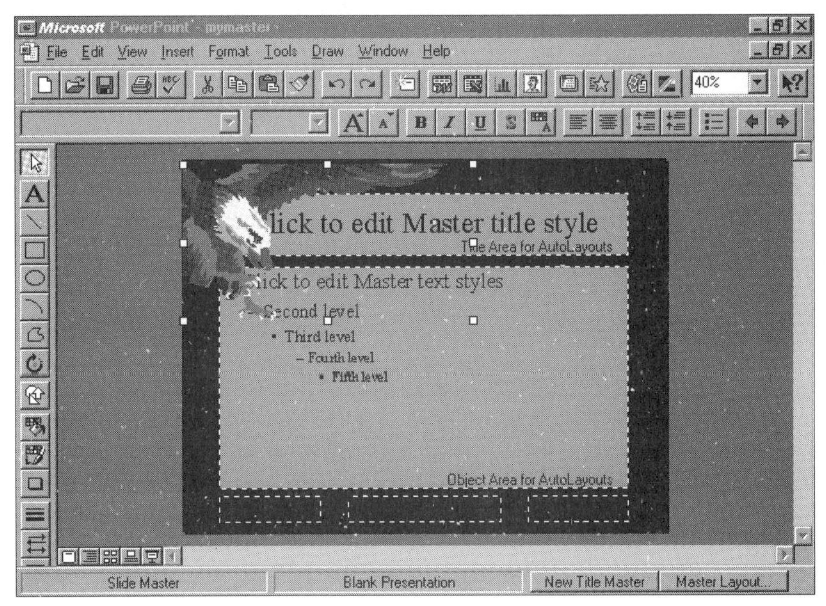

Now let's move and resize the Title Area and Object Area boxes to dovetail with the eagle:

1. Use the shortcut menu to display the guides. To open the correct shortcut menu, click the **right mouse** button on the slide background (black).
2. Resize the Title Area and Object Area boxes to align their edges as shown in the table below. Positive (+) numbers indicate positions above the slide center (for the horizontal guide) or to the right of the slide center (for the vertical guide). Negative (–) numbers indicate positions below or to the left of the center. For help, refer to Figure 6.7.

	Title Area	**Object Area**
Top Edge	+2.50	–0.00
Bottom Edge	+1.25	–2.75
Left Edge	–2.25	–4.25
Right Edge	+4.25	+4.25

Figure 6.7 **Mymaster, after resizing the Text and Object boxes**

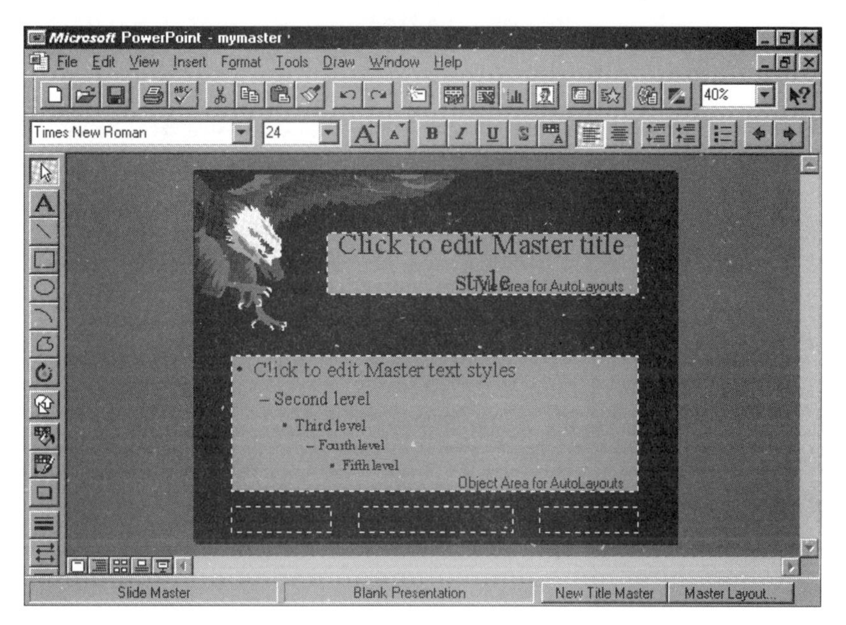

3. Remove the guides. Your Slide Master should match that shown in Figure 6.7. If necessary, proportionally resize the eagle object to fine-tune its fit with the Title and Object Area.

Now let's change the format of the Title Area and Object Area text:

1. Select the entire **Title Area** and bold it.
2. Deselect the Title Area, and select the entire **Object Area.**
3. In the Font Size list box, select **24** to change the size of all five levels of the Object Area text to 24 points.
4. Click on the **Center Alignment** button to center the Object Area text.
5. Select all the Object Area's level-2 through level-5 text. Do not select the level-1 text.
6. Press **Del** to delete the level-2 through level-5 text. All that should remain is the level-1 text.
7. Click on the **Bullet On/Off** button to remove the bullet from this text.

8. Display the ruler.
9. Drag the **trailing-line indent triangle** (the lower triangle) as far to the left as possible. The two indent triangles should now both be set to 0.
10. Click on a blank area of the Slide Master to deselect the Object Area.
11. Remove the ruler.

Now let's enter a title for slide 1 of mymaster and then copy some body text from mypres1:

1. Change to Slide view. Observe your modified slide 1. As expected, its appearance matches that of the Slide Master.
2. Enter the title **Competitors beware!**
3. In the Object Area, enter the text shown in Figure 6.8. (Look familiar?)
4. Deselect.

Figure 6.8 **Mymaster, after adding text and increasing box margins**

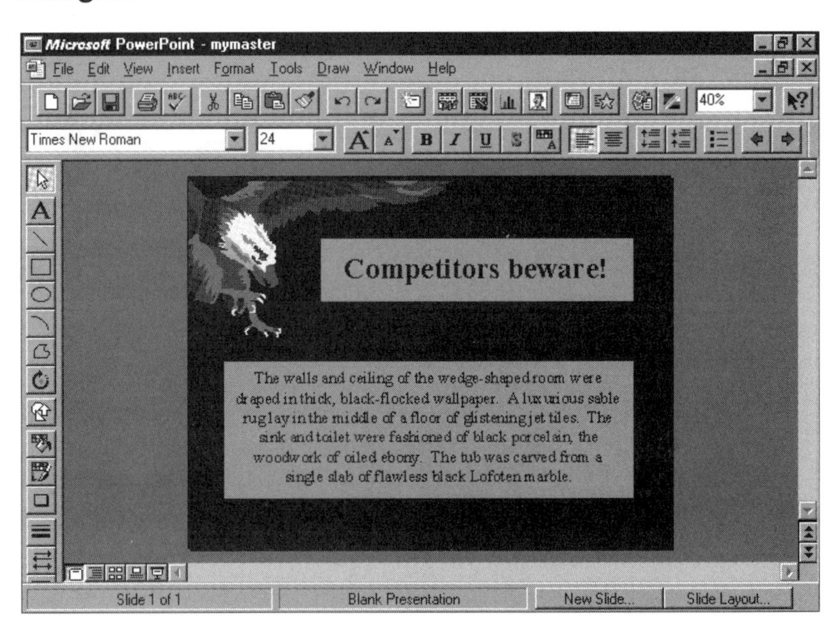

Your text extends all the way to the top and side edges of the bulleted-list object box, resulting in a somewhat cramped and unbalanced appearance. Let's fix things up by increasing the *box margins*, the spaces between the object box's edges and the text:

1. Display the Slide Master, and select the **Object Area**.
2. Choose **Format, Text Anchor** to open the Text Anchor dialog box. You use this command to change an object box's margins.
3. In the Box Margins box, increase the left and right margins (the upper option) to **.25** inches and the top and bottom margins (the lower option) to **.15** inches.
4. Click on **OK** to return to the Slide Master.
5. Change to Slide view. Observe your modified body-text layout, which should match that shown in Figure 6.8. Note how the increased box margins add a sense of balance to the object.

We're almost home! Just one more small refinement. Let's add a border to the Title and Object Areas:

1. Display the Slide Master, and select both the **Title Area** and the **Object Area**.
2. Choose **Format, Colors And Lines** to open the Colors And Lines dialog box.
3. In the Color list box, select the **red** color (you may have to click on **Other Color** to see a palette containing red).
4. In the Styles list box, select the second style from the bottom, a double (thick/thin) line.
5. Click on **OK** to apply your line changes.
6. Deselect the Title and Object Areas.
7. Change to Slide view. Click on the **Slide Show** button to view slide 1 as it would appear in a slide show. Your screen should match that shown in Figure 6.9. Note how much stronger the text objects look with their new red borders.
8. Press **Esc** to return to Slide view.
9. Use the **New Slide** button to create a new bulleted-list slide (slide 2). Observe that its appearance matches that of the Slide Master, as will the appearance of every slide you add to this presentation.
10. Save the file and then close it.

Figure 6.9 **Mymaster, completed**

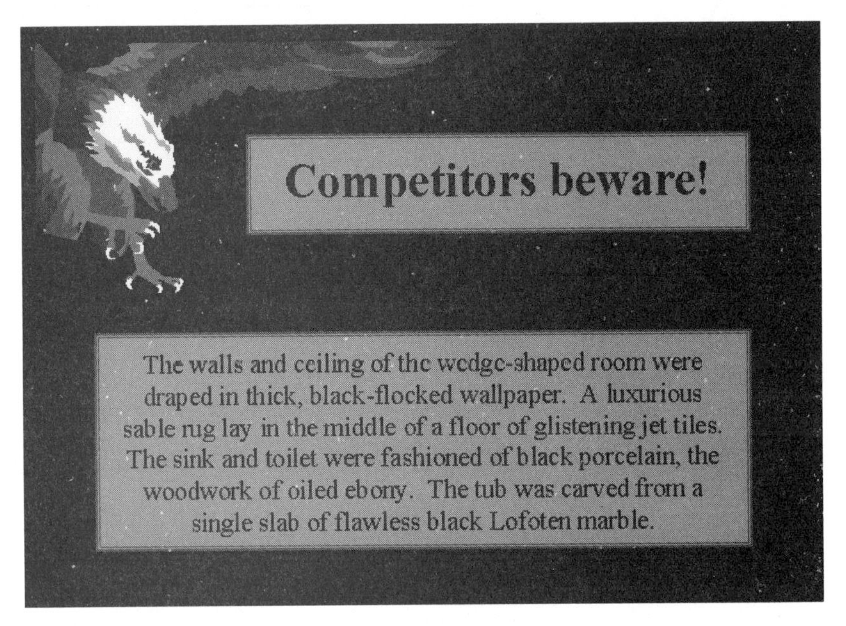

Congratulations on completing this gargantuan group of activities! Pat yourself on the back several times, breathe deeply, shake the kinks out of your mousing hand, and take a nice long break before diving into the next section.

WORKING WITH TEMPLATES

As you know now, creating a sophisticated Slide Master can be a long and arduous task. To simplify this task, PowerPoint provides you with a library of *templates*.

When you apply a template to a presentation, the presentation's Slide Master is replaced with the template's Slide Master. Thus, the presentation takes on all the characteristics of the template's Slide Master: the format of the title and bulleted-list text, the color scheme, the background graphics (such as borders, lines, and logos), and automatic page numbering and date and time stamping.

In effect, when you apply a template to a presentation, you create a new, sophisticated Slide Master for the presentation. Only you do it in a fraction of the time.

APPLYING A TEMPLATE TO A PRESENTATION

Here's the general procedure to apply a template to a presentation:

- Open the presentation to which you want to apply the template. If the presentation does not already exist, open a new presentation.
- Choose *Format, Apply Design Template* or click on the *Apply Design Template* button on the Standard toolbar to open the Apply Design Template dialog box.
- If necessary, change the current drive and folder to that in which the template is stored.
- In the Name list box, select your desired template.
- Click on *Apply.*

Note: You can use any PowerPoint presentation as a template. For example, you could use the Format, Presentation command to apply mymaster—the presentation that you created in the previous activity—to another presentation. The target presentation would then have the same black-background, eagle-clip-art Slide Master as mymaster.

Let's apply a template to mypres1, the active presentation:

1. Press **Ctrl+Home** to display slide 1 of mypres1.
2. Choose **Format, Apply Design Template** to open the Apply Design Template dialog box.
3. Observe the Look In box. You need to make Templates the current folder to get at PowerPoint's template files. If Templates is already the current folder—that is, if Templates appears in the Look In box—skip directly to step 6.
4. If you see *Templates* in your Look In box, double-click on it to make it current, and then skip directly to step 6.
5. If you do not see *Templates* in your Look In box, double-click on **c:** . Then, locate and double-click on **powerpnt** or **MSOffice,** depending on how you've installed PowerPoint. Finally, double-click on **Templates** to make it the current folder.
6. Observe the folders listed under Templates. Find the Presentation Designs folder and double-click on it. Scroll to see PowerPoint's vast library of templates.
7. Click on **Azure**. The Preview box displays the template.

8. Click on **Apply** to apply the Azure template to mypres1, as shown in Figure 6.10. Take a look at slides 1 through 4. Note that applying this template did not change any of its slide text or layout, but instead added background graphics, color, and text enhancements. Note also that the word *Azure* appears in the status bar at the bottom of the window.

Figure 6.10 **Applying the template file Azure**

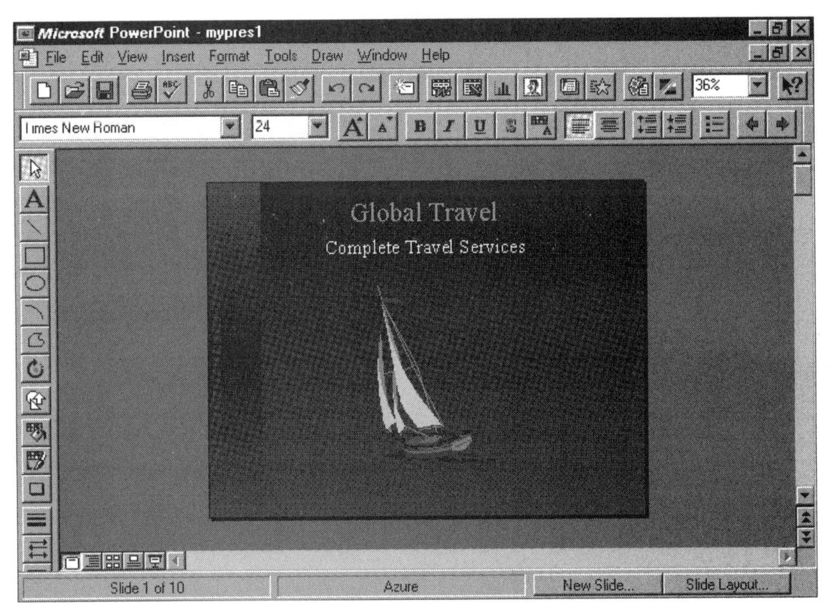

9. Display the Slide Master. When you applied the Azure template to your mypres1 presentation, you replaced mypres1's Slide Master with Azure's Slide Master, which is what you see right now on your screen.
10. Change to Slide view.

PRACTICE YOUR SKILLS

1. Repeat steps 6 through 8 to apply a new template of your choice to mypres1. Observe slides 1 through 4. Repeat this step for as many different templates as you wish to apply. Note how powerful the Template command is; with a few

mouse clicks, you can create an entirely different, professional-looking visual world for your presentation!

2. Save the file and then close it.

CREATING THE DEFAULT TEMPLATE

Whenever you open a new presentation file—by choosing File, New and selecting the Blank Presentation option—PowerPoint automatically applies the Default template, if there is one, to your new presentation. If PowerPoint finds no Default template at start-up, it applies its built-in default settings to all your new presentations.

Although you do not technically need a Default template to run PowerPoint, it is good to have one, especially when you get around to wanting to customize your default settings. For example, let's say that you preferred beginning work on your new presentations in Outline view, rather than in the current default, Slide view. You could either open each new presentation and then change from Slide to Outline view, or you could customize your Default template to open new presentations in Outline view.

Let's create a Default template for your system. In order to match your Default settings with ours, you'll exit PowerPoint, and then restart it. Our defaults will match upon start-up, so you can then safely create your Default template:

1. Choose **File, Exit** to exit PowerPoint.
2. Restart PowerPoint.
3. In the PowerPoint dialog box, select **Blank Presentation** and click on **OK**. In the New Slide dialog box, select **Title Slide** and click on **OK**. Maximize the presentation, if necessary.
4. Choose **File, Save As** to open the Save As dialog box. Chances are, the Save In box is not displaying the correct folder in which to store your Default template.
5. Click on the **down arrow** in the Save As Type list box at the bottom of the window. Click on **Presentation Templates**. Note that your Save In box now displays the Templates folder. All you need to know is what kind of file you're saving, and PowerPoint makes sure that you put it in the right place.
6. Click on the **File Name** text box and type **Default**.

7. Click on **Save**.
8. If asked whether you want to replace the existing Default template, click on **OK**.
9. Close the file.

Congratulations! You now have a Default template. For now, we'll just let our Default files sit there and be innocuous, well-behaved default templates.

PRACTICE YOUR SKILLS

In this activity, you will make some final changes to mypres1 and then run a slide show of the presentation:

1. Open **mypres1** from your Power Work folder (Chapter 1).
2. Apply the template Soaring to mypres1 (Chapter 6). Your screen should match that shown in Figure 6.11.

Figure 6.11 **Applying the template file Soaring**

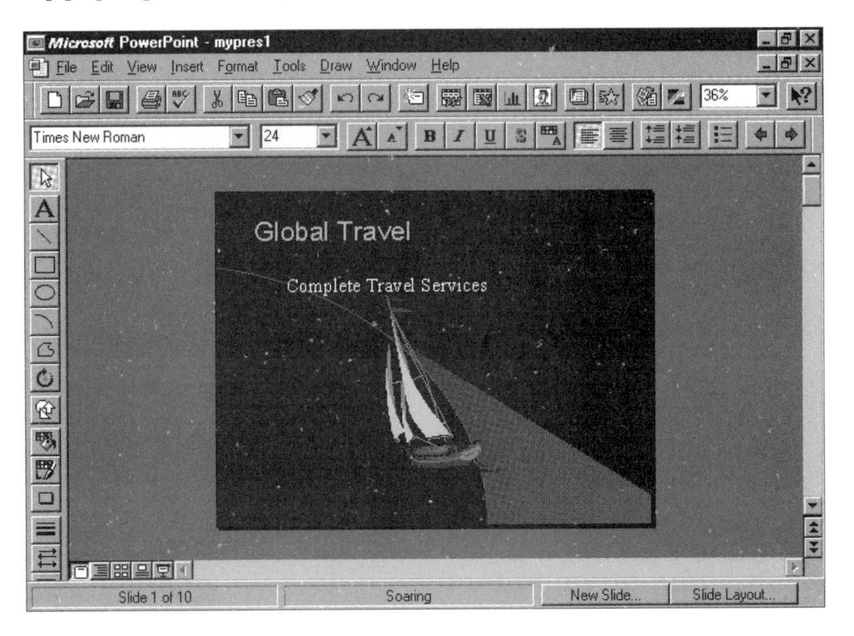

3. Display slides 1 through 4, the Global Travel slides. Note the shaded background, the yellow title text, and the circular level-1 bullets. All in all, a great-looking template!
4. Display slide 5, your eagle slide. Note that it does not look like the other slides. Why not? Because you changed its color scheme in Chapter 5, and this change overrides most of the attributes of the Soaring template. To change the slide back to its original format, do the following:
   - Choose *Format, Custom Background* to open the Custom Background dialog box.
   - Click on the *down arrow* to open the color palette.
   - Click on the *black box* to return the background color to black.
   - Click on *Apply.*
5. Display slide 10, your text-object slide. Note that it doesn't really fit in with this presentation. Let's get rid of it.
6. Choose **Edit, Delete Slide** to delete the current slide (slide 10). Slide 9 appears; it is the new current slide.

And there you have it: the nine slides that you previewed at the beginning of Chapter 2. You've come a long way in these last five chapters! Let's end this activity by running a slide show of your entire presentation:

1. Display slide 1 and run a slide show. Advance through all nine slides. Make sure to admire your handiwork—and then return to Slide view (Chapter 2).
2. Save the file, and then close it (Chapter 1).

SUMMARY

In this chapter, you explored two closely related topics, slide masters and templates. You now know how to change the Slide Master's font size, bullet character, and bullet indent; how to enhance the Slide Master; how to apply a template to a presentation; and how to create the Default template.

Here's a quick reference for the techniques you learned in this chapter:

Desired Result	How to Do It
Display the Slide Master	Choose **View, Master, Slide Master** or **Shift**+click on the **Slide View** button
Change the Title Area and Object Area font size	In the Slide Master, select the Title Area and/or Object Area text you want to resize; use the **Increase/Decrease Font Size** buttons or the **Font Size** list box to increase or decrease the font size
Change an Object Area bullet character	In the Slide Master, select the **Object Area**; place the insertion point in the desired text level; choose **Format, Bullet** (or use the shortcut menu) to open the Bullet dialog box; to change the bullet-character font, select a new font in the Bullets From drop-down list box; to select the bullet character, click on any of the characters in the character grid; to resize the bullet character, increase or decrease the percentage value in the Size box; to change the color of the bullet character, check the **Special Color** option and choose your new color from the drop-down list box; click on **OK**
Change an Object Area bullet indent	In the Slide Master, select the **Object Area** to display the ruler; drag the desired **trailing-line indent triangle** to your desired new position; remove the ruler
Apply a template to a presentation	Open the presentation; choose **Format, Apply Design Template** or click on the **Apply Design Template button**; choose **Presentation Templates** from the File Of Type drop-down list box; select your desired template; click on **Apply**
Delete a slide	Select the slide; choose **Edit, Delete Slide**

In the next chapter, you will learn how to create and modify an organization chart.

CHAPTER 7: WORKING WITH ORGANIZATION CHARTS

Sneak Preview, Part 2

Creating an Organization Chart

Editing the Organization Chart

Formatting the Organization Chart

In Chapters 2 through 6, you learned the basics of working with slides. Now you're ready to use those basics to tackle some real-world presentation challenges. Over the next several chapters, you will create a sophisticated presentation that makes use of several new PowerPoint features. In this chapter, you will learn how to use Microsoft Organization Chart to create, edit, and enhance an *organization chart*, a diagram depicting the structure of a hierarchical organization, such as a company.

When you're done working through this chapter, you will know

- How to create an organization chart
- How to add a subordinate to the organization chart
- How to promote and demote levels in the organization chart
- How to change box color in the organization chart
- How to add a drop shadow to the boxes in the organization chart
- How to change the style of your organization chart

SNEAK PREVIEW, PART 2

Over the course of Chapters 7 through 12, you will create a ten-slide presentation that uses many of PowerPoint's advanced slide creation and editing features. We'll begin this chapter with a sneak preview of this presentation. As you observe these ten slides, remember that you'll soon possess the technical mastery to create them yourself!

If you are not running PowerPoint on your computer, please start it now.

Let's run a slide show of Preview2, a presentation that contains copies of the ten slides you'll create throughout this and the next five chapters:

1. Open **Preview2** from your Power Work folder.
2. Maximize your presentation window, if necessary.
3. Click on the **Slide Show** button (a miniature screen located to the left of the horizontal scroll bar) to run the slide show with the default settings. You'll learn more about running a slide show in Chapter 12.
4. Choose **File, Close** to close Preview2.

CREATING AN ORGANIZATION CHART

An organization chart is a diagram that depicts the structure of a hierarchical organization. You can also use an organization chart to show structures that don't include people; for example, a diagram might show the relationship of a main office to its branch offices.

Figure 7.1 shows a simplified version of the Global Travel organization chart that you'll create over the course of this chapter. As this figure shows, organization charts identify the names and functions of an organization's members, the hierarchical relationships among its upper-level and lower-level positions, and the relationships among its various departments.

Figure 7.1 **The Global Travel organization chart, simplified**

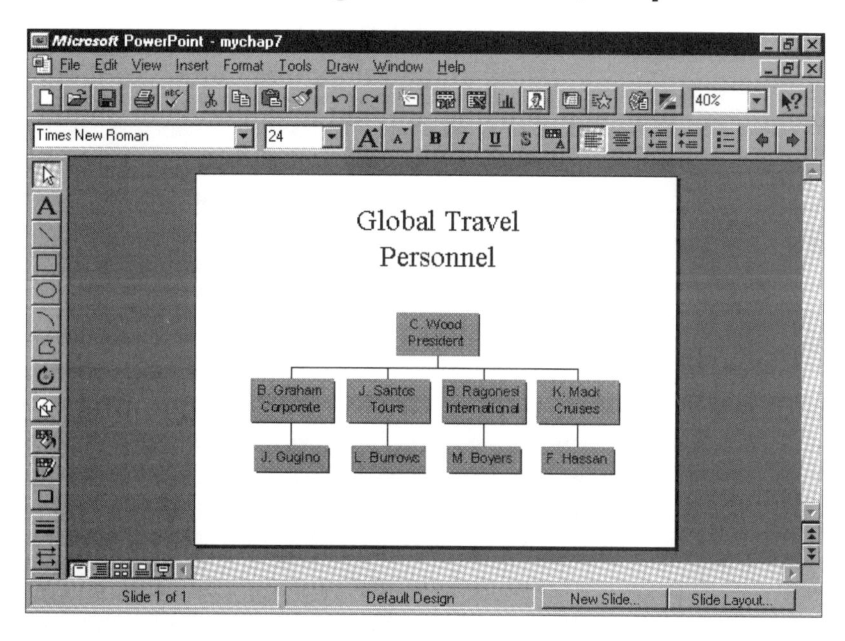

Each box on this chart represents a person and a position in the organization. The lines connecting the boxes indicate the reporting relationship (who reports to whom). For example, a person on the second level reports to a person on the first level.

The Global Travel organization chart that you are going to create in this chapter has three levels: president, division manager, and subordinate. However, you can create as many levels as you need. PowerPoint comes with an embedded application called Microsoft Organization Chart that makes creating and editing organization charts quick and easy.

Here's the general procedure to start Microsoft Organization Chart:

- Move to the slide you want to place the organization chart after.
- Click on the *New Slide* button.
- Select the *Organization Chart* autolayout.
- Click on *OK*.
- Click on the *Title* object and type a title for the organization chart.
- Double-click on the *Organization Chart* object to open Microsoft Organization Chart.

Let's begin creating an organization chart:

1. Choose **File, New** to open the New Presentation dialog box.
2. Click on the **Blank Presentation** icon under the General tab, and then click on **OK** to create a new presentation based on a blank presentation. The New Slide dialog box opens to display the available autolayouts for the first slide in the presentation (as shown in Figure 7.2).

Figure 7.2 **The New Slide dialog box**

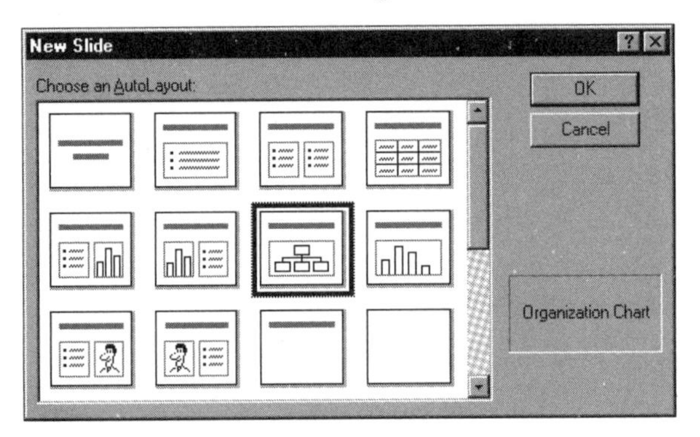

3. Click on the **Organization Chart** autolayout and click on **OK** to create the new presentation and display the first slide with an organization chart layout.
4. Double-click on the **Organization Chart** object to start Microsoft Organization Chart (see Figure 7.3).
5. Choose **File, Save As** and then type **mychap7** to name the new presentation. **Note:** Make sure that you click on File in the

Figure 7.3 **Microsoft Organization Chart upon start-up**

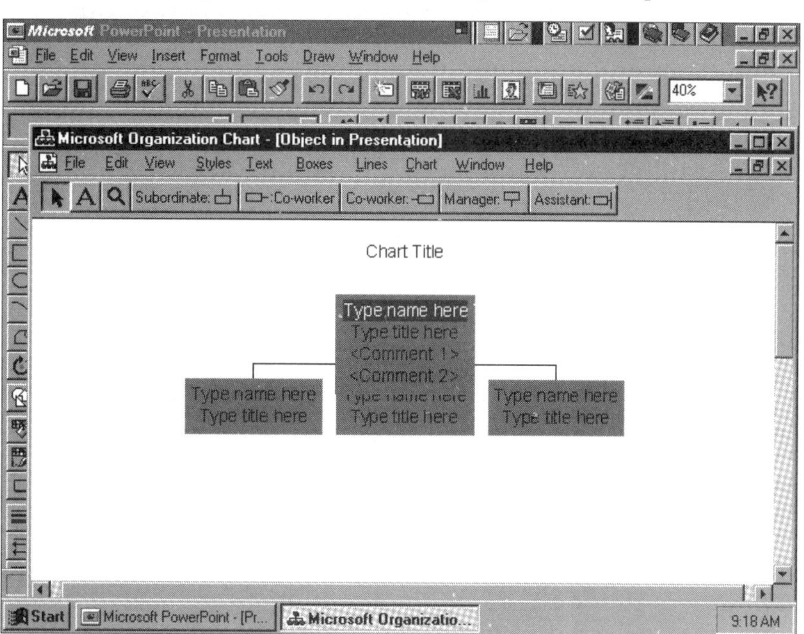

main PowerPoint window, not in the Microsoft Organization Chart window.

6. Make the Power Work folder the current folder. Click on **Save** to close the Save As dialog box and save the presentation.
7. Select the **Title** object and type **Global Travel**; press **Enter** to create a new line for the title and type **Personnel**.
8. Double-click on the **Organization Chart** object to again start the Microsoft Organization Chart.

EXPLORING THE MICROSOFT ORGANIZATION CHART WINDOW

When you double-click on an Organization Chart object in PowerPoint, the Microsoft Organization Chart window opens displaying a chart *template* (a pattern) containing four boxes. Microsoft Organization Chart has its own menu bar and toolbar as well. Let's explore the Microsoft Organization Chart menus and tools:

1. Click on the **Maximize/Restore** button to maximize the Microsoft Organization Chart window. (It's less confusing if there's only one window, menu bar, and toolbar visible.)

2. Click on **File** to open the File drop-down menu. You can use the File menu to open a new or existing chart, close or save a chart, or exit from Microsoft Organization Chart. (**Note**: You can have up to four organization charts open at a time.)
3. Click on **Edit** to open the Edit drop-down menu. You can use the Edit menu commands to edit and select objects in your organization chart.
4. Click on **View** to open the View drop-down menu. You can use the View menu to change the magnification of your organization chart. By default, Microsoft Organization Chart displays an organization chart at 50 percent magnification. You can also use the View menu to display the Custom Drawing tools that you can use to draw on your organization charts.
5. Click on **Styles** to open the Styles drop-down menu. You can use the Styles menu to change the look of your organization chart.
6. Open the **Text** menu. It displays a list of formatting commands.
7. Open the **Boxes** menu and then the **Lines** menu. You use these menus to change the look of the boxes and lines in the organization chart.
8. Open the **Chart** menu. You use the Chart menu to change the background color.
9. Now observe the toolbar. The Microsoft Organization Chart toolbar contains tools to create and change your chart. There are three types of tools on the toolbar:
   - *General purpose tools* are for selecting, editing, and viewing objects in your chart. They include:
     - *Selection Arrow tool*—used to select and drag objects.
     - *Text tool*—used to enter text into boxes.
     - *Zoom tool*—used to magnify any part of your chart.
   - *Box tools* are for creating boxes in your chart. They include:
     - *Subordinate box tool*—used to create a *subordinate box* (a box that reports to a manager box).
     - *Left Co-worker box tool*—used to create a *co-worker box* (a box with the same manager) above or to the left of an existing box.

- *Right Co-worker box tool*—used to create a co-worker box below or to the right of an existing box.
- *Manager box tool*—used to create a *manager box* (a box which has subordinate boxes reporting to it) for an existing box.
- *Assistant box tool*—used to create an *assistant box* (a box providing administrative or managerial assistance to its manager) for an existing box.

ADDING TEXT TO THE ORGANIZATION CHART

Each box in the organization chart has several field labels you can use as prompts for entering organization chart information.

Here's the general procedure to enter text in an organization chart box:

- Select the box in which you want to enter text.
- Type the text you want in the first field.
- Press *Tab* to move to the next field in the organization chart box.
- Type the text you want in the second field.
- Repeat the steps above, as necessary, to enter text in each of the fields for the box. **(Note:** You don't have to enter text in every field.)
- Select the next box in which you want to enter text, if necessary.

Let's begin entering text in our organization chart:

1. Select the top box in the organization chart, if necessary. When the box is selected, its background turns black and its field text turns white.
2. Type **C. Wood** to replace the Name field with the text *C. Wood.*
3. Press **Tab** to select the *Title* field.
4. Type **President** to replace the Title field with the text.
5. Select the first box from the left in the bottom row (see Figure 7.4).

Figure 7.4 **Selecting a box and entering text**

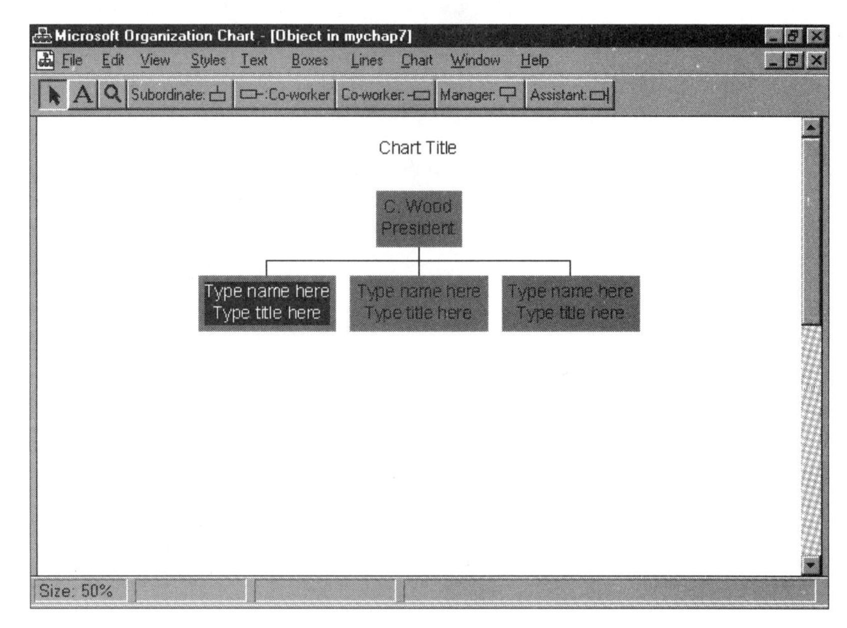

6. Type **B. Graham**, press **Tab** and type **Corporate** to add the text to the selected box. (**Note:** When you are finished typing, you can press **Esc** to deselect the box.)

PRACTICE YOUR SKILLS

Let's complete the organization chart text:

1. Using Figure 7.5 as a guide, complete the text in the remaining boxes:

J. Santos	B. Ragonesi
Tours	International

   Note: The background color in the organization chart boxes was changed to make Figure 7.5 easier to read. Your screen will not exactly match that shown in the figure.

2. Choose **File, Update Presentation** to save the presentation. (**Note:** This updates the presentation, not the chart.)

Figure 7.5 **Completing the organization chart**

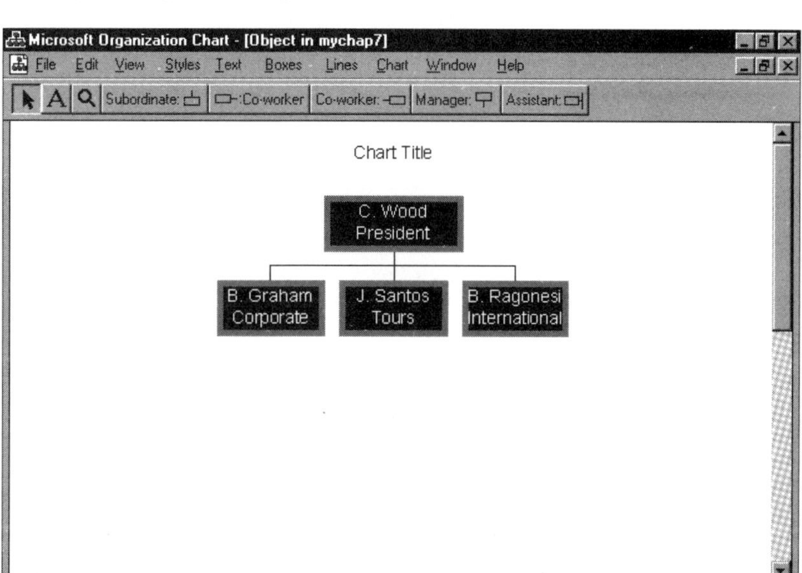

CHANGING THE MAGNIFICATION OF THE ORGANIZATION CHART

As you learned earlier in this chapter, Microsoft Organization Chart opens at 50 percent magnification. While this is generally a good magnification, you might need to enlarge a part of the chart in order to edit it. Or, if your organization chart is huge, you may want to reduce the magnification to see the whole chart.

You can use the Zoom tool to change the chart magnification. This tool (the third tool from the left on the toolbar) has two faces. When you can see the entire chart, the tool displays as the Enlarge tool. After you use the Enlarge tool to zoom in on a portion of the screen, the tool displays as the Reduce tool.

Here's the general procedure for using the Zoom tool to change the magnification of the chart:

- To enlarge a portion of the chart, click on the Enlarge tool (it displays as a magnifying glass) and click on the box you want to enlarge.
- To view the entire chart, click on the Reduce tool (it displays as a miniature organization chart) and click anywhere on the chart.

In addition to the Zoom tool, you can use the Chart menu to change the magnification. The View menu is more versatile because you can access all four of Microsoft Organization Chart's magnification levels simply by choosing View, and selecting the magnification level you want (*Size to Window, 50% of Actual, Actual Size,* and *200% of Actual*).

Let's increase the magnification of the chart:

1. Click on the **Zoom** tool (the third tool from the left on the toolbar, it displays a magnifying glass).
2. Click on the **C. Wood** box to enlarge the organization chart. Note that the magnification level in the status line now says *size: 100%* and that the Zoom tool displays a miniature organization chart (as shown in Figure 7.6).

Figure 7.6 **The chart at 100 percent magnification**

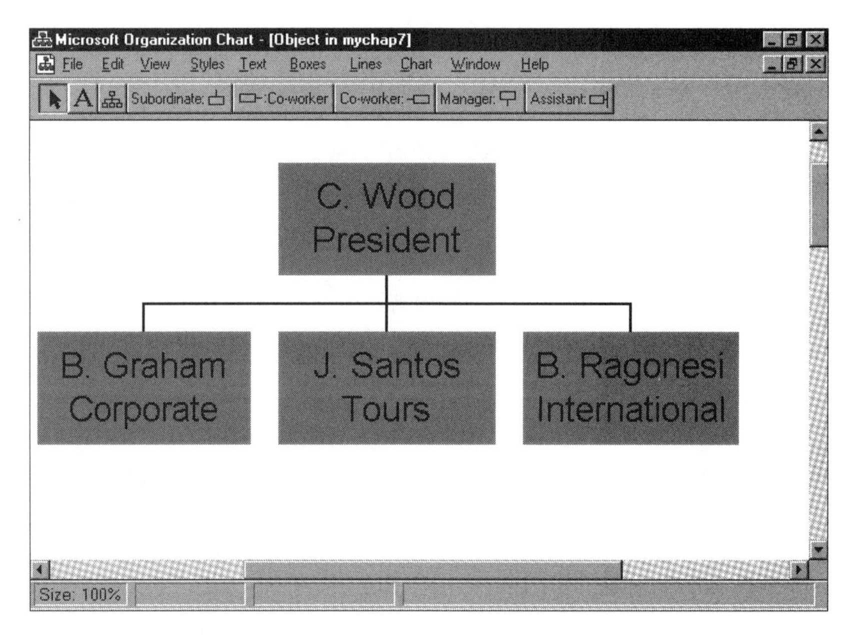

3. Open the **View** menu and note that the *Actual Size* command is checked.
4. Close the **View** menu without selecting any of the commands.

5. Click on the **Zoom** tool (still the third tool from the left).
6. Click anywhere on the chart and compare your screen to Figure 7.7. Microsoft Organization Chart changes the chart magnification so you can view the entire chart page.

Figure 7.7 **The chart at Size To Window magnification**

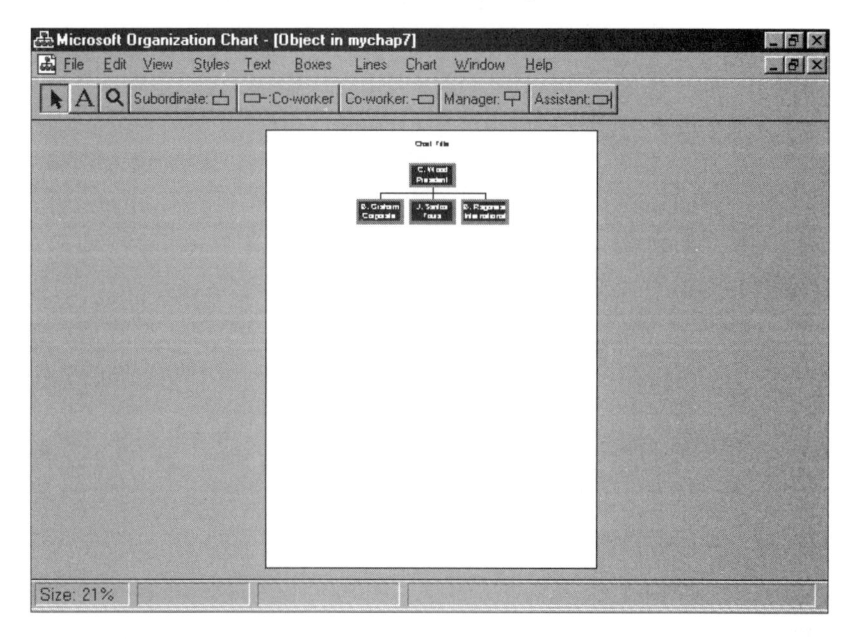

7. Choose **View, 50% of Actual** to return to the default magnification.

PLACING A CHART ON A SLIDE

Once you've created your chart, you need to exit from Microsoft Organization Chart and place that chart on the slide in your presentation.

Here's the general procedure for exiting Microsoft Organization Chart and placing the chart on the slide:

- Choose *File, Exit And Return To Presentation.*
- Click on *Yes* to update your presentation and return to the slide. (Or, choose *File, Update* to update any changes on your slide while keeping Microsoft Organization Chart open.)

Let's place our newly created organization chart on the slide:

1. Choose **File, Exit And Return To mychap7**. A message box displays a prompt asking you to update the presentation.
2. Click on **Yes,** if necessary, to update your presentation and return to the slide. The organization chart appears on the slide as an object.
3. Save the file.
4. Double-click on the chart to reopen Microsoft Organization Chart. The organization chart is displayed in the Microsoft Organization Chart window.
5. Maximize the Microsoft Organization Chart window, if necessary.

EDITING THE ORGANIZATION CHART

In today's world, hardly anyone stays in the same job forever. So, once you have created your basic organization chart, you'll probably find that you need to edit it by adding or deleting boxes when someone is hired or quits. Or, you might need to promote or demote someone. In the next section, we'll focus on adding, moving, and deleting boxes within our organization chart.

ADDING A BOX TO THE ORGANIZATION CHART

Global Travel is growing so fast that the company needs to hire some people to keep up with the work load.

Here's the general procedure to add a box to the organization chart:

- Click on the appropriate box tool to add a manager, co-worker, or subordinate.
- Select the box to which you want to add a manager, co-worker, or subordinate box.

Let's add subordinates to the *B. Graham* box.

1. Click on the **Subordinate** box tool (the fourth tool from the left on the toolbar).
2. Click on the **B. Graham** box to add a subordinate box.

3. Click on the **Subordinate** box tool and click on the **B. Graham** box again to add another subordinate (see Figure 7.8).

Figure 7.8 **Adding subordinate boxes**

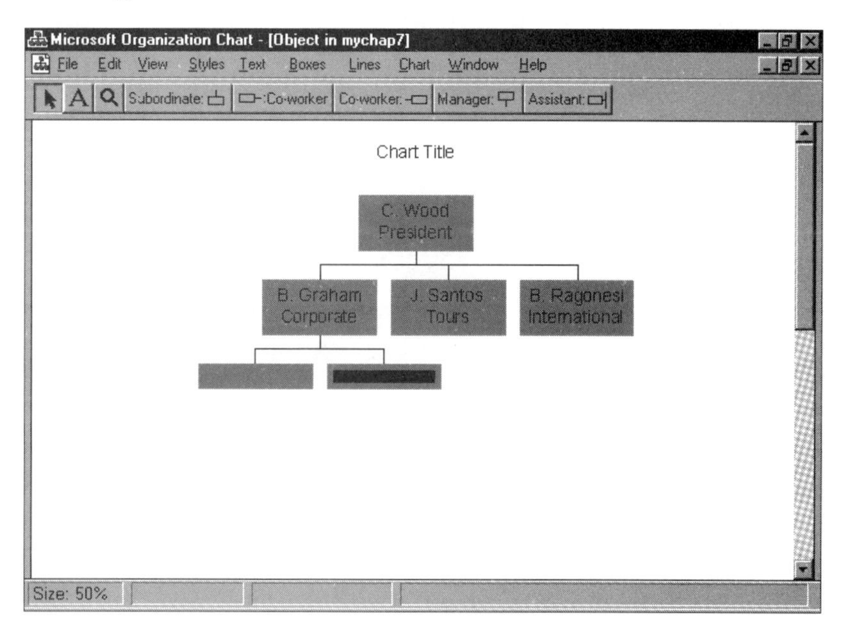

That wasn't too difficult. But why should you have to add boxes one at a time? Here's the general procedure to add multiple boxes:

- Click on the box tool once for each box you want to create (2 clicks = 2 boxes, 3 clicks = 3 boxes, and so on).
- Click on the box to which you want to attach the new boxes.

Note: When you create multiple new boxes, you can only attach them to one existing box.

Let's add two boxes to the *J. Santos* box:

1. Click on the **Subordinate** box tool twice.
2. Click on the **J. Santos** box to attach the new boxes to it.

PRACTICE YOUR SKILLS

1. Attach two new subordinate boxes to the *B. Ragonesi* box.
2. Using Figure 7.9 as a guide, add the following text to the new boxes:

B. Graham	J. Santos	B. Ragonesi
K. Mack	L. Burrows	M. Duncanson
B. Jakat	L. Nimue	M. Boyers

Figure 7.9 **Global Travel's new hires**

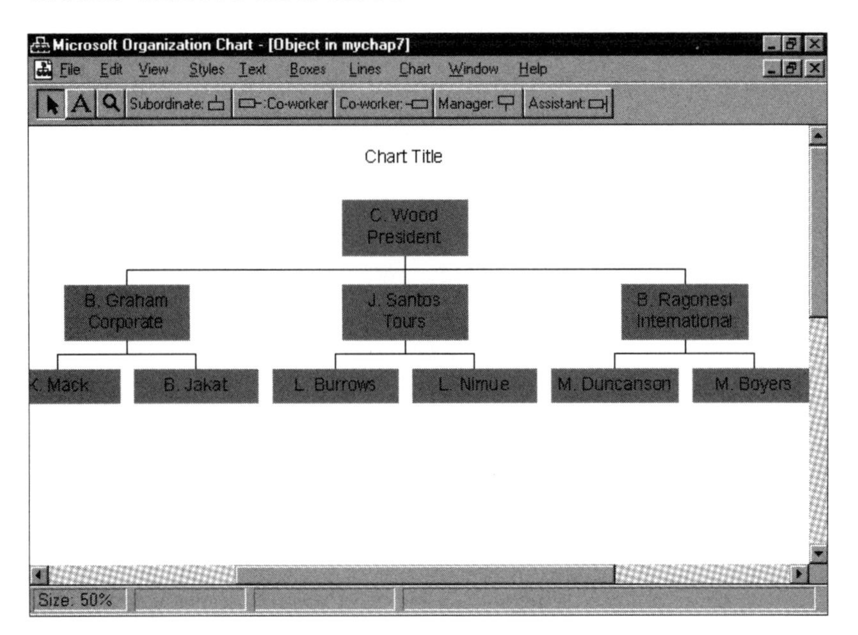

3. Change the magnification to view the entire chart. (Hint: Choose **View, Size To Window**.)
4. Change the magnification to **50% of Actual**.

MOVING BOXES IN THE ORGANIZATION CHART

People are constantly changing jobs within a company. Hopefully, the people in your company are climbing up the corporate ladder instead of falling down it. Whatever the case, you can quickly and easily promote and demote boxes in the organization chart. Here's the general procedure to move a box in the organization chart:

- Select the box you want to move.
- Choose *Edit, Cut*.
- Select the box to which you want to attach the box you are moving.
- Choose *Edit, Paste Boxes*.

Let's move a box:

1. Select the **K. Mack** box. The company is doing so well that they need a new Cruise department, and K. Mack is being promoted to manager.
2. Choose **Edit, Cut** to remove the *K. Mack* box from the organization chart and place a copy of it on the clipboard.
3. Select the **C. Wood** box.
4. Choose **Edit, Paste Boxes**. K. Mack now reports directly to C. Wood (see Figure 7.10).

PRACTICE YOUR SKILLS

Now that K. Mack is a manager, she needs some subordinates to report to her. B. Graham needs to hire someone, too:

1. Add two new subordinate boxes below the *K. Mack* box.
2. Add the text **F. Hassan** and **N. Szafranski** to the new boxes.
3. Add a new subordinate to the *B. Graham* box and add the text **J. Gugino** to the new box.
4. Add the Title text **Cruises** to the *K. Mack* box.
5. Change the magnification to **Size To Window** and compare your chart to that shown in Figure 7.11.
6. Return the magnification to **50% Of Actual**.

Figure 7.10 **Promoting K. Mack**

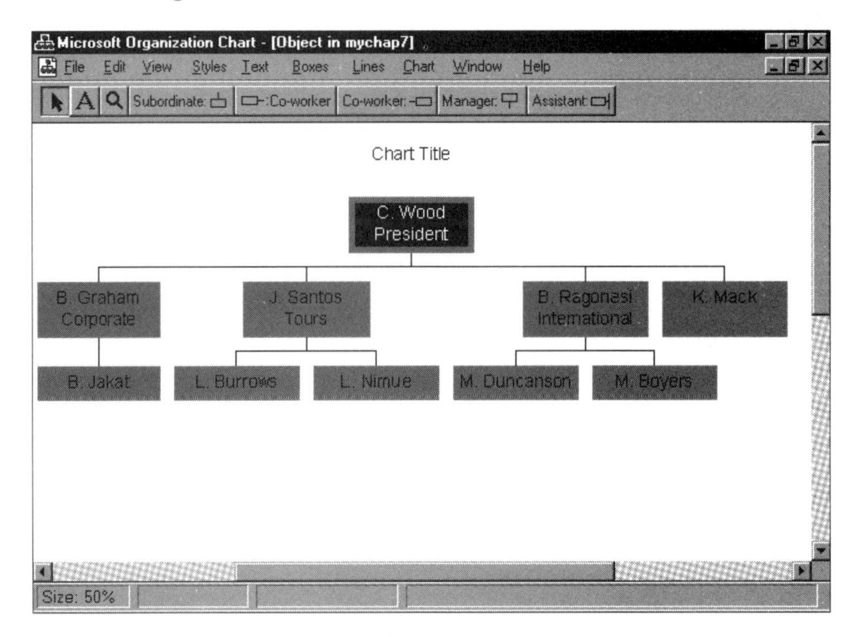

Figure 7.11 **Global Travel's glory days**

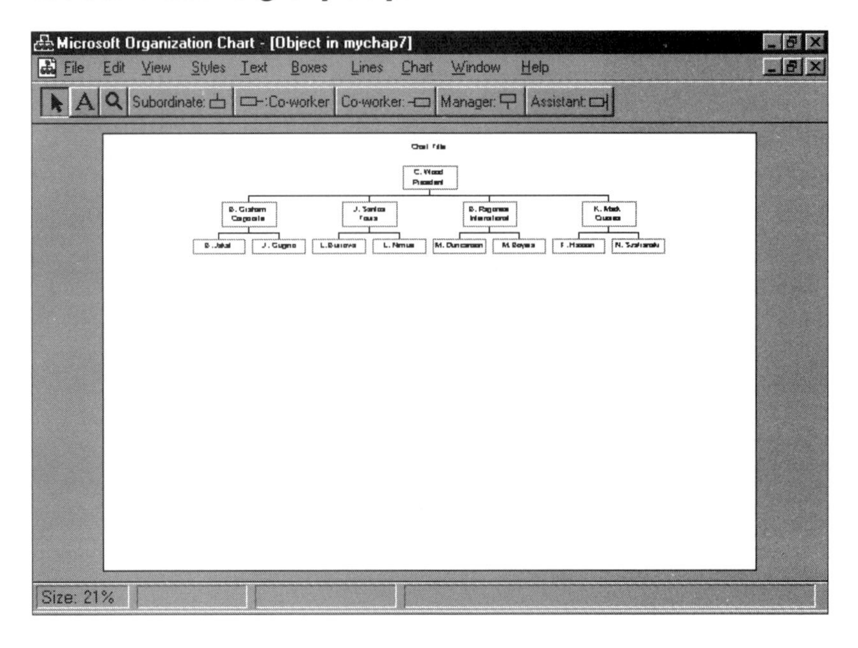

DELETING A BOX FROM THE ORGANIZATION CHART

If you find you no longer need a box in the organization chart, you can quickly remove it.

Here's the general procedure to delete a box from the organization chart:

- Select the box you want to delete.
- Press *Del*.

Let's delete one of the boxes in the organization chart:

1. Select the **M. Duncanson** box. M. Duncanson was offered a better job, so she's leaving Global Travel.
2. Press **Del** to delete the *M. Duncanson* box from the chart.

PRACTICE YOUR SKILLS

M. Duncanson found that new job just in time. Global Travel is downsizing. Delete the following boxes from the organization chart:

B. Jakat

L. Nimue

N. Szafranski

FORMATTING THE ORGANIZATION CHART

There are many ways to change the appearance of your organization chart. For example, you can change the fill color of the boxes, or add a drop shadow to the boxes to set them off from the background of the chart. Or, if you're feeling really radical, you can change the style of the entire chart.

CHANGING THE FILL COLOR OF THE BOXES

Here's the general procedure to change box color:

- Select the box whose color you want to change (press *Shift* to select multiple boxes).

- Choose *Boxes, Color.*
- Select a new color for the boxes.

You probably noticed that the black text is hard to read on the green boxes in our organization chart. So, let's change the color of the Global Travel organization chart boxes:

1. Select the **C. Wood** box.
2. Press and hold the **Shift** key and click on each of the other boxes in the organization chart; then release the **Shift** key. **Note:** Do not release the Shift key until you have selected all of the boxes in the organization chart.
3. Choose **Boxes, Color** to display the box color options.
4. Select the box color of your choice. Click on **OK**.
5. Click anywhere to deselect the boxes—you can't see how the new color looks until you deselect.

ADDING A DROP SHADOW TO THE BOXES

Here's the general procedure to add a drop shadow to a box:

- Select the box to which you want to add a drop shadow (press Shift to select more than one box).
- Choose *Boxes, Shadow.*
- Select the shadow style you want.

Let's add a drop shadow to the boxes in the organization chart:

1. Choose **Edit, Select, All** to select all of the boxes in the organization chart.
2. Choose **Boxes, Shadow** to display the shadow options (see Figure 7.12).
3. Click on the **Drop Right** shadow option (the second option in the second row).
4. Deselect the chart and compare your screen to that shown in Figure 7.13.

Figure 7.12 **Box Shadow options**

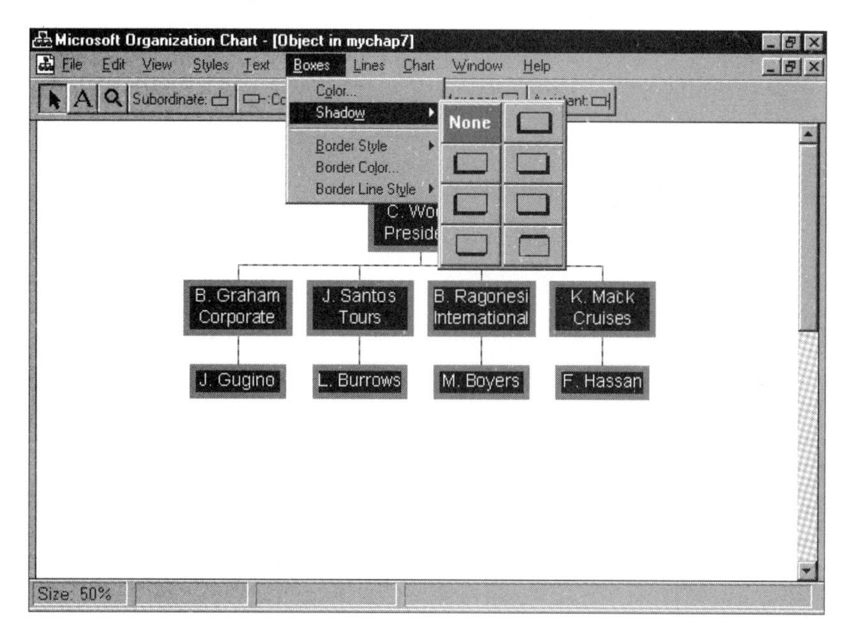

Figure 7.13 **The completed chart**

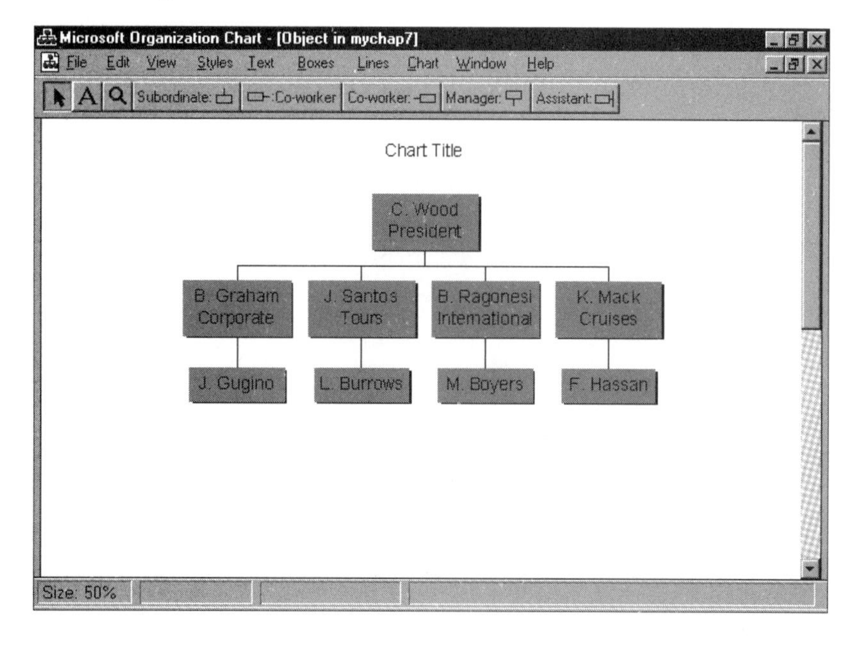

CHANGING THE STYLE

If you want to completely change the look of your organization chart, you can select a new style from the Styles menu.

Here's the general procedure to change the style of an organization chart:

- Select the entire organization chart.
- Open the *Styles* menu.
- Select a new chart style.

Let's change the style of the organization chart:

1. Choose **Edit, Select, All** to select the entire organization chart.
2. Click on **Styles** to open the Styles drop-down menu.
3. Click on the third style in the top row.
4. Choose **File, Exit And Return To mychap7** and click on **Yes** to return to the slide. Compare your screen to that shown in Figure 7.14. **Note:** If you are prompted to save to the Clipboard, click on **No**.
5. Close mychap7 (save changes, if necessary).

SUMMARY

In this chapter, you explored the techniques involved in creating organization charts. You now know how to apply an orgchart autolayout to a slide, how to start Microsoft Organization Chart, how to change the magnification of the organization chart, how to add a box to an organization chart, how to promote and demote workers in an organization chart, and how to use styles in an organization chart.

Figure 7.14 **Changing the organization chart style**

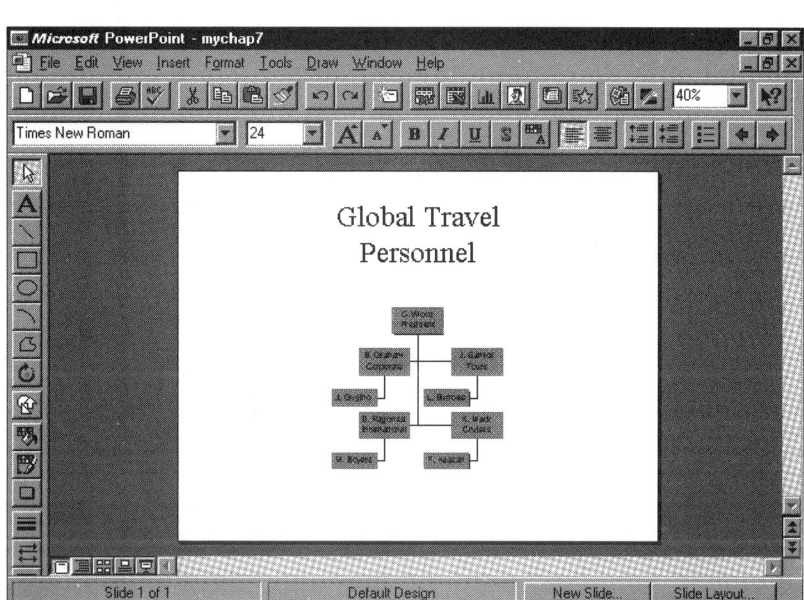

Here's a quick reference for the techniques you learned in this chapter:

Desired Result	**How to Do It**
Start Microsoft Organization Chart	Move to the slide after which you want to place the organization chart; click on the **New Slide** button; select the **Organization Chart** autolayout; click on **OK**; click on the **Title** object and type a title for the organization chart; double-click on the **Organization Chart** object to open Microsoft Organization Chart
Enter text in an organization chart box	Select the box in which you want to enter text; type the text you want in the first field; press **Tab** to move to the next field in the organization chart box; type the text you want in the second field; repeat the steps above, as necessary, to enter text in each of the fields for the box

Desired Result	How to Do It
Enlarge or reduce magnification of an organization chart	To enlarge a portion of the chart, click on the **Zoom** tool (it displays as a magnifying glass) and click on the box you want to enlarge; to view the entire chart, click on the **Zoom** tool (it displays as a miniature organization chart) and click anywhere on the chart
Exit Microsoft Organization Chart	Choose **File, Exit And Return To Presentation**; click on **Yes** to update your presentation and return to the slide, or choose **File, Update** to update any changes on your slide while keeping Microsoft Organization Chart open
Add a box to the organization chart	Click on the appropriate box tool to add a manager, co-worker, or subordinate; select the box to which you want to add a manager, co-worker, or subordinate box
Add multiple boxes	Click on the box tool once for each box you want to create (2 clicks = 2 boxes, 3 clicks = 3 boxes, and so on); click on the box to which you want to attach the new boxes
Move a box in the organization chart	Select the box you want to move; choose **Edit, Cut**; select the box to which you want to attach the box you are moving; choose **Edit, Paste**
Delete a box from the organization chart	Select the box you want to delete; press **Del**
Change the color	Select the box whose color you want to change (press **Shift** to select multiple boxes); choose **Boxes, Color**; select a new color for the boxes; deselect the box
Add a drop shadow to a box	Select the box to which you want to add a drop shadow (press **Shift** to select more than one box); choose **Boxes, Shadow**; select the shadow style you want; deselect the box
Change the style of an organization chart	Select the entire organization chart; open the **Styles** menu; select a new chart style; deselect the chart

In the next chapter, you'll find out how to use Microsoft Graph to create column charts for your presentation. You will learn how to open Microsoft Graph, how to enter data in the datasheet, how to exclude a row or column of data from the chart, how to edit a cell, how to change the width of a column in the datasheet, and how to delete a row or column from the datasheet. You will also learn how to place a chart on the slide, how to change the placement of the legend, how to format numbers along the y-axis of the chart, and how to add a text label to the chart.

CHAPTER 8: WORKING WITH COLUMN CHARTS

Using Microsoft Graph

Creating a Column Chart

Enhancing a Column Chart

In this chapter, you'll add to your repertoire of chart types by learning how to create, edit, and enhance a *column chart,* a chart in which items of data (such as quarterly sales figures) are displayed as rectangular columns. Column charts are among the most popular and easy-to-understand charts for displaying data trends (growth, decline, and so on) and for comparing related data.

When you're done working through this chapter, you will know

- How to open Microsoft Graph
- How to enter data in the datasheet
- How to exclude a row or column of data from the chart
- How to edit a cell
- How to change the width of a column in the datasheet
- How to delete a row or column from the datasheet
- How to place a chart on the slide
- How to change the placement of the legend
- How to format numbers along the y-axis of the chart
- How to add a text label to the chart

USING MICROSOFT GRAPH

Microsoft Graph is an embedded application that allows you to create charts for your presentations. You can choose from eight two-dimensional chart types (area, bar, column, line, pie, doughnut, radar, and scatter) and six three-dimensional chart types (area, bar, column, line, pie, and surface), each of which is available in several variations. In total, you can format your chart 103 different ways. By default, Graph plots your data as a column chart. However, you can change the chart type (we'll show you how in Chapter 9).

Microsoft Graph consists of two windows: the *Chart window* and the *Datasheet window*. When you first open Microsoft Graph, the Datasheet window displays sample data and the Chart window contains a sample chart plotted from that data.

Note: PowerPoint uses the terms *chart* and *graph* interchangeably. In this book, we will use *Graph* to refer to the Microsoft Graph application window and *chart* to refer to anything we create.

Here's the general procedure for starting Graph from the Presentation window:

- Move to the slide after which you want to place the chart.
- Click on the *New Slide* button.

- Click on the *Graph* autolayout.
- Click on *OK.*
- Add a title to the slide.
- Double-click on the *Graph* object. Microsoft Graph opens, displaying a sample datasheet and chart (see Figure 8.1).

Figure 8.1 **The Microsoft Graph window**

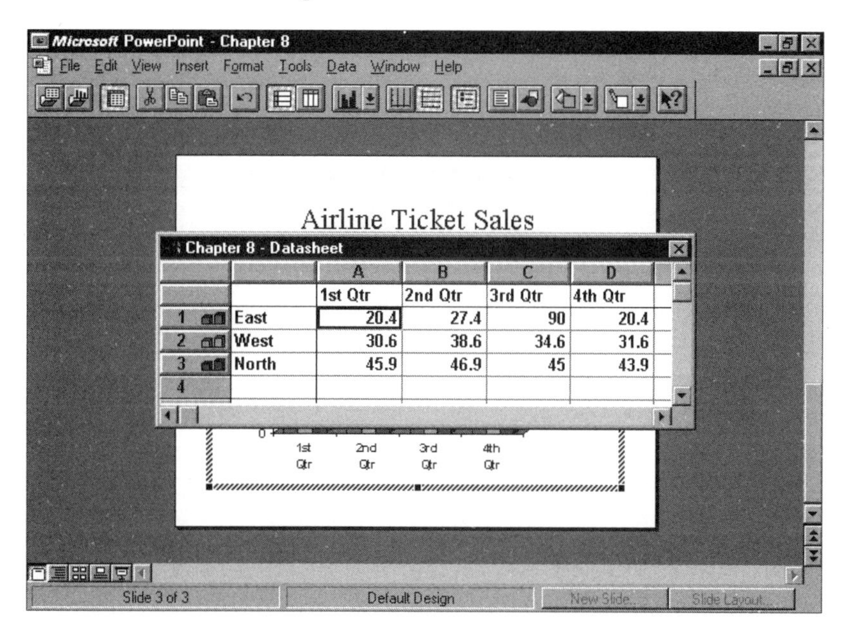

Note: Microsoft Graph doesn't have its own window in PowerPoint—when you create a chart, it opens right on your slide. Anytime you click outside of the datasheet or chart, Microsoft Graph automatically returns you to Slide view and updates the chart on the slide, so be careful not to click outside the datasheet or chart when working in Graph. If you *are* accidentally returned to the slide, simply double-click on the chart again to reopen Graph. Once you reopen Graph, you may not see the datasheet. To display the datasheet, click on the View Datasheet button.

If you are not running PowerPoint on your computer, please start it now. Close all open presentations. Let's start Microsoft Graph and take a look at the Graph window:

1. Open **Chapter 8** from your Power Work folder and maximize the presentation window, if necessary.
2. Display the last slide in the presentation (slide 1), and click on the **New Slide** button to add a slide to the end of the presentation.
3. In the New Slide dialog box, select the **Graph** autolayout (see Figure 8.2)

Figure 8.2 **The graph autolayout**

4. Click on **OK** to create the new graph slide.
5. Select the **Title** object and type the title **Airline Ticket Sales**.
6. Double-click on the **Graph** object to start Microsoft Graph.
7. Move the datasheet to the upper-left corner of the window (place the mouse pointer on the title bar and drag). Your screen should resemble that shown in Figure 8.3.

Now that Microsoft Graph is running, let's take a look at the Graph window.

1. Observe the menu options. File, Edit, Window, and Help are standard menu options available in most Windows programs. View, Insert, Format, and Tools are Microsoft Windows application menus. Data is a Microsoft Graph–specific menu.

Figure 8.3 **Moving the datasheet**

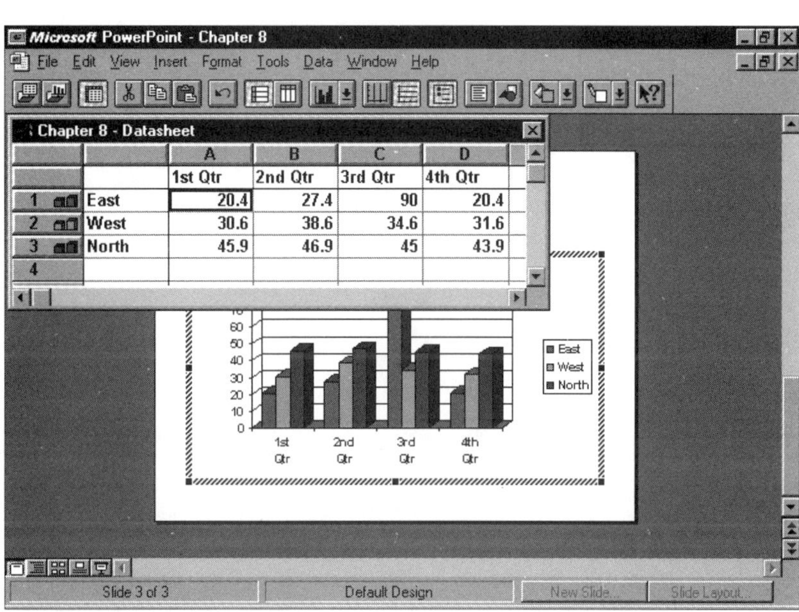

2. Click on **Data** and observe the drop-down Data menu. You use this menu to set up the options on your data sheet. For example, if you create a bar chart, you need the data in your datasheet to be set up in columns instead of rows.

3. Click on **Format** and observe the drop-down Format menu (do not select any of the commands in the Format menu). Notice the AutoFormat command. This command opens the AutoFormat dialog box, which shows several formatting options for whichever basic chart type you select in the Galleries list. Figure 8.4 shows the chart formatting options available for a 3-D Column chart.

4. Open the **Insert** menu. With this menu, you can add titles, data labels, a legend, axes labels, and gridlines to your chart.

5. Press **Esc** twice to close the Insert menu.

6. Observe the toolbar (as shown in Figure 8.5). Its tools allow quick access to some of Graph's basic commands and formatting techniques.

Figure 8.4 **3-D column chart options in the AutoFormat dialog box**

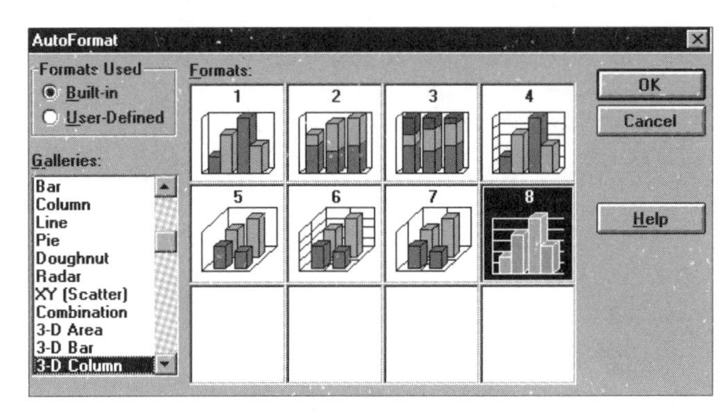

Figure 8.5 **The Microsoft Graph toolbar**

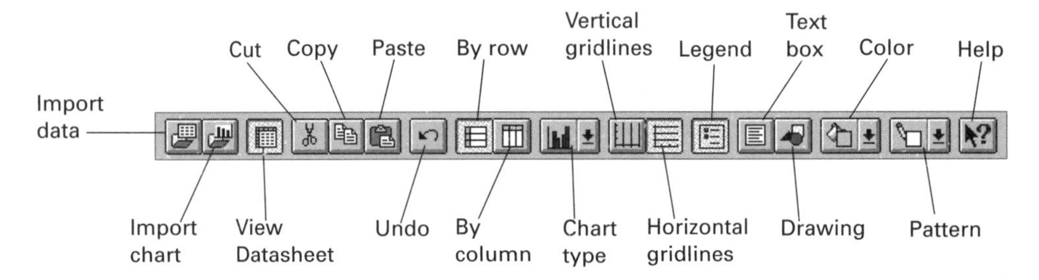

THE DATASHEET WINDOW

As mentioned earlier, Graph consists of the Datasheet window and the Chart window. You enter and edit your data in the datasheet, and it is formatted as a chart.

The datasheet itself is divided into 4,000 rows and 4,000 columns, in which you can enter numbers and labels. You might think that because the datasheet looks like a spreadsheet it therefore must be one. Don't be fooled. You cannot enter formulas into the datasheet, as you can into a spreadsheet.

You enter labels for your data in the first row and leftmost column of the datasheet. The first row and column are always visible in the Datasheet window. No matter how much data is in your datasheet, you can always see your labels while scrolling through the datasheet. Table 8.1 defines the elements of the Microsoft Graph Datasheet window. Figure 8.6 illustrates where some of these elements are located.

Figure 8.6 **The Datasheet window**

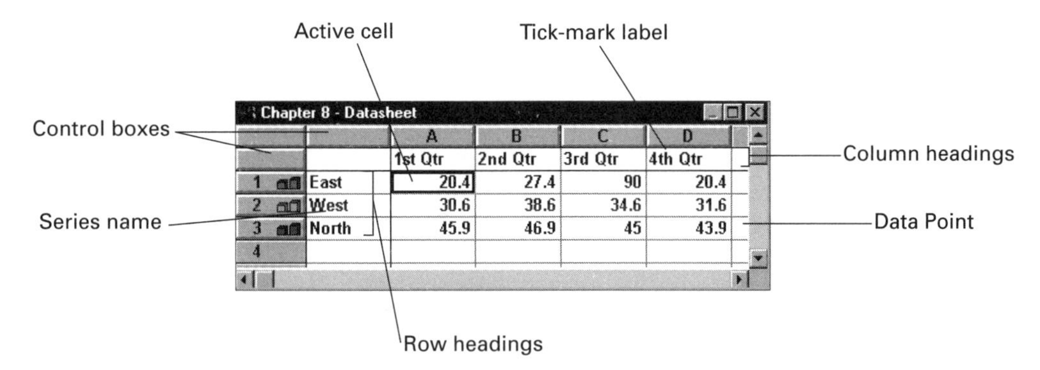

Table 8.1 **The Elements of the Datasheet Window**

Term	Definition
Row and column headings	The top row and the left column of cells on the datasheet. This is where your labels are entered.
Column and row control boxes	Located above column headings and to the left of row headings, you use these to select and deselect rows and columns or to exclude rows and columns from your chart. A control box appears extruded when the row or column is included, and pushed in when it is not. Column control boxes display column letters, while row control boxes display row numbers. In addition, control boxes indicate whether data series are read in columns or rows.
Cell	An intersection of a row and a column on the datasheet. You enter data into cells.
Active cell	The currently selected cell, indicated by a heavy border.

Table 8.1 **The Elements of the Datasheet Window (Continued)**

Term	Definition
Data series	A row or column of data used to plot one set of bars or columns, or one line or pie.
Data point	A single cell value, representing a single item in a data series.
Series name	A name that identifies a row or column of data. These names appear in the legend.
Tick-mark labels	The names that appear along the horizontal axis of an area, column, or line chart, and along the vertical axis of a bar chart. When data series are in rows, the tick-mark labels identify the columns. When data series are in columns, the tick-mark labels identify rows.

Now let's explore the Datasheet window:

1. Observe the cells. Each cell contains a data point (one piece of information that will be plotted on the chart).
2. Observe the column and row headings. The top row of the datasheet contains the column headings, while the first column displays the row headings. These headings appear as labels in the chart.
3. Observe the row and column control boxes. These are the boxes above the column headings and to the left of the row headings. They are used to select and deselect columns and rows of the datasheet. If a control box is extruded, the information in that column or row is currently selected to be included in the chart. If a control box is pushed in, any information in that column or row will be excluded from the chart.
4. Open the **Data** menu. The *Series In Rows* option is checked, indicating that the information on the datasheet is read row by row, each row forming a separate data series. This is reflected on the datasheet by the graph symbols to the right of the row number.

5. Choose **Series In Columns** and observe the datasheet. The graph symbols display to the right of the column letters, indicating that each column is a separate data series.
6. Observe the chart. When the Series In Columns option is checked, the row headings in the datasheet become the x-axis labels in the chart. The column headings become the legend.
7. Choose **Data, Series In Rows**. The datasheet and chart change back.

THE CHART WINDOW

The Chart window shows you the pictorial representation of the data you enter in the datasheet. After entering data in the datasheet, you can change the look of the chart in the Chart window.

Table 8.2 defines the elements of the Microsoft Graph chart. Figure 8.7 illustrates where some of these elements are located.

Table 8.2 **The Elements of a Chart**

Term	Definition
Data marker	A bar (in column and bar charts), shape (in area and pie charts), or dots and symbols (in line and xy, or *scatter*, charts) that mark a single data point or value. Related markers in a chart make up a data series.
Data series	A group of related data points. For example, one region's airline-ticket sales figures for all four quarters make up a data series. In the sample chart, each region (East, West, and North) is a data series. A chart can have one or more data series.
Axis	A line that serves as a major reference for plotting data in a chart.
X-axis	The horizontal or category axis.
Y-axis	The vertical or value axis.

Table 8.2 The Elements of a Chart (Continued)

Term	Definition
Tick mark	A short line that crosses an axis and marks off a category, scale, or data series.
Tick-mark label	Text that appears beside or below a major tick mark to identify it.
Plot area	The area in which Graph plots your data. It includes the axes and all markers that represent data points.
Grid lines	Optional lines that extend from the tick marks on an axis across the plot area to make it easier to view data values.
Chart text	Text that describes data or items in a chart. Text can be attached or unattached.
Attached text	Any label linked to a chart object such as an axis or a data marker. Attached text moves with the item when it is repositioned, but cannot be moved independently of the chart object.
Unattached text	Text you add by just typing whenever the chart is active and then pressing Esc. You can move unattached text anywhere on the chart.
Legend	A key that identifies a data-series name and the patterns, colors, or symbols associated with that data series.

Let's take a quick tour of the Chart:

1. Click on the **View Datasheet** button (the third button from the left on the toolbar) to close the datasheet, displaying only the chart.

Figure 8.7 **The Chart window**

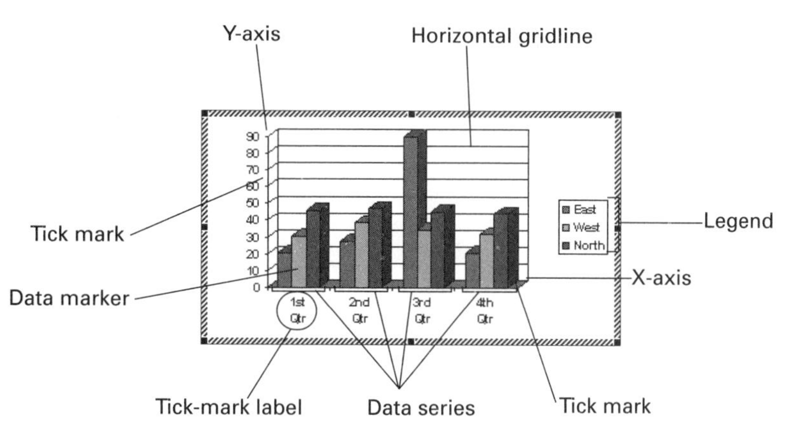

2. Observe the x-axis (the horizontal axis). It displays the category—in this case, periods of time—being graphed.
3. Observe the y-axis (the vertical axis). This shows the values being graphed; in our example, the number of sales.
4. Observe the legend. Located on the right side of the Chart window, it serves as a key identifying the different data series in the chart.
5. Observe the data series. Each data series consists of all the columns that have the same color or pattern. For example, the first column in each quarter is the data series for East.

CREATING A COLUMN CHART

A column chart depicts data graphed against an x-axis (horizontal axis) and a y-axis (vertical axis). The x-axis shows the *category* being graphed, such as products, regions, or periods of time. The y-axis shows the *values* being graphed, such as dollars or numbers of products sold.

Figure 8.8 shows a simplified version of the Airline Ticket Sales column chart that you'll create over the course of this chapter. In this figure, the x-axis categories are regions (North America, Europe, and Far East), and the y-axis values are thousands of dollars.

Figure 8.8 **Airline Ticket Sales column chart, simplified**

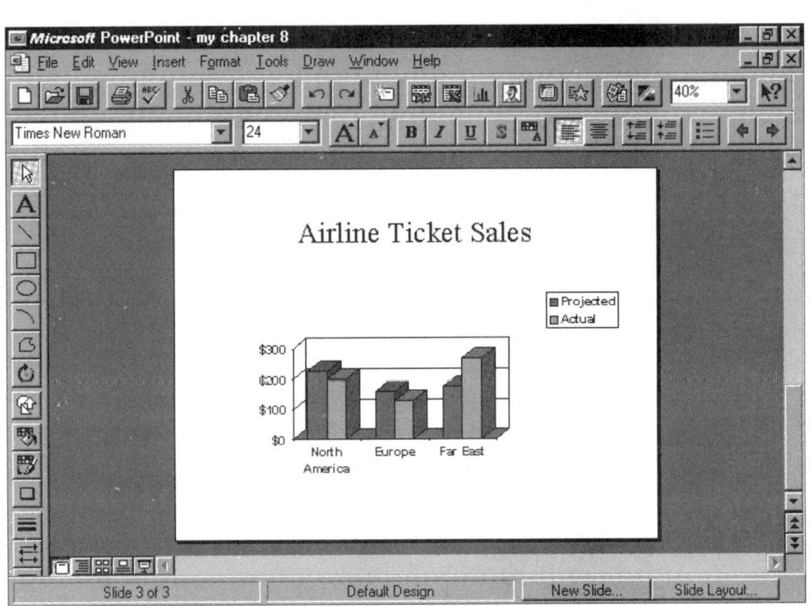

Column charts are useful for showing variation over a period of time. Each number in the datasheet is represented by a column in the chart. Data is entered into the datasheet by row. This means that the information in the first column of your datasheet appears in your chart as the legend, and the contents of the first row become the labels along the horizontal axis.

SELECTING CELLS AND ENTERING DATA

To enter data on the datasheet, you first need to make the cell active by selecting it. The cell surrounded by a darkened border is the active cell. You can use the mouse or the keyboard to select a cell. Then, simply type the data. If there is any data in the cell you selected, the new data you type will replace it. If you are going to be entering a row or column of numbers, you can select all the cells in that row or column and then enter your data.

Here's the general procedure for entering data into a selected row or column:

- Click on the *View Datasheet* button to open the datasheet, if necessary.

- Drag to select the cells in which you want to enter information.
- Type the data, and press *Enter* to advance to the next selected cell.
- Repeat the previous step until data has been completely entered.

Let's begin creating our column chart:

1. Click on the **View Datasheet** button to open the datasheet.

2. Drag from the **1st Qtr** to the **3rd Qtr** cell to select three cells.
3. Observe the selected cells. The active cell always has a darkened border. Any data you type will be entered in the active cell.
4. Type **Canada**. The text you type replaces the contents of the first selected cell.
5. Press **Enter** to make *2nd Qtr* the active cell.
6. Observe the Chart window. The first tick-mark label along the horizontal axis reflects the change made on the datasheet.
7. Type **Europe** and press **Enter** to replace *2nd Qtr* with *Europe* and to make *3rd Qtr* the active cell.
8. Type **Far East** to replace *3rd Qtr.*
9. Press **Enter**. Canada becomes the active cell). Because you selected only three cells, pressing Enter toggles you through those cells only.

EXCLUDING A DATASHEET ROW OR COLUMN FROM THE CHART

Excluding a row or column from the datasheet will remove that data from the chart without actually deleting the data from the datasheet.

Here's the general procedure for excluding a row or column of data in the datasheet from the chart:

- Double-click on the control box for the row or column you want to exclude from the chart.

Because we want our chart to include only three data series, we need to exclude the fourth sample data series from the datasheet. Let's do that now:

1. Observe the Chart window. The 4th Qtr data series should be excluded from the chart data.
2. Double-click on the **column D** control box above the 4th Qtr cell to exclude the 4th Qtr column. Clicking once will only select the column or row, not mark it for exclusion.
3. Observe the chart. The modified column chart has three regions displayed along the horizontal axis. The data in the 4th Qtr column is still on the datasheet, but it does not appear in the current chart (see Figure 8.9).

Figure 8.9 **The datasheet and chart with the 4th Qtr data excluded**

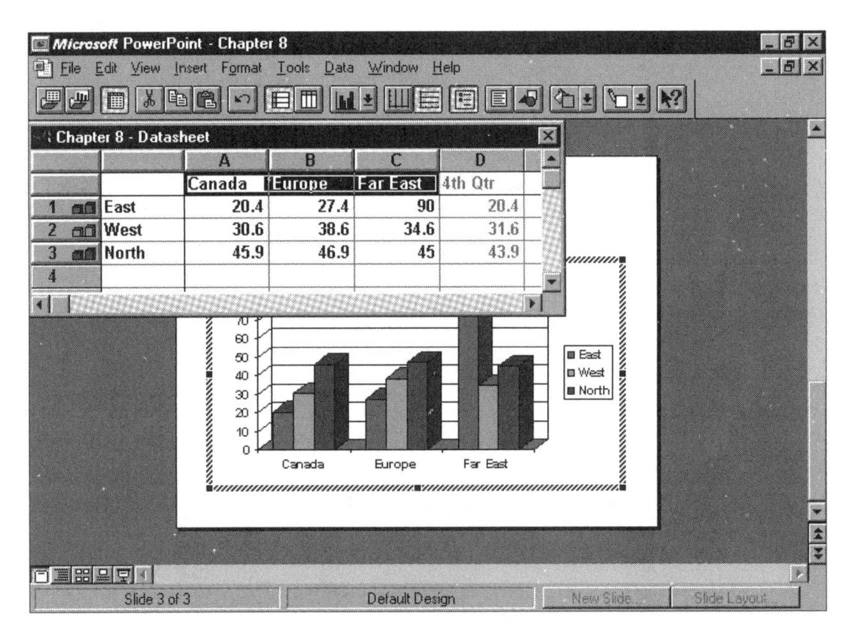

EDITING A CELL

It is not necessary for you to retype all the information in a cell every time you want to change it. If you would like to modify the data in a cell instead of replace it, you can edit the cell.

Here's the general procedure for editing a cell in the datasheet:

- In the Datasheet window, double-click on the cell that you want to edit. The insertion point is placed in the text in the cell.
- Place the insertion point and enter the new text, or press the *Backspace* and *Del* keys to edit the text.

Now let's edit a cell in the datasheet:

1. Click on the **Canada** cell to select it.
2. Type **America** and press **Enter** to replace *Canada* with *America*.
3. Double-click on the **America** cell to place the insertion point in the text. You can edit a cell without retyping all the text.
4. Press **Home** to place the insertion point at the beginning of *America*.
5. Type **North** and press **Spacebar**. Now the region covered by the chart will include both Canada and the United States.
6. Press **Enter** to register the change.

CHANGING THE COLUMN WIDTH

Your datasheet has default column widths. If you enter a number that is longer than the cell is wide, Graph will solve the difficulty by expressing the number exponentially. For example, if you enter the number 1,000,000,000 in a narrow cell, the number will be expressed as *1E + 09* (1 + nine zeros). When you enter text that is wider than the cell, only the characters that fit in the cell will be displayed; however, all the text characters will be displayed on your chart.

You can increase or decrease the column width as needed to make it easier for you to work with your data on the datasheet. Datasheet columns may be as narrow as the width of one character or wide enough to hold 255 characters. Keep in mind, however, that the width of the column in your datasheet has nothing to do with how the data will be displayed on your chart.

Here's the general procedure for changing column widths:

- Click on the control box for the column whose width you want to change.

- Choose *Format, Column Width* to open the Column Width dialog box.
- Type a number between 1 and 255 that represents the new character width for the selected column.
- Click on *OK* to change the column width and return to the datasheet.

Let's widen column A to view all the text in each cell:

1. Observe the North America cell. You cannot see all of that cell's text on the datasheet.
2. Click on the **column A** control box (above the North America cell) to select the column.
3. Choose **Format, Column Width** to open the Column Width dialog box. The standard width for columns is nine characters.
4. Type **13** to widen the column to 13 characters, as shown in Figure 8.10.

Figure 8.10 **The Column Width dialog box**

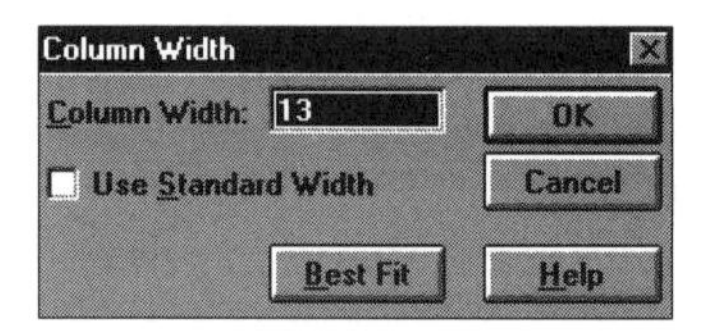

5. Press **Enter** to register the new column width and close the dialog box.
6. Observe the datasheet. It is now possible to see all the text in the North America cell. Note that in order to change the width of one cell, it is necessary to change the width of the entire column.
7. Observe the chart. Changing the column width on the datasheet has no effect on the Chart window.

DELETING A ROW OR COLUMN FROM THE DATASHEET

To delete a row or column from the datasheet, you can use the *Edit, Delete* command.

You can delete one cell or a range of cells. Of course, deleted data is not displayed on the chart.

Here's the general procedure for deleting a row or column:

- Select the entire row or column (click on the control box).
- Choose *Edit, Delete.*

Note: If you select only a cell or range of cells in a row or column, then the Delete dialog box appears. Make the appropriate choice in the dialog box and then click on OK.

Let's continue working on the datasheet:

1. Drag down from the **East** cell to the **West** cell to select the East and West cells. The East cell is active.
2. Type **Projected** and press **Enter** to replace *East* with *Projected* and to move to the West cell.
3. Type **Actual** and press **Enter** to replace *West* with *Actual.*
4. Observe the Chart window. The label for the first set of bars in the legend has changed from *East* to *Projected,* and *Actual* has replaced *West.* (**Note:** You might need to drag the chart down to see the entire legend.)
5. Observe the Datasheet window. Projected and Actual are the only two series of numbers we need for the modified chart. Therefore, we should eliminate the North series. (**Note:** If you moved the chart in step 4, you might need to click on the **View Datasheet** button to reopen the datasheet.)
6. Click on the **row 3** control box (to the left of the North cell) to select the row containing the North data.
7. Choose **Edit, Delete** to delete the row from the datasheet and to remove the North column of data from the current chart.
8. Observe your chart and datasheet. They should match those shown in Figure 8.11.

Figure 8.11 **The Graph window, after deleting a row**

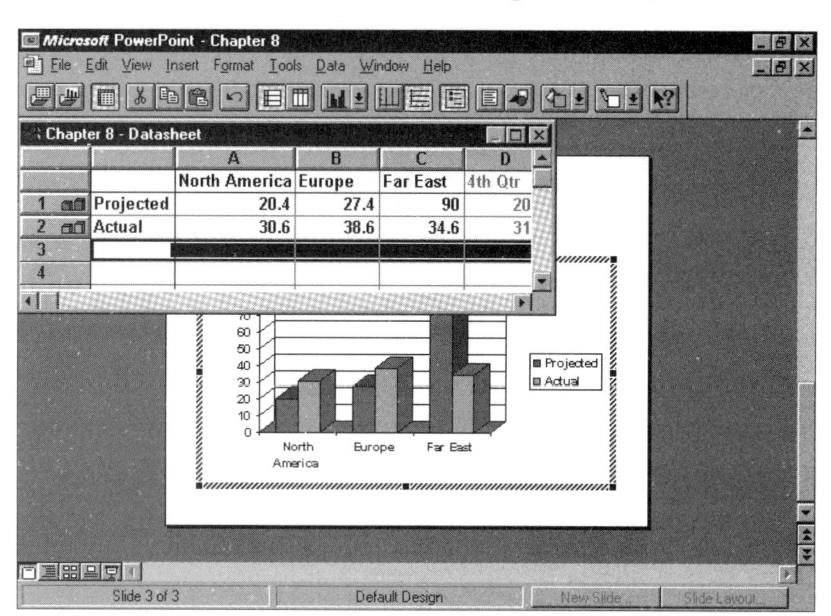

PRACTICE YOUR SKILLS

Now let's complete the datasheet so that it matches that shown in Figure 8.12:

1. Select all the cells from **20.4** in the Projected row through **34.6** in the Actual row. (Hint: Drag to select the cells.)
2. Enter the following Projected and Actual values for the North America, Europe, and Far East columns so that your window matches that shown in Figure 8.12:

	North America	**Europe**	**Far East**
Projected	225	160	175
Actual	200	130	270

Figure 8.12 **The completed datasheet**

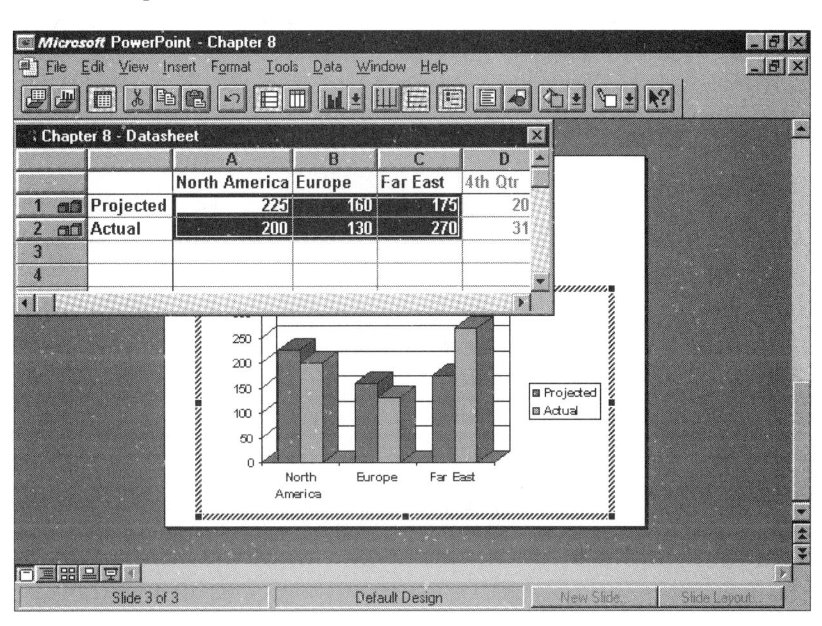

PLACING A CHART ON A SLIDE

Once you have entered your data and created your chart, you need to exit from the Graph window and place that chart on the slide in your presentation.

Here's the general procedure for exiting the Graph window and placing the chart on the slide:

- Close the datasheet, if necessary.
- Click anywhere on the slide workspace (except on the chart). Graph closes and returns you to the PowerPoint slide. The chart appears on the slide in the position of the Graph object.

Let's place our newly created column chart on the slide and see what it looks like:

1. Click on the **View Datasheet** button to close the datasheet.
2. Click on the slide above the title *Airline Ticket Sales* to return to the slide. The column chart Airline Ticket Sales that we created in this chapter appears on the slide as an object.
3. Save the file as **my chapter 8**.

4. Double-click on the chart to reopen Microsoft Graph. The Airline Ticket Sales chart and chart toolbar are displayed in the Graph window. The datasheet is still closed.

ENHANCING A COLUMN CHART

Charts are created with certain defaults, depending on the template you are using for your presentation. However, you are not stuck with these settings. Once you have created a chart, you can enhance it in many ways.

CHANGING THE LEGEND FORMAT

Each group of related data points has a particular pattern, color, or symbol in the chart. The legend is a key that identifies these patterns. By default, the legend appears in the upper-right corner of your chart; however, you can move the legend anywhere on the chart.

Here's the general procedure for changing the placement of the legend:

- Click on the chart to make it active, if necessary.
- Click on the legend.
- Choose *Format, Selected Legend.*
- Click on *Placement* and select a legend type.
- Click on *OK.*

Note: You can also move the legend to a new location by dragging it.

Let's change the position of the legend on the chart we created in this chapter:

1. Click on the chart, if necessary, to activate it.
2. Click on the legend to select it.
3. Choose **Format, Selected Legend** to open the Format Legend dialog box. This dialog box consists of three parts: *Pattern options* to control the border and background of the legend; *Font options* to control the size and appearance of the legend text; and *Placement options* to control the position of the legend.

4. Click on **Placement** to display the Placement options (see Figure 8.13).
5. Choose **Corner** and click on **OK** to place the legend at the corner of the chart.

Figure 8.13 The Format Legend dialog box

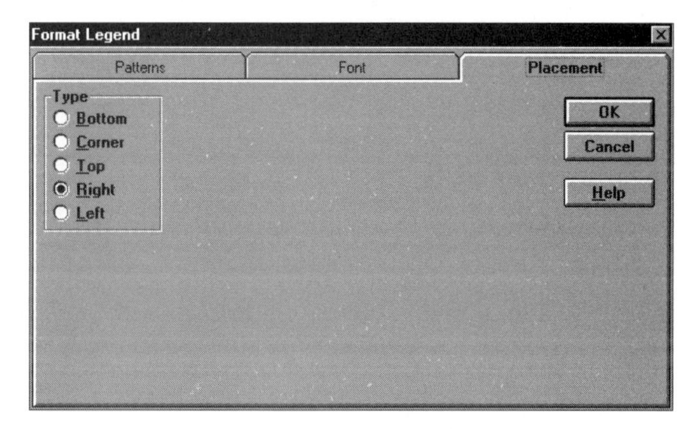

FORMATTING Y-AXIS NUMBERS

Your default chart style does not include any formatting for the numbers along the y-axis, so you can't tell if they are supposed to represent currency, percentages, or some other measurement. You can quickly and easily add formatting—such as dollar signs, decimal places, or commas—by formatting the cell at the intersection of the second row and second column of the datasheet.

Here's the general procedure for changing formatting of y-axis numbers:

- Click on the *View Datasheet* button to open the datasheet, if necessary.
- Click on cell *A1* (the cell at the intersection of row 1 and column A of the datasheet).
- Choose *Format, Number.*
- Click on the number format desired for the y-axis.
- Click on *OK.*

Let's add dollar signs to the numbers along the y-axis of our chart:

1. Open the Datasheet, if necessary, by clicking on the **View Datasheet** button.
2. Click on **A1** (the cell in row 1, column A). The format of this cell controls the format of the numbers along the vertical axis of the chart.
3. Choose **Format, Number** to open the Number Format dialog box. This dialog box, shown in Figure 8.14, displays a list of possible formats for numbers. (**Note:** You can use the Shortcut menu to open the Number Format dialog box.)
4. Choose **$#,##0_);($#,##0)** from the Format Codes list to format the vertical axis numbers as currency. (**Note:** You might need to scroll down to view the correct number format.)
5. Click on **OK** to register the formatting and close the dialog box.
6. Close the datasheet and observe the chart. The numbers along the y-axis are formatted as currency.
7. Click anywhere on the slide (outside of the chart) to return to the slide.

Figure 8.14 **The Number dialog box**

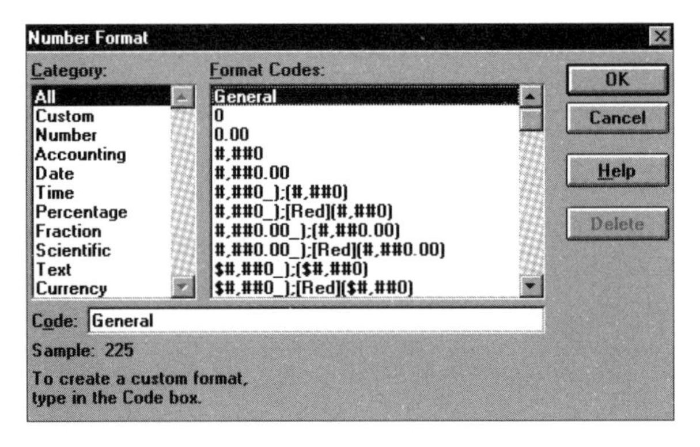

ADDING A TEXT LABEL ON A SLIDE

As a finishing touch, you can add text labels to clarify or explain parts of your chart. Here's the general procedure for adding a text label to the chart:

- Return to your slide.
- Select the *Text* tool.
- Click to place an insertion point on the slide workspace.
- Type the text.
- Select the text and format it as needed.
- Drag the text to the desired location on the slide.

Let's add a text label like the one shown in Figure 8.15:

1. Select the **Text** tool (located on the Drawing toolbar; it displays the letter *A*).
2. Place the insertion point anywhere on the slide workspace.
3. Type **Sales in thousands**.
4. Press **Esc** to select the text.
5. Move the text label to the location shown in Figure 8.15. (**Note**: Don't panic if your figure doesn't exactly match ours.)
6. Save the file.
7. Close the file.

SUMMARY

In this chapter, you explored column charts. You now know how to open Microsoft Graph, how to create a column chart, how to exclude a row or column of data from the chart, how to edit a cell, how to change the width of a column in the datasheet, and how to delete a row or column from the datasheet. You also learned how to place a chart on the slide, how to change the placement of the legend, how to format numbers along the y-axis of the chart, and how to add a text label to the chart.

Figure 8.15 **The completed column chart**

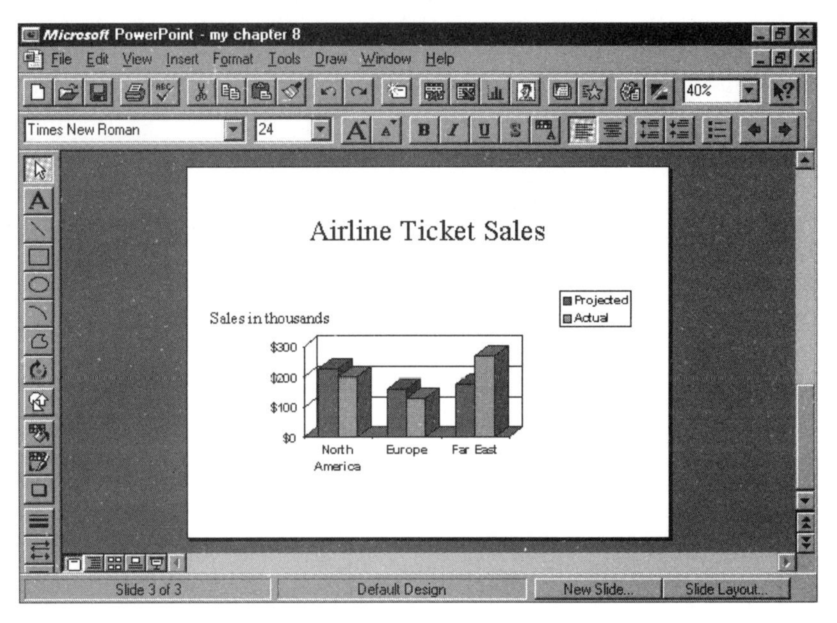

Here's a quick reference for the techniques you learned in this chapter:

Desired Result	How to Do It
Open Microsoft Graph	Move to the slide after which you want to place the chart; click on the **New Slide** button; click on the **Graph** autolayout; click on **OK**; add a title to the slide; double-click on the **Graph** object
Enter data into the datasheet	Open Microsoft Graph; drag to select the cells in which you want to enter information; type the data and press **Enter** to advance to the next selected cell; repeat the previous step until all the data has been entered
Exclude a row or column of data	Double-click on the **control box** for the row or column you want to exclude from the chart

Desired Result	How to Do It
Edit a cell	Double-click on the cell that you want to edit to place the insertion point in the cell; edit as necessary
Change column width	Click on the **control box** for the column whose width you want to change; choose **Format, Column Width** to open the Column Width dialog box; type a number between 1 and 255 that represents the new character width for the selected column; click on **OK**
Delete a row or column	Select the entire row or column (click on the **control box**); choose **Edit, Delete**
Place the chart on the slide	Click on the slide (not on the chart)
Change the placement of the legend	Click on the legend; choose **Format, Selected Legend**; click on **Placement**; select a legend type; click on **OK**
Change the format of y-axis numbers	Select **cell A1**; choose **Format, Number**; click on the desired number format for the y-axis; click on **OK**
Add a text label to the chart	Return to the slide; select the **Text** tool; click to place an insertion point; type the label text; press **Esc** to select the text; format the text as needed; drag the text to the desired location on the slide

In the next chapter, you'll find out how to modify Microsoft Graph to suit your needs and how to create and edit pie charts on your slides. You will learn how to clear the datasheet, how to change the chart type, how to change the data series, and how to change legend options. You will also learn how to explode a pie chart, how to create a double-exploded pie chart, how to copy a chart, how to resize a chart, and how to recolor a chart.

CHAPTER 9: WORKING WITH PIE CHARTS

Creating a Pie Chart

Enhancing a Pie Chart

Charts can be an integral part of any presentation. PowerPoint provides you with the tools to create several different kinds of charts. In Chapter 8, you learned how to create column charts for your presentation. In this chapter, you'll learn how to create, edit, and enhance a *pie chart,* a circular diagram that depicts numerical as well as textual information. Both kinds of chart can make your presentation more interesting.

When you're done working through this chapter, you will know

- How to create a pie chart
- How to clear the datasheet
- How to change the chart type
- How to change the data series
- How to change legend options
- How to explode a pie chart
- How to create a double-exploded pie chart
- How to copy a chart
- How to resize a chart
- How to recolor a pie slice

CREATING A PIE CHART

A pie chart is a circular diagram that depicts that relationship between a whole and its parts. Figure 9.1 shows a simplified version of the Global Travel pie chart that you'll create over the course of this chapter. As you can see from this figure, each slice of the pie represents one part of the whole pie. The percentages indicate the size of each part in relation to the whole; for example, the Europe slice is 41 percent of the whole pie. Pie charts are particularly useful for comparing the relative size of a whole's constituent parts.

Here's the general procedure for creating a pie chart:

- Move to the slide to which you want to add the pie chart.
- If necessary, click on *Slide Layout.*
- Select the *Graph* autolayout.
- Press *Enter.*
- Add a title for the chart.
- Double-click on the *Graph* object.
- Choose *Format, AutoFormat* to open the AutoFormat dialog box.
- In the Galleries list, select *Pie* to display the format options for pie charts.

Figure 9.1 **Global Travel pie chart, simplified**

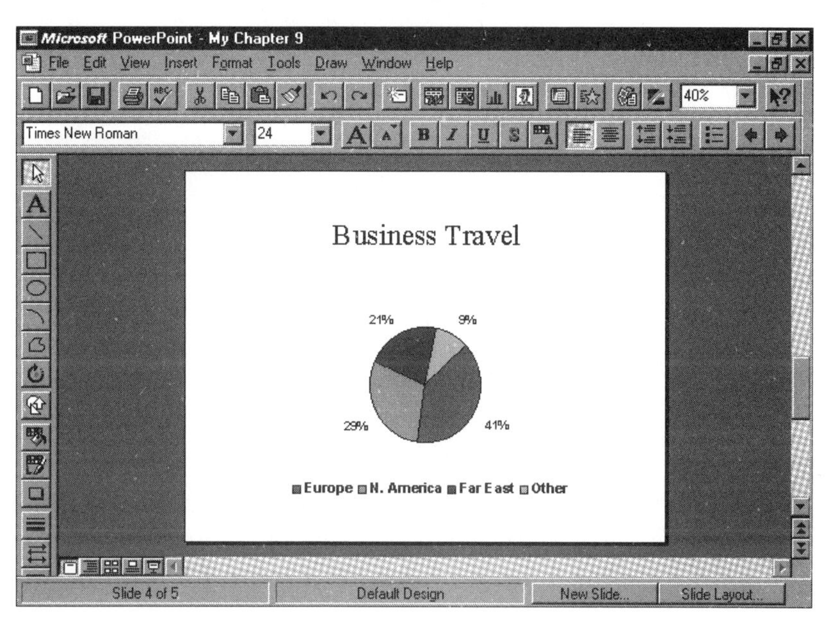

- Choose the pie-chart format you want.
- Click on *OK.* Any data you enter in the datasheet will be formatted as a pie chart.

CLEARING DATA FROM THE DATASHEET

As you know, when you create a chart, Microsoft Graph always opens with sample data and a chart based on that data. In Chapter 8, you learned how to edit the sample data to create your own chart. In some cases, you will want to clear all the data from the datasheet and enter your own, instead of editing the sample data.

Here's the general procedure for clearing all data from the datasheet:

- In the datasheet, click on the corner *control box* to select all the cells in the datasheet.
- Choose *Edit, Clear* and select the clear option you want: *All* clears both the data and the number format; *Contents* clears only the data; *Formats* clears only the number format, leaving the data intact.

- Click on *OK.* All the data is cleared from the datasheet.

If you are not running PowerPoint on your computer, please start it now. Close all open presentations. Let's clear the data from the datasheet:

1. Open **Chapter 9** from your Power Work folder.
2. Add a new graph slide (slide 3) to the end of the presentation. (Click on **New Slide**, click on the **Graph** autolayout, and click on **OK**.)
3. Add the title **Business Travel**.
4. Double-click on the **Graph** object. The Graph window opens, displaying the sample data and chart.
5. Move the datasheet up so that the chart is visible (place the mouse pointer on the Datasheet title and drag upward).
6. Click on the corner **control box** to select all the data. Figure 9.2 shows the corner control box.

Figure 9.2 **The corner control box**

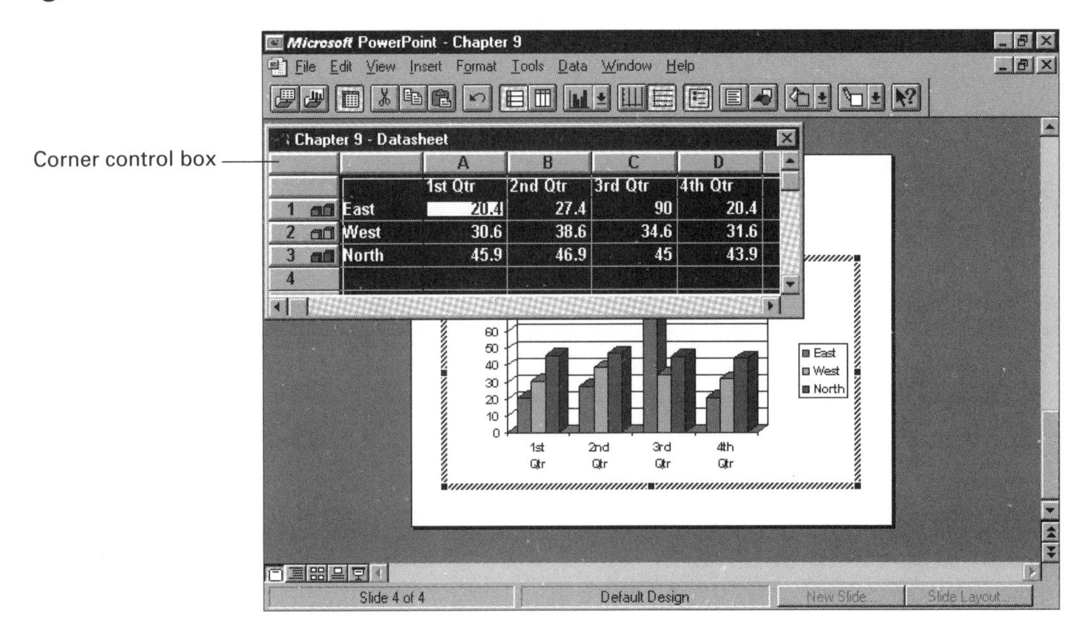

7. Choose **Edit, Clear, Contents** to clear only the data. If you want to remove only the number format, choose Clear, Formats; to clear both data and number format, choose Clear, All.
8. Click anywhere on the datasheet to deselect the cells, and observe your datasheet. It should match that shown in Figure 9.3.
9. Observe the Chart window. When you clear the datasheet, there is no information available for Graph to plot.

Figure 9.3 **The empty datasheet**

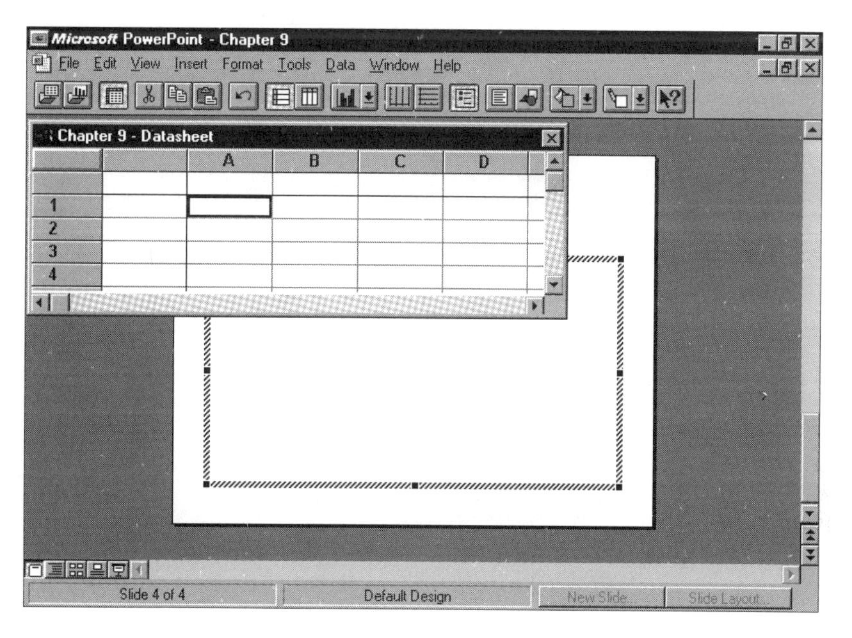

ENTERING DATA FOR THE PIE CHART

As you learned in Chapter 8, a data series is a group of related values, such as all the sales for a particular region. Each individual piece of data in a series is called a data point. In a pie chart, each data point is represented by a *data marker*, or slice of the pie.

A pie chart always consists of one data series and as many data points as necessary. The pie chart you are creating has one data series with four data points.

Let's enter the labels for the pie chart:

1. Select the heading cells for row 1 through row 4, (refer to Figure 9.4). Remember, the top unnumbered row of the datasheet is reserved for labels. If you accidentally place data there, it will not be plotted in the chart.

Figure 9.4 **The completed labels**

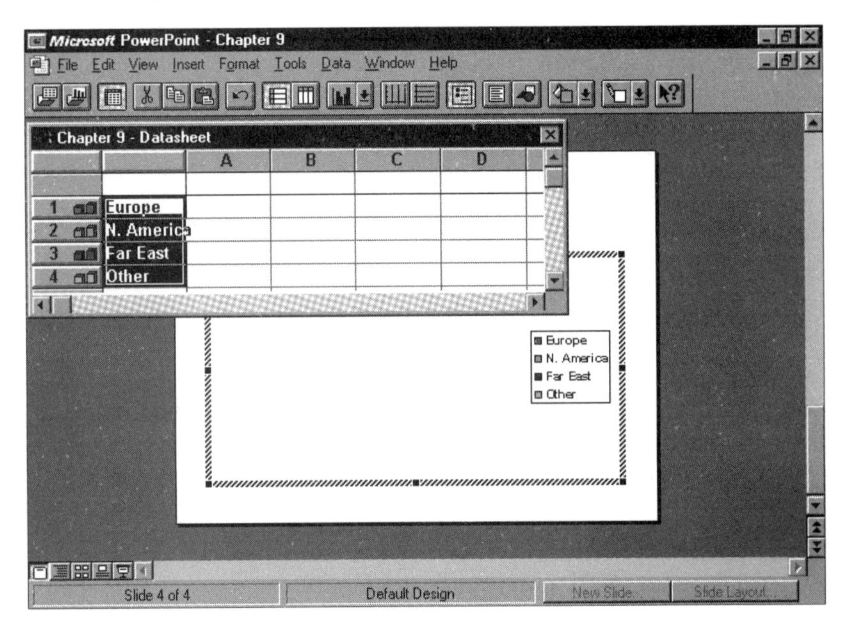

2. Starting in row 1 (the second row of the datasheet), enter the following data, pressing **Enter** after each label:

   Europe

   N. America

   Far East

   Other

PRACTICE YOUR SKILLS

Let's complete the data for the pie chart:

1. Starting in row 1, enter the following values in column A:

   551

   406

   295

   130

   (Hint: Select the four cells and press **Enter** after each entry.)

2. Observe your chart and datasheet. They should match those shown in Figure 9.5. Graph plots the data as a column chart, the default chart type.
3. Save the file as **My Chapter 9**.

Figure 9.5 **The completed datasheet and default chart**

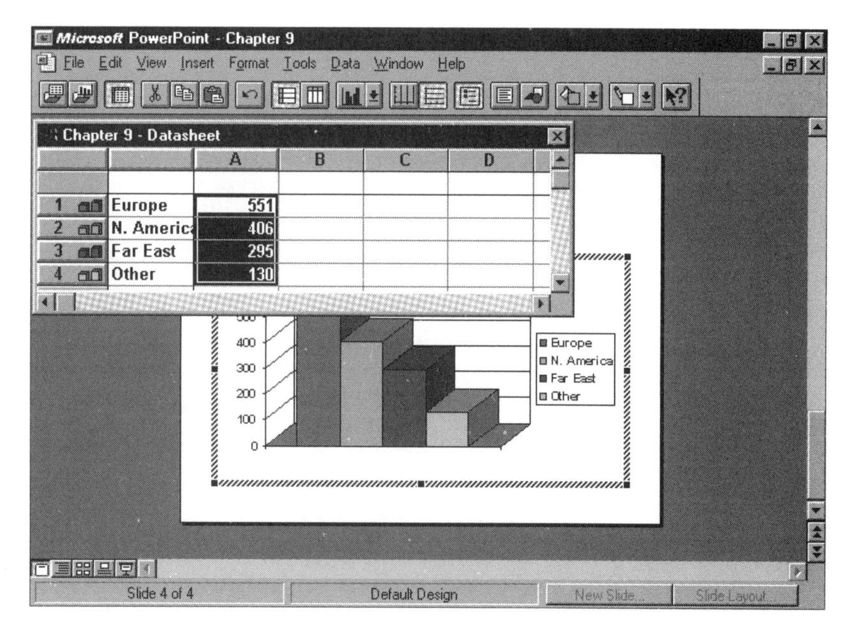

CHANGING THE CHART TYPE

You can use the Format, AutoFormat command to change the chart type from the default column chart. When you choose a chart type from the Galleries list in the AutoFormat dialog box, Graph displays a gallery of chart formats from which to choose.

Figure 9.6 illustrates the pie-chart styles available in the Chart Gallery for pie charts.

Figure 9.6 **The AutoFormat dialog box**

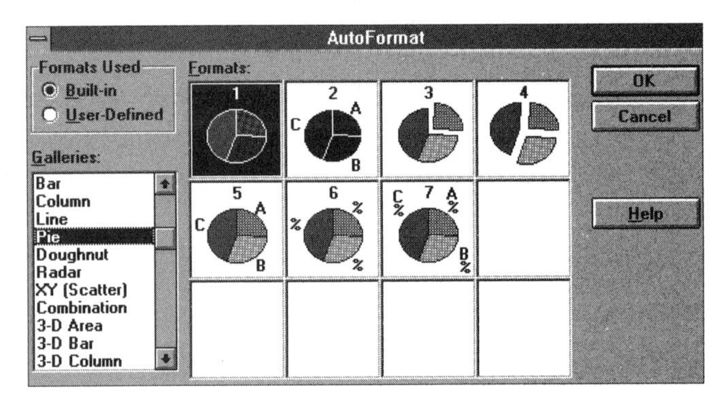

Here's the general procedure for changing the chart type:

- Choose *Format, AutoFormat.*
- Select a chart type from the Galleries list.
- Select the chart format of your choice.
- Click on *OK.*

Let's change the chart type:

1. Choose **Format, AutoFormat** to open the AutoFormat dialog box.
2. Choose **Pie** from the Galleries list (as shown in Figure 9.6). The pie-chart formatting options are displayed.
3. Click on pie style **6** (the format for a colored pie chart with labeled percentages) to choose that chart format.
4. Click on **OK**. The bar chart changes to a pie chart.

5. Observe the chart—but don't panic. Your chart should have one visible data marker and match that shown in Figure 9.7. In the next section, you will fix the chart so that you can see all the data markers.

Figure 9.7 **The pie chart with one data marker**

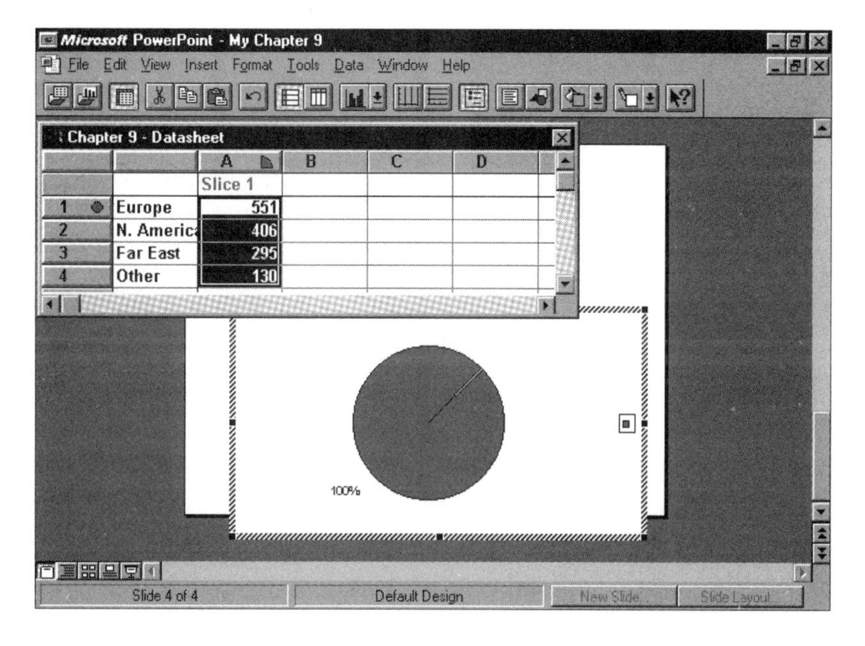

CHANGING THE DATA SERIES

Earlier in this chapter, you learned that a pie chart consists of only one data series and as many data points as necessary. Microsoft Graph provides you with two data-series options: You can enter data series into the datasheet either in rows or in columns.

The *Series setting* (rows or columns) affects the way Graph plots your chart. If you enter your data in columns but have the Series option set to rows, then Graph plots the chart using each row as a separate data series. A pie chart can have only one data series, so if you have the Series option incorrectly set, Graph will plot the first data point as the entire series. A pie chart with one pie slice? No thanks. You need to make sure that Graph reads the data series as you intend.

You can create a pie chart by using either Series setting, as long as you understand these rules:

- If the series is set to rows, the first row of the datasheet, starting with the second cell, is reserved for legend labels. The second row, starting with the second cell, starts the data to be plotted.
- If the series is set to columns, the first column of the datasheet, starting with the second cell, is reserved for legend labels. The second column, starting with the second row, starts the data to be plotted.

So, if you create a pie chart and find that only one data point has been plotted, check the Series option before you panic.

Let's change the Series option for your pie chart:

1. Observe the datasheet. The whole-pie symbol to the right of row 1 control box indicates that Graph is set to read each row of the datasheet as a separate data series. Because a pie chart has only one data series, Graph can plot only the data for Europe. This is why our pie chart shows only one data marker (or slice).
2. Choose **Data, Series In Columns** to change the datasheet so that Graph reads each column as a data series.
3. Observe the datasheet. The pie-slice symbols to the right of the row numbers in the row control boxes indicate that the Series In Columns option is selected.
4. Observe the chart. It shows all four data markers and should match that shown in Figure 9.8.

CHANGING LEGEND OPTIONS

The legend works as a key to identify the data markers or slices in your pie chart. By default, when you create a chart, Graph displays the legend somewhere on the right side of your Chart window. It has a thin line border and the text is 18 point. You can change any of these defaults.

Here's the general procedure for changing the legend options:

- From Microsoft Graph, select (click on) the legend in the Chart window.

Figure 9.8 **The pie chart with data in columns**

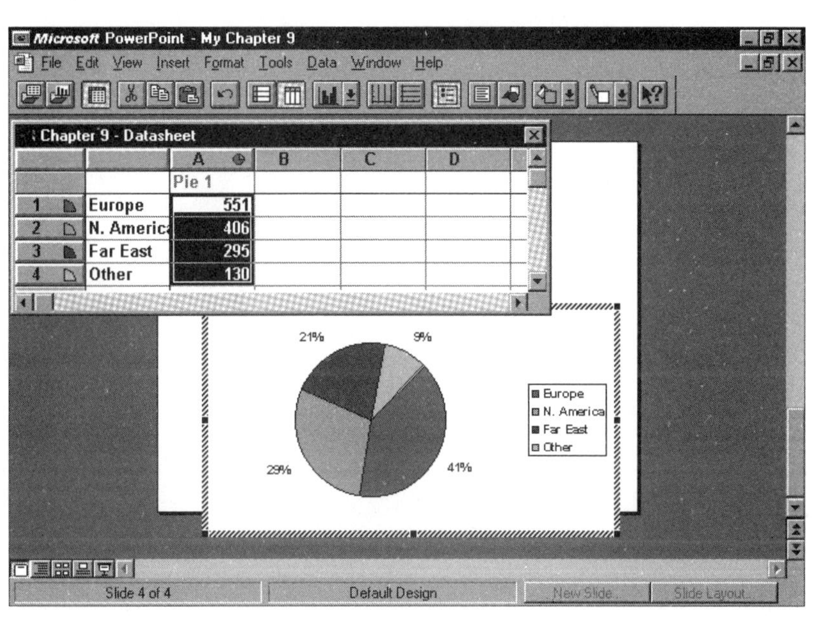

- Double-click on the legend in the Chart window. The *Format Legend* dialog box opens.
- Select the border and area options desired.
- Click on *Font* to change the format of the legend text.
- Click on *Placement* to reposition the legend.
- Click on *OK.*

Let's change the legend options:

1. Close the datasheet, if necessary.
2. Observe the legend. It is on the right side of your chart.
3. Double-click on the legend to open the Format Legend dialog box. This dialog box includes options to change the pattern, font, and placement of the legend (as shown in Figure 9.9).
4. Under Border, choose **None** to remove the border around the legend.

Figure 9.9 **The Pattern options in the Format Legend dialog box**

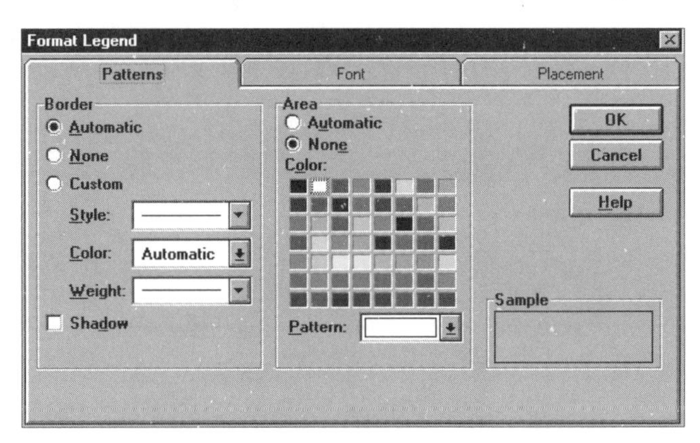

5. Click on **Font** to display the font options (as shown in Figure 9.10).
6. From the Size list box, select **20**.
7. Click on **Placement** to display the Placement options.
8. Select **Bottom** to position the legend at the bottom of the chart.

Figure 9.10 **Font options in the Format Legend dialog box**

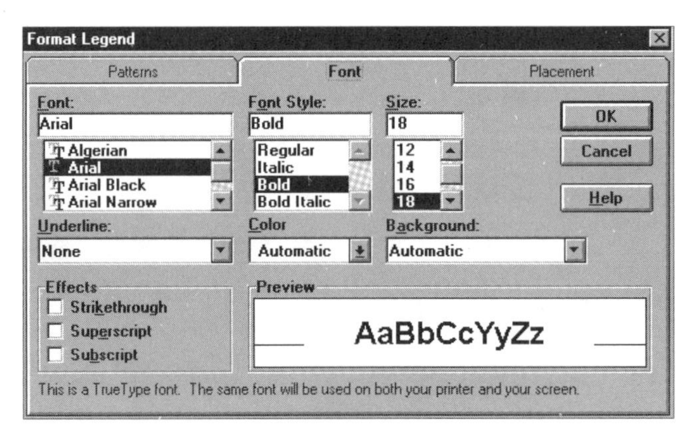

9. Click on **OK**. The border around the legend is removed, the text is slightly larger, and the legend appears at the bottom of the chart.
10. Select the legend and center it under the chart, if necessary.
11. Return to the presentation (click anywhere on the slide, except on the chart).
12. If necessary, center the chart on the slide (use the guides to center the chart).
13. Deselect the chart and compare your slide to that shown in Figure 9.11.
14. Save the file.

Figure 9.11 **The pie chart with formatted legend**

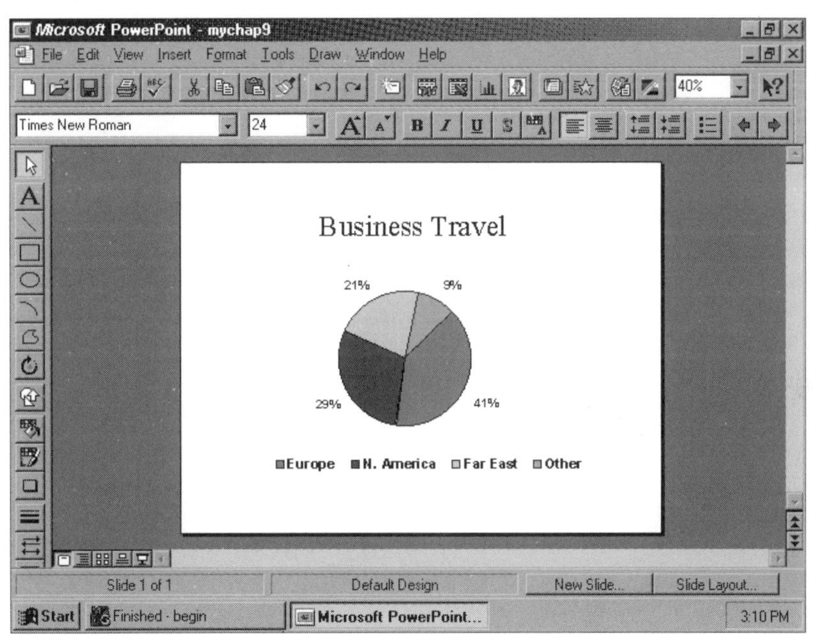

ENHANCING A PIE CHART

If a plain pie chart looks great in a presentation, think how much nicer a customized pie chart will look. As with everything in PowerPoint, there is a lot you can do to enhance your pie chart. For example, you can add emphasis to certain slices either by separating them from the rest of the chart or by recoloring them.

EXPLODING A PIE CHART

One way to enhance your pie chart is by *exploding*, or dragging away from the pie, one or more sections. If there is a particular piece of data that you want to emphasize, you can explode the pie slice representing that data. For example, if the data representing European sales is the most important part of your pie chart, you can drag the Europe slice away from the pie chart to draw attention to it.

You can explode as many slices as you want to; in fact, you can explode *all* the slices.

Here's the general procedure for exploding a pie-chart slice:

- Open Microsoft Graph.
- Click on the chart. Handles appear around the chart.
- Click on the desired slice of the pie. Handles appear around the slice.
- Place the mouse pointer on the slice.
- Press and hold the mouse button.
- Drag the slice away from the pie.
- Release the mouse button.

Now let's explode the Europe slice in your pie chart:

1. Double-click on the chart to reopen Microsoft Graph.
2. Close the datasheet, if necessary.
3. Click on the chart to select it.
4. Click on the **Europe** pie slice (41%). Handles appear around the pie slice, indicating that it is selected.
5. Place the mouse pointer on the **Europe** pie slice and drag the slice out slightly. Your chart should match that shown in Figure 9.12.
6. Return to the presentation to update the chart (click anywhere on the presentation window).
7. Deselect the chart.
8. Save the file.

Figure 9.12 The exploded pie in the Graph window

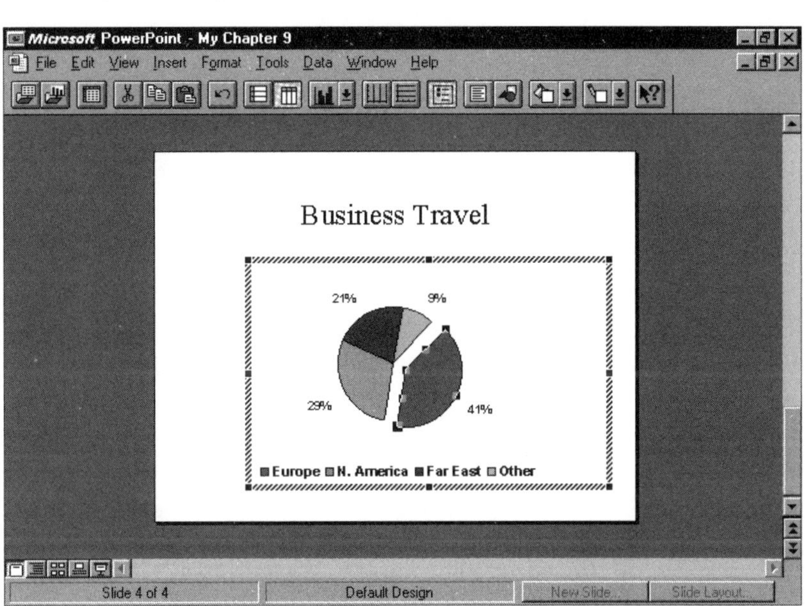

CREATING A DOUBLE-EXPLODED PIE CHART

You can fit more than one pie chart on a slide, which can be useful when you want to compare data. For example, in the first part of this chapter, you created a pie chart showing the breakdown of Global Travel business travelers by region and exploded the European region from the pie. You might want to create another pie chart to display detailed information about this European pie slice.

When you create a double-exploded pie chart, you place two charts on one slide. The first chart gives an overview; for example, the number of business travelers by region. The second chart then shows a breakdown of one section of the first pie chart. To continue our example, if Europe accounts for 41 percent of business travelers, then a second pie chart might show the breakdown of the European countries to which business people travel.

COPYING CHARTS

You can create two charts from scratch on the same slide. However, if you have already created one or both of the charts you want to use in the double-exploded pie, why do all that work again? You can copy an existing chart and paste it on another slide.

Here's the general procedure for copying a chart:

- Select the chart you want to copy.
- Choose *Edit, Copy* to place a copy of the chart on the Clipboard.
- Move to or add the slide on which you want to place a copy of the chart.
- Choose *Edit, Paste.* A copy of the chart is pasted on the new slide.
- Double-click on the chart to edit it, if necessary.

Let's begin creating a double-exploded pie chart:

1. Add a new graph slide (slide 5) to the end of the presentation.
2. Add the title **European Travel**.
3. Delete the Graph object (click once on the **Graph** object and press **Del**).
4. Move to slide 4. This slide displays the pie chart you just created.
5. Select the pie chart and choose **Edit, Copy** to place a copy of the chart on the Clipboard.
6. Move to slide 5 and choose **Edit, Paste** to paste the pie chart on the new slide.
7. Observe the slide. The pie chart you copied from slide 4 now appears on slide 5. You will use this pie chart as the basis for a double-exploded pie chart.
8. Observe the legend. It stretches across the bottom of the screen and takes up a lot of space. It's a good idea to condense the legend before you add another chart to the slide.
9. Double-click on the chart to open the Microsoft Graph window.
10. Close the datasheet, if necessary.
11. Click on the legend to select it; then choose **Format, Selected Legend**.

12. Click on **Font**; choose **14** in the Size list and **Regular** in the Font Style list.
13. Click on **Placement** and select **Left** to move the legend to the left of the chart.
14. Click on **OK** to apply the formatting changes to the legend.
15. Drag the legend to the upper-left corner of the chart window, so it's even with *21%*.
16. Return to the presentation to update the chart.

RESIZING CHARTS

Right now, the first pie chart is taking up most of the workspace on your slide. In order to fit a second chart on the slide, you need to resize the first chart. There are three ways you can do this:

- *Cropping* changes the frame, but not the chart. In other words, you eliminate the empty white space around the chart without changing the size of the chart itself.
- *Scaling* resizes the entire chart window proportionally.
- *Resizing* changes the size of the chart, but not necessarily proportionally.

If you are trying to place two charts on one slide, it is a good idea to try cropping the charts before you resize them.

Here's the general procedure for cropping a chart:

- Select the chart in Slide view.
- Choose *Tools, Crop Picture*. The mouse pointer turns into a Cropping tool.
- Place the Cropping tool over one of the selection handles so that you can see the handle through the hole in the center of the Cropping tool.
- Drag the Cropping tool up or down and over until you cannot see any extra white space.
- Repeat the above steps as necessary to remove white space from the rest of the chart.

Use this option when you want to reduce the white space around a chart without affecting the size of the chart.

Here's the general procedure for scaling the chart:

- Select the chart in Slide view.
- Choose *Draw, Scale.*
- Type the percentage by which you want to scale the chart.
- Click on *OK.* The chart is scaled by the percentage you indicated.

Scale the chart when you want to resize the chart proportionally.

Here's the general procedure for resizing the chart manually:

- Select the chart in Slide view.
- Place the mouse pointer on one of the selection handles.
- Drag the selection handle to resize the chart.

If you need to resize the chart, but it doesn't matter if you keep the original proportions, use the above option.

Let's crop the pie chart:

1. Click on the pie chart to select it.
2. Choose **Tools, Crop Picture**. The mouse pointer becomes a Cropping tool, as shown in Figure 9.13.

Figure 9.13 **The Cropping tool**

3. Place the center of the Cropping tool over the lower-right selection handle of the chart.
4. Press and hold the **left mouse button**. The mouse pointer becomes a 90-degree angle and a dotted line appears around the chart.
5. Drag in and up until the dotted outline is just below and to the right of the chart (refer to Figure 9.14).
6. Release the mouse button. The chart is redrawn with the new, smaller frame.
7. Place the Cropping tool on the upper-left selection handle.

Figure 9.14 **Cropping the chart**

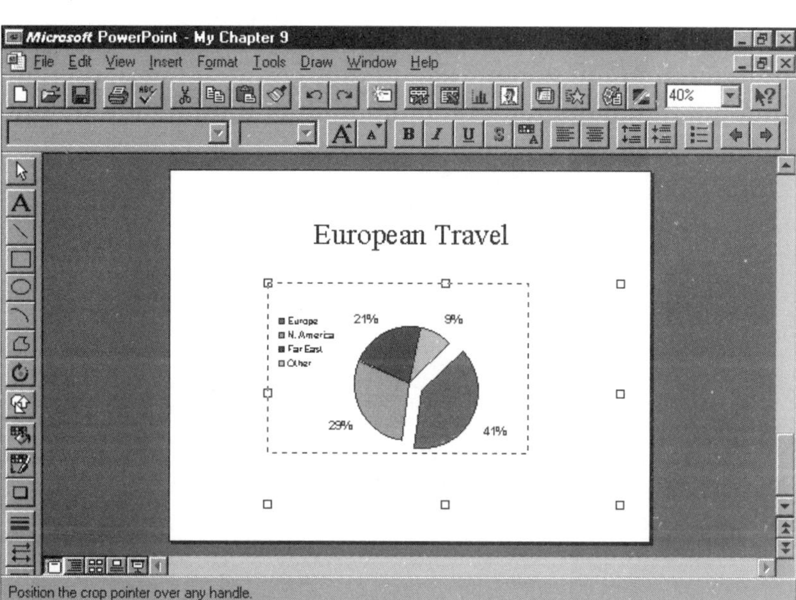

8. Press the **left mouse button** and drag in and down until the dotted outline is just above and to the left of the chart.
9. Release the mouse button and observe the slide. The chart now takes up less work space.
10. Click anywhere to deselect the chart.

Now let's move the chart to the left edge of the slide:

1. Select the chart.
2. Place the mouse pointer on the chart and drag it to the left edge of the slide. Refer to Figure 9.15 to position the chart.
3. Save the file.

ADDING A SECOND CHART TO THE SLIDE AND DELETING THE LEGEND

You don't have to display the legend as part of your chart. In fact, if you choose one of the pie-chart styles that includes labels for each pie slice, you might not want to have a legend, too.

Figure 9.15 **The chart after resizing and moving**

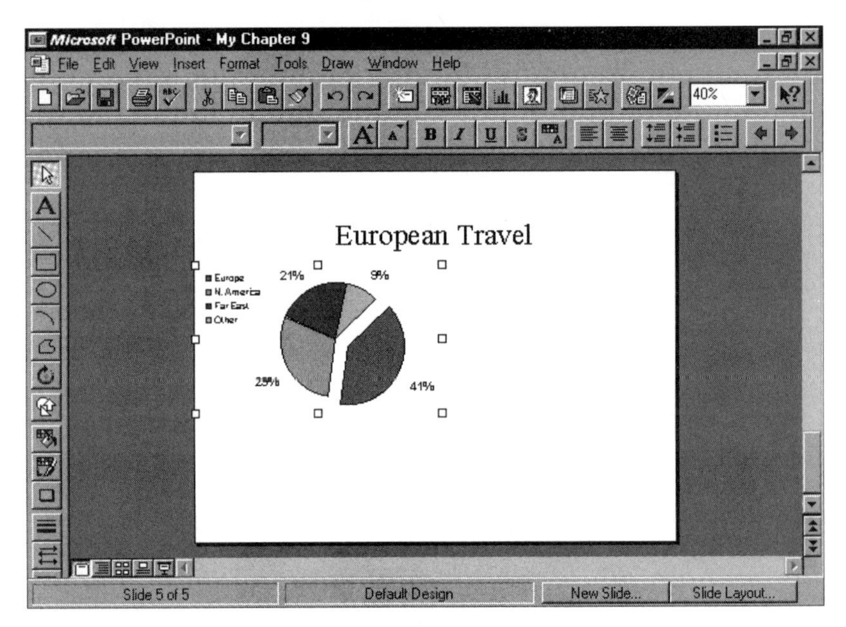

Here's the general procedure for deleting the legend from your chart:

- Start Microsoft Graph.
- Click on the *Legend* button on the toolbar.

Note: If you decide at a later date that you need the legend, you can display it again by clicking on the Legend button again.

1. Click on the **Insert Graph** tool to insert a second Graph object on the slide. Of course, this places it on top of the first chart, but don't worry about that, we'll move it later.

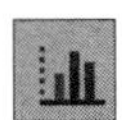

2. Double-click on the new **Graph** object to open Microsoft Graph, if necessary.
3. Move the datasheet to the upper-left corner of the window, if necessary. Then, clear the datasheet by clicking on the corner **control box** and choosing **Edit, Clear, Contents**.

4. Choose **Format, AutoFormat** to open the AutoFormat dialog box.
5. In the Galleries list, select **Pie** to display the pie chart formats.
6. Select pie-chart style **5** and click on **OK**; this creates a labeled pie chart when you enter data in the datasheet. You don't need to wait until you enter data to select the type of chart you want.
7. Choose **Data, Series in Columns**.
8. Click on the **Legend** button (the sixth button from the right on the toolbar) to delete the legend.

PRACTICE YOUR SKILLS

Let's enter data for the second pie chart:

1. Enter the following data in the datasheet:

Spain	**77**
Germany	**191**
England	**235**
Other	**48**

2. Compare your slide to that shown in Figure 9.16.
3. Return to the slide to update the chart.
4. Move the second chart to the lower-right corner of the slide.
5. Crop the excess white space from the second chart. (Hint: Use the **Tools, Crop Picture** command to select the Cropping tool.)
6. Choose **Draw, Scale** and scale the second chart to **80%**, then press **Enter**.
7. Move the chart to the lower-right corner of the slide again and compare your slide to that shown in Figure 9.17.
8. Save the file.

Figure 9.16 **The second pie chart**

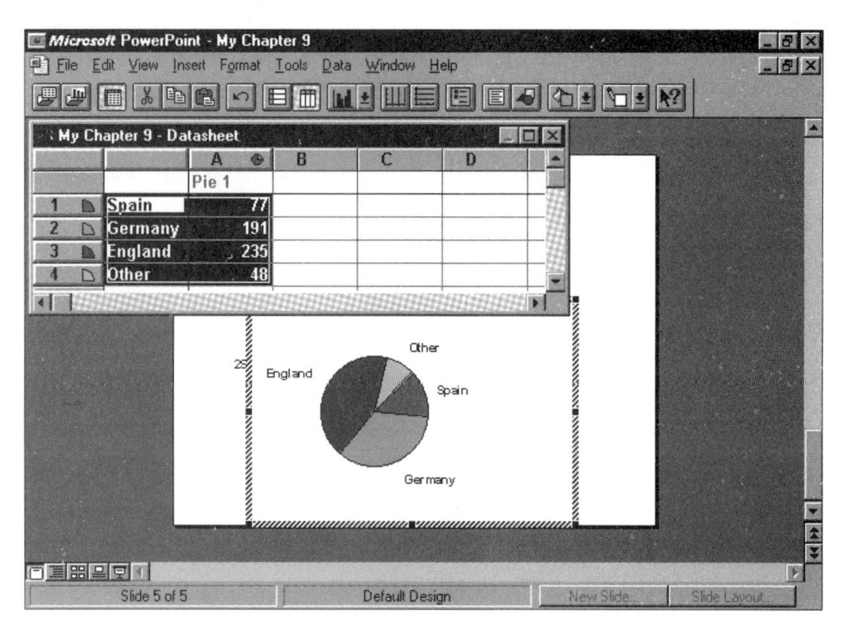

Figure 9.17 **The cropped, scaled chart**

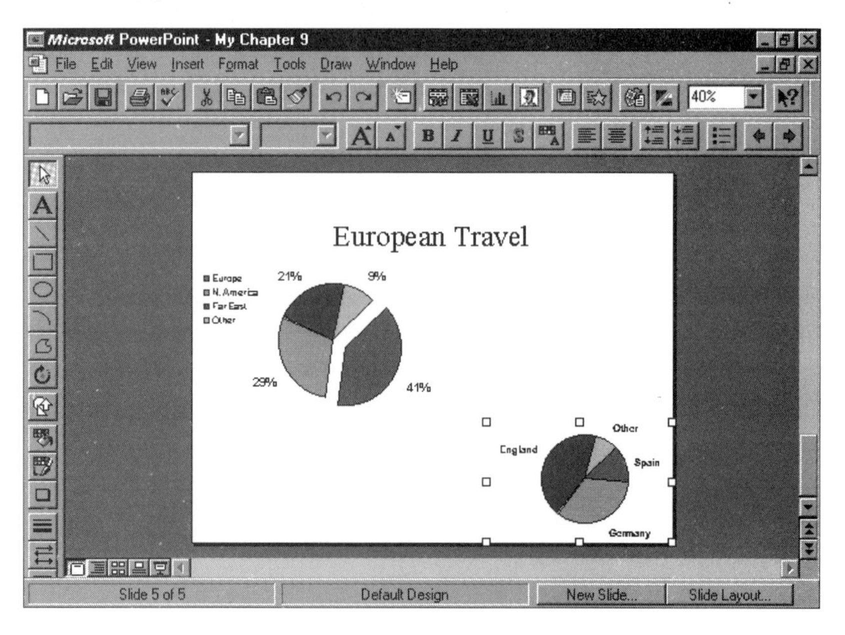

RECOLORING A PIE SLICE

You have two pie charts on your slide and they look fine, but both use the default colors, so your audience might find it difficult to distinguish between them. You can recolor the second pie to indicate its relationship to the first pie. For example, if the second pie shows a breakdown by country of the Europe pie slice, you might want to change the color of the second pie so that all the slices are the same color as the first pie's Europe slice. Then, you could change the patterns in the second pie to distinguish between those slices.

Here's the general procedure for recoloring a chart:

- Double-click on the chart to open Microsoft Graph.
- Select the pie slice you want to recolor.
- Double-click on the pie slice to open the Format Data Point dialog box.
- From the Area box, select a color.
- From the Pattern drop-down list, select a pattern.
- Click on *OK.*

Let's recolor the second pie chart:

1. Double-click on the second pie chart to open Microsoft Graph and edit that chart.
2. Close the datasheet, if necessary.
3. Click on the chart and then click on the **Spain** pie slice to select it. The Spain pie slice is the same color as the European pie slice.
4. Double-click on the **Spain** pie slice in the Chart window to open the Format Data Point dialog box. This dialog box gives you several options for changing the color and pattern of the selected pie slice, as well as the style, color, and weight of the border. The Pattern and Color options work together to determine the pattern and color of the selected item.
5. Observe the Area box. The pattern and color are set to Automatic. If you return to the chart now, the chart colors will not change because they are already formatted with the automatic (default) colors.

6. Click on the **Pattern** drop-down list to display the available pattern options for the pie slice.
7. Select your desired pattern. Since the pie slice is already the same color as the European slice, you don't have to change the color.
8. Click on **OK** to close the Format Data Point dialog box and format the slice with the new pattern.
9. Double-click on the **Germany** pie slice.
10. Click on the **Pattern** drop-down list and select a pattern for your pie slice.
11. Select the color of the European slice (the first color from the left in the third row of the color palette) for the Germany pie slice.
12. Click on **OK**.

PRACTICE YOUR SKILLS

Let's finish customizing the pie chart:

1. Change the pattern and color for each of the other slices in the pie chart. Make sure that you use a different pattern and the color the color of the European slice for each pie slice. (Hint: You must select each slice of the pie to change it's pattern.)
2. Return to the slide to update the chart.
3. Save the file.

CREATING TITLES FOR PIE CHARTS

If you have two pie charts on a slide, it helps lessen the confusion if you add a title to each chart. As you know, you can add unattached text labels to charts in Slide view.

Here's the general procedure for adding a title to the chart in Slide view:

- Select the *Text* tool.
- Place the insertion point on the slide above the chart.
- Type a title for the chart.
- Select the title.

- Change the format, if necessary.
- Move the title to center it above the chart, if necessary.

Let's add a title to each of the pie charts:

1. Select the **Text** tool.
2. Place the insertion point on the slide above the first pie chart.
3. Type **Business Travel**.
4. Press **Esc** to select the text you typed in step 3.
5. Click on the **Underline** button (located on the toolbar, it displays as an underlined *u*) to underline the text.
6. Position the title above the Business Travel chart as shown in Figure 9.18. (**Note**: You might need to move the chart object down to make room for the title.)
7. Save the file.

Figure 9.18 **The double-exploded pie chart**

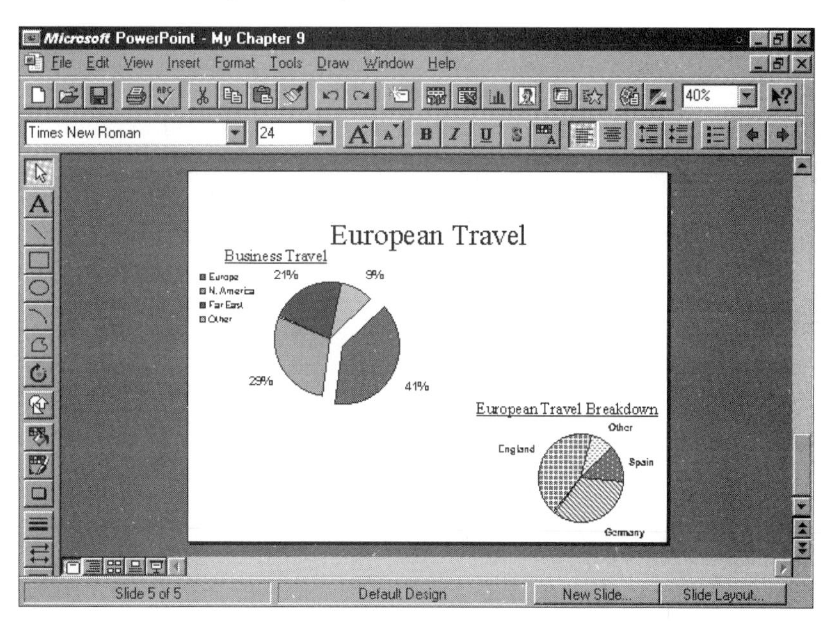

PRACTICE YOUR SKILLS

Let's create a title for the second chart:

1. Create the 24-point, underlined, Times New Roman title **European Travel Breakdown** for the second chart.
2. Refer to Figure 9.18 to position the title above the European Travel chart.
3. Save the file.
4. Close the presentation.

PRACTICE YOUR SKILLS

Wow, now you know everything you've ever wanted to about charts! Congratulations on making it this far. You've learned several important PowerPoint charting techniques in the past three chapters. The following group of activities gives you an opportunity to practice these techniques.

Note: In case you need to refresh your memory about a certain procedure, the relevant chapter number is included in parentheses at the end of each step.

Follow these steps to create the organization chart shown in Figure 9.19:

1. Create a new, blank presentation (Chapter 7).
2. Choose **Organization Chart** as the autolayout for the first slide in the new presentation.
3. Click on **OK**.
4. Add the title **Travel Literature** to the new slide (Chapter 7).
5. Open **Microsoft Organization Chart** (Chapter 7).
6. Type the following text into the organization chart (Chapter 7):

top box:	**Brochures**
second row, left:	**Entertainment**
second row, middle:	**Hotels/Motels**
second row, right:	**Tours**

Figure 9.19 **The completed organization chart**

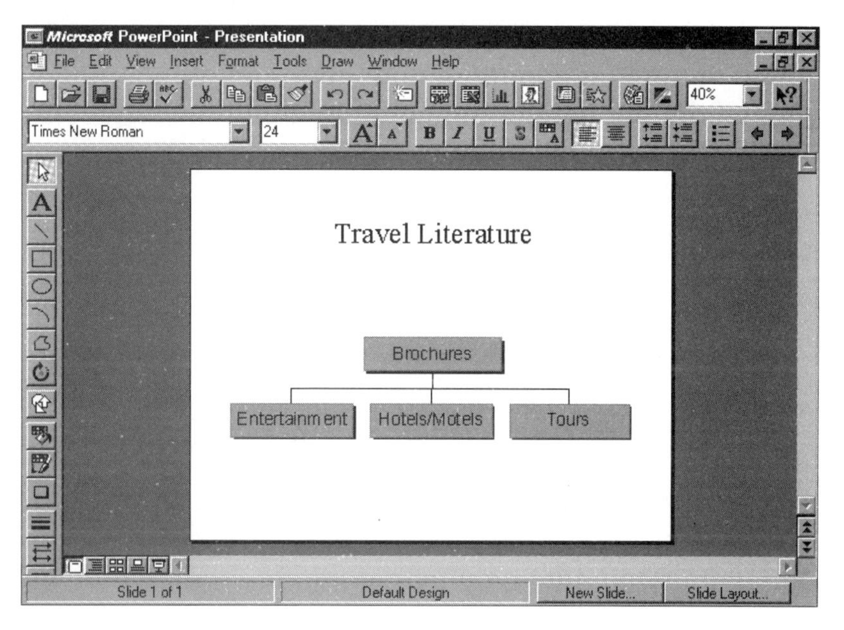

7. Select and delete the text *Type Title Here* from each of the organization chart boxes.
8. Change the color of the boxes (Chapter 7).
9. Add a drop shadow to each of the boxes (Chapter 7).
10. Return to the slide (Chapter 7). (Hint: Choose **File, Exit And Return To Presentation** and click on **Yes**.)
11. Save the presentation as **my skills 3** (Chapter 7).
12. Compare your slide with Figure 9.19.

Follow these steps to create the slide shown in Figure 9.20:

1. Add a new graph slide to the presentation (Chapter 7).
2. Add the title **Sales Report (in thousands)** (Chapter 7).
3. Start Microsoft Graph (Chapters 8 and 9).

Figure 9.20 **The completed column chart**

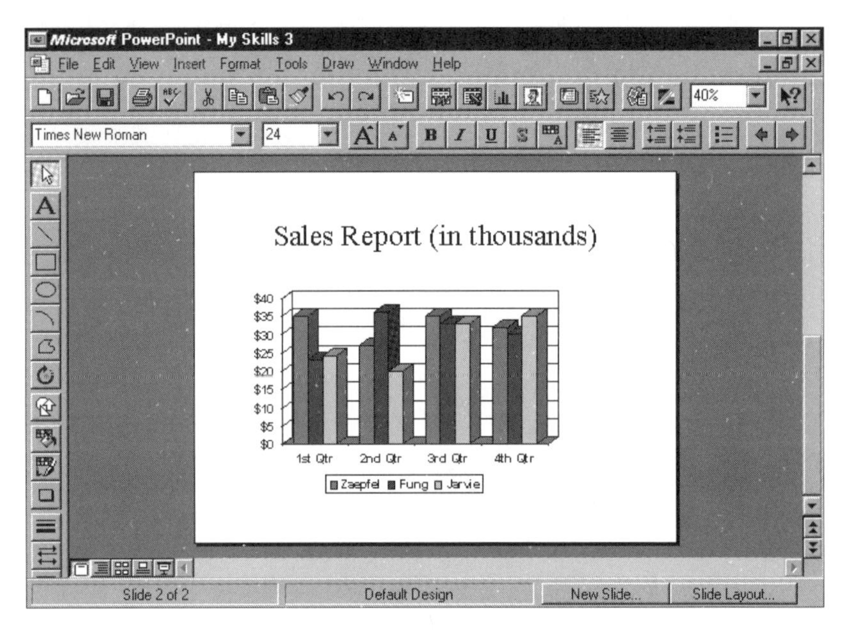

4. Enter the following labels in the first unlettered column (Chapter 8). (Hint: Begin entering the labels in the second row of the first column.)

   Zaepfel

   Fung

   Jarvie

5. Type in the following new data (Chapter 8):

	1st Qtr	**2nd Qtr**	**3rd Qtr**	**4th Qtr**
Zaepfel	**35**	**27**	**35**	**32**
Fung	**23**	**36**	**33**	**30**
Jarvie	**24**	**20**	**33**	**35**

6. Change the y-axis format to **$#,##0;_)($#,##0)** (Chapter 8).
7. Place the legend at the bottom of the chart (Chapter 8).

8. Return to the presentation to place the chart on the slide (Chapter 8).
9. Save the presentation (Chapter 2).
10. Compare the slide to Figure 9.20. (The y-axis values displayed will vary, depending on the size of the chart.)

Follow these steps to create the slide shown in Figure 9.21:

Figure 9.21 **The completed pie chart**

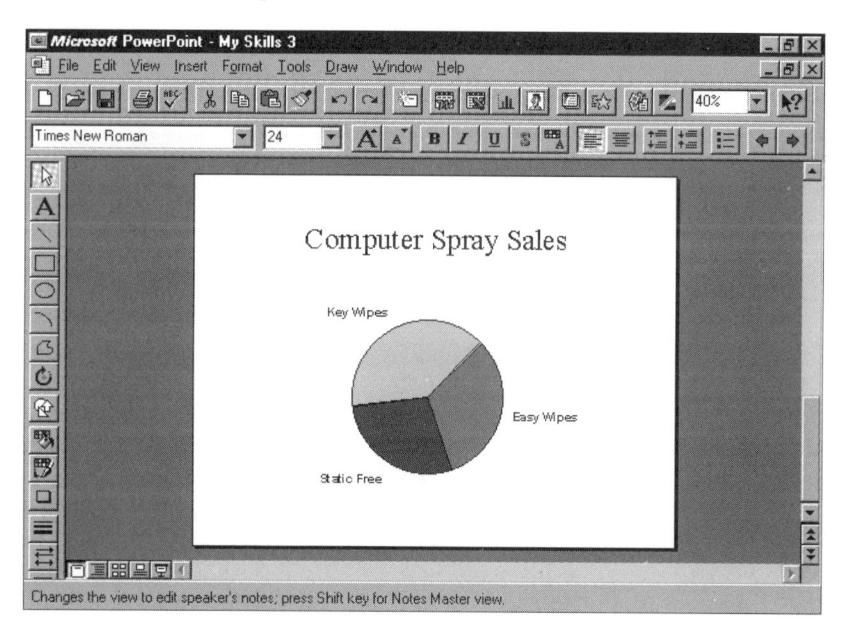

1. Add a new graph slide (slide 3) to the end of the presentation (Chapter 7).
2. Add the title **Computer Spray Sales** (Chapter 7).
3. Start Microsoft Graph (Chapters 8 and 9).
4. Change the Series setting to read in columns (Chapter 9).
5. Clear all the data from the datasheet (Chapter 9).

6. In the first column, add the following labels (Chapter 9):

   Easy Wipes

   Static Free

   Key Wipes

7. In the second column, add the following values (Chapter 9):

   82

   73

   101

8. Change the chart type to **Pie** and select style **5** (Chapter 9).
9. Remove the legend from the chart (Chapter 9).
10. Return to the presentation to place the chart on the slide (Chapter 8).
11. Save the presentation (Chapter 2).
12. Compare the slide to Figure 9.21.
13. Close the presentation (Chapter 7).

SUMMARY

In this chapter, you explored pie charts. You now know how to create a pie chart, how to clear the datasheet, how to set Microsoft Graph defaults, how to change the chart type, how to change the data series, and how to change legend options. You also learned how to explode a pie chart, how to create a double-exploded pie chart, how to copy a chart, how to resize a chart, and how to recolor a pie slice.

Here's a quick reference for the techniques you learned in this chapter:

Desired Result	**How to Do It**
Create a pie chart	Move to the slide to which you want to add the pie chart; click on the **Layout** button; choose the **Graph** autolayout; click on **OK**; add a title to the slide; double-click on the **Graph** object; choose **Format, AutoFormat**; select **Pie** from the Galleries list; choose the pie-chart format you want; click on **OK**
Clear data from the datasheet	Click on the corner **control box** to select all the cells; choose **Edit, Clear** and choose the clear option you want
Change the chart type	Choose **Format, AutoFormat**; in the Galleries list, select the chart type you want; select the chart format you want; click on **OK**
Change the legend options	Double-click on the legend; select the border and area options desired; click on **Font**; select the text format options desired; click on **Placement**; select the position; click on **OK**
Explode a slice from the pie chart	Click on the desired slice of pie; place the mouse pointer on the slice; press and hold the **left mouse button**; drag the slice away from the pie; release the mouse button
Copy a chart	Select the chart you want to copy; choose **Edit, Copy**; move to the slide on which you want to place the chart; choose **Edit, Paste**; double-click on the chart to edit it, if necessary

Desired Result	**How to Do It**
Crop a chart	Select the chart; choose **Tools, Crop Picture**; place the Cropping tool over one of the selection handles so that you can see the handle through the hole in the center of the Cropping tool; drag the Cropping tool up or down and over until you cannot see any extra white space; repeat the above steps as necessary to remove white space from the rest of the chart
Scale a chart	Select the chart; choose **Draw, Scale**; type the percentage by which you want to resize the chart; click on **OK**
Resize a chart	Select the chart; place the mouse pointer on one of the selection handles; drag the handle to resize
Delete the legend from a chart	Open Microsoft Graph; click on the **Legend** button
Recolor a chart	Open Microsoft Graph; select the pie slice you want to recolor; double-click on the pie slice; select a color; select a pattern from the Pattern drop-down list; click on **OK**
Add a title to the chart in Slide view	Select the **Text** tool; place the insertion point on the slide; type a title; press **Esc**; change the format and move the title to center it above the chart, if necessary

In the next chapter, you'll further explore templates and slide masters. You will learn how to apply a template to a presentation, how to change the background color of a template, how to change chart colors in a template, how to create a logo for a template, how to insert slide numbers, how to remove background items from a slide, and how to apply a presentation as a template.

CHAPTER 10: ADVANCED TEMPLATES AND SLIDE MASTERS

Customizing a Template

The AutoContent Wizard

In Chapter 6, you learned that you can apply any one of PowerPoint's many design templates to your presentation. The *template* is a set of masters and a color scheme that give consistency. In this chapter, you will create your own template by customizing a PowerPoint template.

When you are done working through this chapter, you will know

- How to apply a design template to a presentation
- How to change the background color of a template
- How to change chart colors in a template
- How to create a logo for a template
- How to insert slide numbers
- How to remove background items from a slide
- How to use the AutoContent wizard

CUSTOMIZING A TEMPLATE

As you learned in Chapter 6, a design template consists of a set of slide masters and their color scheme. It includes all the basic elements—colors and formatting—that you need to create a presentation. You can use any of the design templates that come with PowerPoint as a basis for creating your own design template.

APPLYING A DESIGN TEMPLATE TO THE PRESENTATION

Before you can customize a PowerPoint design template, you have to apply one to your presentation.

To add a template to your presentation:

- Choose *Format, Apply Design Template* (or click on the *Apply Design Template* button).
- Move to the folder that holds the template you want to apply, if necessary.
- Select the template you want to apply to your presentation.
- Click on *Apply.*

If you are not running PowerPoint on your computer, please start it now. Close all open presentations. Let's apply a template to your presentation:

1. Open **Chapter 10** from your Power Work folder.

2. Save the file. It is a good idea to save your presentation before you apply a template. Then, if something goes wrong, you lose nothing but time.
3. Choose **Format, Apply Design Template** (or click on the **Apply Design Template** button in the Standard toolbar).
4. Move to the Presentation Designs folder, if necessary.
5. Scroll down and select **Metal Bar** in the Name list box.
6. Observe the preview box. Your screen should match that shown in Figure 10.1.

Figure 10.1 **The Apply Design Template dialog box with Metal Bar selected**

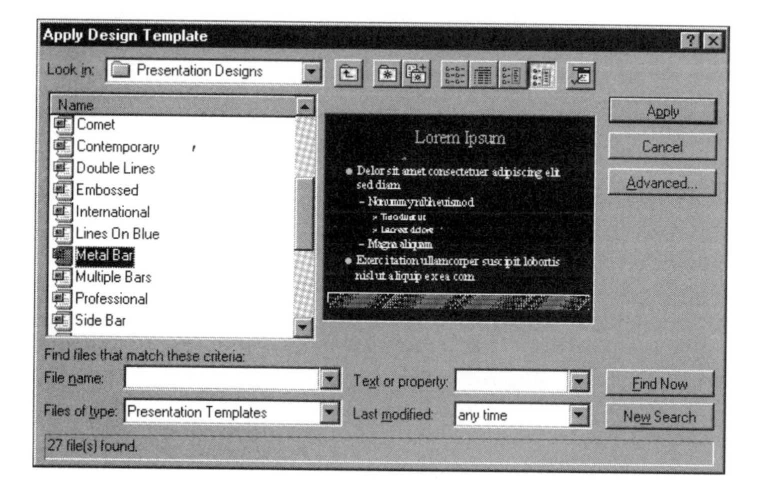

7. Click on **Apply** to apply the design template Metal Bar to Chapter 10. The Slide Master, Notes Master, Title Master, and Handout Master from the template become the masters for the Chapter 10 presentation. At this point, you need to be concerned only with the Slide Master. You will learn more about the other masters in Chapter 12.
8. Observe the screen message: *Charts are being updated with new color scheme.* Depending on the speed of your computer and the number of charts in your presentation, this might take quite a while, so relax and enjoy a cup of coffee. If after

five minutes the color scheme still has not been updated, you might need to turn off your computer and start again.

Note: Your computer might freeze up if you have several charts in the presentation to which you are applying a design template. If you reboot your computer and still are unable to apply a design template to the presentation, you may have to apply design templates to your presentations before you create charts.

9. Observe the screen. The slides are formatted with the color scheme and design of the Metal Bar design template.
10. Save the file as **My Chapter 10**.

MODIFYING THE DESIGN TEMPLATE

PowerPoint formats your presentation based on the formats saved in the Slide Master of the design template you apply. You can change any or all of the design template formats once you have applied the design template.

For example, if you like the look of a certain design template, but not its colors, you can apply the design template and then change the colors to ones that you find more appealing.

To change a color in a design template:

- Apply the design template you want to the presentation.
- Choose *Format, Slide Color Scheme*.
- Click on *Custom* to display the Custom tab.
- From the Scheme Colors box, select the color you want to change.
- Click on *Change Color* to open the Color dialog box.
- Select a new color from the grid, or you can click on the Custom tab and create your own color.
- Click on *OK* to return to the Color Scheme dialog box.
- Click on *Apply* to return to your presentation and register the color change only on the selected slide. Or click on *Apply To All* to change the color on all the slides in the presentation.

Let's change the color of the Title text:

1. Choose **Format, Slide Color Scheme** to open the Slide Color Scheme dialog box. Then click on **Custom** to display the Custom tab, if necessary.
2. Click on the title-text color (**yellow**) to select the color that you want to change.
3. Click on **Change Color** to open the Title Text Color dialog box.
4. Observe the dialog box, shown in Figure 10.2. As you learned in Chapter 5, the Color dialog box displays a grid of available colors and the current color of the selected item. You can also use the Custom tab to create a custom color.
5. In the color grid, click on **blue-green** (the fourth color from the left in the fourth row of the grid—refer to Figure 10.2).

Figure 10.2 **The Title Text Color dialog box with blue-green selected**

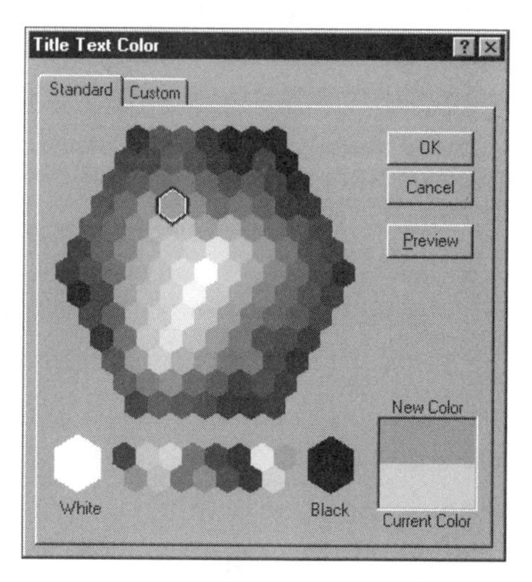

6. Click on **OK** to return to the Color Scheme dialog box. Blue-green replaces yellow as the scheme color for title text.
7. Observe the Apply and Apply To All buttons at the top right corner of the dialog box. If you click on Apply To All, PowerPoint recolors the title text for all the slides in your presentation. If you click on Apply, PowerPoint recolors the title text for the selected slide only.

8. Click on **Apply To All** to close the Color Scheme dialog box, return to the presentation, and recolor the title text on every slide.
9. Observe the slide. The title color is blue-green instead of yellow.
10. Save the file.

CHANGING THE DEFAULT CHART COLORS

In the last chapter, you learned that you can change colors for any or all of the data markers on a particular chart without affecting the default colors for the rest of the charts in your presentation. You can also change default colors for all of the charts in a presentation. If there is a particular color that you hate, this is the perfect opportunity to change that color in the Color Scheme dialog box so you will never be bothered by it again.

Data markers for charts are formatted using the fills and accent colors in the Scheme list. The first data marker uses the fill color, the second data marker uses the first accent color (the accent color below the fills color), the third data marker uses the second accent color (the accent color to the right of the fills color), and so on. To change default chart colors, you need only change any or all of these colors.

To change the chart color scheme:

- Choose *Format, Slide Color Scheme* to open the Color Scheme dialog box. Charts are formatted using the fills or accent colors in the Scheme Colors box.
- Select the color you want to change. It must be one of the fills or accent colors in the Scheme Colors box.
- Click on *Change Color.*
- Select the color you want from the color grid or click on the *Custom* tab and create your own color.
- Click on *OK.*
- Repeat the above steps as necessary until you are satisfied with the chart colors.

Let's change the color scheme for the charts:

1. Move to slide 2 and observe the column chart. Let's change the color of the first data marker.

2. Choose **Format, Slide Color Scheme**.
3. Move the **Color Scheme dialog box** to the left side of the screen until the Far East data series is visible. It's okay if the left side of the dialog box isn't visible.
4. Observe the chart. The first data marker is gold. This corresponds with the color in the Fills box. The second data marker is red. This corresponds with the first accent color in the scheme.
5. In the Color Scheme dialog box, select the fills color. Let's change it.
6. Click on **Change Color**.

You want to select a color that will work well with the background and the other chart colors. Red and yellow provide a good contrast, so let's change the first data marker to yellow and the second to red:

1. In the color grid, select **yellow** (the color immediately to the left of the selected color).
2. Click on **OK** and observe the new fills color.
3. In the Scheme Colors box, select the first accent color (below the fills color) and click on **Change Color**.
4. In the color grid, select **red** (the third color from the right in the second row from the bottom of the grid).
5. Click on **OK** and observe the new accent color.
6. Click on **Apply To All**. Using this method to change the chart colors changes the color on every chart in the presentation.
7. Observe the slide. The column chart now looks like a hot dog stand.

INSERTING SLIDE NUMBERS

You can use the View, Header And Footer command to add a slide number to one or all of the slides in your presentation.

To use the View, Header And Footer command to insert slide numbers:

- Move to the slide on which you want a slide number.
- Choose *View, Header And Footer.*

- Check *Slide Number.*
- Click on *Apply* to add a number to only the selected slide. Or click on *Apply To All* to add a number to all of the slides in the presentation.

PowerPoint displays the slide numbers in the lower-right corner of the slide.

Let's insert a slide number on each slide:

1. Choose **View, Header And Footer** to open the Header And Footer dialog box (see Figure 10.3).

Figure 10.3 **The Header And Footer dialog box**

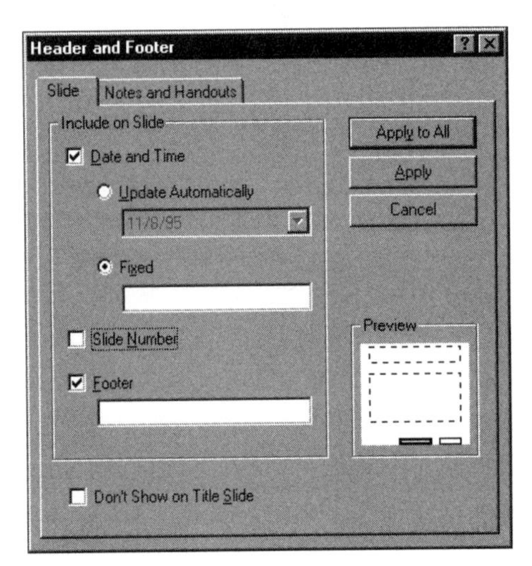

2. Observe the Slide tab. It includes several options for the slides in your presentation.
   - *Date and Time*—You can add either a date and time that will automatically update, or a fixed date and time. If you choose to include a fixed date and time, you must type the information in the Fixed text box, or nothing will appear on the slide.
   - *Slide Number*—This numbers the slides in your presentation. This number automatically updates when you insert, delete, or move slides.

- *Footer*—You can add text that appears on each slide. If you choose to add footer text, you must type the text in the Footer text box, or—you guessed it—nothing will appear on the slide.

3. Click on the **Slide Number** check box to select it.
4. Click on **Apply To All** to close the Header And Footer dialog box and add a slide number to each of the slides in your presentation.
5. Observe the slide. The slide number appears in the lower-right corner of the slide.
6. Save the file.

CREATING A LOGO

You can further enhance the appearance of your presentation by adding a logo to the slides. One effective way of customizing your presentations is to combine clip art, text, and drawn objects to create your own logos. You can create the logo directly on the Slide Master so that it appears in the same position on every slide.

Here's the general procedure for adding a logo to your presentation:

- Choose *View, Master, Slide Master.*
- Choose *Insert, Clip Art.*
- Click on *Yes* to add clip art to PowerPoint, if necessary. (**Note:** You only have to do this the first time you use clip art.)
- Choose a clip-art category from the Categories list box.
- Double-click on the clip-art slide you want to use.
- Choose *Draw, Scale* to resize the graphic, if necessary.
- Type a percentage by which you want to scale the clip art.
- Click on *OK.*
- Move the graphic to the appropriate place on your slide.
- Select the *Text* tool.
- Type the text for your logo.
- Select the *Selection* tool.
- Select and format the logo text, if necessary.

- Move the logo text to the appropriate place on your slide, if necessary.
- Move to Slide view to see the logo on the slide.

Let's create a logo to add to the Slide Master. First, we must copy the clip art on which we want to base the logo:

1. Choose **View, Master, Slide Master**. Because you want the logo to appear on every slide, you need to create it on the Slide Master.
2. Choose Insert, Clip Art.

   Note: If this is the first time you're using clip art, click on **Yes** to add the clip art to PowerPoint.
3. From the Categories list, select **Travel** to display the Travel clip art.
4. Select the ship's wheel on the third picture in the second row and click on **Insert**.

The ship's wheel that appears on your screen is not big enough for our purposes (as shown in Figure 10.4). It needs to be edited so that it can serve as part of the logo:

1. Select the clip art, if necessary, and choose **Draw, Scale**.
2. In the Scale dialog box, type **125** and click on **OK** to increase the ship's wheel to 125 percent of its original size.
3. Move the ship's wheel to the lower-left corner of the window (refer to Figure 10.5).

After you complete the graphic part of your logo, you might want to add text, such as the company name. Let's do that now:

1. Click on the **Date Area** box, press **Esc**, and then press **Del** to delete the Time And Date placeholder. Since we're not going to add the time and date to our presentation, we don't need this placeholder.
2. Select the **Text** tool and click below the horizontal bar at the bottom of the screen to place the insertion point.
3. Type **Global Travel**.
4. Press **Esc** to select the text you just typed.
5. Change the font size to **18** point.
6. Refer to Figure 10.6 to move the text below the ship's wheel.

Figure 10.4 **The ship's wheel before scaling**

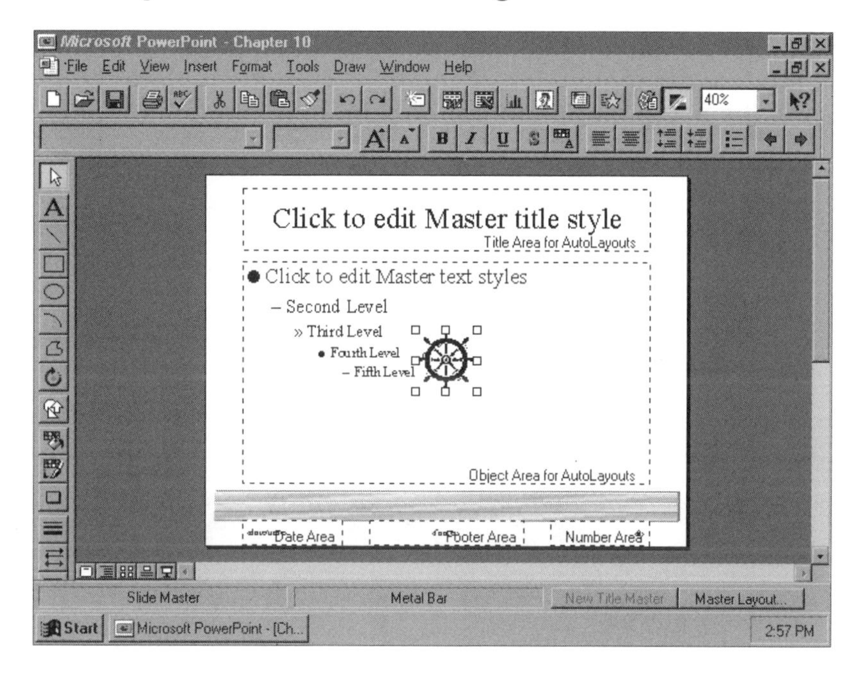

Figure 10.5 **Moving the clip art**

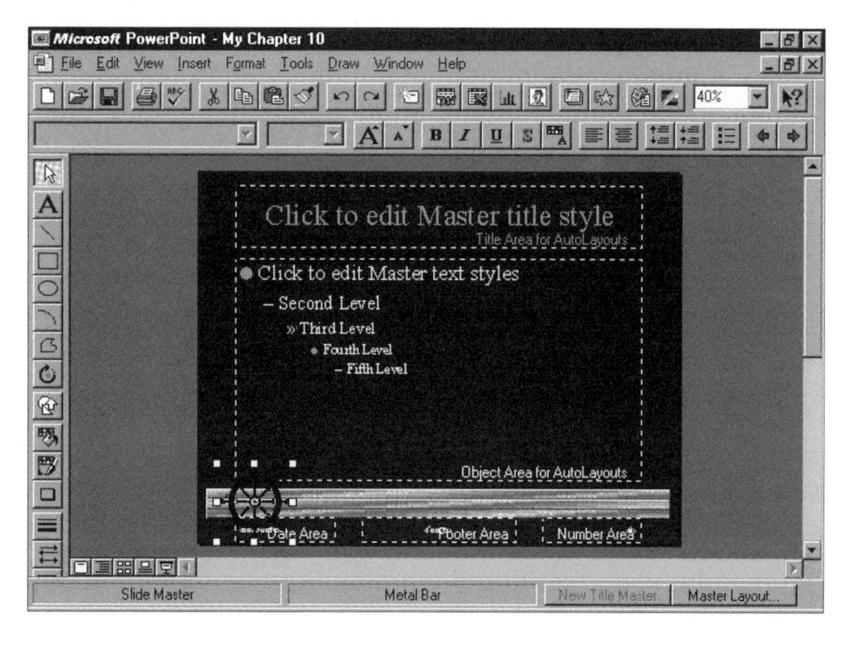

Figure 10.6 The Global Travel logo

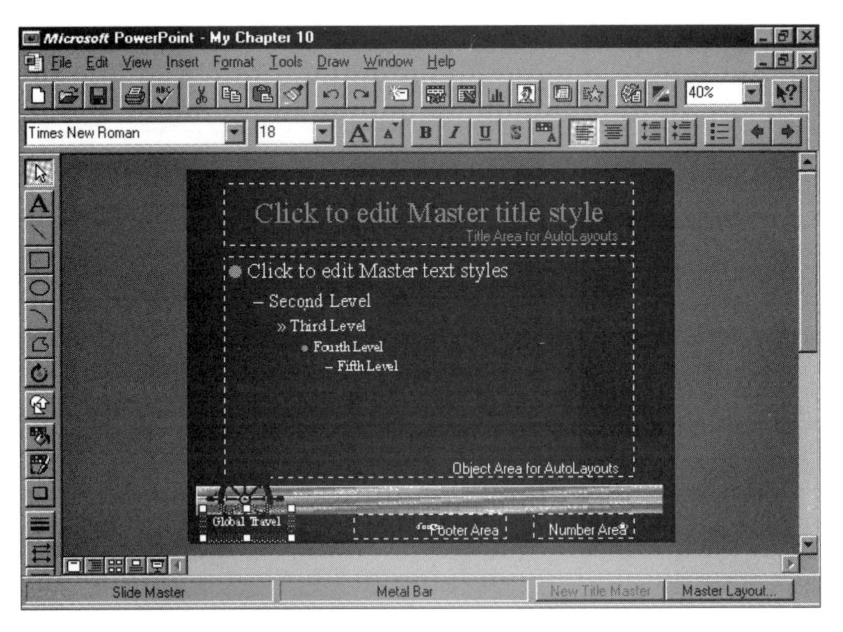

PRACTICE YOUR SKILLS

Let's make the logo match that shown in Figure 10.7:

1. Add a thin line border around the logo text. (Hint: You must select the text in order to change its attributes.)
2. Add a fill color and shadow to the logo. (Hint: Use the Format menu to add fill and shadow.)
3. Go to Slide view and view the logo on the first slide.
4. Save the file.

DELETING BACKGROUND ITEMS FROM A SLIDE

There may be times when you do not want background items to appear on an individual slide. For example, you might want to create a title slide to introduce the presentation, or you might create a chart that overlaps several of the background items. In these cases, you don't want the distraction of background items. When you turn off the display of background items on a slide, any objects placed on the Slide Master will be hidden.

Figure 10.7 **The completed logo**

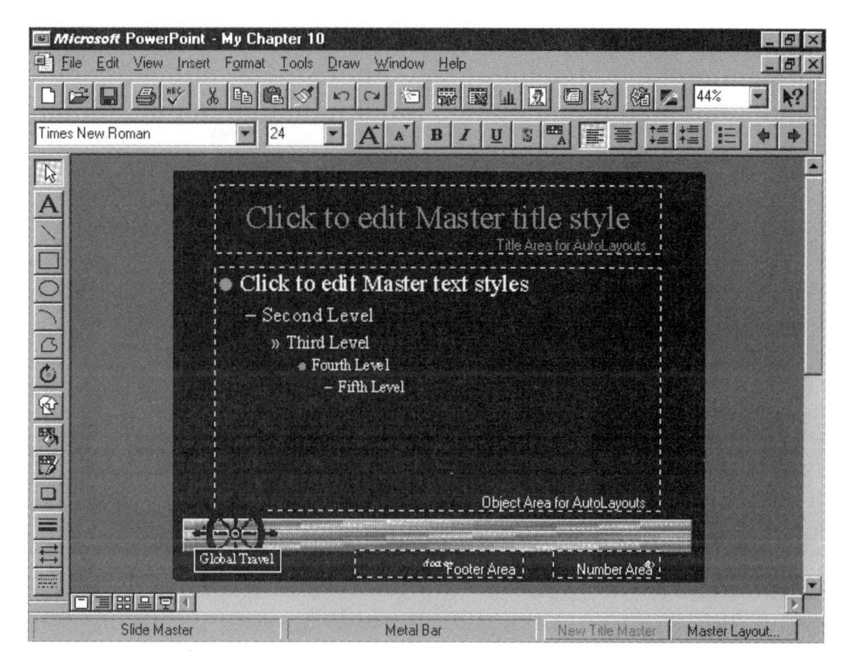

Here's the general procedure for turning off the display of background items on a slide:

- Move to the slide on which you want to hide the background items.
- Choose *Format, Custom Background.*
- Check *Omit Background Graphics From Master.*
- Click on *Apply.*

Here's the general procedure for returning the background items to the slide:

- Move to the slide on which you want to view the background items.
- Choose *Format, Custom Background.*
- Uncheck *Omit Background Graphics From Master.*
- Click on *Apply.*

Let's turn off the display of background items on the double exploded pie chart slide:

1. Move to slide 4 and observe it. The pie chart overlaps the bar at the bottom of the screen.
2. Choose **Format, Custom Background** to open the Custom Background dialog box, as shown in Figure 10.8.

Figure 10.8 **The Custom Background dialog box**

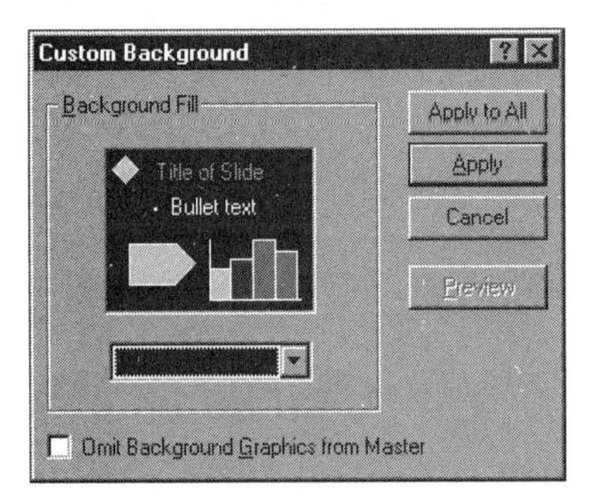

3. Check **Omit Background Graphics From Master**.
4. Click on **Apply** and observe the slide. The background items disappear from slide 4, allowing you to see both charts without the distraction of background graphics (see Figure 10.9).
5. Choose **Format, Custom Background** and observe that there is a check mark in the *Omit Background Graphics From Master* check box. To display the items once more, you would uncheck the check box and click on Apply.
6. Press **Esc** and move to slide 3. When you turn off the display of background items, it affects only the active slide. Therefore, you can still see the background items on this slide.
7. Move to slide 1.
8. Save and close the file.

Figure 10.9 **The slide with background items hidden**

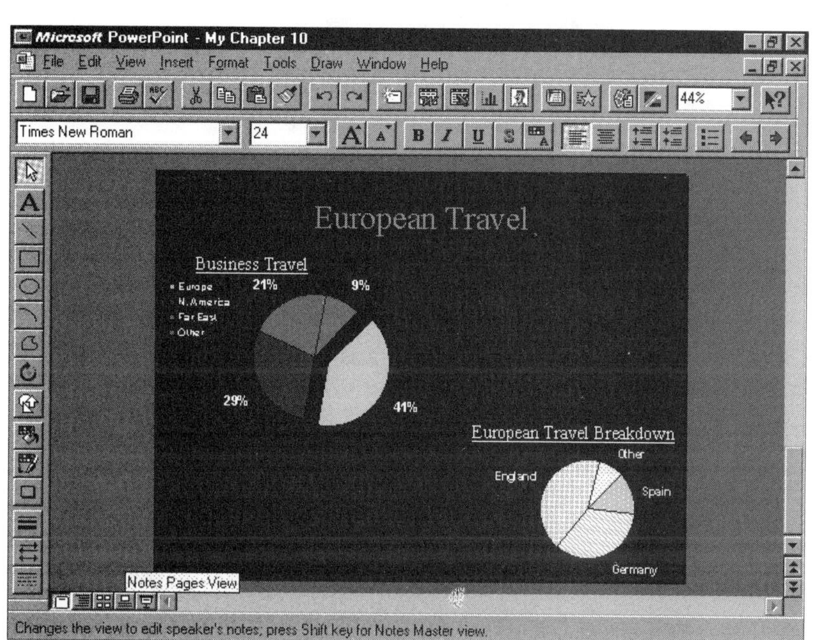

THE AUTOCONTENT WIZARD

A *wizard* is a guided approach to creating a presentation. It's PowerPoint's way of helping you to quickly create presentations with a professional look. Wizards can help you develop ideas and design the look of your presentation. All you do is answer the questions that appear on your screen.

The AutoContent wizard starts by creating a title slide, and then allows you to choose a presentation category. For example, you can choose between selling a product, service, or idea; recommending a strategy; or communicating bad news.

Once you have a title and subject, PowerPoint creates an outline for you to follow based on your answers to the wizard's prompts. You simply type your information over the placeholder text in the outline. Switch into Slide view to see your slides and change the slide layout.

Here's the general procedure to start the AutoContent wizard:

- Choose *File, New.*
- Click on *Presentations.*
- Click on *AutoContent Wizard.*
- Click on *OK.*
- Click on *Next.*
- Type the title slide information and click on *Next.*
- Select a presentation category and click on *Next.*
- Continue to answer the prompts and click on *Next* until you reach the last screen of the AutoContent wizard.
- Click on *Finish.*

Let's use the AutoContent wizard to create a new presentation:

1. Choose **File, New**.
2. Click on **Presentations** to display the Presentations tab.
3. Click on **AutoContent Wizard** and click on **OK** to start the AutoContent wizard. The first screen of the AutoContent Wizard dialog box opens (as shown in Figure 10.10).

Figure 10.10 The first screen of the AutoContent Wizard

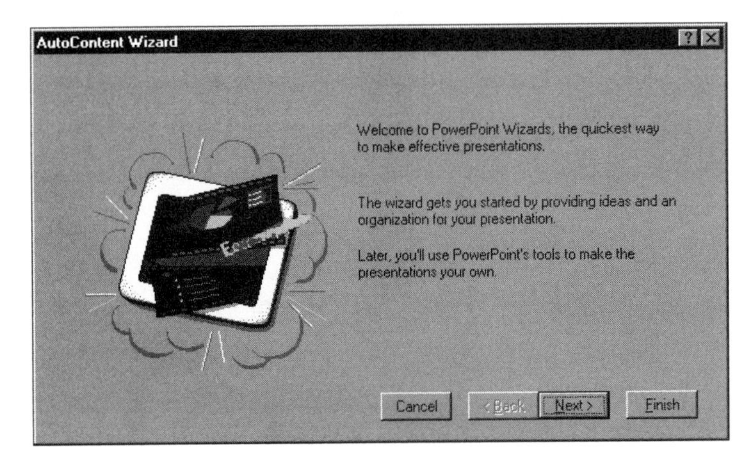

4. Click on **Next** to move to the second AutoContent wizard screen.
5. In the *What Are You Going To Talk About box*, type **Global Travel**.
6. In the *What Is Your Name box*, type your name.
7. Delete any text in the Other Information You'd Like To Display box.
8. Click on **Next** to move to the third screen. On the third screen, you select a presentation format. The AutoContent wizard creates a different outline for each of the options listed. If you don't like the options listed, you can click on Other and select another presentation type.
9. Click on **Reporting Progress** and click on **Next** to create a progress report presentation.
10. Click on **Next** twice to accept the defaults for presentation style, length, and output.
11. Click on **Finish** to create the presentation. Now take a look at the presentation. It opens in Slide view. The first slide contains the title and your name.
12. Switch to Outline view. The rest of the slides contain a sample outline for a Reporting Progress presentation. You select the sample text and replace it with your text.
13. Select the text for slide 2 and type **Sales - Fourth Quarter**.
14. Select the text for slide 3 and type **Sales - Year to Date**.
15. Delete the remaining slides in the presentation.
16. Move to the first slide in the presentation and run a slide show. (**Note:** To move to the next slide of the slide show, click the **left mouse button**.) Notice that PowerPoint applied a template and made the presentation look nicer. You can continue to add and delete slides and modify the presentation any way you like.
17. Save the file as **My Auto Presentation**.
18. Close the file.

SUMMARY

In this chapter, you explored templates and slide masters. You now know how to apply a template to a presentation, how to change the background color of a template, and how to change chart colors in a template. You also learned how to create a logo for a template, how to insert slide numbers, how to remove background items from a slide, and how to use the AutoContent wizard to create a presentation.

Here's a quick reference for the techniques you learned in this chapter:

Desired Result	How to Do It
Apply a template to your presentation	Choose **Format, Apply Design Template;** move to the folder that holds the template you want to apply; select the template; click on **Apply**
Change a color in a template	Apply the template you want to the presentation; choose **Format, Slide Color Scheme**; click on **Custom**; from the Scheme Colors box, select the color you want to change; click on **Change Color**; select a new color from the grid or click on **Custom** and create your own color; click on **OK**; click on **Apply** or **Apply To All**
Change the chart color scheme	Choose **Format, Slide Color Scheme** to open the Color Scheme dialog box; click on **Custom**; select the color you want to change; click on **Change Color**; select the color you want from either the color grid or click on **Custom** and create your own color; click on **OK**; repeat the above steps as necessary; click on **Apply** or **Apply To All**
Insert slide numbers	Choose **View, Header And Footer**; check **Slide Number**; click on **Apply** or **Apply To All**

Desired Result	How to Do It
Add a logo to your presentation	Choose **View, Master, Slide Master**; choose **Insert, Clip Art**; choose a clip-art category; click on the clip art you want to use; click on **OK**; choose **Draw, Scale**; type a percentage by which to scale the clip art; click on **OK**; move the clip art to the appropriate place on your slide; select the **Text** tool; type the text for your logo; select the **Selection** tool; select and format the logo text, if necessary; move the logo text to the appropriate place on your slide, if necessary; move to Slide view to see the logo on the slide
Turn off the display of background items on a slide	Move to the slide on which you want to hide the background items; choose **Format, Custom Background**; check **Omit Background Graphics From Master**; click on **Apply**
Return the background items to the slide	Move to the slide on which you want to view the background items; choose **Format, Custom Background**; uncheck **Omit Background Graphics From Master**; click on **Apply**
Use the AutoContent wizard	Choose **File, New**; click on **Presentations**; click on **AutoContent Wizard**; click on **OK**; click on **Next**; type a topic; press **Tab**; type any other information and click on **Next**; choose a presentation type and click on **Next**; select options as necessary and click on **Next**; click on **Finish**; create the presentation

In the next chapter, you'll explore two closely related topics: importing and exporting files. You will learn how to import an outline, how to import data and charts from other applications, how to import a picture, how to export a PowerPoint presentation as an outline, and how to export a PowerPoint slide as a graphic.

CHAPTER 11: IMPORTING AND EXPORTING

Importing Data and Charts from Other Applications

Importing an Outline

Importing a Picture

Exporting Powerpoint Presentations and Slides

Throughout this book, you learned how to create the different PowerPoint slides that make up a presentation. In this chapter, you will learn how to *import* (use files or objects that were created in another presentation or application) and *export* (use PowerPoint slides and presentations in other applications). You can import data, outlines, and pictures from other sources into your presentation, saving you the work of creating them more than once. In addition, you can export PowerPoint slides and presentations to enhance your spreadsheets or word-processing documents.

When you are done working through this chapter, you will know

- How to import data from a Microsoft Excel worksheet
- How to import a chart from Microsoft Excel workbook
- How to import an outline from Word for Windows
- How to import a picture
- How to export a PowerPoint presentation as an outline
- How to export a PowerPoint slide as a Windows metafile

IMPORTING DATA AND CHARTS FROM OTHER APPLICATIONS

Computer software allows you to automate your office. There is an application for every use, and chances are you use another application besides PowerPoint, such as Microsoft Excel or Lotus 1-2-3. If this is the case, you can import data from the other application into Graph. You can either directly import the data, or you can copy and paste the data from another document.

If you have a spreadsheet that shows the monthly sales for a company, for example, and you want to create a chart for your PowerPoint presentation based on that information, you can use the information from your Excel or Lotus spreadsheet to plot the PowerPoint chart. Instead of taking the time to create your Excel or Lotus data all over again in PowerPoint, you import data from the other application directly into a Graph datasheet. You don't even have to run the other application. There are several applications from which you can use data from applications such as Excel and Lotus 1-2-3 to create PowerPoint charts.

Note: When you import data or charts from Excel 5 or 7, PowerPoint can only read the first page of the workbook. You might need to move the worksheet or chart so it is the first page of the workbook before you can import it.

IMPORTING DATA FROM MICROSOFT EXCEL

If you have a Microsoft Excel worksheet that contains the information you want to plot in your PowerPoint chart, you can import the data from the worksheet directly into your PowerPoint presentation.

Note: You can only import the first worksheet in an Excel workbook file.

Here's the general procedure for importing data from Microsoft Excel:

- Move to the slide on which you want to create the chart.
- Add a title to the slide.
- Double-click on the *Graph* object.
- Clear the datasheet.
- Select the cell where the data will begin (usually this is the first cell of the datasheet).
- Click on the *Import Data* button.
- Select the file name.
- Click on the *Entire File* button at the bottom of the dialog box to import all the data, or click on the *Range* button and type the data range in the Range box to import a range of data.
- Click on *OK*.

If you are not running PowerPoint on your computer, please start it now. Close all open presentations except the start-up presentation. Let's create a PowerPoint chart with data imported from Microsoft Excel:

1. Open and maximize **Chapter 11**.
2. Add a new graph slide (slide 5) to the end of the presentation.
3. Add the title **Global Travel Package Rates**.
4. Double-click on the **Graph** object.
5. Drag the datasheet up and to the left to display the datasheet and the chart.
6. Select all the data in the datasheet, then choose **Edit, Clear, Contents** to clear all the data from the datasheet. If you do not clear data from the datasheet before importing data, Graph asks if you want to overwrite the existing data.
7. Select the first cell of the datasheet, as shown in Figure 11.1. Graph will place the imported data in the datasheet beginning with the selected cell.
8. Click on the **Import Data** button (the first button from the left on the toolbar) to open the Import Data dialog box, shown in Figure 11.2.

Figure 11.1 **The first cell of the datasheet**

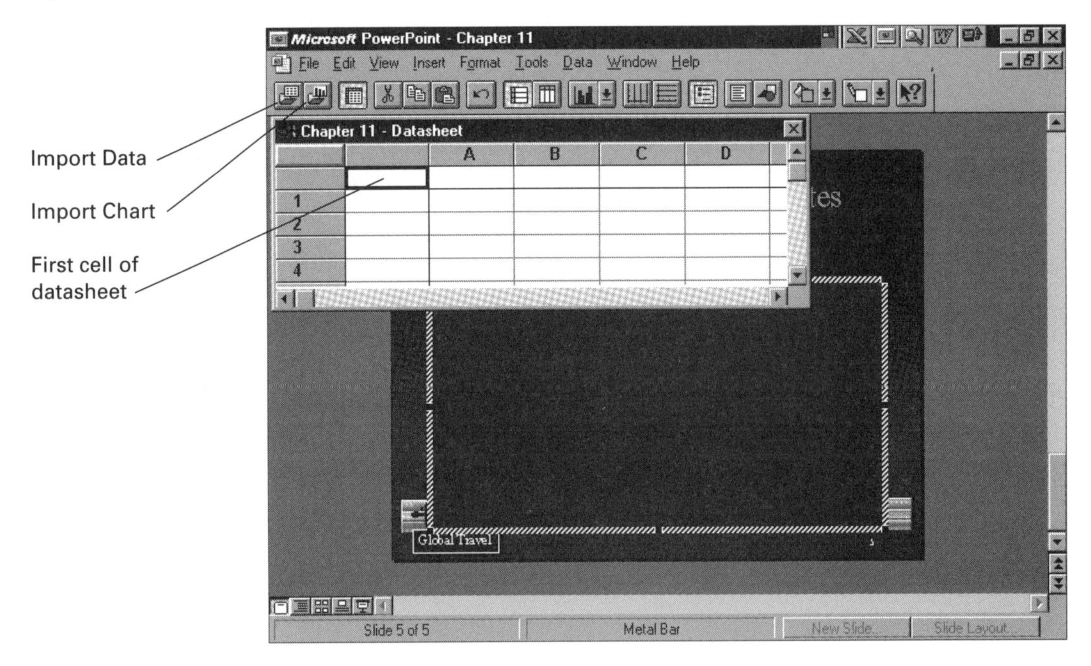

Figure 11.2 **The Import Data dialog box**

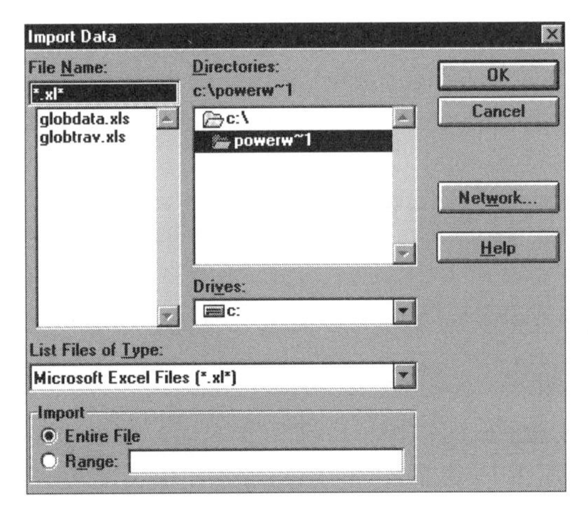

9. If necessary, move to your Power Work folder (it displays as powerw~1).

10. Select the file name **globdata.xls**. This is the workbook containing the worksheet on whose data we want to base a PowerPoint chart.

11. Click on **Entire File** (at the bottom of the dialog box), if necessary. When you select Entire File, Graph imports all the information in the worksheet. If you wanted to import only a portion of the worksheet, you would click on Range and type in the range you wanted to plot as a chart. For example, to create a chart from a worksheet like the one shown in Figure 11.3, based on the vacation package data without including the extra text, you would select Range and type the range A3:E7. Only the information in cell A3 through cell E7 would be plotted.

Figure 11.3 **Sample Excel worksheet**

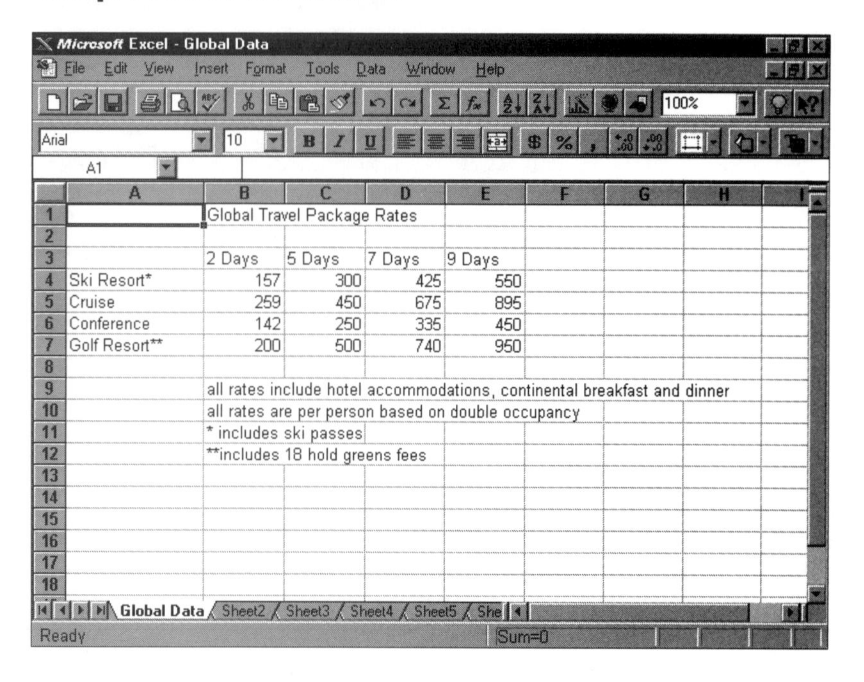

	A	B	C	D	E
1		Global Travel Package Rates			
2					
3		2 Days	5 Days	7 Days	9 Days
4	Ski Resort*	157	300	425	550
5	Cruise	259	450	675	895
6	Conference	142	250	335	450
7	Golf Resort**	200	500	740	950
8					
9		all rates include hotel accommodations, continental breakfast and dinner			
10		all rates are per person based on double occupancy			
11		* includes ski passes			
12		**includes 18 hold greens fees			

12. Click on **OK** to import all the data from the first worksheet of globdata into the Graph datasheet.

13. Observe the Datasheet window. The Excel data is pasted into the datasheet.
14. Observe the chart. Graph plots a chart based on the Excel data.
15. Click on the slide to exit from Microsoft Graph and to update the chart on the slide.
16. Save the file as **My Chapter 11**. Your chart should match the one in Figure 11.4.

Figure 11.4 **The completed chart**

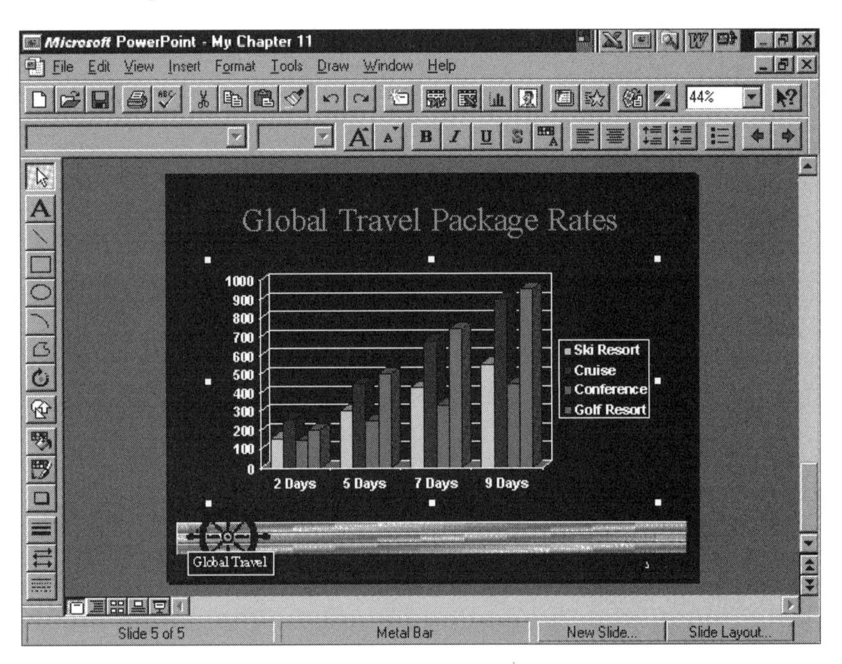

IMPORTING A MICROSOFT EXCEL CHART

You can use Microsoft Excel to create charts as well as worksheets. If you do use Excel to create a chart and then decide you must have that chart in your PowerPoint presentation, you can import the chart itself without importing the Excel data. Once you import the Microsoft Excel chart, the chart is *embedded* in your presentation—the original information is stored in your PowerPoint presentation file, allowing you to edit the object in PowerPoint.

Here's the general procedure for importing an Excel chart into Graph:

- Move to or create the slide on which you want to add the Excel chart.
- Add a title for the chart.
- Double-click on the *Graph* object.
- Drag the Datasheet window up, if necessary.
- Click on the *Import Chart* button.
- Select the name of the file containing the chart you want to import. (The chart must be the first sheet in the file.)
- Click on *OK*. The Excel chart opens in Graph, and the data used to create the chart is displayed in the datasheet.

Let's import an Excel chart:

1. Add a new graph slide (slide 6) to the end of the presentation.
2. Add the title **Package Sales**.
3. Double-click on the **Graph** object.
4. Move the Datasheet window up and to the right and select the first cell of the datasheet.
5. Click on the **Import Chart** button to open the Import Chart dialog box. Move to your Power Work folder, if necessary.

6. From the List Files of Type list box, select **Microsoft Excel 5.0 Charts.**
7. Select **globTrav.xis**. You can only import a chart if it is the first sheet in an Excel workbook.
8. Click on **OK**. You should see the message *Opening a Microsoft Excel chart will overwrite existing data and chart formatting. Continue?* When you import a Microsoft Excel chart, the Excel chart formatting will overwrite any PowerPoint formatting defaults. Even if you cannot see a chart, PowerPoint default formatting is still there each time you open Graph—you must confirm overwriting the existing chart every time you import an Excel chart.

9. Click on **OK** to overwrite the PowerPoint chart formatting. The Microsoft Excel chart opens in Graph, and its data is included in the Graph datasheet.
10. Return to the slide and update the chart.
11. Observe the slide—the chart is small. Let's enlarge it.
12. Select the chart, if necessary.
13. Choose **Draw, Scale**, type **90**, and click on **OK** to enlarge the chart to 90 percent of its original size.
14. Center the chart on the slide, if necessary.
15. Open Microsoft Graph and double-click on the chart's **y-axis** to open the Format Axis dialog box.
16. Click on **Font** to display the Font tab.
17. Select **opaque** from the Background drop-down list, and click on **OK**. The y-axis numbers are easier to read with an opaque background.
18. Return to the slide.
19. Compare your chart to that shown in Figure 11.5.
20. Save the file.

IMPORTING AN OUTLINE

In PowerPoint, you can import an outline to begin a new presentation or to add to an existing presentation. You can import outlines from Microsoft Word or other word-processing applications. PowerPoint can read Microsoft Word files directly, as well as *RTF* (Rich Text Format) and plain text (.TXT) files.

When reading a Microsoft Word or an RTF file, PowerPoint picks up the outline structure from the styles used in the file (a heading 1 in Microsoft Word becomes a title in PowerPoint, a heading 2 becomes the first level of a Body object, and so on). If the file contains no outline styles, PowerPoint uses the paragraph indents or tabs to determine titles and body-text levels.

In plain text files, PowerPoint uses tabs at the beginning of paragraphs to determine the outline structure. For example, if there is no tab at the beginning of a line, PowerPoint imports it as a slide

Figure 11.5 **The completed slide**

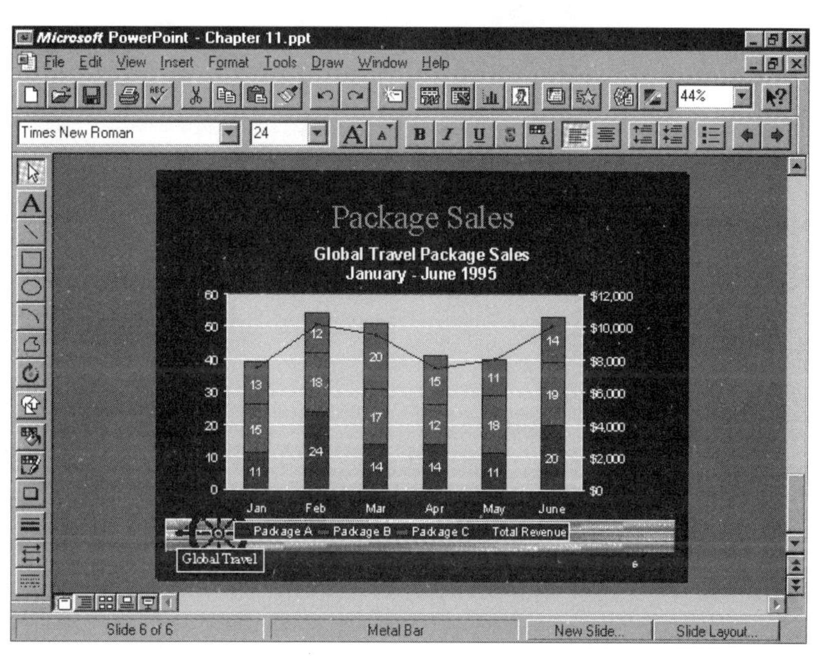

title. If there is one tab at the beginning of the line, PowerPoint imports the paragraph as level-1 body text.

Note: Microsoft Word outlines can have up to nine indent levels, but PowerPoint outlines have only six (one for titles and five for body text). When you import a Word for Windows outline, PowerPoint discards all text that is not part of a six-level outline.

Figure 11.6 illustrates the Word for Windows outline with outline styles applied. Figure 11.7 shows the same outline delineated with tabs.

You can import an outline in any of PowerPoint's views. PowerPoint inserts slides after the current slide in Slide view and Outline view, and after the selected slide in Slide Sorter view.

Here's the general procedure for importing an outline into a PowerPoint presentation:

- Move to the slide after which you want to insert the outline.
- Choose *Insert, Slides From Outline.*

Figure 11.6 **A Word for Windows outline formatted with outline styles**

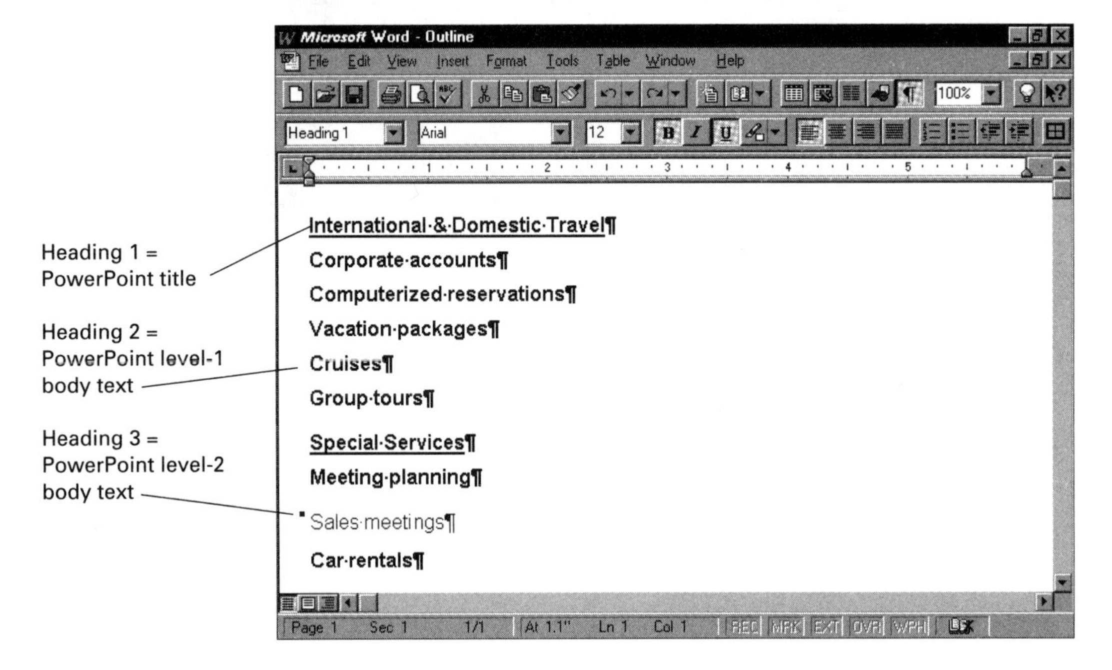

- Move to the appropriate drive and folder and select the file that contains the outline you want to import.
- Click on *OK*. The new slides are added after the current or selected slide and are formatted according to the Microsoft Word outline style applied to them, or the number of tab markers at the beginning of the paragraph.

Let's import an outline to add text slides to My Chapter 11:

1. Move to the last slide in the presentation (slide 6), if necessary.
2. Choose **Insert, Slides From Outline** to open the Insert Outline dialog box, shown in Figure 11.8.
3. Move to the Power Work folder, if necessary, and select **Outline**. This is a Word for Windows file containing text for the new PowerPoint slides.
4. Click on **Insert**. PowerPoint imports the file, adding its text to your presentation.

Figure 11.7 **A Word for Windows outline delineated with tabs**

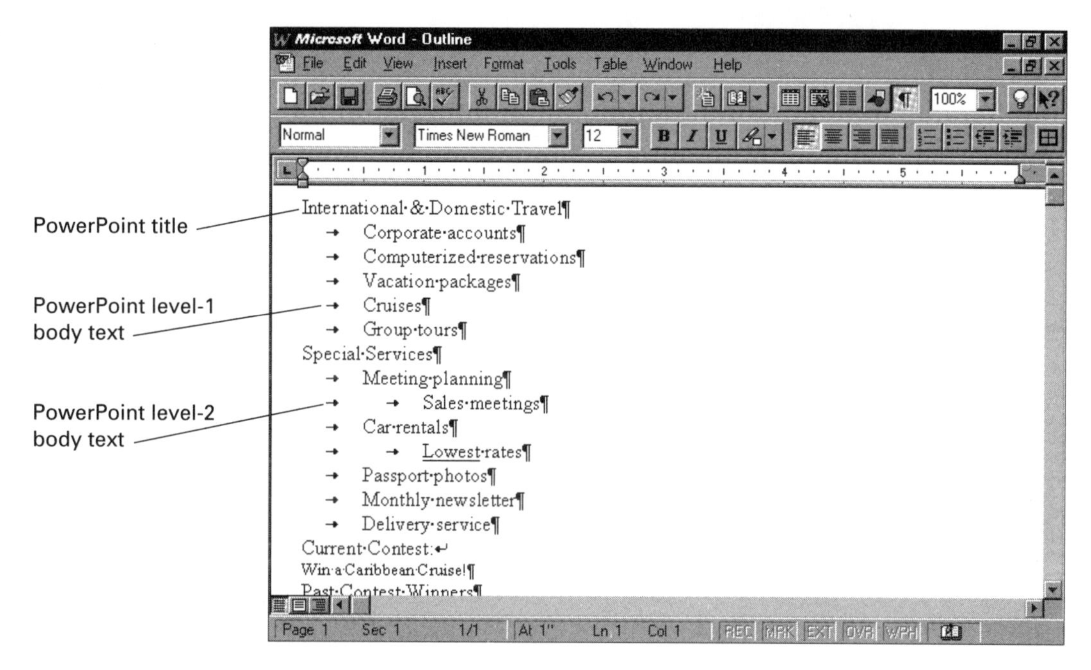

Figure 11.8 **The Insert Outline dialog box**

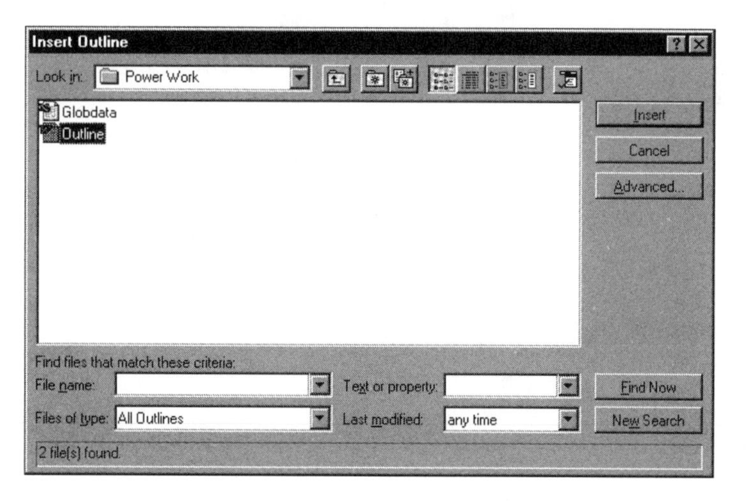

PowerPoint creates a new slide for each level-1 heading and adds the other headings as body text. The slides appear after the current slide in your presentation and follow the format of the template.

Before we do anything to the text slides, let's take a look at the new slides. As you learned in Chapter 1, you can use Slide Sorter view to get an overview of your presentation:

1. Choose **View, Slide Sorter** to view all the slides you imported.
2. Scroll down to view the new slides (slides 7 through 11). All the new slides, except the last, contain text only, as shown in Figure 11.9. The last slide is blank.
3. Save the file.

Figure 11.9 **The new slides in Slide Sorter view**

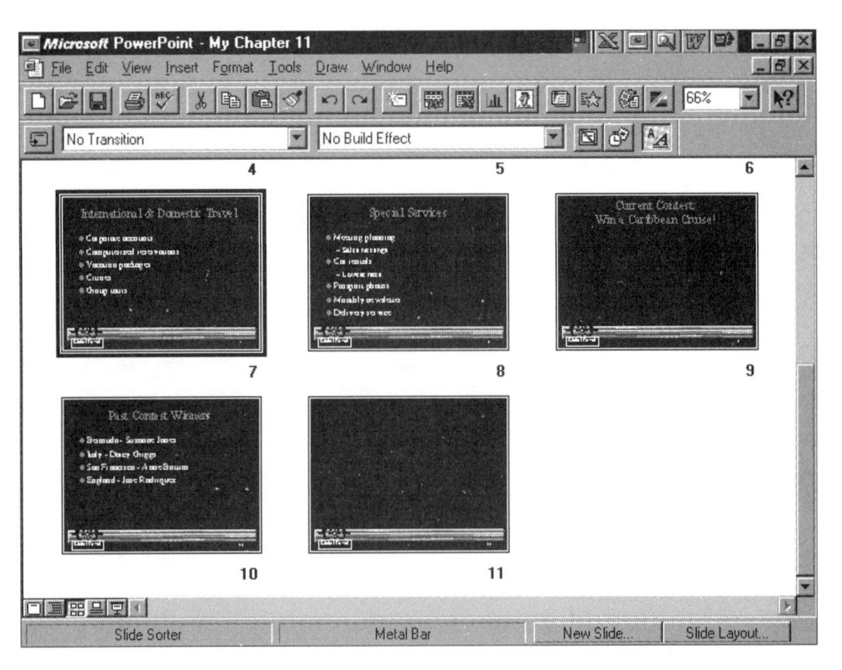

IMPORTING A PICTURE

As you learned in Chapter 5, PowerPoint comes with several clip-art files containing many graphics you can use in your presentations. However, if you want to use a particular *picture* (a drawing created in another application), you can import it into your presentation. This allows you to create an illustration in a graphics application and have that illustration placed on a slide in your presentation. You cannot, however, edit an imported picture in PowerPoint, because an imported graphic does not retain any information about the application in which it was created.

Here's the general procedure for importing a picture:

- Move to the slide on which you want to add the picture.
- Choose *Insert, Picture* to open the Insert Picture dialog box. This dialog box shows a list of available picture files in the current drive and folder.
- Choose the drive and folder that contains the picture file you want to import.
- Choose the picture file you want.
- Click on *OK*. PowerPoint places the picture on the active slide.

Let's import a picture into My Chapter 11:

1. Double-click on slide **9** (Current Contest). When you double-click on a slide in Slide Sorter view, PowerPoint returns you to Slide view for that slide.
2. Delete the Text object (use Shift+click to select the entire text object). Because you are placing a picture on the slide, the Text object is not necessary.
3. Choose **Insert, Picture** to open the Insert Picture dialog box, shown in Figure 11.10.
4. Move to your Power Work folder, if necessary.
5. Select **Tropics** and click on **OK** to import the tropics graphic.
6. Choose **Draw, Scale** to open the Scale dialog box.
7. Type **125** and click on **OK** to enlarge the picture 125 percent.
8. Observe the slide. PowerPoint places the tropics graphic in the center of the slide, as shown in Figure 11.11.

Figure 11.10 The Insert Picture dialog box

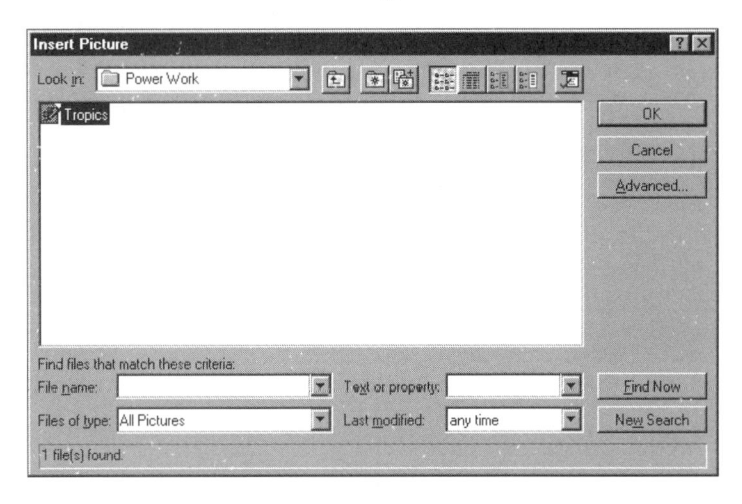

Figure 11.11 The tropics graphic on the slide

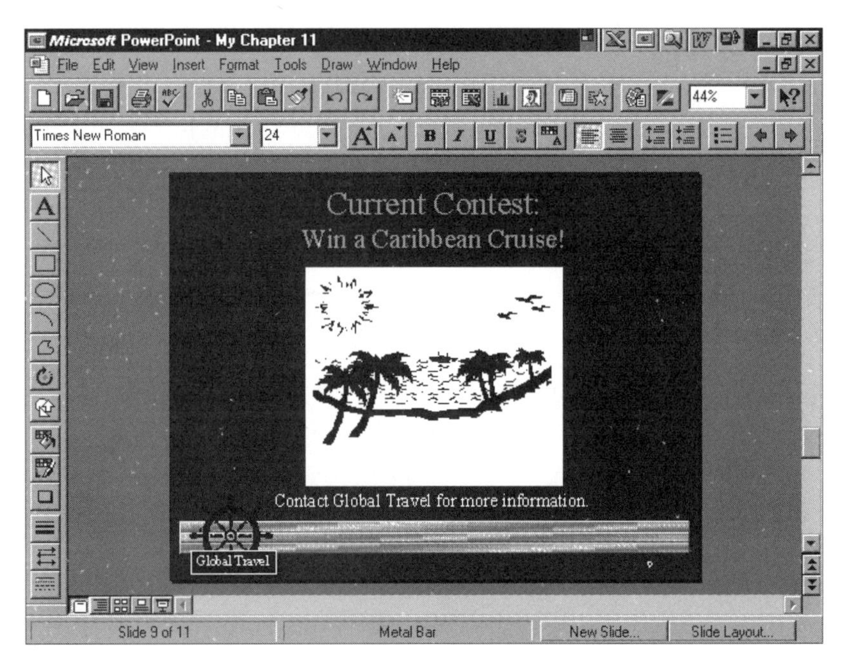

9. Select the text **Win a Caribbean Cruise!**
10. Change the font size of the selected text to **36** points.
11. Select the **Text** tool, place the insertion point on the slide workspace, and type the text **Contact Global Travel for more information.**
12. Move the text so that its position matches that shown in Figure 11.11. (Hint: Select the text and then move it.)
13. Save the file.

EXPORTING POWERPOINT PRESENTATIONS AND SLIDES

Exporting means using PowerPoint presentations or slides in documents created with other applications. You can export a presentation as an outline, or export a slide by attaching it to another document or saving it as a *Windows metafile* (a Windows graphical format). You can use PowerPoint and any other applications to make your life easier and your work more consistent.

EXPORTING A PRESENTATION AS AN OUTLINE

If you create a PowerPoint presentation and then decide that you want to create a document explaining the presentation, you can save the PowerPoint presentation as an outline and open it in a word-processing application. Only text is saved when you save a presentation as an outline.

Here's the general procedure for saving a PowerPoint presentation as an outline:

- Choose *File, Save As* to open the File Save dialog box.
- Type a name for the outline.
- Select the appropriate drive and folder.
- From the Save As Type drop-down list, select *Outline/RTF*.
- Click on *Save*. The presentation is saved as an outline and you can open it in any word-processing application that will read RTF files.

Let's save your PowerPoint presentation as an outline:

1. Choose **File, Save As** to open the File Save dialog box.

2. From the Save As Type drop-down list, select **Outline/RTF**. In order to save your presentation as an outline, you have to tell PowerPoint that's what you want to do.
3. Click on **Save** to close the File Save dialog box and save the presentation as an outline.
4. Choose **Insert, Slides From Outline** to open the Insert Outline dialog box.
5. Observe that My Chapter 11 is available in the File Name list box. You can use it in any application that reads RTF files.
6. Click on **Cancel** to close the dialog box without inserting the outline.

EXPORTING THE CURRENT SLIDE AS A WINDOWS METAFILE

If you save a slide as a Windows metafile, you save all graphics and text on the slide. Then, you can use PowerPoint to export the Windows metafile to another document.

Here's the general procedure for saving a slide as a Windows metafile:

- Move to the slide you want to save as a metafile. (You can save only one slide at a time.)
- Choose *File, Save As* to open the File Save dialog box.
- Type a name for the metafile.
- Choose the appropriate folder.
- From the Save As Type list, select *Windows Metafile*.
- Click on *Save*. The current slide is saved as a Windows metafile and can be used in another presentation.

Let's save a slide as a Windows metafile:

1. Move to slide 2 (Airline Ticket Sales). You can save only one slide at a time as a Windows metafile, and you have to move to the slide you want before you can save it.
2. Choose **File, Save As** to open the File Save dialog box.
3. Type **sales chart** to name the Windows metafile.
4. From the Save As Type list, select **Windows Metafile**.

5. Click on **Save**. Your slide is saved as a Windows metafile, ready to be used in another presentation or application.
6. Close My Chapter 11. Do not save changes.

SUMMARY

In this chapter, you added slides to My Chapter 11 by importing objects and files created in other applications. You also learned how to export PowerPoint presentations and slides. Now that you are finished working through this chapter, you know how to import data from Microsoft Excel, how to import a Microsoft Excel chart, how to import an outline from Word for Windows, how to import a picture, how to save a PowerPoint presentation as an outline, and how to save the current slide as a Windows metafile.

Here's a quick reference of the techniques covered in this chapter:

Desired Result	How to Do It
Import data from Microsoft Excel	Move to the slide on which you want to create the chart; add a title to the slide; double-click on the **Graph object**; clear the datasheet; select the cell where the data will begin; click on the **Import Data** button; select the appropriate drive and directory; select the file; click on the **Entire File** button (at the bottom of the dialog box) to import all the data, or, click on the **Range** button and type the data range; click on **OK**
Import an Excel chart into Graph	Move to or create the slide on which you want to add the Excel chart; add a title for the chart; double-click on the **Graph** object; drag the datasheet window up, if necessary; select the first cell in the datasheet; click on the **Import Chart** button; select the name of the file containing the chart you want to import; click on **OK** twice
Import a picture	Move to the slide on which you want to add the picture; choose **Insert, Picture**; choose the folder that contains the picture file you want to import; choose the picture file you want; click on **OK**

Desired Result	How to Do It
Import an outline into a PowerPoint presentation	Move to the slide after which you want to insert the outline; choose **Insert, Slides From Outline**; move to the appropriate folder and select the file that contains the outline you want to import; click on **Insert**
Save a PowerPoint presentation as an outline	Choose **File, Save As**; type a name for the outline; select the appropriate folder; from the Save As Type drop-down list, select **Outline/RTF**; click on **Save**
Save a slide as a Windows metafile	Move to the slide you want to save as a metafile (you can save only one slide at a time); choose **File, Save As**; type a name for the metafile; choose the appropriate folder and directory; from the Save As Type list, select **Windows Metafile**; click on **Save**

In the next chapter, you'll find out how to add the finishing touches to your presentation. You will learn how to change the order of slides in Outline view and in Slide Sorter view, how to delete slides from your presentation, how to add transition effects to your slides, how to add builds to text slides, how to run the slide show, and how to add notes to your presentation.

CHAPTER 12: PRESENTATION OPTIONS

Rearranging Slides in a Presentation

Adding Transitions And Builds to the Presentation

Running a Slide Show

Adding Notes to a Presentation

So far, you have created and enhanced text slides, graphics slides, and chart slides to create a presentation. In this chapter, you will add the finishing touches to your presentation to prepare it for viewing by the general public.

When you are done working through this chapter, you will know

- How to change the order of slides in Outline view
- How to change the order of slides in Slide Sorter view
- How to delete slides from your presentation
- How to add transition effects to your slides
- How to add builds to text slides
- How to run a slide show
- How to add notes to your presentation

REARRANGING SLIDES IN A PRESENTATION

When you create your slides, you really don't need to worry about placing them in a particular order. Finish all the slides first, and then move them around until you have them in the order that best fits your presentation. You can reorder your slides in either Outline view or Slide Sorter view.

CHANGING THE ORDER OF SLIDES IN OUTLINE VIEW

If you move a slide title, all its subheadings move with it. However, if you move a subheading, only that subheading moves. Therefore, if you want to change the order of your slides in Outline view, it is generally a good idea to first collapse your outline by clicking on the *Show Titles* button. Just the titles of your slides will then be displayed, making it easier to view all the slides and ensure that all the text on each slide moves with that slide.

Here's the general procedure for rearranging slides in Outline view:

- Click on the *Show Titles* button.
- Select the slide you want to move.
- Click on the *Move Up* or *Move Down* button to move the slide up or down in the outline. Or, place the mouse pointer on the slide icon and drag it up or down in the outline.
- Click on the *Show All* button to return body text to the outline.

If you are not running PowerPoint on your computer, please start it now. Let's move a slide in Outline view:

1. Open and maximize **Chapter 12** from your Power Work folder.
2. Click on the **Outline View** button (located at the bottom of the screen, it displays a miniature outline) to move to Outline view.

3. Observe the outline. The slides containing graphs and other graphics show only their titles. You can see only title and body text in Outline view.
4. Click on the **Show Titles** button to collapse all text in the outline except the slide titles (see Figure 12.1). You don't have to collapse slides before you rearrange them, but it is easier if you do.

5. Observe the slide icons. On those for slides containing graphs or graphics, shapes are displayed.
6. Select slide 7 (International & Domestic Travel).
7. Click on the **Move Up** button to move the slide above the Package Sales slide.

8. With the International & Domestic Travel slide still selected, click on the **Move Up** button four times to move the slide up to slide 2. Your International & Domestic Travel slide is now slide 2.
9. Click on the **Show All** button to return all the text to the outline.

Figure 12.1 The presentation in Outline view with titles only

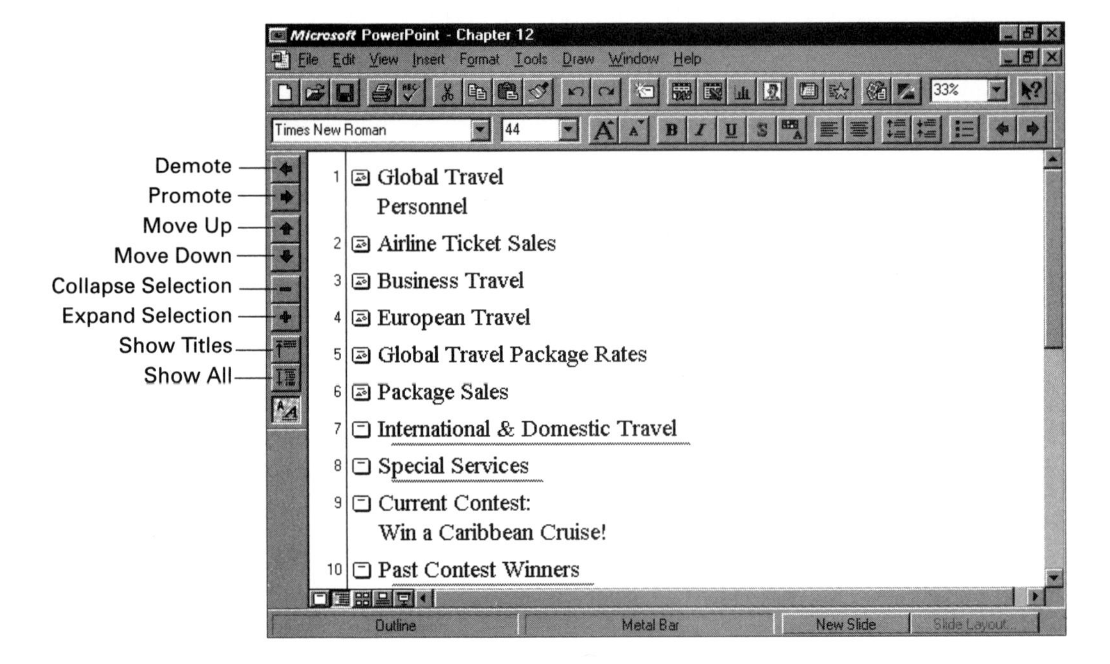

10. Observe slide 2. All the subheadings moved with the slide title.

PRACTICE YOUR SKILLS

Let's make slide 8 (Special Services) the third slide in the outline:

1. Display only the slide titles.
2. Move the **Special Services** slide in front of the Airline Ticket Sales slide. (Hint: You must select the slide before you can move it.)
3. Compare your outline to that shown in Figure 12.2.
4. Display all the slide text.
5. Save the file as **My Chapter12**.

Figure 12.2 The outline after rearranging the slides

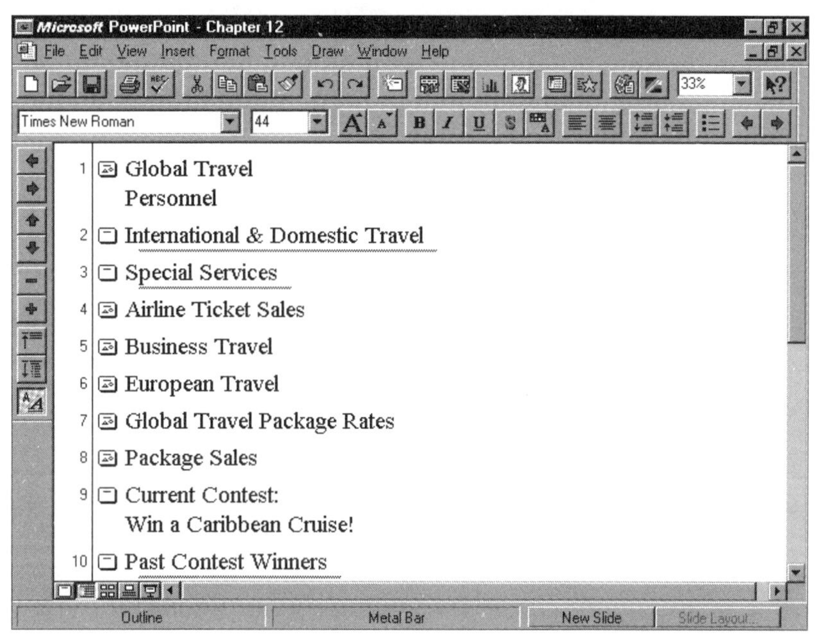

CHANGING THE ORDER OF SLIDES IN SLIDE SORTER VIEW

The only disadvantage to moving slides in Outline view is that you can't see what the slide looks like. If you want to see how the presentation actually looks as you rearrange it, you might want to rearrange slides in Slide Sorter view.

Here's the general procedure for changing the order of slides in Slide Sorter view:

- Move to Slide Sorter view.
- Select the slide you want to move.
- Start dragging the slide. The mouse pointer becomes a slide icon.
- Drag the slide icon to a new position.

Let's change the order of slides in Slide Sorter:

1. Click on the **Slide Sorter View** button.

2. Observe the Slide Sorter. You can see a miniature representation of each slide, and beneath each slide is its slide number.
3. Place the mouse pointer on slide 6. You are going to move the European Travel slide to a new location.
4. Press and hold the **left mouse button** and move the mouse pointer. The pointer changes to a slide icon.
5. Drag the **slide icon** to the right of slide 8 (Package sales).
6. Release the mouse button. The European Travel slide is now the eighth slide in the presentation, as shown in Figure 12.3.

Figure 12.3 **The presentation after moving the European Travel slide**

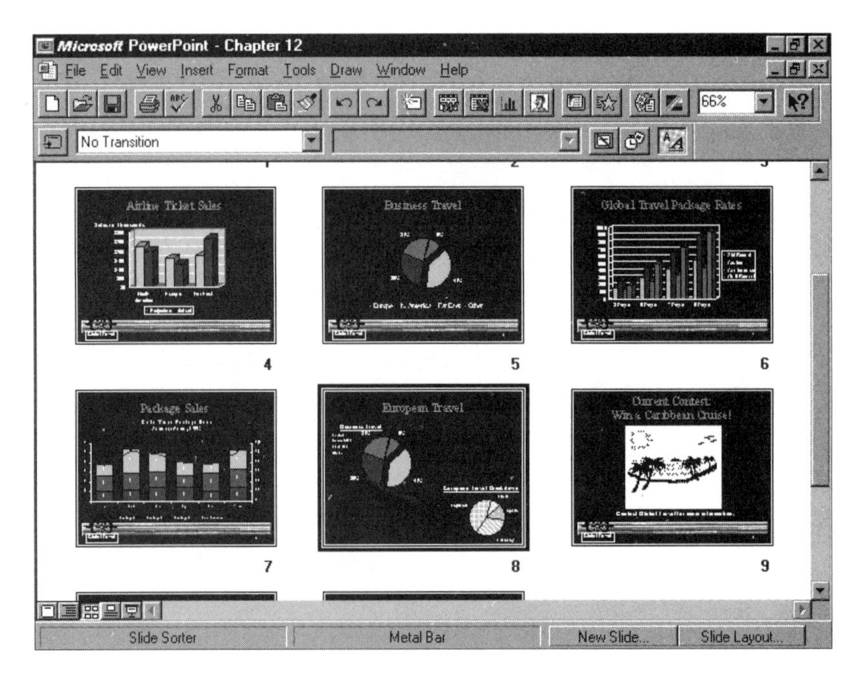

7. Observe the slide numbers. The slides have been automatically renumbered.
8. Select slide **5** (Business Travel).
9. Drag the **slide icon** to a position between slides 7 and 8 to place the Business Travel slide in front of the European Travel slide.

PRACTICE YOUR SKILLS

Let's move another slide in Slide Sorter view, so that your presentation matches that shown in Figure 12.4:

1. Move the Airline Ticket Sales slide (slide 4) in front of the Special Services slide (slide 3).
2. Save the file.

Figure 12.4 **The presentation in Slide Sorter view, after rearranging the slides**

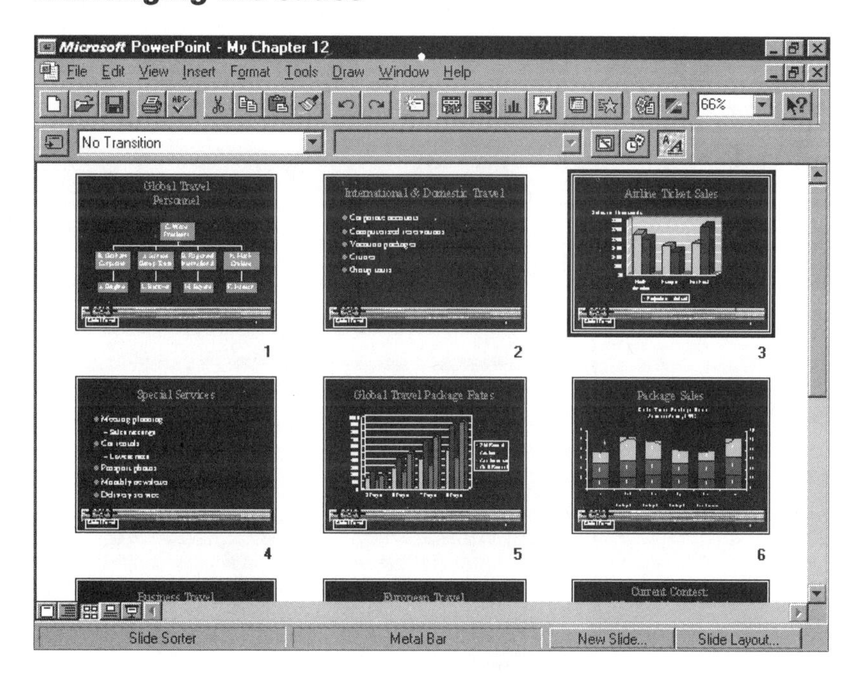

DELETING A SLIDE

As you look at your presentation, you may find that there is a slide you really don't need. PowerPoint allows you to quickly and easily delete any unnecessary slides.

Here's the general procedure for deleting slides in Outline view and Slide Sorter view:

- Select the slide you want to delete.

- Press *Del.*

Here's the general procedure for deleting slides in Slide view:

- Move to the slide you want to delete.
- Choose *Edit, Delete Slide.*

Let's delete a slide in Slide Sorter view:

1. Select **slide 8, European Travel**.
2. Press **Del** to delete the slide from the presentation.
3. Observe the presentation (see Figure 12.5). The slide has been removed and the remaining slides have been renumbered.

Figure 12.5 **The presentation, after deleting a slide**

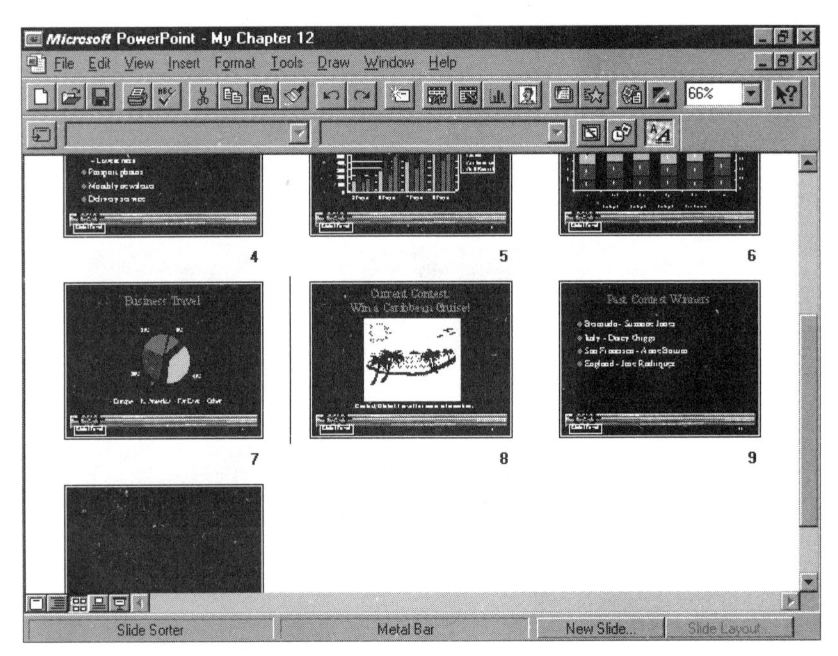

4. Choose **Edit, Undo Clear** to undelete the slide.
5. Save the file.

HIDING A SLIDE

If you aren't sure whether you really need a slide, you can hide it instead of deleting it. A hidden slide is still part of your presentation, but it doesn't display during a slide show. You might choose to hide a slide containing information that clarifies information on another slide. For example, you could hide a slide containing a spreadsheet that gives a detailed breakdown of a chart on another slide.

Here's the general procedure to hide a slide:

- Select the slide.
- Choose *Tools, Hide Slide.*

If, during the slide show, you decide that the information on the hidden slide is vital, you can simply select the slide and choose Tools, Hide Slide again to return the slide to the presentation.

ADDING TRANSITIONS AND BUILDS TO THE PRESENTATION

Once you have your presentation in the order in which you want to present it, you can make it more interesting by adding transitions and builds. PowerPoint gives you several options to control how your slides are displayed during a slide show. You can set a *transition effect* (the method by which one slide moves off the screen and the next slide moves on). You can also control whether the slides advance automatically, and set the amount of time each slide is displayed. In addition, you can *build* body text—add a major bullet and its subpoints one by one—on each slide.

TRANSISITION EFFECTS

For each slide, you can set a different transition effect, as well as determine how quickly the transition will take place. You can set transition effects in Slide view or in Slide Sorter view. When you set a transition effect in Slide view, the effect applies only to the current slide. So, if you want to set transition effects for more than one slide at a time, select the slides in the Slide Sorter and then apply the effects.

Here's the general procedure for setting transition effects:

- Display the slide in Slide view, or select the slide(s) in Slide Sorter view.

- Choose *Tools, Slide Transition* (or click on the *Slide Transition* button in Slide Sorter view) to open the Transition dialog box.
- Select the transition effect from the drop-down list box.
- Select the transition speed (*Slow, Medium, Fast*).
- Select whether to advance to the next slide by clicking the mouse or automatically.
- Click on *OK*.

Note: If you have the necessary equipment, you can add sound to your transition effects. For more information, see your PowerPoint documentation.

Let's add transition effects to your presentation:

1. Switch to Slide view.
2. Move to slide 1, if necessary.
3. Choose **Tools, Slide Transition** to open the Slide Transition dialog box, shown in Figure 12.6. Here you can set a transition effect, tell PowerPoint how fast or slow you want the effect to take place, determine whether the slide will advance automatically or when you click the mouse, and select a sound option. (The picture of a dog in the lower-right corner of the dialog box represents a slide graphic.) You can see what a transition effect will look like in your presentation by watching the dog when you choose an effect from the Effect drop-down list box.

Figure 12.6 **The Transition dialog box**

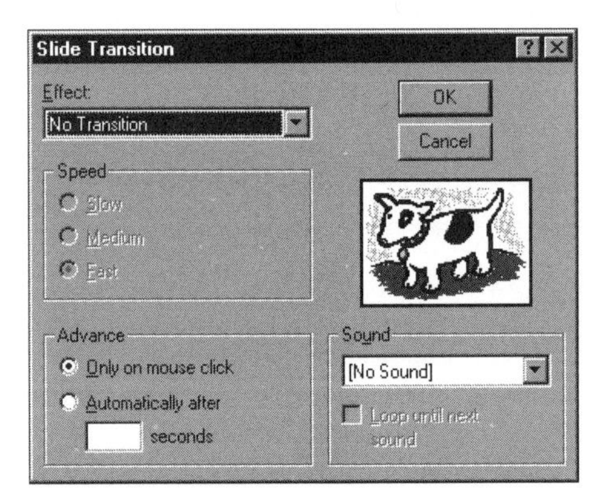

4. Click on the **down arrow** to display the transition options available in the Effect drop-down list box.
5. Select **Box Out**. When you select a transition effect, it is applied to the picture of the dog.
6. Click on **Medium** to set the speed for the transition.
7. In the Advance box, click on **Automatically After** to advance to the next slide automatically.
8. Type **3** to display the slide for 3 seconds before advancing to the next slide.
9. Click on **OK**.
10. Switch to Slide Sorter view.
11. Observe slide 1. Below it, you see a transition icon and the number *:03* (refer to Figure 12.7). The slide icon with an arrow indicates that a transition effect has been applied to the slide. The number :03 indicates that the slide will automatically advance in 3 seconds. (**Note:** You can click on the transition icon to see what the transition effect looks like.)

Figure 12.7 **The slide with transition effect in Slide Sorter view**

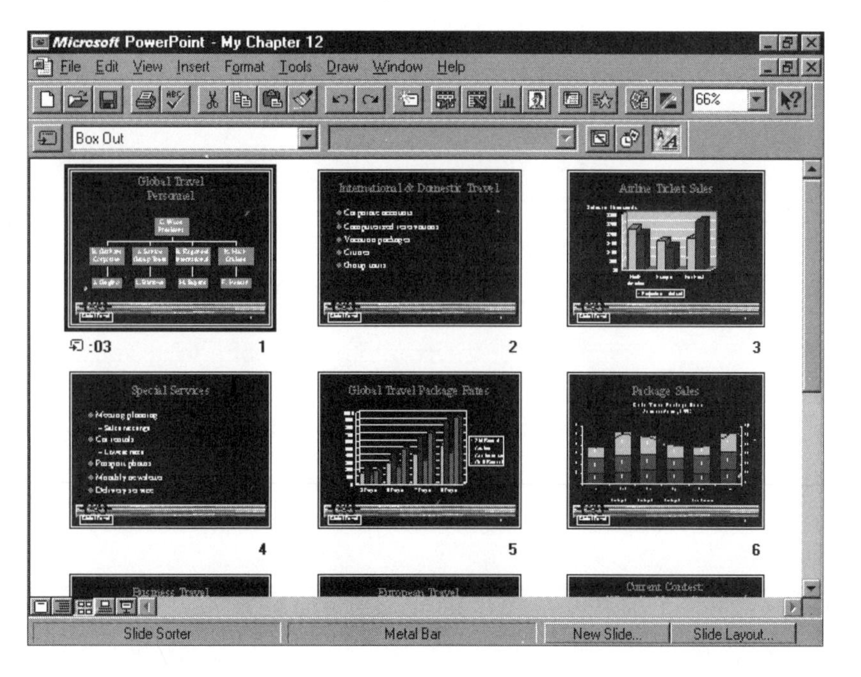

12. Observe slide 2. Because there is no transition effect set for this slide, there are no icons or numbers beneath it. Let's set a transition effect for slide 2.
13. Select slide 2.
14. Click on the **Slide Transition** button to open the Transition dialog box.

15. Choose **Box In** from the Effect drop-down list box.
16. Set the speed to **Medium**, if necessary.
17. Set the slide to advance automatically after 3 seconds.
18. Click on **OK**.
19. Select slides 3 through 6 (while holding **Shift**, click on each slide). Your screen should now look like that shown in Figure 12.8. You can apply a transition effect to more than one slide at a time in Slide Sorter view.
20. Click on the **Slide Transition** button to open the Slide Transition dialog box, and choose **Dissolve** from the Effect drop-down list box.
21. Set the speed to **Medium**, if necessary.
22. Set the slides to advance automatically after 3 seconds.
23. Click on **OK**.

PRACTICE YOUR SKILLS

1. Set the transition effect and speed of your choice for the remaining slides.
2. Set all the slides to advance automatically after 3 seconds.
3. Save the file.

Figure 12.8 **Selecting multiple slides**

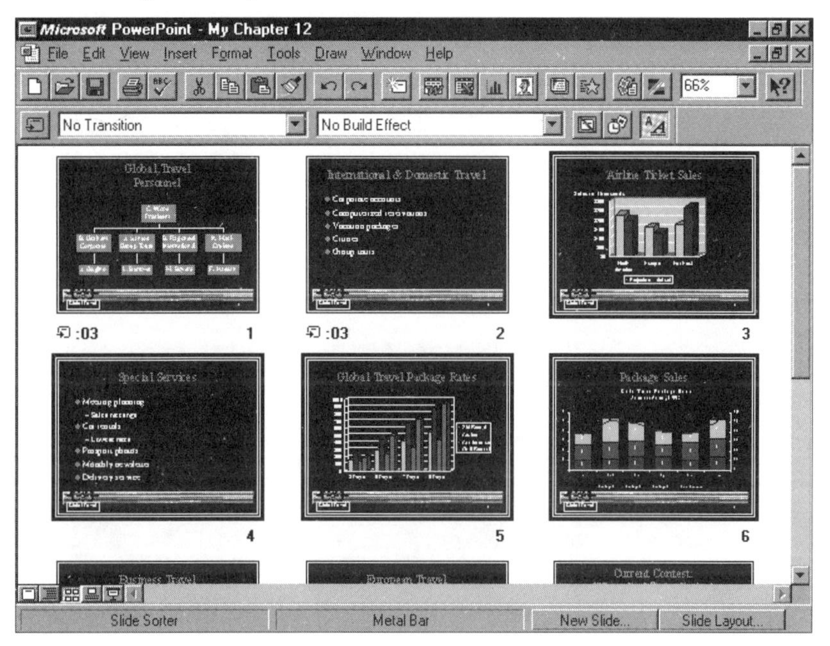

ADDING BUILDS

Text slides are a necessity for imparting information during your presentation, but they can be boring. You can keep your audience interested in your presentation during text slides if you use the *Build* command to add each major bullet (and its subpoints) to the slide one at a time. You choose the effect you want to see as each new bullet point is added to the slide and presto, your boring old text slides have new life.

If you add a build to a slide and the slide is set to advance automatically, each bulleted item on the slide is displayed for an equal portion of the time set for that slide. For example, if a slide is timed to advance after 8 seconds and there are four bullets, each bullet will be displayed for 2 seconds.

Here's the general procedure for adding builds to slides:

- Move to the slide with the bulleted list.
- Choose *Tools, Build Slide Text.*
- Select a build effect from the submenu or click on *Other* to display the Animation Settings dialog box.

- If necessary, set Build Options and Effects and click on *OK*.

Let's add builds to the text slides in your presentation:

1. Double-click on slide 2 (International & Domestic Travel) to return to Slide view.
2. Choose **Tools, Build Slide Text** to display the submenu shown in Figure 12.9.

Figure 12.9 **The Build submenu**

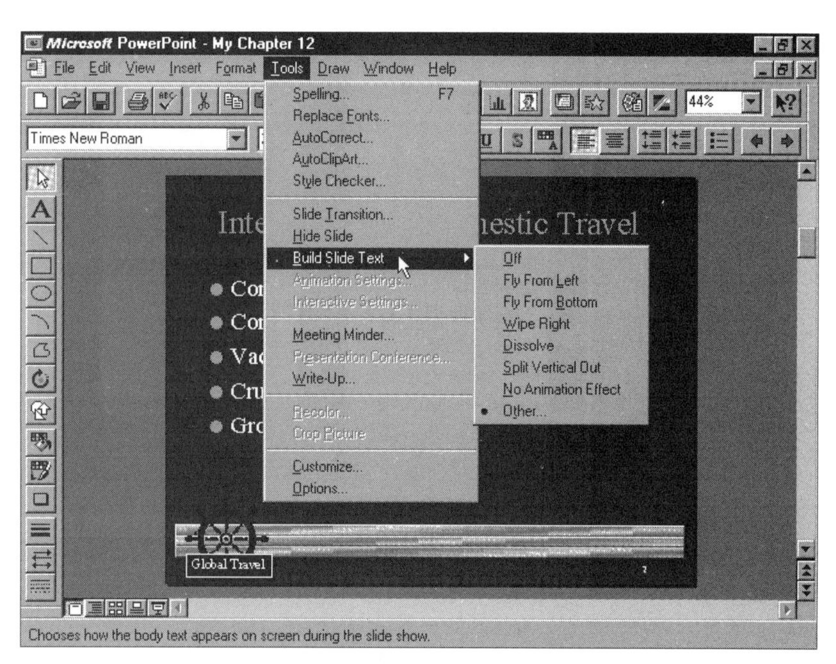

3. Select **Fly From Left**. Each bulleted item on the International & Domestic Travel slide will "fly" in from the right side of the screen when you run your slide show.
4. Switch to Slide Sorter view.
5. Observe slide 2. The bulleted icon below the slide indicates that when you run the slide show, the body text will build one item at a time.
6. Select slide 4. You can set a build in Slide Sorter view, as well as in Slide view.

7. Click on the **Text Build Effects** button to display available build effects.
8. Select the effect of your choice.

PRACTICE YOUR SKILLS

Let's add a build to Past contest winners slide in your presentation:

1. Add the build effect of your choice to slide 10.
2. Save the file.

RUNNING A SLIDE SHOW

As you learned in Chapter 2, you can display a presentation on your computer screen by running a slide show. Running a slide show is an excellent way to rehearse before giving your presentation. You can see the effect each slide has, try different transitions, change the timing to suit your script, and generally design your electronic presentation so that it gets your point across in a clear, professional manner.

If the timing of your slide show is not quite right, you can change it during your rehearsal, or you can wait and change it in the Transition dialog box. Use whichever method is most convenient for you.

Here's the general procedure for running a slide show:

- Choose *View, Slide Show* to open the Slide Show dialog box.
- Choose either *All* or *From/To*, depending on how many of the presentation slides you want in the slide show.
- Choose the method you want to use to advance the slides. Choose *Manual Advance* to change slides by clicking the mouse button. Choose *Use Slide Timings* to advance the slide show automatically, using the timings you set in the Transition dialog box. Choose *Rehearse New Timings* to check timings and adjust them as necessary during the slide show.
- If you want the slide show to run continuously until you press Esc, check *Loop Continuously Until 'Esc'*.
- Click on the *Show* button. Either the first slide in the presentation, or the first slide in the range you specified, appears in slide-show format.

Now that you have added transition and build effects to your slides, let's see how they look in the slide show:

1. Switch to Slide Sorter view, if necessary.
2. Choose **View, Slide Show** to open the Slide Show dialog box.
3. Click on **All**, if necessary, to view all the slides in the presentation.
4. Click on **Use Slide Timings**, if necessary, to run the slide show with the timings you set earlier in this chapter.
5. Click on **Show**. The slide show runs, with each slide advancing automatically after 3 seconds. This means that the slides with text builds are moving too fast to be really effective.

PRACTICE YOUR SKILLS

Obviously, if you want to talk during this presentation, you need to reset the timings. Let's do so:

1. Change the slide timings for the following slides:

slide 2:	12 seconds
slide 4:	12 seconds
slide 10:	10 seconds

   (Hint: You can change the timings in the Slide Transition dialog box.)
2. Make any transition or build changes you want.
3. Run a slide show to check the new timings, transitions, and builds.
4. Save the file.

ADDING NOTES TO A PRESENTATION

You can create a *Notes page*, containing a slide image and additional space for your speaker notes, for every slide in your presentation. This can be a helpful reference tool. The Notes page is formatted based on the *Notes Master*.

The Notes Master controls the format and placement of the following items:

- *Background items.* Anything you add to the Notes Master is displayed on each Notes page.
- *Text style attributes.* Like the Slide Master, the Notes Master has a Master Body object with five indent levels that you can format. If you change the format of any master text, that format change affects every Notes page.
- *Slide image.* You can change the size and position of the slide image.

Here's the general procedure for adding notes to a presentation:

- Move to the slide for which you want to create a Notes page.
- Choose *View, Notes Pages.* The Notes page for the current slide appears.
- Type notes in the Notes Body Area.
- Use the Tool Palette to add any graphics you want.
- Click on the *Slide Changer* to move to the Notes page for the next slide.
- Repeat the above steps until you are finished writing notes.

Let's take a look at the Notes Master page before adding notes to your presentation:

1. Choose **View, Master, Notes Master** to display the Notes Master page.
2. Observe the Notes Master, shown in Figure 12.10. The Notes Master page contains a slide placeholder and a Master Body object for your notes. The bottom-left corner of the screen displays the words *Notes Master,* indicating that anything you change or add here will be displayed on every Notes page.
3. Click on the **Notes Body Area** object to select it.
4. Change the magnification to 66 percent. The text in the Notes Area object is easier to read now, as you can see in Figure 12.11. The Master Body object contains five text levels.
5. Click on the **Line Color** tool and click on **Automatic** to add a line around the Notes body text. Because you added a line

Figure 12.10 The Notes Master

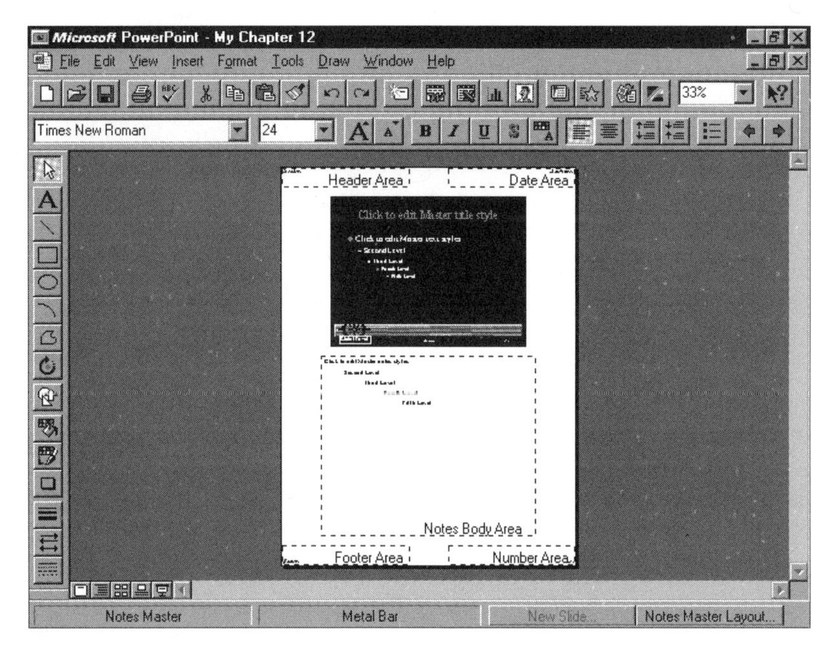

Figure 12.11 The Master Body object at 66 percent magnification

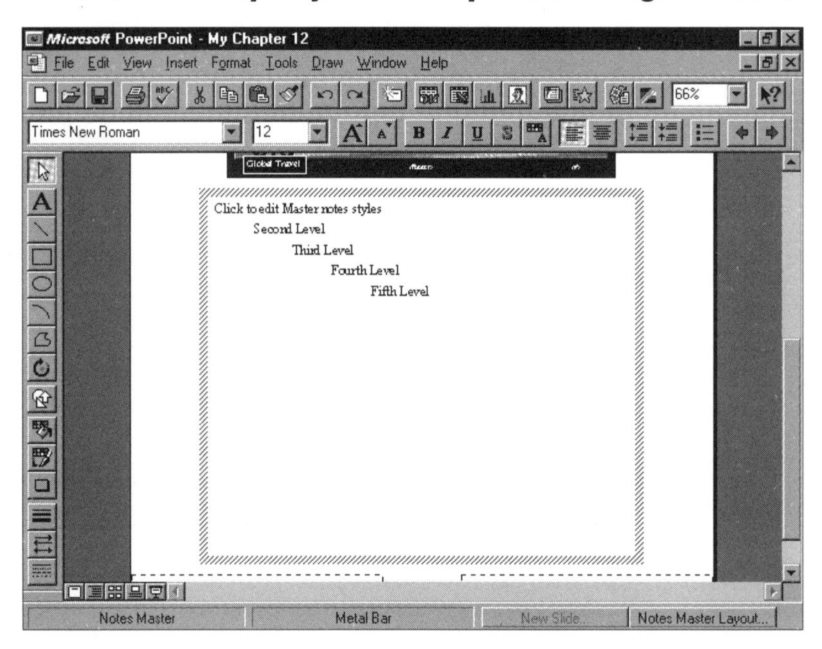

around the Master Body object, it will appear on every Notes page. (**Note**: The Drawing toolbar is the vertical toolbar along the left side of the window.)

Now, let's add notes to the presentation:

1. Choose **View, Notes Pages** to leave the Notes Master and move to a Notes page.
2. Move to Notes 1, if necessary.
3. Click on the **Notes Body Area** for Notes 1 to select it.
4. Type the following:

   Global Travel, a full-service travel agency, was founded in 1970. Our office is operated by a team of qualified managers and experienced assistants whose goal is to provide you with quality service at the lowest price.

5. Observe your slide. It should match that shown in Figure 12.12.

PRACTICE YOUR SKILLS

Let's create a Notes page that matches that shown in Figure 12.13:

1. Move to Notes 9. (Hint: Your Notes 9 should display the Current Contest slide.)
2. Add the following speaker's note:

   Four times a year, Global Travel offers clients the chance to enter a drawing for a free trip. This quarter, one lucky person will win an all-expenses paid, seven-day Caribbean cruise.

   (Hint: You must select the **Notes Body Area** before you can type.)

3. Return to Slide view and save the file.
4. Close the file.

Figure 12.12 The Notes page, after adding text

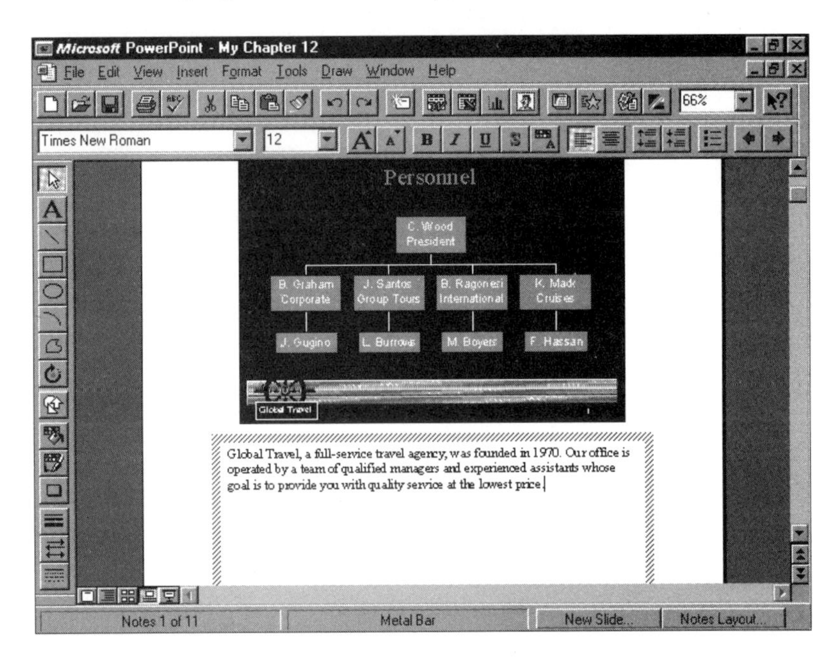

Figure 12.13 Notes page 9

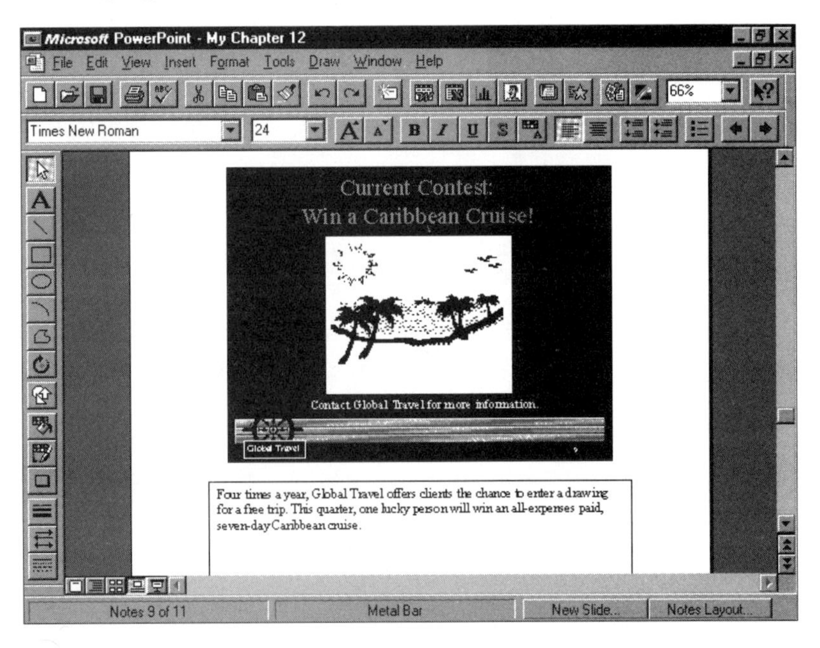

SUMMARY

Congratulations—you've completed your presentation! Doesn't it feel great? In this chapter, you learned how to change the order of slides in Outline view, how to change the order of slides in Slide Sorter view, and how to delete slides from your presentation. You also learned how to add transition effects to your slides, how to add builds to text slides, how to run a slide show, and how to add notes to your presentation.

Here's a quick reference of the techniques you learned in this chapter:

Desired Result	How to Do It
Rearrange slides in Outline view	Click on the **Show Titles** button to view slide titles only; select the slide you want to move; click on the **Move Up** or **Move Down** button to move the slide up or down in the outline, or place the mouse pointer on the **slide icon** and drag it up or down in the outline; click on the **Show All** button to restore the complete outline
Change the order of slides in Slide Sorter view	Move to Slide Sorter view, select the slide you want to move, start dragging the slide, drag the **slide icon** to a new position
Delete slides in Outline and Slide Sorter views	Select the slide you want to delete and press **Del**
Delete slides in Slide view	Move to the slide you want to delete; choose **Edit, Delete Slide**
Hide a slide	Select the slide; choose **Tools, Hide Slide**
Display a hidden slide	Select the slide; choose **Tools, Hide Slide**

Desired Result	How to Do It
Set transition effects	Display the slide in Slide view, or select the slide(s) in Slider Sorter view; choose **Tools, Slide Transition** (or click on the **Slide Transition** button in Slide Sorter view) to open the Slide Transition dialog box; select the transition effect from the drop-down list box; select the transition speed (**Slow**, **Medium**, **Fast**); select whether to advance to the next slide by clicking the mouse or automatically; click on **OK**
Add builds to slides	Move to the slide with the bulleted list; choose **Tools, Build Slide Text**; select an effect
Run a slide show	Choose **View, Slide Show** to open the Slide Show dialog box; choose either **All** or **From/To**, depending on how many of the presentation slides you want in the slide show; choose **Manual Advance** to change slides by clicking the mouse button, choose **Use Slide Timings** to advance the slide show automatically using the timings you set in the Transition dialog box, or choose **Rehearse New Timings** to check timings and allow you to change them during the slide show; click on the **Show** button
Add notes to a presentation	Move to the slide for which you want to create a Notes page; choose **View, Notes Pages** to display the Notes page for the current slide; type notes in the Body object; use the Tool Palette to add any graphics you want; click on the **Slide Changer** to move to the Notes page for the next slide; repeat the above steps until you are finished writing notes

In the next chapter, you will explore the various options available for printing your presentation. You will learn how to change the slide setup, how to print black-and-white slides, how to set a print range, how to scale your slides to fit your paper size, how to print a presentation, how to print handouts, how to print an outline, and how to print notes.

CHAPTER 13: PRINTING

The Slide Setup Command

Using Printing Options

Printing Slides, Notes, Handouts, and an Outline

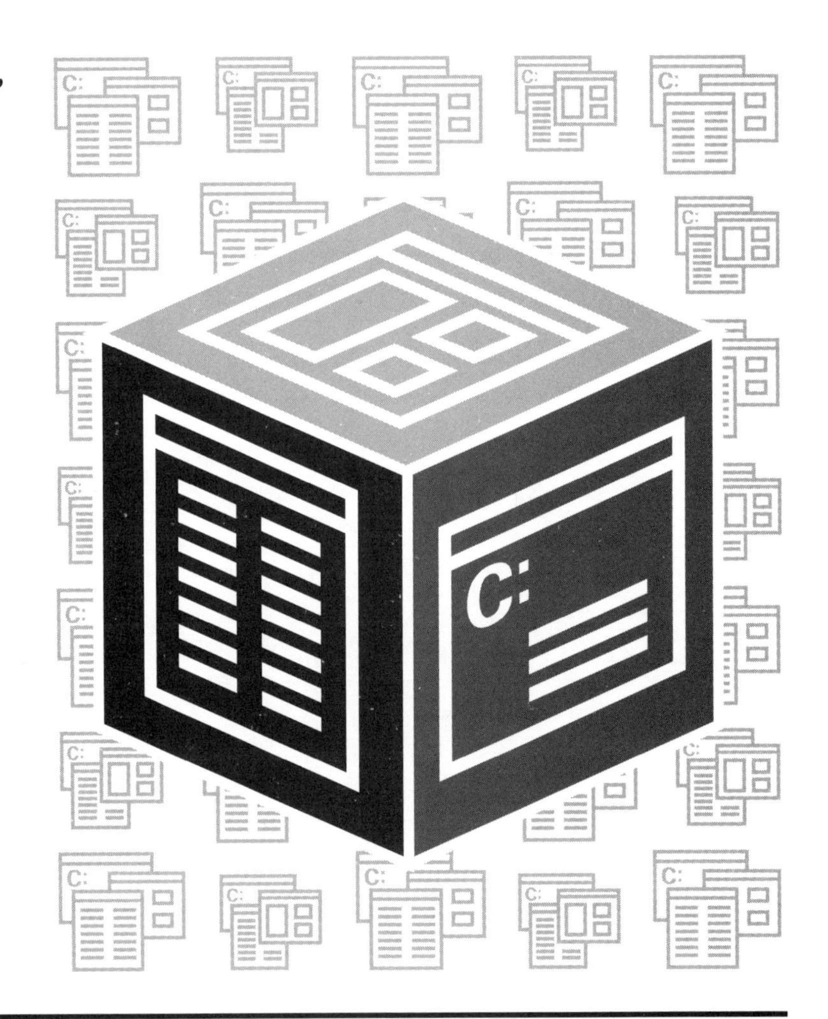

Until now, you have viewed all the parts of your presentation only on your screen. Eventually, you will probably need to create and print a complex presentation. This chapter introduces various techniques to help you manage the printing of a presentation (the slides themselves), an outline, notes, and handouts.

When you're done working through this chapter, you will know

- How to change the slide setup
- How to set print options
- How to print slides
- How to print Handout pages
- How to print an outline
- How to print Notes pages

THE SLIDE SETUP COMMAND

When you open a new presentation, PowerPoint creates slides that have a width of 10 inches, a height of 7.5 inches, and *landscape orientation* (the slide is wider than it is tall). However, you can use the *Slide Setup* command to change these settings as well as to set the number with which to begin numbering your slides.

Note: The default orientation for Notes, Handout, and Outline slides is *portrait orientation* (the slide is taller than it is wide).

Figure 13.1 shows the Slide Setup dialog box with the default setting, and Table 13.1 describes the elements of the dialog box.

Figure 13.1 The Slide Setup dialog box with default settings

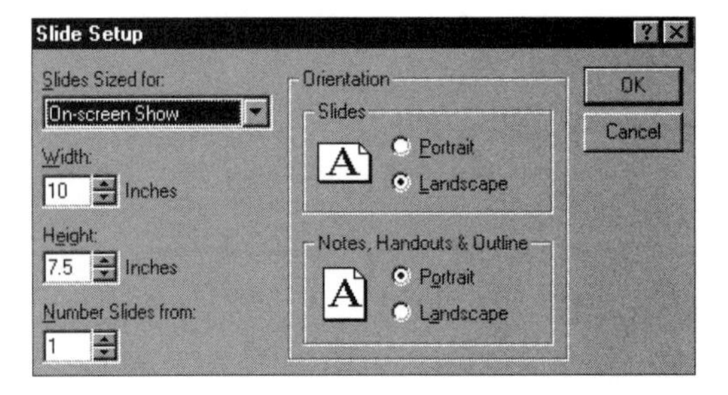

You can modify the slide setup at any time, but if you change settings *after* creating your slides, PowerPoint must adjust the slides to fit the new size.

Table 13.1 Elements of the Slide Setup Dialog Box

Element	Purpose
Slides Sized For box	Allows you to select a size for your slides. There are five standard slide-size options and a custom option that allows you to specify a nonstandard size.
Width and Height boxes	Located below the Slides Sized For box, these show the width and height of the slide workspace. If you choose one of the standard sizes in the Slides Sized For box, slides have a 1-inch margin. For example, if you choose Letter Paper (8.5 × 11 in), your slide width is set to 10 inches and the height to 7.5 inches. If you choose the Custom option, then you can set your own slide width and height.
Number Slides From box	Allows you to set the number to be assigned to the first slide in the presentation. Usually, it is fine to start numbering your presentation from 1. However, if you have a very long presentation that has been split into two or more files, you might want to start the numbering in the second and following files with something other than 1. As you learned in Chapter 10, you must first insert page numbers before you can print those numbers.
Orientation box	Allows you to set the orientation of the slides as well as the orientation for the Notes, Handouts, and Outline. You can choose Landscape (wide) or Portrait (tall).

When you change the settings for existing slides, PowerPoint politely lets you know that you might need to edit your slides. We advise that, if possible, you choose a slide setup *before* you begin creating slides.

Note: If you change the slide setup after creating slides, it is a good idea to take a look at the entire presentation on screen and print a draft copy to make sure it looks okay in the new size or orientation.

Here's the general procedure for changing the slide setup:

- Choose *File, Slide Setup.*

- Choose the appropriate Slides Sized For option for your presentation output.
- Set a number with which to begin numbering the slides.
- Choose an orientation option.
- Click on *OK*.
- If you already have slides in your presentation and you change the size setting, you may see a message saying that you may need to edit your slides to fit. If you decide to go ahead with the change, click on *Change*.
- Look at your presentation on screen and print a draft copy to make sure the old format and content fit appropriately in the new size.
- If necessary, edit the slides or change the size again.

If you are not running PowerPoint on your computer, please start it now. Close all open presentations except the start-up presentation. Let's take a look at the Slide Setup dialog box:

1. Open **Chapter 13** and move to Slide view, if necessary.
2. Choose **File, Slide Setup** to open the Slide Setup dialog box. You can change the size and orientation of your slides and choose the page number for the first slide here.
3. Click on the **down arrow** in the Slides Sized For box to display the slide-size options (as shown in Figure 13.2). There are five slide-size options you can choose from. *On-screen Show* is for a presentation that you run on your computer. *Letter Paper* (8.5 × 11 in) is for a presentation you print on regular-size U.S. paper. *A4 Paper* (210 × 297 mm) is for slides printed on regular-size International paper. *35mm Slides* is for slides printed as 35mm color slides. *Overhead* is for slides you print as overhead transparencies. *Custom* allows you to set your own slide size.

Let's change the slide size and see what happens:

1. Choose **35mm Slides** from the Slides Sized For list to resize the slides, preparing them as 35mm color slides.
2. Observe the Width and Height boxes. The contents of the Width box change to *11.25* inches. The Height box setting stays the same.

Figure 13.2 **The Slide Setup dialog box with slide-size options displayed**

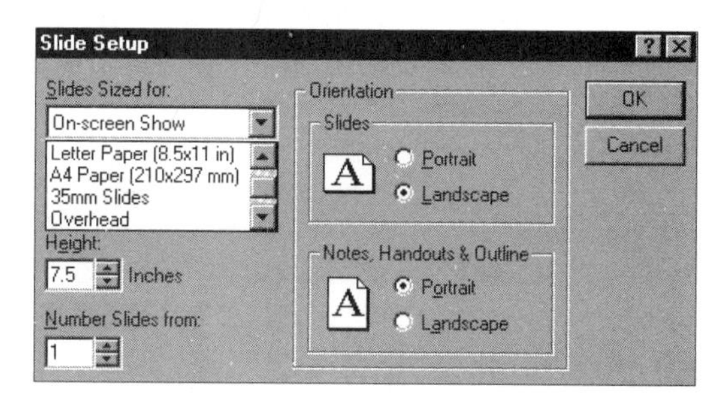

3. Click on **OK**. PowerPoint swiftly resizes every slide and Notes page, making them wider.
4. Observe the first slide. The slide itself is slightly wider, though the organization chart is the same size.

PRACTICE YOUR SKILLS

Let's reset the Slide Setup dialog box to letter-sized paper:

1. Choose **File, Slide Setup**.
2. From the Slides Sized For list, select **Letter Paper** (8.5 × 11 in) to reset the slides to print on U.S. letter paper.
3. Click on **OK**.
4. Save the file as **My Chapter 13**.

USING PRINTING OPTIONS

Once your slides are set up the way you want them, you are ready to print all or part of the presentation. As you know, PowerPoint has four views. You can print hard copy for any of these views and customize the printed copy with the print options available in the Print dialog box (shown in Figure 13.3). We will look at a few of these options in the following sections.

Note: Depending on the printer you have installed, you may have different options available to you in the Print dialog box. For the purpose of this chapter, we are assuming that you are using a laser printer. If you are using a dot-matrix or bubble-jet printer,

Figure 13.3 **The Print dialog box**

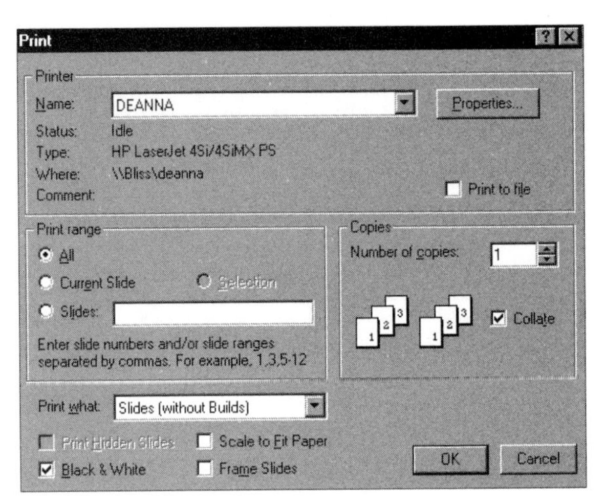

you may see different options in the Print dialog box. Don't panic. Choose the options that are appropriate for your printout. If you do not have a printer, you can still walk through most of the steps in this chapter.

If you aren't sure whether you have a printer installed, you can open the Print dialog box and check. The installed printer is displayed at the top of the dialog box.

THE PRINT RANGE OPTION

You can choose to print all the slides in your presentation, just the current slide, or a specific range of slides. This is helpful if you have a long presentation and want to see how one of the slides will look when you print it out, or if you want to show someone part of your presentation to give them an idea of what it looks like without giving the whole thing away.

Here's the general procedure for printing all the slides or just the current one:

- Choose *File, Print.*
- Click on the appropriate *Print Range* option.
- Click on *OK.*

Here's the general procedure for printing a range of slides:

- Choose *File, Print.*
- Click on *Slides.*
- Type the number of the first slide in the range you want to print.
- Type a comma (,) or hyphen (-).
- Type the number of the last slide in the range you want to print.
- Click on *OK.*

THE BLACK & WHITE OPTION

If you check the *Black & White* option, then all the slides in your presentation will be printed in black ink. The program will interpret all colors and fills as areas that are to be left white, and all text and lines will be converted to black.

This can be particularly useful if you want to quickly print draft copies of color presentations. It is also standard practice to print speaker's notes or handouts (we will discuss Handout pages later in this chapter) in black and white, to make them easier to read.

Figure 13.4 shows a Notes page printed in black and white. Figure 13.5 shows the same Notes page printed with the Black & White option turned off.

THE SCALE TO FIT PAPER OPTION

The Scale To Fit Paper option automatically sizes slides to fit the paper loaded in the printer. If you are creating a presentation that is to be printed on 5 × 7 paper or 11 × 14 paper, all you have to do is put the paper in the printer. This option will then be chosen for you if the paper in the printer doesn't correspond to the slide size and orientation specified in the Slide Setup box.

THE FRAME SLIDES OPTION

If you check the Frame Slides option, then PowerPoint adds a thin frame around the border of the printed slides, handouts, and Notes pages.

Figure 13.4 The Notes page printed in black and white

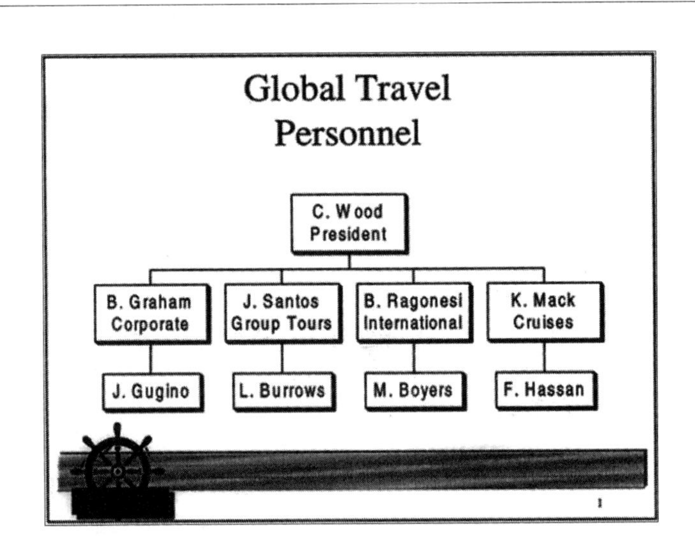

Global Travel, a full-service travel agency, was founded in 1970. Our office is operated by a team of qualified managers and experienced assistants whose goal is to provide you with quality service at the lowest price.

Figure 13.5 The Notes page printed regularly

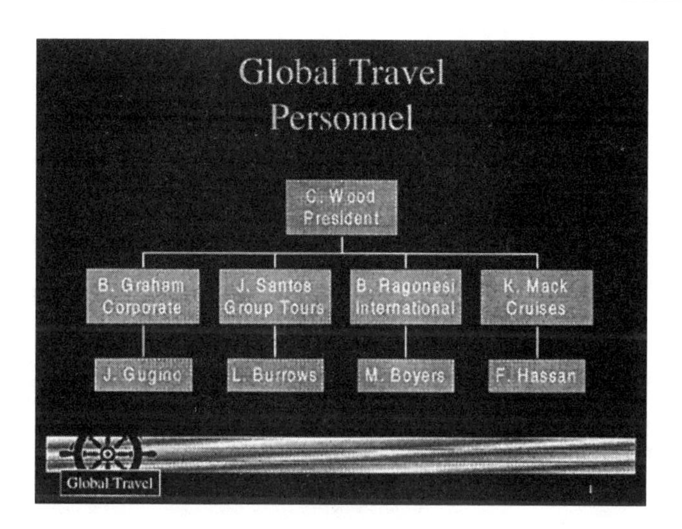

Global Travel, a full-service travel agency, was founded in 1970. Our office is operated by a team of qualified managers and experienced assistants whose goal is to provide you with quality service at the lowest price.

PRINTING SLIDES, NOTES, HANDOUTS, AND AN OUTLINE

Once you understand some of the print options that you can choose from, you are ready to look at the different output options PowerPoint offers you. Besides choosing a print range and print options in the Print dialog box, you can choose to print any part of your presentation—a slide, a Notes page, a Handout page, or an outline.

PRINTING SLIDES

When you print the slides in your presentation, you have two options:

- *Slides (With Builds)* prints each bulleted item of a build slide as a separate slide, beginning with the slide title. One bulleted item is added on each subsequent printout until all the bulleted items are printed.
- *Slides (Without Builds)* prints one page per slide, with all the bulleted items present, even though the slide builds when you run the Slide Show.

Figure 13.6 shows a printed slide without builds, and Figure 13.7 shows the first printout of the same slide when the Slides (With Builds) option is selected.

Here's the general procedure for printing slides:

- Choose *File, Print* to open the Print dialog box.
- Select the type of slide printout from the *Print What* drop-down list box.
- Select the number of slides to print from the Print Range box. You can print all slides, the current slide, or a range of slides.
- Set the number of copies you want to print.
- Click on *OK*.

Let's print a slide from My Chapter 13:

1. Save the file. It is a good idea to save the file before you print. Then, if anything goes wrong, you still have a good copy of the presentation.
2. Move to slide 2.

Figure 13.6 Slide 2 without builds

International & Domestic Travel

- Corporate accounts
- Computerized reservations
- Vacation packages
- Cruises
- Group tours

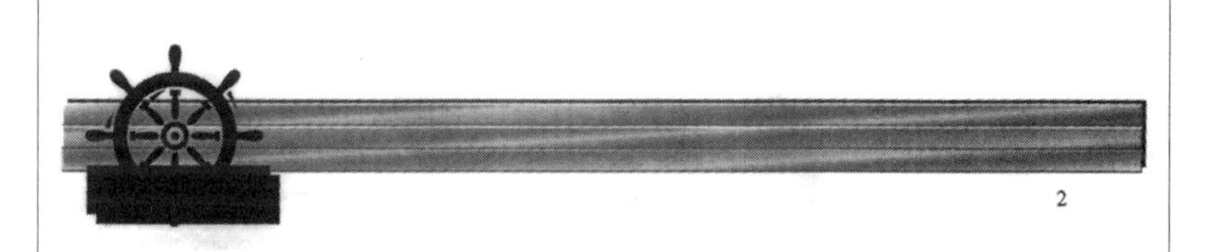

2

3. Choose **File, Print** to open the Print dialog box.
4. In the Print What box, select **Slides (Without Builds)**, if necessary.
5. In the Print Range box, click on **Current Slide** to print only the current slide (slide 2).
6. Set the number of copies to **1**, if necessary. (It is a good idea, whenever possible, to print out only one copy and then photocopy it as necessary. This is especially true with laser printers, which are sometimes warrantied for a certain number of copies rather than for a given length of time.)
7. Click on **OK** to print slide 2. Your printout should resemble that shown in Figure 13.6.

PRACTICE YOUR SKILLS

Now that you have printed a slide without builds, let's try printing a slide with builds:

Figure 13.7 **Slide 2 with builds**

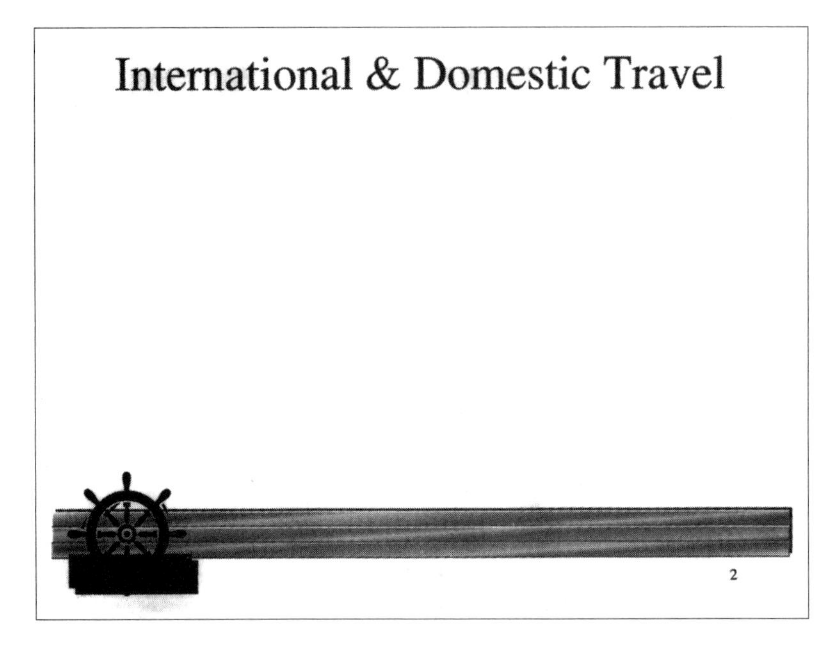

1. Print slide 2 with builds. The first page of your output should resemble that shown in Figure 13.7.
2. Save the file.

PRINTING HANDOUTS

If you are giving a presentation, you frequently will find it helpful to have handouts for your audience. PowerPoint allows you to print Handout pages showing your presentation in miniature. This allows your audience to follow along more easily as you give your presentation.

You can choose from three options when printing handouts:

- 2 Slides Per Page
- 3 Slides Per Page
- 6 Slides Per Page

You can see what these options look like in the *Handout Master*. The Handout Master, shown in Figure 13.8, allows you to format and place the text and graphics that you want on each page. It has placeholders showing what two, three, and six slides per page will look like when printed.

Figure 13.8 **The Handout Master**

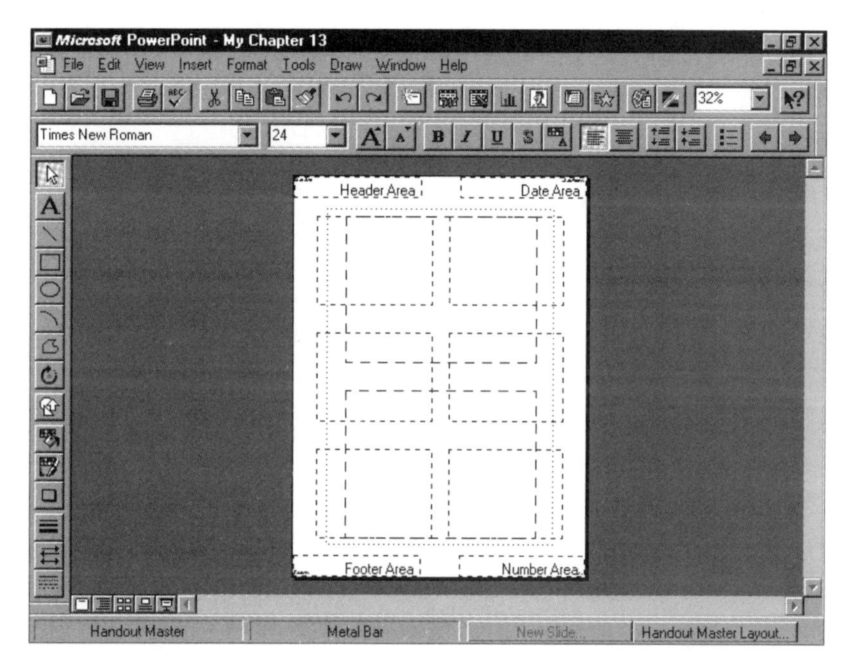

Here's the general procedure for adding text or graphics to the Handout Master:

- Choose *View, Master, Handout Master.*
- Select the *Text* tool and place the insertion point on the slide workspace.
- Type the text you want to appear on every Handout page.
- Reposition the text, if necessary, so that it is not overlapping the Handout placeholder for the option (2, 3, or 6) that you want to print.
- Add any clip art or drawings that you want on each Handout page.

Here's the general procedure for printing audience handouts:

- Add the text and graphics you want on each Handout page to the Handout Master.
- Choose *File, Print*.
- From the Print What box, select the appropriate Handout option.
- From the Print Range box, select the range you want to print.
- If necessary, set the number of copies you want to print.
- Check the *Black & White* print option, if necessary.
- Click on *OK*.

Let's print Handout pages for My Chapter 13. We'll begin by adding the company name to the Handout Master:

1. Choose **View, Master, Handout Master** to move to the Handout Master.
2. Reduce the magnification to **33%**, if necessary.
3. Select the **Text** tool and place the insertion point anywhere on the slide workspace.
4. Type **Global Travel Sales Presentation**.
5. Select the text you typed in step 3 and move it to the top and center of your Handout Master.
6. Save the file.

Now that you've added the presentation title to your Handout pages, let's print them and see how they look:

1. Choose **File, Print** to open the Print dialog box.
2. From the Print What box, select **Handouts (3 Slides Per Page)** to print three slide images per page.
3. In the Print Range box, click on **All** to print all the slides on Handout pages. You can choose to print a range of slides, too.
4. Check the **Black & White** option, if necessary. Because handouts are easier to read if they are black and white, we suggest that you always check this option when printing them.
5. Click on **OK**. PowerPoint prints Handout pages that should resemble those shown in Figure 13.9.

Figure 13.9 The Handout pages

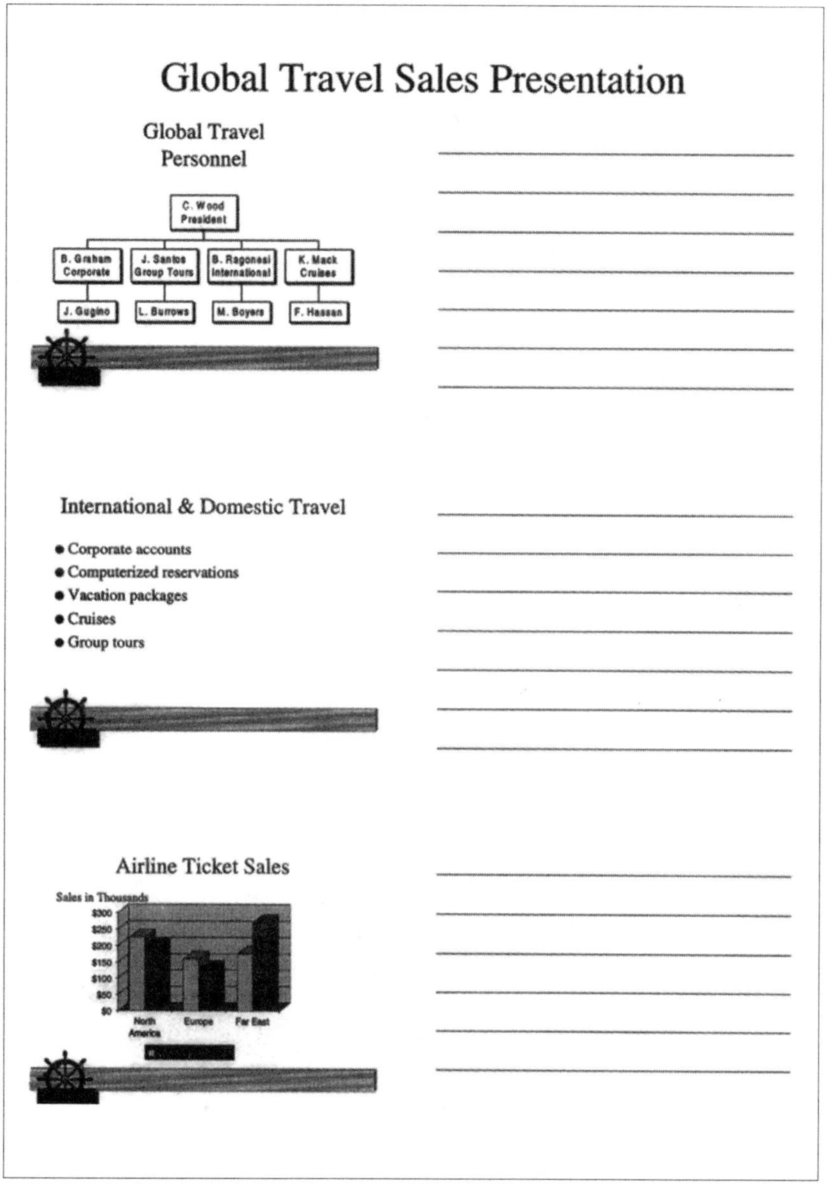

Global Travel Sales Presentation

Global Travel Personnel

C. Wood President

B. Graham Corporate

J. Santos Group Tours

B. Ragonesi International

K. Mack Cruises

J. Gugino

L. Burrows

M. Boyers

F. Hassan

International & Domestic Travel

- Corporate accounts
- Computerized reservations
- Vacation packages
- Cruises
- Group tours

Airline Ticket Sales

Sales in Thousands

$300
$250
$200
$150
$100
$50
$0

North America
Europe
Far East

Figure 13.9 The Handout pages (Continued)

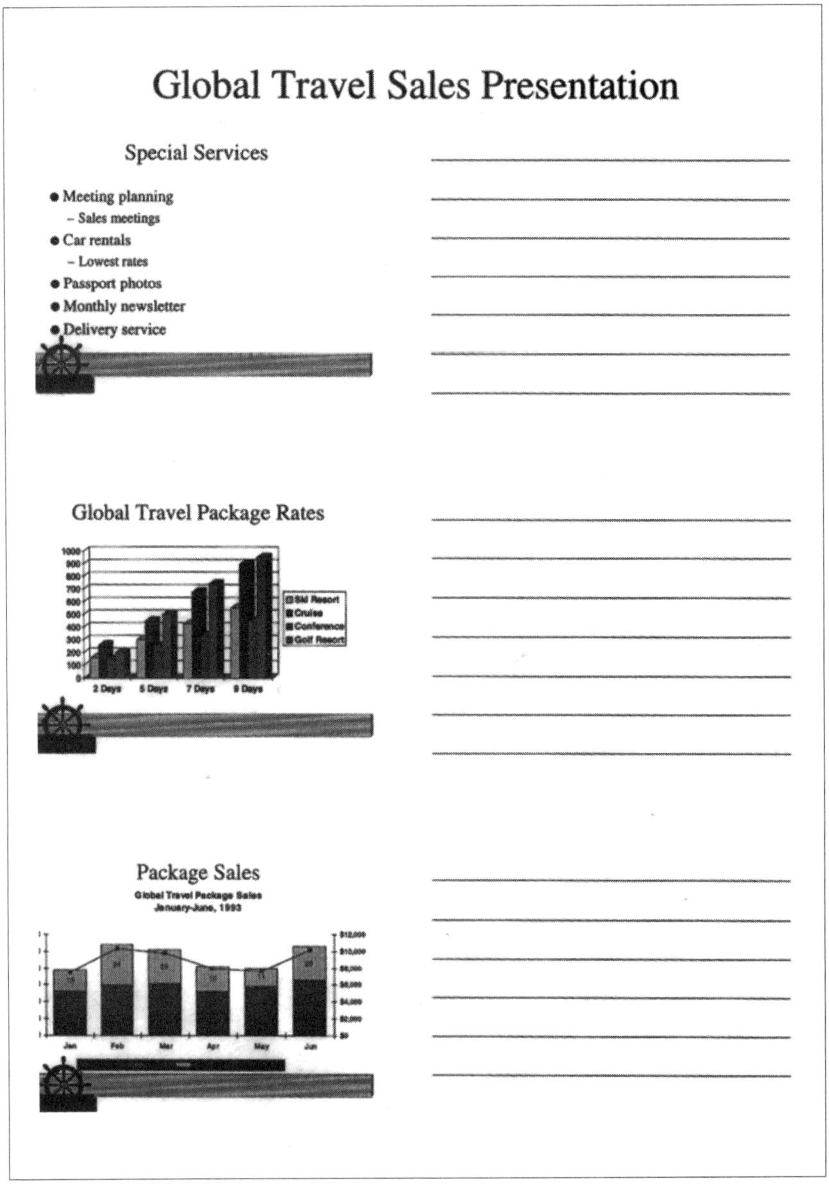

Global Travel Sales Presentation

Special Services

- Meeting planning
  - Sales meetings
- Car rentals
  - Lowest rates
- Passport photos
- Monthly newsletter
- Delivery service

Global Travel Package Rates

Ski Resort
Cruise
Conference
Golf Resort

2 Days 5 Days 7 Days 9 Days

Package Sales

Global Travel Package Sales
January-June, 1993

Jan Feb Mar Apr May Jun

Figure 13.9 The Handout pages (Continued)

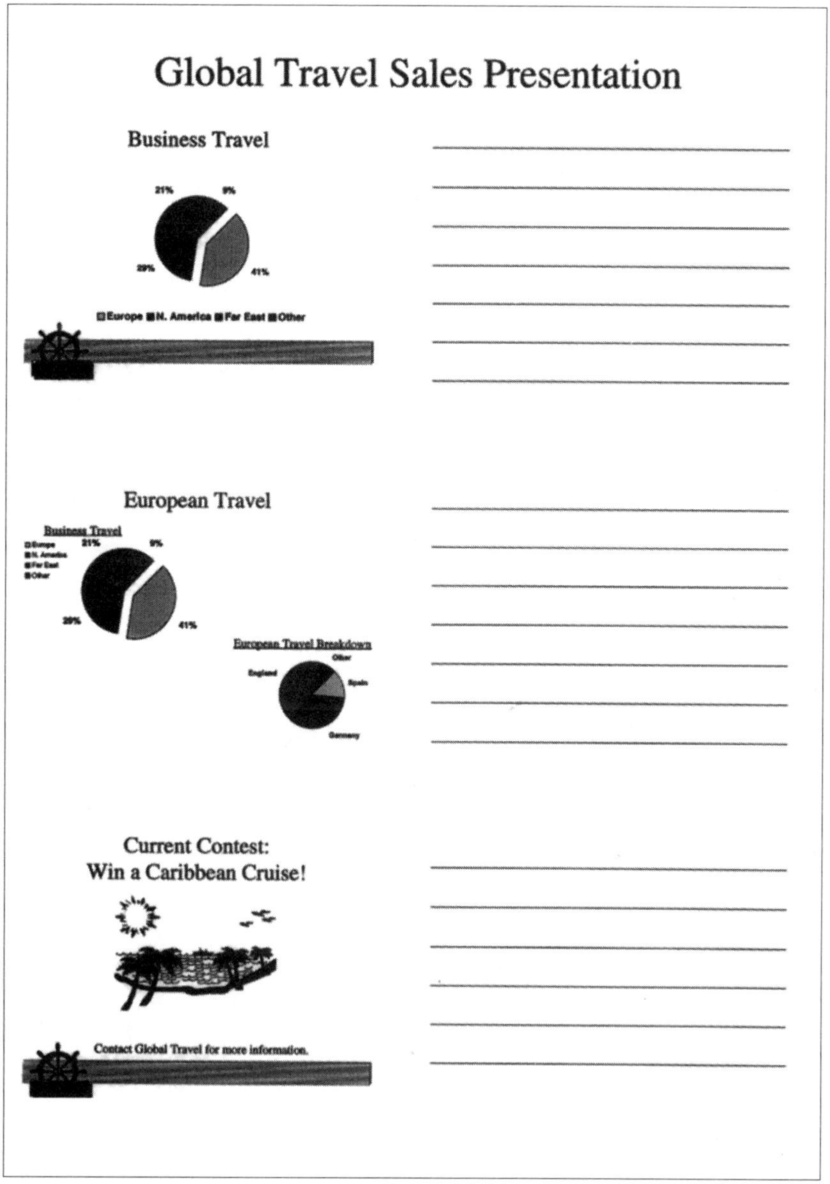

Global Travel Sales Presentation

Business Travel

21% 9% 29% 41%

Europe N. America Far East Other

European Travel

Business Travel

21% 9% 29% 41%

European Travel Breakdown

Other England Spain Germany

Current Contest:
Win a Caribbean Cruise!

Contact Global Travel for more information.

Figure 13.9 The Handout pages (Continued)

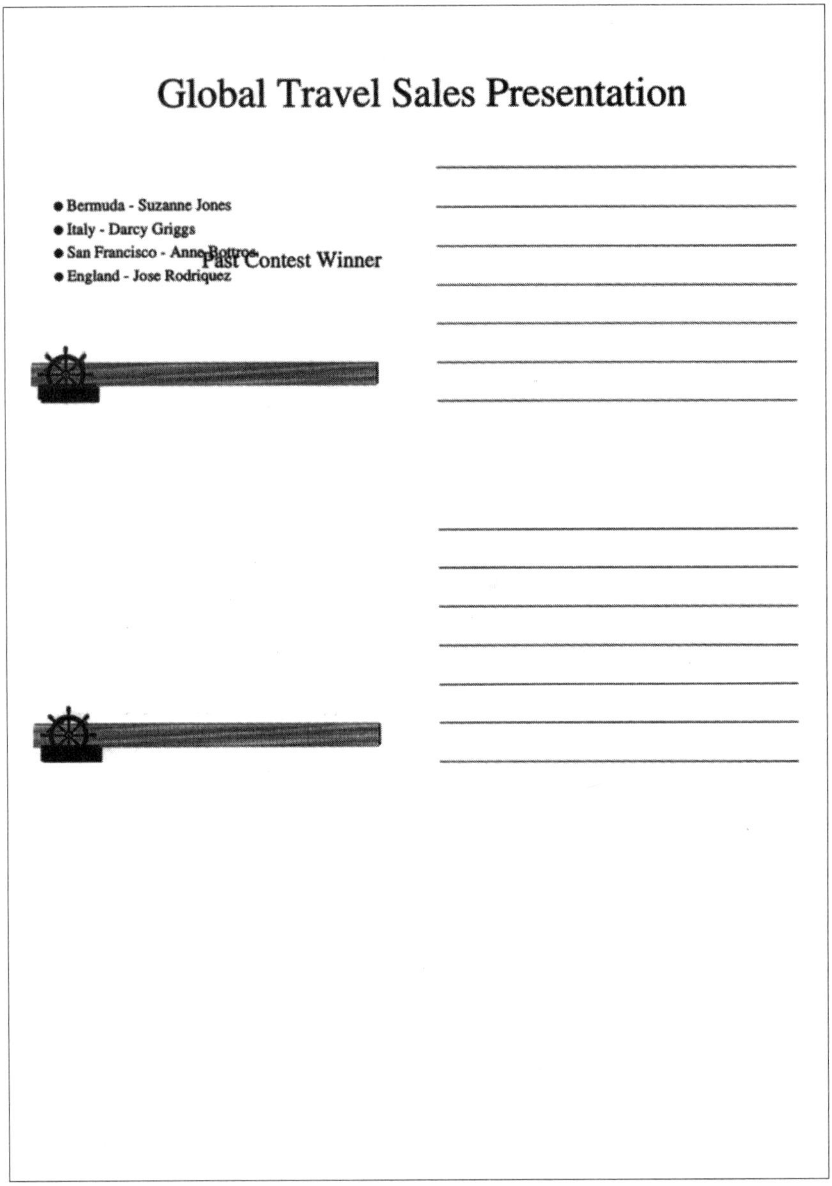

Global Travel Sales Presentation

Past Contest Winner

- Bermuda - Suzanne Jones
- Italy - Darcy Griggs
- San Francisco - Anne Bottroe
- England - Jose Rodriquez

PRINTING AN OUTLINE

PowerPoint prints an outline just as it appears on your screen. To add background items to the printed outline, you use the *Outline Master*. The Outline Master, like the Handout Master, contains a placeholder. You can add text, dates, or borders that you want to appear on every page of your outline.

Your outline prints according to the way you format it in Outline view. For example, if you display only the slide titles and increase the view to 50 percent, then your printed outline will show only slide titles at a text size comparable to a 50 percent view.

Here's the general procedure for printing an outline:

- In Outline view, format your outline: collapse or expand the titles and body text, and choose an appropriate view scale and font.
- Choose *File, Print.*
- From the Print What drop-down list, select *Outline View.*
- Click on *OK.*

Let's print an outline that resembles the one shown in Figure 13.10:

1. Choose **View, Outline**. You want to print an outline that contains only slide titles.
2. Click on the **Show Titles** button, if necessary, to collapse the body text. Printing titles only gives you a list of your slides and their slide numbers. You can then use this list to keep track of slides as you run your presentation.
3. Increase the magnification to 50 percent, if necessary.

Now that your outline is formatted the way you want it, you're ready to print:

1. Save the file. Remember, it is a good idea to save your presentation before you print it.
2. Choose **File, Print**.
3. From the Print What drop-down list box, select **Outline View**.
4. From the Slide Range box, select **All**, if necessary, to print the entire outline.
5. Click on **OK**.
6. Compare your printout to that shown in Figure 13.10.

Figure 13.10 The Printed Outline

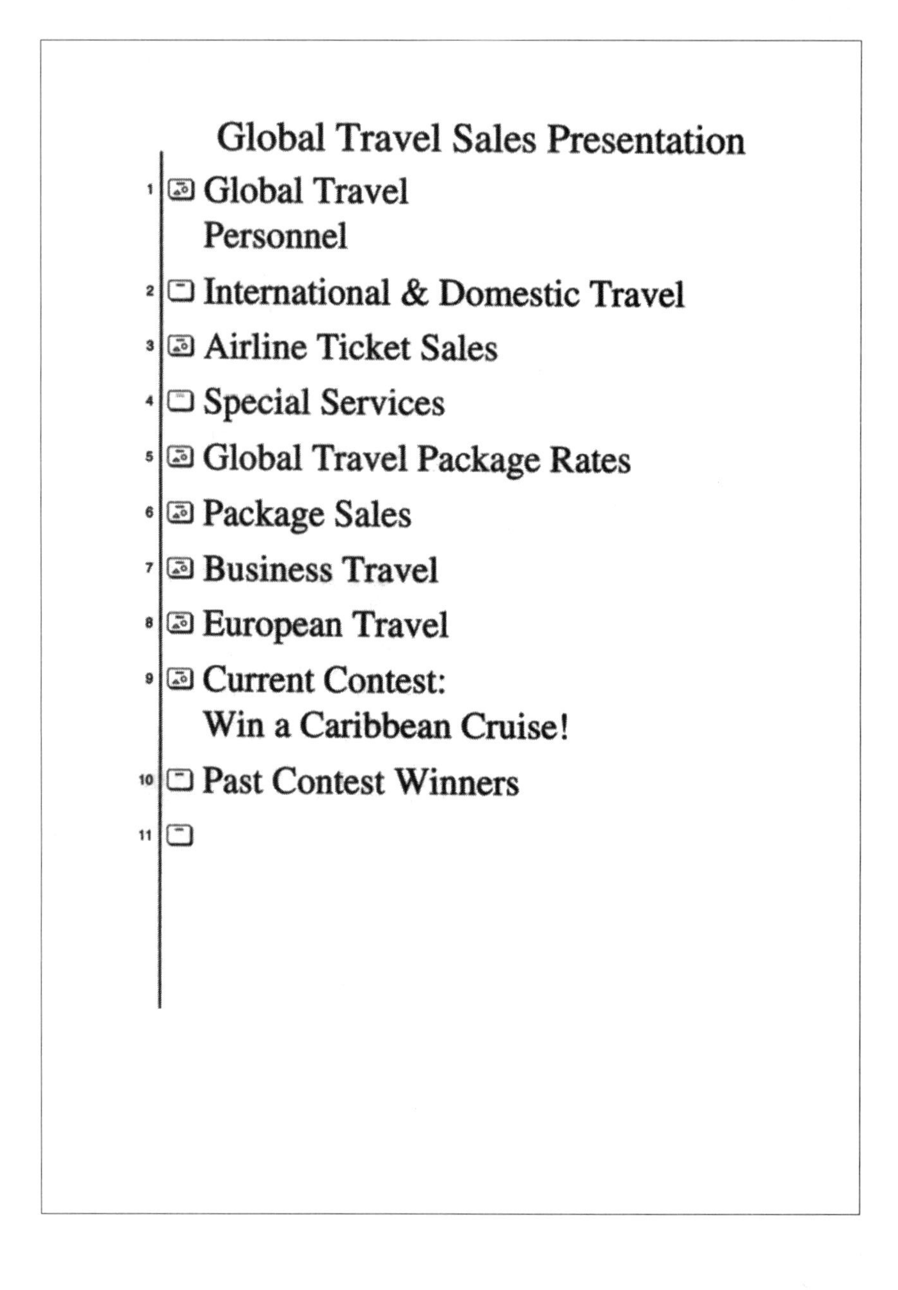

PRINTING NOTES

In addition to slides, handouts, and an outline, you can print the Notes pages you learned to create in Chapter 12. These can be used as speaker notes for yourself, or as a reference for your audience.

Here's the general procedure for printing Notes pages:

- Choose *File, Print.*
- From the Print What drop-down list, select *Notes Pages.*
- From the Print Range box, select the range option you want.
- Check the *Black & White* print option.
- Click on *OK.*

Let's print a Notes page:

1. Move to slide 9 in Slide view.
2. Click on the **Notes Pages** view button (located at the bottom of the screen, it displays a miniature slide with notes below it) to move to Notes view.
3. Observe the notes. You created a Notes page for this slide in Chapter 12.
4. Choose **File, Print**.
5. From the Print What drop-down list, select **Notes Pages**.
6. In the Slide Range box, select **Current Slide** to print the Notes page for only the current slide.
7. Check the **Black & White** option, if necessary, and click on **OK**.
8. Observe your Notes page printout. It should resemble that shown in Figure 13.11.
9. Save the file
10. Close the file.

PRACTICE YOUR SKILLS

Throughout the course of this book, you have learned how to create a professional-looking presentation. Now you'll use several of these skills to create the presentation shown in Figure 13.12 (located at the end of the exercise). **Note:** This practice exercise is

Four times a year, Global Travel offers clients the chance to enter a drawing for a free trip. This quarter, one lucky person will win an all-expenses paid, seven-day Caribbean cruise.

Figure 13.11 The Notes page for slide 9

quite long. It is not necessary to finish the entire practice in one sitting, however. Feel free to work on it over an extended period of time. Make sure you save it whenever you stop, though. Then, next time you sit down, you can begin where you left off.

Let's begin creating the presentation:

1. Create a new blank presentation (Chapter 7).
2. Choose **Title Only** as the autolayout for the first slide in the new presentation. (Hint: It's in the third row of autolayouts.)
3. Type the title **Global Travel** (Chapter 7).
4. Use the **Text** tool to type the following text at the left center of the slide:

   Training

   Perspectives

5. Change the size of the text you typed in step 4 to **60 point** and add a text shadow. (Hint: Use the **Format, Font** command to add a text shadow.)
6. Select the text object **Training Perspectives** and use the **Format** menu to add a gray shadow.
7. Add a new bulleted-list slide and type the title **Training Philosophy** (Chapter 7).
8. Type the following bulleted body text for slide 2 (Chapters 2 and 3):

   Teach consistent methodology to provide consistent quality

   Build internal talents and capabilities

   Respond quickly to anticipated market shifts

   Share ideas and solutions through worldwide team approach

9. Switch to Outline view (Chapter 2).
10. Create a new slide and increase the view to 50 percent (Chapter 7).
11. Type the title **The focus...** for slide 3 (Chapter 3).

12. Type the following Body text for slide 3 (Chapter 3):

    Teams of internal experts

    Build curriculum

    Monitor results to ensure effective training

    5.5% of revenue reinvested in training

    6 million hours of training per year

    138 hours per person per year

13. Demote the following lines one level:

    Build curriculum

    Monitor results to ensure effective training

    138 hours per person per year

14. In Slide view, move the bulleted item **5.5% of revenue reinvested in training** below the bulleted item *6 million hours of training per year* (Chapter 3).
15. Change the Body object's line spacing to **1.10** for slides 2 and 3 (Chapter 3).
16. Insert a new Title Only slide after slide 1 (Chapter 2).
17. Type the title **Global Travel**.
18. Save the file as **Skills 4**.
19. Run the slide show.
20. Apply the **Twinkle** design template to the presentation (Chapters 6 and 10).
21. Add a new graph slide (slide 5) to the end of the presentation, then type the title **How we train...**.
22. Start Microsoft Graph (Chapters 8 and 9).
23. Clear the data from the datasheet (Chapter 9).

24. Input the following information into the datasheet (Chapter 8 and 9):

	Instructor led	**Self-study**	**Seminars**
Customer Service	**27.4**	**20.7**	**90**
Computer Skills	**83**	**38.6**	**34.6**
Time Management	**45.9**	**46.9**	**45**

(Hint: You can resize the cells in the datasheet to see all the data in each cell.)

25. Move the legend to the bottom of the chart (Chapter 9).
26. Change the data to **Series In Columns** (Chapter 9).
27. Return to the presentation, updating the chart on the slide.
28. Scale the chart to **115** percent.
29. Reposition the chart, if necessary.
30. Add the label **Hours** to the y-axis (Chapter 8).

Now let's edit the Slide Master:

1. Move to the Slide Master.
2. Display the **Academic** clip art category and view the magnifying glass (Chapters 5 and 10). (Hint: Select the category from the categories list.)
3. Select the magnifying glass and click on **Insert**.
4. Scale the magnifying glass to **35** percent (Chapter 10). (Hint: Select the magnifying glass and use the **Draw, Scale** command.)
5. Move the magnifying glass to the lower-right corner of the Slide Master.
6. Save the file.
7. Run the slide show.
8. Turn off the background items on slide 5 (Chapter 10).

9. Move to slide 2 and insert the picture **Focus Object** (Chapter 11).
10. Move slide 2 ahead of slide 1 (Chapter 12).
    (Hint: Switch to Slide Sorter view to move the slides.)
11. Add transitions to the slides. Have the slides advance automatically after 6 seconds (Chapter 12).
12. Add builds to slides 3 and 4 (Chapter 12).
13. Add the following speaker's note to slide 5 (Chapter 12):

    Global Travel believes that better training makes better employees and happier customers.

14. Save the file.
15. Run the slide show.
16. Print the Notes page for slide 5.
17. Close the presentation and exit PowerPoint.

Figure 13.12 **The completed Skills 4 presentation, printed as slides**

Figure 13.12 **The completed Skills 4 presentation, printed as slides (Continued)**

Training
Perspectives

Figure 13.12 **The completed Skills 4 presentation, printed as slides (Continued)**

Training Philosophy

- Teach consistent methodology to provide consistent quality
- Build internal talents and capabilities
- Respond quickly to anticipated market shifts
- Share ideas and solutions through worldwide team approach

Figure 13.12 The completed Skills 4 presentation, printed as slides (Continued)

- Teams of internal experts
  - Build curriculum
  - Monitor results to ensure effective training
- 6 million hours of training per year
  - 138 hours per person per year
- 5.5% of revenue reinvested in training

Figure 13.12 The completed Skills 4 presentation, printed as slides (Continued)

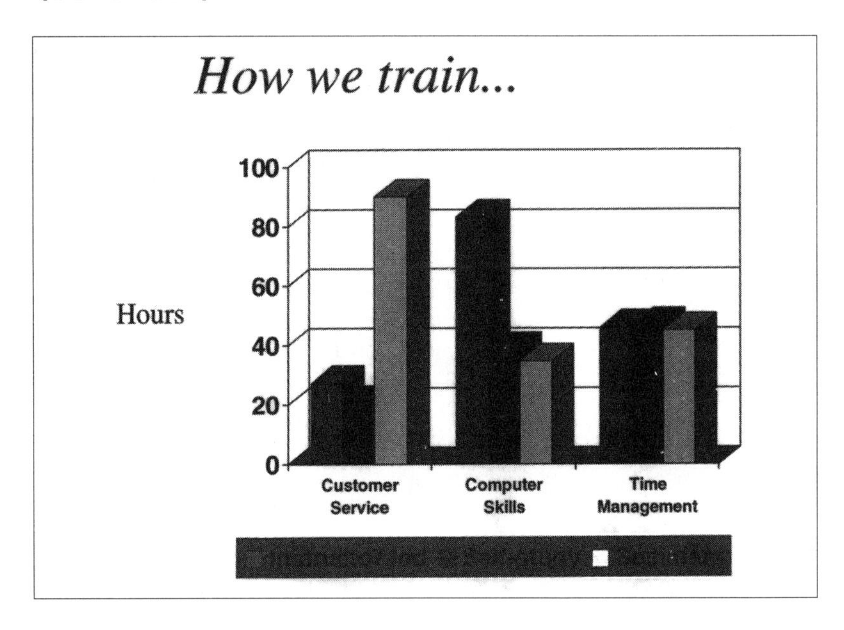

SUMMARY

In this chapter, you learned various techniques to help you manage the printing of your presentation. You learned how to change the slide setup, how to change print options, how to print all or part of a presentation, how to print an outline, how to print Notes pages, and how to print Handout pages.

With this chapter, you have completed your foundation of PowerPoint skills. Congratulations! You can now venture out into the real world to create and print handsome, sophisticated PowerPoint presentations.

Here's a quick reference guide to the PowerPoint features introduced in this chapter:

Desired Result	**How to Do It**
Change the slide setup	Choose **File, Slide Setup**; choose the appropriate Slides Sized For option for your presentation output; choose an orientation option; select a number with which to begin numbering the slides; click on **OK**
Print all or just the current slide	Choose **File, Print**; click on the appropriate Print Range option; click on **OK**
Print a range of slides	Choose **File, Print**; click on **Slides**; type the number of the first slide in the range you want to print; type a comma (,) or hyphen (-); type the number of the last slide in the range you want to print
Print slides	Choose **File, Print**; select the type of slide printout from the Print What drop-down list box; select the number of slides to print from the Print Range box; set the number of copies you want to print; click on **OK**

Desired Result	**How to Do It**
Add text or graphics to the Handout Master	Choose **View, Master, Handout Master**; select the **Text** tool and place the insertion point on the slide workspace; type the text you want to appear on every Handout page; reposition the text, if necessary, so that it is not overlapping the Handout placeholder for the option (2, 3, or 6) that you want to print; add any clip art or drawings that you want on each Handout page
Print Handout pages	Add the text and graphics you want on each Handout page to the Handout Master; choose **File, Print**; from the Print What drop-down list box, select the appropriate Handout option; from the Print Range box, select the range you want to print; if necessary, set the number of copies you want to print; check the **Black & White** print option; click on **OK**
Print an outline	Choose **View, Master, Handout Master** and add any elements that you want on every page; in Outline view, format your outline; choose **File, Print** to open the Print dialog box; from the Print What drop-down list box, select **Outline** view; in the Print Range box, click on **All**; click on **OK**
Print Notes pages	Choose **File, Print**; from the Print What drop-down list box, select **Notes Pages**; from the Print Range box, select the range option you want; check **Black & White**; click on **OK**

Following this chapter are three appendices: Appendix A, "Installation," walks you through PowerPoint 7.0 installation and printer selection; Appendix B, "Toolbar Reference," lists the buttons for the Toolbar in each of PowerPoint's views; and Appendix C, "Keystroke Reference," lists the keystroke equivalents of the mouse and menu commands in this book.

APPENDIX A: INSTALLATION

Before You Begin Installing

Installing PowerPoint On Your Computer

This appendix contains instructions for installing PowerPoint 7.0 for Windows 95 on your computer.

BEFORE YOU BEGIN INSTALLING

Please read through the following two sections before beginning the installation procedure.

PROTECTING YOUR ORIGINAL INSTALLATION DISKS

PowerPoint comes with several floppy disks or a CD-ROM that you'll need in order to install the program on your computer. Before you begin, you should protect your original installation disks from accidental erasure. When a disk is protected, its data can be read but not modified.

To protect a 3½-inch disk:

- Slide the plastic locking button in the corner of the disk to its uppermost position.

REQUIRED HARD-DISK SPACE

You need to have at least 24MB of free hard-disk space to install PowerPoint 7.0 for Windows 95. (While this is the amount required for complete installation, not the installation we will perform, we recommend this upper limit in order to be safe.) If you do not have this much free hard-disk space, you will have to delete enough files from your hard disk to bring the total free space up to 24MB. For help in doing this, please refer to your DOS or Windows manual.

Note: Remember to *back up* (copy to a floppy disk) any files that you wish to preserve before deleting them from your hard disk.

INSTALLING POWERPOINT ON YOUR COMPUTER

Follow these steps to install PowerPoint 7.0 for Windows 95:

1. Start Windows 95. (If you have not already installed Windows 95 on your system, please do so now; for help, see your Windows 95 reference manuals.)
2. Insert the installation disk labeled *Setup* in the appropriate drive. If you are installing PowerPoint from a network, you will be prompted for the drive and folder later in the installation process.

3. In the taskbar, click on **Start**, point to **Settings**, and choose **Control Panel**.
4. Double-click on the **Add/Remove Programs** icon and then verify that the Install/Uninstall tab is active.
5. Click on the **Install** button to begin the installation.
6. Follow the on-screen instructions to complete the installation. Here are some guidelines:
    - For help understanding the contents of an installation dialog box, click on its *Help* button.
    - In general, accept all installation defaults (by clicking on *Continue* or *OK*).
    - When prompted to select an installation option, choose either *Typical* or *Custom* to install PowerPoint. The *Typical option* installs the basic PowerPoint setup, which will still give you access to many features. The *Custom option* allows you to install the PowerPoint components of your choice. The hard-disk space required for each component is listed next to it.
    - If you discover that you don't have enough free hard-disk space to install the option of your dreams, either exit the installation procedure, free up some space on your hard disk and repeat the installation, or try life without it.
7. When the installation is complete, you are returned to Windows 95. To start PowerPoint, click on **Start**, point to **Programs**, and click on **Microsoft PowerPoint**. If you've installed Microsoft Office, you'll need to click on **Microsoft Office** in the Program menu and then click on **Microsoft PowerPoint**.

APPENDIX B: TOOLBAR REFERENCE

Your PowerPoint application and presentation windows are chock-full of interactive screen elements—buttons, tools, drop-down list boxes, tear-off palette boxes, and so on—so many that it's positively daunting to try to remember them all! The ToolTips feature, which lets you display a button's name and function by pointing to it, makes life somewhat easier. However, you can only examine one button at a time. The figures and tables in this appendix provide you with an overview of PowerPoint's grand gaggle of screen elements. If you take the time to learn what these elements do, they'll help you to work more quickly and increase your overall PowerPoint fluency.

Figure B.1 **The Standard toolbar**

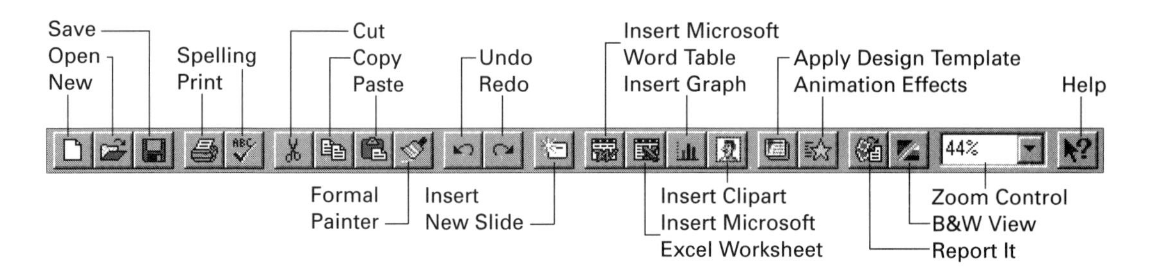

Table B.1 **The Standard Toolbar**

Button	**Function**
New	Creates a new presentation
Open	Opens an existing presentation
Save	Saves the active presentation
Print	Prints the active presentation
Spelling	Spell-checks the active presentation
Cut	Moves the selected object to the Clipboard
Copy	Copies the selected object to the Clipboard
Paste	Pastes the Clipboard contents to the slide
Format Painter	Copies the selected format
Undo	Undoes the last action
Redo	Redoes the last action that was undone
Insert New Slide	Adds a new slide after the current slide
Insert Microsoft Word Table	Adds a Microsoft Word table to the slide
Insert Microsoft Excel Worksheet	Adds an Excel worksheet to the slide

Table B.1 **The Standard Toolbar (Continued)**

Button	Function
Insert Graph	Adds a Microsoft graph to the slide
Insert Clip Art	Adds clip art to the slide
Apply Design Template	Opens the Apply Design Template dialog box
Animation Effects	Displays the Animation Effects toolbar
Report It	Saves the active presentation's contents to a Microsoft Word outline
B&W View	Displays the active presentation in black and white
Zoom Control	Changes the magnification at which you edit
Help	Provides context-sensitive help

Figure B.2 **The Formatting toolbar**

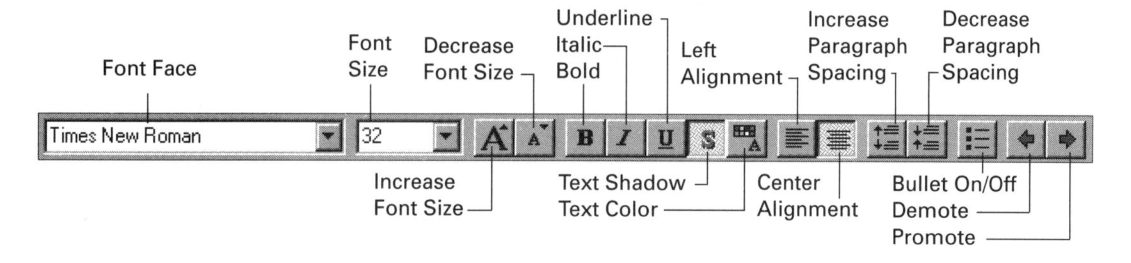

Table B.2 **The Formatting Toolbar**

Button	Function
Font Face	Changes the selected text's font
Font Size	Changes the selected text's font size
Increase Font Size	Enlarges the font size
Decrease Font Size	Reduces the font size
Bold	Bolds the selected text
Italics	Italicizes the selected text
Underline	Underlines the selected text
Text Shadow	Shadows the selected text
Text Color	Changes the color of the selected text
Left Alignment	Left-aligns the selected text
Center Alignment	Centers the selected text
Increase Paragraph Spacing	Adds more space between selected paragraphs
Decrease Paragraph Spacing	Reduces space between selected paragraphs
Bullet On/Off	Adds/removes the default bullet from the selected paragraphs
Promote	Unindents the selected paragraphs by one level
Demote	Indents the selected paragraphs by one level

Figure B.3 **The Formatting toolbar (in Slide Sorter view)**

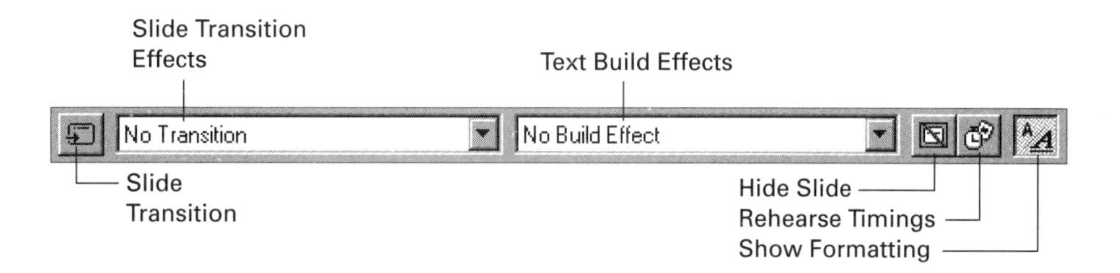

Table B.3 **The Formatting Toolbar (in Slide Sorter View)**

Button	Function
Slide Transition	Determines the transition attributes for the selected slide
Slide Transition Effects	Determines the transition effect for the selected slide
Text Build Effects	Determines the build effect for the selected slide
Hide Slide	Skips the selected slide(s) in a slide show
Rehearse Timings	Runs and rehearses a slide show
Show Formatting	Displays all character formatting (in Outline view) or titles (in Slide view)

Figure B.4 **The Drawing toolbar**

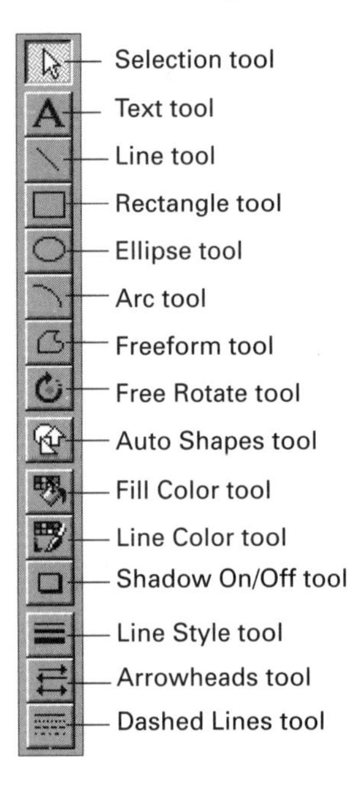

Table B.4 **The DrawingToolbar**

Button	Function
Selection tool	Selects and edits objects
Text tool	Creates text objects
Line tool	Creates straight lines
Rectangle tool	Creates rectangles
Ellipse tool	Creates ellipses
Arc tool	Creates arcs
Freeform tool	Creates freeform objects
Free Rotate tool	Rotates the selected object
AutoShapes tool	Creates autoshapes
Fill Color tool	Adds/removes default fill color

Table B.4 **The DrawingToolbar (Continued)**

Button	Function
Line Color tool	Adds/removes default line color
Shadow On/Off tool	Adds/removes default shadow color
Line Style tool	Changes the thickness of a line
Arrowheads tool	Adds arrowheads to selected lines, arcs, or open free forms
Dashed Lines tool	Changes the style of the selected line to dashed

Figure B.5 **The Outline toolbar (in Outline view)**

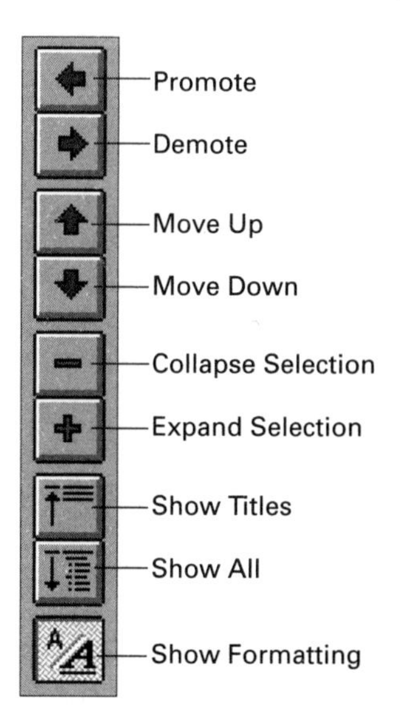

Table B.5 **The Outline Toolbar (in Outline View)**

Button	Function
Promote	Promotes the selected paragraphs one level
Demote	Demotes the selected paragraphs one level

Table B.5 **The Outline Toolbar (in Outline View) (Continued)**

Button	Function
Move Up	Moves the selected text above the previous outline text
Move Down	Moves the selected text below the next outline text
Collapse Selection	Displays only the titles of the selected text
Expand Selection	Displays all levels of the selected text
Show Titles	Displays only the slide titles
Show All	Displays all the slide text
Show Formatting	Displays all character formatting (in Outline view) or titles (in Slide view)

Figure B.6 **The View buttons**

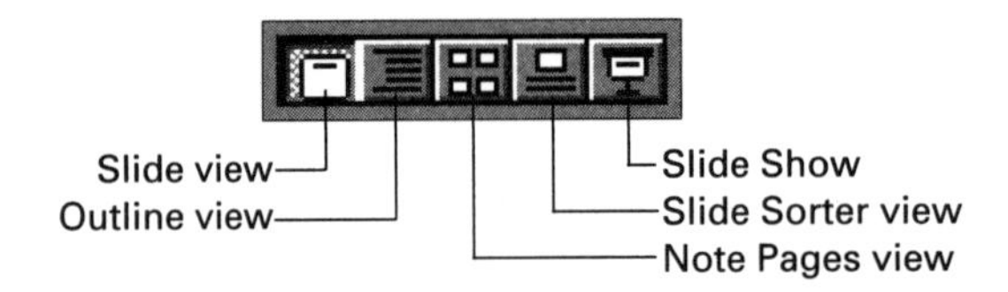

Table B.6 **The View Buttons**

Button	Function
Slide View	Changes to Slide view
Outline View	Changes to Outline view
Slide Sorter View	Changes to Slide Sorter view
Notes Pages View	Changes to Notes Pages view
Slide Show	Runs a slide show of active presentation

APPENDIX C: KEYSTROKE REFERENCE

In PowerPoint, many of the actions that can be performed with the mouse can also be performed with the keyboard. Choose the method—or combination of methods—that works best for you. Tables C.1 through C.8 list PowerPoint actions and the corresponding keystrokes required to perform them.

Table C.1 **Deleting and Copying**

Action	Keystroke
Delete character left	Backspace
Delete word left	Ctrl+Backspace
Delete character right	Delete
Delete word right	Ctrl+Delete
Cut	Ctrl+X
Copy	Ctrl+C
Paste	Ctrl+V
Undo	Ctrl+Z

Table C.2 **Formatting**

Action	Keystroke
Change font	Ctrl+Shift+F
Change point size	Ctrl+Shift+P
Increase font size	Ctrl+Shift+>
Decrease font size	Ctrl+Shift+<
Bold	Ctrl+B
Underline	Ctrl+U
Italic	Ctrl+I
Subscript	Alt+Ctrl+Shift+<
Superscript	Alt+Ctrl+Shift+>
Plain text	Ctrl+Shift+Z
Toggle case	Shift+F3
Format character	Ctrl+T

Table C.2 **Formatting (Continued)**

Action	Keystroke
Center paragraph	Ctrl+E
Justify paragraph	Ctrl+J
Left-align paragraph	Ctrl+L
Right-align paragraph	Ctrl+R

Table C.3 **Menu Commands**

File Commands	
Action	**Keystroke**
New	Ctrl+N
Open	Ctrl+O or Ctrl+F12
Close	Ctrl+W or Ctrl+F4
Save	Ctrl+S or Shift+F12
Print	Ctrl+P or Ctrl+Shift+F12
Exit	Ctrl+Q or Alt+F4
Edit Commands	
Undo	Ctrl+Z
Redo	Ctrl+Y
Clear	Delete
Cut	Ctrl+X or Shift+Delete
Copy	Ctrl+C or Ctrl+Insert
Paste	Ctrl+V or Shift+Insert
Select all	Ctrl+A
Find	Ctrl+F

Table C.3 **Menu Commands (Continued)**

File Commands	
Replace	Ctrl+H
Edit Commands	
Duplicate	Ctrl+D
View Commands	
Show guides	Ctrl+G
Normal view to Master view	Shift+click View button
Insert Commands	
Date	Alt+Shift+D
Time	Alt+Shift+T
Page number	Alt+Shift+P
New slide	Ctrl+M
Tools	
Spelling	Ctrl+Alt+L or F7
Draw Commands	
Group	Ctrl+Shift+G
Ungroup	Ctrl+Shift+H
Regroup	Ctrl+Shift+J
Help	
Contents	F1
Context-sensitive help	Shift+F1

Table C.4 **Navigating**

Action	Keystroke
Character right	Right Arrow
Character left	Left Arrow
Line up	Up Arrow
Line down	Down Arrow
Word left	Ctrl+Left Arrow
Word right	Ctrl+Right Arrow
End of line	End
Beginning of line	Home
Paragraph up	Ctrl+Up Arrow
Paragraph down	Ctrl+Down Arrow
End of page object (Outline view	Ctrl+End
Start of page object (Outline view)	Ctrl+Home
Move from title to text	Ctrl+Enter
Go to first slide	Ctrl+Home
Go to last slide	Ctrl+End

Table C.5 **Outlining**

Action	Keystroke
Promote paragraph	Alt+Shift+Left Arrow
Demote paragraph	Alt+Shift+Right Arrow
Move selected paragraph(s) up	Alt+Shift+Up Arrow
Move selected paragraph(s) down	Alt+Shift+Down Arrow
Show heading level 1	Alt+Shift+1

Table C.5 Outlining (Continued)

Action	Keystroke
Expand text under a heading	Alt+Shift+Plus (+)
Collapse text under a heading	Alt+Shift+Minus (–)
Show all text and headings	Alt+Shift+A
Display character formatting	/ (Numeric keypad)

Table C.6 Selecting

Action	Keystroke
Character right	Shift+Right Arrow
Character left	Shift+Left Arrow
End of word	Ctrl+Shift+Right Arrow
Beginning of word	Ctrl+Shift+Left Arrow
Line up	Shift+Up Arrow
Line down	Shift+Down Arrow
Select all objects (in Slide view)	Ctrl+A
Select all slides (in Slide Sorter view)	Ctrl+A
Select all text (in Outline view)	Ctrl+A
Any text	Drag with left mouse button
Word	Double-click
Paragraph	Triple-click
Drag and drop	Select and drag
Drag and drop copy	Ctrl+select and drag

Table C.7 **Activating Windows and Menus**

Action	Keystroke
Go to previous presentation window	Ctrl+Shift+F6
Go to next presentation window	Ctrl+F6
Maximize application window	Alt+F10
Display shortcut menu	Click right mouse button

Table C.8 **Slide Shows**

Action	Keystroke
Go to slide <*number*>	<*Number* >+Enter
Black/unblack screen	B or . (period)
White/unwhite screen	W or , (comma)
Show/hide pointer	A or =
Stop/restart automatic show	S or +
End show	Esc, Ctrl+Break, or -
Erase screen annotations	E
Use new time	T
Use original time	O
Advance on mouse click	M
Advance to hidden slide	H
Advance to next slide	Click, Spacebar, N, Right Arrow, Down Arrow, or Page Down
Return to previous slide	Backspace, P, Left Arrow, Up Arrow, or Page Up

INDEX

Note: Italicized page numbers denote figures.

A

B

C

R

S

T

U

V

W

X

Y

Z

■ END-USER LICENSE AGREEMENT

READ THIS AGREEMENT CAREFULLY BEFORE BUYING THIS BOOK. BY BUYING THE BOOK AND USING THE PROGRAM LISTINGS, CD-ROM, AND PROGRAMS REFERRED TO BELOW, YOU ACCEPT THE TERMS OF THIS AGREEMENT.

The program listings included in this book and the programs included on the CD-ROM contained in the package at the back of the book ("CD-ROM") are proprietary products of Ziff-Davis Press and/or third party suppliers ("Suppliers"). The program listings and programs are hereinafter collectively referred to as the "Programs." Ziff-Davis Press and the Suppliers retain ownership of the CD-ROM and copyright to the Programs, as their respective interests may appear. The Programs and the copy of the CD-ROM provided are licensed (not sold) to you under the conditions set forth herein.

License. You may use the CD-ROM on any compatible computer, provided that the CD-ROM is used on only one computer and by one user at a time.

Restrictions. You may not commercially distribute the CD-ROM or the Programs or otherwise reproduce, publish, or distribute or otherwise use the CD-ROM or the Programs in any manner that may infringe any copyright or other proprietary right of Ziff-Davis Press, the Suppliers, or any other party or assign, sublicense, or otherwise transfer the CD-ROM or this agreement to any other party unless such party agrees to accept the terms and conditions of this agreement. This license and your right to use the CD-ROM and the Programs automatically terminates if you fail to comply with any provision of this agreement.

U.S. GOVERNMENT RESTRICTED RIGHTS. The CD-ROM and the programs are provided with **RESTRICTED RIGHTS**. Use, duplication, or disclosure by the Government is subject to restrictions as set forth in subparagraph (c)(1)(ii) of the Rights in Technical Data and Computer Software Clause at DFARS (48 CFR 252.277-7013). The Proprietor of the compilation of the Programs and the CD-ROM is Ziff-Davis Press, 5903 Christie Avenue, Emeryville, CA 94608.

Limited Warranty. Ziff-Davis Press warrants the physical CD-ROM to be free of defects in materials and workmanship under normal use for a period of 30 days from the purchase date. If Ziff-Davis Press receives written notification within the warranty period of defects in materials or workmanship in the physical CD-ROM, and such notification is determined by Ziff-Davis Press to be correct, Ziff-Davis Press will, at its option, replace the defective CD-ROM or refund a prorata portion of the purchase price of the book. **THESE ARE YOUR SOLE REMEDIES FOR ANY BREACH OF WARRANTY.**

EXCEPT AS SPECIFICALLY PROVIDED ABOVE, THE CD-ROM AND THE PROGRAMS ARE PROVIDED "AS IS" WITHOUT ANY WARRANTY OF ANY KIND. NEITHER ZIFF-DAVIS PRESS NOR THE SUPPLIERS MAKE ANY WARRANTY OF ANY KIND AS TO THE ACCURACY OR COMPLETENESS OF THE CD-ROM OR THE PROGRAMS OR THE RESULTS TO BE OBTAINED FROM USING THE CD-ROM OR THE PROGRAMS AND NEITHER ZIFF-DAVIS PRESS NOR THE SUPPLIERS SHALL BE RESPONSIBLE FOR ANY CLAIMS ATTRIBUTABLE TO ERRORS, OMISSIONS, OR OTHER INACCURACIES IN THE CD-ROM OR THE PROGRAMS. THE ENTIRE RISK AS TO THE RESULTS AND PERFORMANCE OF THE CD-ROM AND THE PROGRAMS IS ASSUMED BY THE USER. FURTHER, NEITHER ZIFF-DAVIS PRESS NOR THE SUPPLIERS MAKE ANY REPRESENTATIONS OR WARRANTIES, EITHER EXPRESS OR IMPLIED, WITH RESPECT TO THE CD-ROM OR THE PROGRAMS, INCLUDING BUT NOT LIMITED TO, THE QUALITY, PERFORMANCE, MERCHANTABILITY, OR FITNESS FOR A PARTICULAR PURPOSE OF THE CD-ROM OR THE PROGRAMS. IN NO EVENT SHALL ZIFF-DAVIS PRESS OR THE SUPPLIERS BE LIABLE FOR DIRECT, INDIRECT, SPECIAL, INCIDENTAL, OR CONSEQUENTIAL DAMAGES ARISING OUT THE USE OF OR INABILITY TO USE THE CD-ROM OR THE PROGRAMS OR FOR ANY LOSS OR DAMAGE OF ANY NATURE CAUSED TO ANY PERSON OR PROPERTY AS A RESULT OF THE USE OF THE CD-ROM OR THE PROGRAMS, EVEN IF ZIFF-DAVIS PRESS OR THE SUPPLIERS HAVE BEEN SPECIFICALLY ADVISED OF THE POSSIBILITY OF SUCH DAMAGES. NEITHER ZIFF-DAVIS PRESS NOR THE SUPPLIERS ARE RESPONSIBLE FOR ANY COSTS INCLUDING, BUT NOT LIMITED TO, THOSE INCURRED AS A RESULT OF LOST PROFITS OR REVENUE, LOSS OF USE OF THE CD-ROM OR THE PROGRAMS, LOSS OF DATA, THE COSTS OF RECOVERING SOFTWARE OR DATA, OR THIRD-PARTY CLAIMS. IN NO EVENT WILL ZIFF-DAVIS PRESS' OR THE SUPPLIERS' LIABILITY FOR ANY DAMAGES TO YOU OR ANY OTHER PARTY EVER EXCEED THE PRICE OF THIS BOOK. NO SALES PERSON OR OTHER REPRESENTATIVE OF ANY PARTY INVOLVED IN THE DISTRIBUTION OF THE CD-ROM IS AUTHORIZED TO MAKE ANY MODIFICATIONS OR ADDITIONS TO THIS LIMITED WARRANTY.

ZIFF-DAVIS PRESS'S LICENSOR(S) MAKES NO WARRANTIES, EXPRESS OR IMPLIED, INCLUDING WITHOUT LIMITATION THE IMPLIED WARRANTIES OF MERCHANTABILITY AND FITNESS FOR A PARTICULAR PURPOSE, REGARDING THE SOFTWARE. ZIFF-DAVIS PRESS'S LICENSOR(S) DOES NOT WARRANT, GUARANTEE OR MAKE ANY REPRESENTATIONS REGARDING THE USE OR THE RESULTS OF THE USE OF THE SOFTWARE IN TERMS OF ITS CORRECTNESS, ACCURACY, RELIABILITY, CURRENTNESS OR OTHERWISE. THE ENTIRE RISK AS TO THE RESULTS AND PERFORMANCE OF THE SOFTWARE IS ASSUMED BY YOU. THE EXCLUSION OF IMPLIED WARRANTIES IS NOT PERMITTED BY SOME JURISDICTIONS. THE ABOVE EXCLUSION MAY NOT APPLY TO YOU.

IN NO EVENT WILL ZIFF-DAVIS PRESS'S LICENSOR(S), AND THEIR DIRECTORS, OFFICERS, EMPLOYEES OR AGENTS (COLLECTIVELY ZIFF-DAVIS PRESS'S LICENSOR) BE LIABLE TO YOU FOR ANY CONSEQUENTIAL, INCIDENTAL OR INDIRECT DAMAGES (INCLUDING DAMAGES FOR LOSS OF BUSINESS PROFITS, BUSINESS INTERRUPTION, LOSS OF BUSINESS INFORMATION, AND THE LIKE) ARISING OUT OF THE USE OR INABILITY TO USE THE SOFTWARE EVEN IF ZIFF-DAVIS PRESS'S LICENSOR HAS BEEN ADVISED OF THE POSSIBILITY OF SUCH DAMAGES. BECAUSE SOME JURISDICTIONS DO NOT ALLOW THE EXCLUSION OR LIMITATION OF LIABILITY FOR CONSEQUENTIAL OR INCIDENTAL DAMAGES, THE ABOVE LIMITATIONS MAY NOT APPLY TO YOU.

Some states do not allow the exclusion or limitation of implied warranties or limitation of liability for incidental or consequential damages, so the above limitation or exclusion may not apply to you.

General. Ziff-Davis Press and the Suppliers retain all rights not expressly granted. Nothing in this license constitutes a waiver of the rights of Ziff-Davis Press or the Suppliers under the U.S. Copyright Act or any other Federal or State Law, international treaty, or foreign law.

YEARS OF EXPERIENCE AT PC LEARNING LABS prove that hands-on learning works best. *PC Learning Labs Teaches Microsoft PowerPoint for Windows 95* makes it easy by including examples on the CD-ROM that work together with instructions in the book. You'll save countless hours of input time by working with sample data on the CD-ROM instead of entering it yourself. Here are some of the examples you'll find on the CD-ROM:

RUNNING A SLIDE SHOW: Open a slide presentation for a travel agency and browse through its contents to get familiar with PowerPoint operations (Chapter 2).

CORRECTING YOUR SPELLING: Open a PowerPoint presentation whose text contains several misspellings and have PowerPoint's spelling checker find and correct the errors (Chapter 3).

CREATING BULLETED LISTS: In the travel agency's presentation, add bulleted lists summarizing the agency's corporate and leisure travel services (Chapter 4).

CHANGING THE COLOR SCHEME: Assign and compare a variety of color schemes, from sedate to dramatic, for the travel agency's slide presentation (Chapter 5).

IMPORTING SPREADSHEET DATA INTO A PRESENTATION: Import a Microsoft Excel worksheet containing comparative rates for travel packages into a PowerPoint presentation (Chapter 11).

IMPORTING A CHART INTO A PRESENTATION: Import a Microsoft Excel chart summarizing the travel agency's package sales into a PowerPoint presentation (Chapter 11).

Tho following files appear under abbreviated file names on the CD-ROM:

In Text	On Disk
Chapter 8	Chap8.ppt
Chapter 9	Chap9.ppt
Chapter 10	Chap10.ppt
Chapter 11	Chap11.ppt
Chapter 12	Chap12.ppt
Chapter 13	Chap13.ppt
focus object	focusobj.wmf